Law, Policy, and Practice on China's Periphery

This book examines the Chinese government's policies and practices for relations with the Inner Periphery areas of Tibet, Xinjiang, and Inner Mongolia, and the Outer Periphery areas of Hong Kong and Taiwan, focusing on themes of political authority, socio-cultural relations, and economic development. China's history may be seen as one of managing the geographic periphery surrounding China proper. Successive imperial, republican, and communist governments have struggled to maintain sovereignty over the regions surrounding the great river valleys of China.

The importance of the periphery is no less real today; concerns over national security, access to natural resources, and long-held concerns about relations between Han and other ethnic groups continue to dominate Chinese law, policy, and practice regarding governance in the Inner Periphery regions of Inner Mongolia, Xinjiang, and Tibet. In the Outer Periphery, Beijing sees engagement with the outside world (particularly the West) as inextricably tied to Chinese sovereignty over former foreign colonies of Hong Kong and Taiwan.

Using the case study of national integration to indicate how policies are articulated and implemented through law and political–legal institutions, this book will be of interest to students and scholars of the peripheral regions. It will also appeal to academic and policy communities interested in legal reform in China

Pitman B. Potter is Hong Kong Bank Chair in Asian Research at the Institute of Asian Research and Professor of Law at the University of British Columbia, Canada.

Routledge Contemporary China Series

1 **Nationalism, Democracy and National Integration in China**
Leong Liew and Wang Shaoguang

2 **Hong Kong's Tortuous Democratization**
A comparative analysis
Ming Sing

3 **China's Business Reforms**
Institutional challenges in a globalised economy
Edited by Russell Smyth and Cherrie Zhu

4 **Challenges for China's Development**
An enterprise perspective
Edited by David H. Brown and Alasdair MacBean

5 **New Crime in China**
Public order and human rights
Ron Keith and Zhiqiu Lin

6 **Non-Governmental Organizations in Contemporary China**
Paving the way to civil society?
Qiusha Ma

7 **Globalization and the Chinese City**
Fulong Wu

8 **The Politics of China's Accession to the World Trade Organization**
The dragon goes global
Hui Feng

9 **Narrating China**
Jia Pingwa and his fictional world
Yiyan Wang

10 **Sex, Science and Morality in China**
Joanne McMillan

11 **Politics in China Since 1949**
Legitimizing authoritarian rule
Robert Weatherley

12 **International Human Resource Management in Chinese Multinationals**
Jie Shen and Vincent Edwards

13 **Unemployment in China**
Economy, human resources and labour markets
Edited by Grace Lee and Malcolm Warner

14 **China and Africa**
   Engagement and compromise
   Ian Taylor

15 **Gender and Education in China**
   Gender discourses and women's schooling in the early twentieth century
   Paul J. Bailey

16 **SARS**
   Reception and interpretation in three Chinese cities
   Edited by Deborah Davis and Helen Siu

17 **Human Security and the Chinese State**
   Historical transformations and the modern quest for sovereignty
   Robert E. Bedeski

18 **Gender and Work in Urban China**
   Women workers of the unlucky generation
   Liu Jieyu

19 **China's State Enterprise Reform**
   From Marx to the market
   John Hassard, Jackie Sheehan, Meixiang Zhou, Jane Terpstra-Tong and Jonathan Morris

20 **Cultural Heritage Management in China**
   Preserving the cities of the Pearl River delta
   Edited by Hilary du Cros and Yok-shiu F. Lee

21 **Paying for Progress**
   Public finance, human welfare and inequality in China
   Edited by Vivienne Shue and Christine Wong

22 **China's Foreign Trade Policy**
   The new constituencies
   Edited by Ka Zeng

23 **Hong Kong, China**
   Learning to belong to a nation
   Gordon Mathews, Tai-lok Lui, and Eric Kit-wai Ma

24 **China Turns to Multilateralism**
   Foreign policy and regional security
   Edited by Guoguang Wu and Helen Lansdowne

25 **Tourism and Tibetan Culture in Transition**
   A place called Shangrila
   Åshild Kolås

26 **China's Emerging Cities**
   The making of new urbanism
   Edited by Fulong Wu

27 **China-US Relations Transformed**
   Perceptions and strategic interactions
   Edited by Suisheng Zhao

28 **The Chinese Party-State in the 21st Century**
   Adaptation and the reinvention of legitimacy
   Edited by André Laliberté and Marc Lanteigne

29 **Political Change in Macao**
   Sonny Shiu-Hing Lo

30 **China's Energy Geopolitics**
The Shanghai Cooperation
Organization
and central Asia
Thrassy N. Marketos

31 **Regime Legitimacy in
Contemporary China**
Institutional change and
stability
*Edited by Thomas Heberer and
Gunter Schubert*

32 **US-China Relations**
China policy on Capitol Hill
Tao Xie

33 **Chinese Kinship**
Contemporary anthropological
perspectives
*Edited by Susanne Brandtstädter
and Gonçalo D. Santos*

34 **Politics and Government
in Hong Kong**
Crisis under Chinese
sovereignty
Edited by Ming Sing

35 **Rethinking Chinese Popular
Culture**
Cannibalizations of the canon
*Edited by Carlos Rojas and
Eileen Cheng-yin Chow*

36 **Institutional Balancing in the
Asia Pacific**
Economic interdependence
and China's rise
Kai He

37 **Rent Seeking in China**
*Edited by Tak-Wing Ngo and
Yongping Wu*

38 **China, Xinjiang and Central Asia**
History, transition and
crossborder interaction into the
21st century
*Edited by Colin Mackerras and
Michael Clarke*

39 **Intellectual Property Rights in
China**
Politics of piracy, trade and
protection
Gordon Cheung

40 **Developing China**
Land, politics and social
conditions
George C.S. Lin

41 **State and Society Responses
to Social Welfare Needs
in China**
Serving the people
*Edited by Jonathan Schwartz
and Shawn Shieh*

42 **Gay and Lesbian Subculture in
Urban China**
Loretta Wing Wah Ho

43 **The Politics of Heritage
Tourism in China**
A view from Lijiang
Xiaobo Su and Peggy Teo

44 **Suicide and Justice**
A Chinese perspective
Wu Fei

45 **Management Training and
Development in China**
Educating managers in a
globalized economy
*Edited by Malcolm Warner
and Keith Goodall*

46 **Patron–Client Politics and Elections in Hong Kong**
Bruce Kam-kwan Kwong

47 **Chinese Family Business and the Equal Inheritance System**
Unravelling the myth
Victor Zheng

48 **Reconciling State, Market and Civil Society in China**
The long march towards prosperity
Paolo Urio

49 **Innovation in China**
The Chinese software industry
Shang-Ling Jui

50 **Mobility, Migration and the Chinese Scientific Research System**
Koen Jonkers

51 **Chinese Film Stars**
Edited by Mary Farquhar and Yingjin Zhang

52 **Chinese Male Homosexualities**
Memba, Tongzhi and Golden Boy
Travis S.K. Kong

53 **Industrialisation and Rural Livelihoods in China**
Agricultural processing in Sichuan
Susanne Lingohr-Wolf

54 **Law, Policy, and Practice on China's Periphery**
Selective adaptation and institutional capacity
Pitman B. Potter

Law, Policy, and Practice on China's Periphery

Selective adaptation and institutional capacity

Pitman B. Potter

LONDON AND NEW YORK

First published 2011
by Routledge
2 Park Square, Milton Park, Abingdon, Oxfordshire OX14 4RN

Simultaneously published in the USA and Canada
by Routledge
711 Third Avenue, New York, NY 10017

First issued in paperback 2014

Routledge is an imprint of the Taylor & Francis Group, an informa business

© 2011 Pitman B. Potter

The right of Pitman B. Potter to be identified as author of this work has been asserted by him in accordance with the Copyright, Designs and Patent Act 1988.

Typeset in Times New Roman by Taylor & Francis Books

All rights reserved. No part of this book may be reprinted or reproduced or utilised in any form or by any electronic, mechanical, or other means, now known or hereafter invented, including photocopying and recording, or in any information storage or retrieval system, without permission in writing from the publishers.

British Library Cataloguing in Publication Data
A catalogue record for this book is available from the British Library

Library of Congress Cataloging in Publication Data
Potter, Pitman B.
Law, policy, and practice on China's periphery: selective adaptation and institutional capacity / Pitman B. Potter.
    p. cm. – (Routledge contemporary China series; 54)
Includes bibliographical references and index.
1. Regionalism–China. 2. Central-local government relations–China.
3. Law–China. 4. China–Politics and government–2002– I. Title.
JQ1506.R43P68 2010
320.80951–dc22   2010003757

ISBN 978-0-415-56405-2 (hbk)
ISBN 978-1-138-85809-1 (pbk)
ISBN 978-0-203-84673-5 (ebk)

**Dedicated to all the peoples of China's periphery,
that their lives may be filled with dignity and promise.**

Contents

	Preface	xii
1	Overview	1
2	Political authority in the Inner Periphery	24
3	Socio-cultural relations in the Inner Periphery	67
4	Economy and development in the Inner Periphery	116
5	Implications for the Outer Periphery	141
6	Conclusion	171
	Notes	183
	Bibliography: Chinese	184
	Bibliography: English	211
	Index	248

Preface

The geographic periphery surrounding China has historically been a contested domain of relationships around sovereignty, society, and development. As a result, management of the periphery has long been a major priority of the Chinese state. Whether in the course of resisting (or succumbing to) invasions from Inner Asia, pacifying (or accommodating) pirates in the South China Sea, or managing relations with foreigners from Japan, Europe, and North America, successive imperial, republican, and communist governments have struggled to maintain control over the regions surrounding the great river valleys of China proper. The importance of the periphery is no less real today. Along the "Inner Periphery" astride China's inland borders, concerns over national security, relations between Han and other ethnic groups (referred to in official Chinese nomenclature as "minority nationalities"), and the challenge of economic development continue to dominate Chinese perspectives on so-called "nationality autonomy regions" such as Inner Mongolia, Xinjiang, and Tibet.

China's approach to governance in the Inner Periphery invites questions about relations with the Outer Periphery—particularly Hong Kong and Taiwan. The two peripheries have generally been considered quite separately in much conventional political thinking. An anecdotal (and possibly apocryphal) story tells of former Politburo member Chen Yonggui speaking in 1980 and rejecting outright (*juedui bu kenengdi*) any suggestion that the "one country–two systems" approach being prepared for Hong Kong in the late 1980s might apply to Tibet. Instead, along the maritime boundaries of the "Outer Periphery," the People's Republic of China (PRC) government sees engagement with the outside world (particularly the West) as tied closely with issues of Chinese sovereignty over former foreign colonies in Hong Kong, Taiwan, and Macao. Protracted negotiations with Britain and Portugal over the return of Hong Kong and Macao, and with the government of Taiwan on reunification, reflect influences of China's policies and practices on local governance in the Inner Periphery and elsewhere. Made distinct by virtue of historical and contemporary circumstances, the Outer Periphery presents particular challenges for China's projects of national sovereignty and integration. Yet the one country–two systems approach to the Outer Periphery has itself become more diversified. Even as it prepared for Hong Kong's reversion to PRC sovereignty, for example, the central government was preparing to offer Taipei much more autonomy that had been allowed for Hong Kong. Such diversity invites questions about links with policies of governance in the Inner Periphery—encouraged in no small part by the central government's linking of relations with the Dalai Lama with his acceptance of PRC sovereignty over Taiwan.

While the central government seems willing to tailor its relations with the periphery according to the particularities of local conditions, it still views the Inner and Outer Peripheries as embodying unified sets of issues. Indeed the emerging field of studies on the "periphery" ("*bianjiang*," or "*bianyuan*") in China proper and on Taiwan suggests an academic and policy perspective that recognizes the fundamental similarity of issues, discourses, and challenges that the Inner and Outer Peripheries present (Xie 1999; Zhang 2005).

China's regulation of its Inner and Outer Peripheries has particular academic and policy significance. Security concerns have driven China to forge political alliances in Central and Southeast Asia, and to pursue vigorous programs of political authority and control. Socio-cultural tensions in the Inner Periphery have driven China to pursue conflicted policies of control and accommodation, while similar conflicts are evident in the Outer Periphery as local communities remain skeptical about China's governance. Economic relations in the Inner Periphery are dominated by development projects aimed at satisfying China's expanding demands for energy and other requirements for growth while also pacifying local minorities, whereas China's economic interaction with the Outer Periphery is an integral component of interaction with the global political economy.

China's management of the periphery is also a measure of the character of the PRC legal system, as policies and practice come increasingly to be explained and justified by reference to legalization (*fazhihua*). As with other aspects of the PRC legal system, the legal regime for relations with the periphery reflects central policy priorities conceived through organs of Party (CPC) and state leadership, which are then expressed and implemented through political–legal texts and organizations. Guided by Party policies, the PRC Constitution provides a general legal framework that supports political–legal regimes for managing the Inner Periphery (relying primarily on the Law on Autonomy in Nationality Areas, and ancillary laws and regulations) and the Outer Periphery (relying mainly on the Special Administrative Region Basic Laws for Hong Kong and Macao and the Anti-Secession Law for Taiwan). Similarly with the expanded application of law to China's economic reforms are, broadly, the "legalization" of China's relations with the periphery is aimed at building legitimacy for central government policies, reforming existing institutional relations, and lending predictability to socio-economic and political behavior.

The legal system is also intended as an instrument of control. Just as the famed Chinese porcelain artists of Jingdezhen who designed the "contending colors" (*doucai*) style of decoration used lines of cobalt blue to confine other hues painted onto various ceramic shapes (Scott 1993; Cort and Stuart 1993), so too does China's legal system seek to impose boundaries constraining China's multiple nationality groups and regional political communities. Thus, the legal system is not intended as a restraint on the powers of the Party/state but rather as an instrument of control by the Party/state over China's people (Lubman 1999). And to the extent that the character of a legal system can be determined based on its response to sensitive political issues, China's law and policy on governance in the periphery may usefully be taken as a measure of the basic tenets and implications of China's socialist legal system generally.

This requires careful scrutiny of political–legal texts on policy priorities, imperatives of practice and implementation, and contexts for institutional behavior. For such texts are much more than simply wooden expressions of government rhetoric. Rather the texts of laws and regulations, administrative orders, governmental notices, and the like reveal the outcome of tendentious politics and decision-making on issues of political authority, socio-cultural relations, and economic development. Official documents illuminate the normative perspectives and institutional relationships that inform interpretation and implementation of policy and law. Revisions to legal and political texts reveal the outcome of political and policy conflict over responses to changing conditions and emerging challenges. To the extent that formal texts serve as benchmarks for organizational behavior, they are invaluable sources for normative and organizational analysis of China's ideals and practices of governance.

This study began amidst a confusing array of observations and ideas emerging over the past few decades. During my residence in Beijing in the 1980s, my impressions about the unruly behavior of migrant Uighurs seemed in conflict with my recollections of the grace and dignity of Turks and Persians from my time in the mid-East as a youth. As a doctoral student in Hong Kong and China in the early 1980s, I was struck by conflicts between international news reporting and scholarship on problems of local development in Tibet, Xinjiang, and Inner Mongolia, and the official imagery of local pastoral bliss and peaceful development. As a witness to the tragedy of Tiananmen in 1989, I noted many parallels and contradictions with the unrest that broke out in Tibet in 1989 and Xinjiang in 1990–1991. And as a frequent visitor to Hong Kong and Taiwan I have been struck repeatedly by the apparent dissonance between Beijing's continued insistence on China's sovereignty over Taiwan despite the operational realities of Taiwan's independence and by the legal and political tensions around the negotiated return of Hong Kong and Macao to Mainland authority. Yet, mindful of the groundbreaking work done by other scholars examining specific areas of China's periphery, I have long been content to remain an interested observer and to confine my work on China to areas of commercial law and human rights.

However, encouraged by colleagues Tim Cheek, Diana Lary, and Daniel Overmyer to work on a variety of issues of local law and policy in China's peripheries, I have gradually steeled myself to stand on the shoulders of giants and attempt a study that examines China's relations with the periphery as a case study of the sustainability of China's socialist rule of law in the context of national integration. Drawing on a range of Chinese and English language archival materials and observations during the course of field visits during 2002–7, I have tried to achieve an understanding of the normative and operational challenges facing China's governance in the periphery. I could hardly aspire to challenge or displace the wonderful work of scholars focused on local knowledge in the periphery itself. Instead I have attempted to build on that knowledge informed by perspectives on Selective Adaptation and Institutional Capacity drawn from my work on other areas of Chinese law and policy.

As a case study in national integration, this book examines the Chinese government's policies and practices for relations with the Inner Periphery areas of Tibet, Xinjiang, and Inner Mongolia, and the Outer Periphery areas of Hong Kong and Taiwan focusing on themes of political authority, socio-cultural relations, and economic development. Chapter 1 provides an overview of China's relations with the Inner and Outer Peripheries, and explains the analytical approach of selective adaptation and institutional capacity used to explain government policies and practices. Chapter 2 reviews the political relationship between Beijing and the Inner Periphery, as articulated in national and local laws, regulations, and political directives on governance. Chapter 3 examines socio-cultural relations in the Inner Periphery, with particular attention to policies on nationalities and religion. Chapter 4 examines the PRC economic policies in the Inner Periphery, focusing on the Western Development Program. Chapter 5 addresses the implications of China's governance of the Inner Periphery for relations with the Outer Periphery areas of Hong Kong and Taiwan. The Conclusion summarizes findings about China's relations with the periphery and suggests longer-term questions and responses.

This project was made possible through the support of the Social Sciences and Humanities Research Council of Canada, for which I am deeply grateful. I am also deeply indebted to University of British Columbia (UBC) colleagues Alison Bailey, Tim Brook, Tim Cheek, Ashok Kotwal, Diana Lary, Daniel Overmyer, Tsering Shakya and Alex Woodside, as well as Elena Caprioni and Sophia Woodman for their encouragement and thoughtful commentary. Invaluable research assistance and copy-editing was provided by a range of graduate students and law students, including Meera Bawa, Eleanor Gill, Jack Hayes, Kang Wei, Matthew Levine, Erika Sedillo, and Tashi Tsering, for which I am very thankful. Veronica Uy, Bridget Phillips, and Megan Coyle at the UBC Centre for Asian Legal Studies and Karen Jew and Rozalia Mate at the UBC Institute of Asian Research provided invaluable staff assistance. I am also grateful for various reviewer reports on the manuscript, which have helped immensely in my efforts to strengthen the work. To other valued colleagues who have shared of their time and insight, I extend my profound thanks. Naturally, despite the best efforts of those who tried to help improve this work, errors and omissions no doubt remain, for which I alone remain responsible.

Pitman B. Potter
Vancouver
April 2010

1 Overview[1]

China exists geographically and conceptually at the center of an ever-widening series of concentric borderlands. The traditional nomenclature of the "Central Kingdom" applied not only to distinguish the China of the Han ethnic nationality group from external principalities, but also to differentiate non-Han groupings within the boundaries of the Chinese empire. Whether we consider the ancient Qin Dynasty with its capital of Chang'an (now Xian) at the bend of the Yellow River or the People's Republic whose heart is Beijing, the North China Plain has served for millennia as both the physical and the spiritual center of China. Although southern China has given rise to numerous cultural achievements in painting, poetry, and other areas, for most of the imperial and modern periods, China's cultural center rested along the course of the Yellow River. And although important dynasties such as the Southern Song and early Ming, as well as the Republic of China were centered or began in the South, this tended to reflect particularities of history—in particular, the extent of intrusion into China proper by non-Han groups through the Yuan and Qing dynasties. Indeed, the retreat of the Southern Song from Mongol power, the circumstances leading Zhu Yuanzhang to defeat the weakened Yuan Dynasty of the Mongols, and later the capacity of Sun Yat-sen and General Yuan Shikai to lead resistance to Manchu-led Qing each reflected particular conditions around Chinese reactions to non-Han control of the North China Plain and the extent to which during periods of dynastic weakness southern China remained freer of control by the non-Han intruders. But these exceptions also suggest how deeply embedded in China's socio-cultural history are tensions with outlying peoples living beyond the domain of Han China.

Looking outward, China's cultural perspective was soon confronted by societies whose structures, belief systems, and behavior conflicted fundamentally with those of the Han. Moving westward, the Chinese came into conflict with Central Asian cultures of the Tarim Basin, whose nomadism and religiosity contrasted with the secular urbanism of the Han (Perdue 2005; Millward and Tursun 2004). Moving north, the Chinese confronted the pastoral societies of the Gobi, with similarly conflicted results (Bulag 2004; Reardon-Anderson 2005). While some of these contacts (especially in the Tarim Basin)

2   *Overview*

were violent, even when relatively peaceful, relentless intrusion from China resulted in displacement and marginalization of local people. In its relations with the borderlands, the Chinese state (whether Imperial, Republican, or Socialist) tended to view local denizens with a mixture of contempt and fear. As the archetypal "other," the peoples of these peripheral regions were considered both inferior and challenging, unequal to the cultural superiority of the Han but also militarily powerful and threatening. Chinese dynasties sought to suppress those barbarians (*yi*, meaning "not yet Sinicized") who ventured too close to the Han homeland, to dominate peaceful border areas through settlement and military garrison, and to convert societies to the benefits of Han culture (Fairbank 1953: 7–10). Thus, through much of Chinese history, management of the periphery has loomed large as an imperative of governance. Even the foreign dynasties of the Yuan and Qing were not exempt from such attitudes, reflecting both the extent of their Sinicization and their appetite for conquest of neighboring peoples (Milward 2007).

Today, China's relations with its borderlands continue to reflect a combination of cultural superiority and deep-seated unease, standing against the context of the policy imperatives of national integration. The concept of the "frontier" (*bianjiang*) wields significant power not only on China's sense of itself and its relations with its neighbors, but also with the communities that live in the frontier areas that comprise China's boundaries (Ma 2005). The periphery of China may be thought of as comprising those regions surrounding China proper that offer both shelter from and interaction with systems, cultures, and peoples outside. China's "Inner Periphery" borderlands have for millennia separated China proper from the pastoral civilizations of inner Asia, while the Outer Periphery has been a maritime boundary against other states and empires in Asia and beyond.

In the Inner Periphery, areas such as Tibet, Xinjiang, and Inner Mongolia constitute administrative components of the People's Republic of China (PRC) state. While questions about sovereignty continue to be addressed by historians (e.g., Smith 2008; Millward and Tursun 2004; Millward and Perdue 2004) and legal specialists (e.g., Sorensen and Phillips 2004; ICLT 1997), China's control over the Inner Periphery remains a political reality. Governance of minority nationality "Autonomous Regions" has long been a central feature of PRC policy, and is presented as an improvement on the policies of domination associated with Imperial China and to some extent the nationalist period (SCIO 1999, 2004a). Despite their formal designations, however, these regions often enjoy less actual autonomy than is conferred by the Center on the Chinese provinces. National integration of minority nationality areas has run the gamut from relatively benign accommodation to military control, but is unavoidably colored by the specter of Han chauvinism (*Da Hanzu zhuyi*)— either as an unfortunate feudal remnant to be gradually educated away or as a subversive complement to socialist transformation that works to displace local socio-cultural arrangements. Thus, China's national integration priorities in Tibet, Xinjiang, and Inner Mongolia have included policies of secularization, economic development, Han dominance, and political control (MacKerras; Rossabi 2004).

From Beijing's perspective, the Outer Periphery comprising Hong Kong, Macao, and Taiwan reflects historical influences of imperialism and internationalization that have drawn these mainly Han societies into greater integration with the world political economy. In the Outer Periphery, national integration policies are reflected in the "one country–two systems" (*yiguo liangzhi or* 1C2S) model applied to Hong Kong and Macao after their return to China in 1997 (Wang 2002). This typology continues to inform China's proposals for unification with Taiwan (Chiu 1993), although with limited success in the face of continued resistance (or at least inconsistent responses) from successive Taiwan governments. While the Anti-Secession Law (2005) eschews direct reference to 1C2S, the Law's promise of a "high degree of autonomy" for Taiwan parallels this foundational principle, which was also relied upon by official commentators about the Law's basic tenets and principles (Wu 2005; Jia 2005).

In both the Inner and the Outer Periphery, relations with China proper and the central government are conflicted by differences of expectation about autonomy; by different perspectives of place that construct the peripheries alternatively as homelands or as border zones of key strategic importance to China; and by differences in ethnicity, language, and culture that affect dynamics of development and organization. Comparison both within and between the Inner and Outer Peripheries can yield important insights not only on China's relations with these areas—an important issue in its own right—but also on China's sense of itself. Such comparisons can reveal the ways in which pursuit of national integration in China remains contingent on central and local conditions, interests, and expectations.

China's Peripheries: local conditions and perspectives

China's policies on governance in the Periphery purport to acknowledge the central government's understanding and appreciation of local conditions (SCIO 1999, 2005). This is a daunting task, however. Each of the areas within the Inner and Outer Peripheries has distinctive local conditions. While their shared status as contested peripheral areas invites generalization, each area under study here has a unique history and culture that defies unified approaches to governance.

The Inner Periphery: governance of minority nationalities

China's Inner Periphery comprises areas traditionally inhabited by societies whose ethnicity is distinct from the Han Chinese, whose numbers are considerably smaller, and whose socio-cultural conditions and aspirations differ considerably from those in Han China. The PRC has defined these peoples as "minority nationalities," acknowledging their distinctiveness yet also asserting their subjugation to a larger Chinese multi-national state (Hao). Large populations of "minority nationalities" reside in the so-called "minority nationality autonomy regions" such as Tibet, Xinjiang, and Inner Mongolia, as well in provinces such as Gansu, Sichuan, and Yunnan. Ningxia is accorded Autonomous Region Status linked to the Hui Nationality—even though these people are considered Han who embraced Islam, their Muslim history, identity, and culture are deemed to warrant a separate social classification from other Han social groups (Lipman 2004). Owing to the role of ethnicity in the nomenclature and political–legal status of Tibet, Xinjiang, and Inner Mongolia Autonomous Regions, the research for this book focused particularly on these three areas of the Inner Periphery.

Tibet Autonomous Region

Tibet's relationship with China reflects a diverse historical legacy characterized by long periods of broad autonomy (Goldstein; Harvard Cold War Project; Norbu 2001; Shakya). Tibet–China ties prior to 1911 under the *Cho-Yan* priest–patron relationship have been likened to a protectorate under international law that did not displace the formal source of local governance in Tibet ("The Legal Status of Tibet": 20–22). In the early twentieth century, the decline of the Qing and British invasion of Tibet led to an Anglo-Tibet treaty (1904), recognized by the Qing government, that sought to preserve Tibet's legal autonomy even while recognizing Britain's sphere of influence. China's dominion over Tibet was reasserted during 1908–11, but waned again with the fall of the Qing and the establishment of the Republic of China. On the other hand, Tibet's efforts to seek international recognition of its statehood achieved mixed results. While formal recognition of Tibetan statehood was not forthcoming, many organizations and individuals in the international community supported Tibetan aspirations for self-determination and cultural protection (Shakya: Chapter 8; International Commission of Jurists: Chapter 6).

Nationalist China's *de facto* control over Tibet was minimal prior to 1949, but afterward the People's Republic began to assert ever more strident claims to authority over Tibet. In the face of Chinese military conquest of Eastern Tibet in 1950, the fourteenth Dalai Lama concluded a "17 Point Agreement" recognizing Chinese sovereignty in return for commitments about local autonomy. Ongoing tensions with China, complicated by US overtures encouraging resistance and by China's socialist transformation policies (most notably collectivization of land), led ultimately to a full-fledged Chinese military occupation in 1959 and the flight of the Dalai Lama to India. Thereafter, the Tibetan government in exile located in Dharamsala repudiated the 17 Point Agreement, while China instituted policies aimed at dismantling traditional Tibetan society and culture and replacing these with Maoist institutions and practices of socialist revolution. China's effects on Tibet were perhaps most destructive during the Cultural Revolution, when, despite the presence of People's Liberation Army (PLA) units in the passes linking Tibet to China proper with orders to prevent intrusion by marauding Red Guards, attacks on monasteries devastated much of Tibet's traditional cultural life. In addition, economic policies emphasizing planting non-local wheat grains instead of the barleys that could survive in Tibet's arid high-altitude climate led to widespread starvation. This combination of Han-chauvinist cultural policies and erratic and unsustainable economic directives not only devastated Tibetan society but also caused deep suspicion locally over China's motives and expectations about Tibet.

During the post-Mao period, the governments of Deng Xiaoping and Jiang Zemin adopted policies aimed at correcting the self-defeating excesses of the Maoist period, in part by promoting economic development and providing broader economic and political opportunities for local Tibetan elites while still imposing severe political controls (Sautman and Dreyer 2006). Following Hu Yaobang's six-point reform proposal announced in 1980, a secret meeting was held between Hu and the Dalai Lama's brother Gyalo Thondup in 1981. Negotiations in Beijing in 1982 ensued over the possible return of the Dalai Lama to China, although success in reconciliation was elusive (Goldstein; Xu 1999). Internal political battles in China leading to the dismissal of Hu in 1987, the launching in 1988 of the International Campaign for Tibet by the government in exile in Dharamsala (which contributed to the award in 1989 of the Nobel Peace Prize to the Dalai Lama), and ultimately the riots in Lhasa in 1987 and 1989 led to a hardening of Beijing's negotiating position. The Dalai Lama's proposed "Middle Way", formalized most prominently in a speech to the European Parliament in Strasbourg in June 1988 (although formulated as early as 1974), offered a modest approach to autonomy coupled with acceptance of Chinese sovereignty over Tibet ("China–Dalai Lama Dialogue"). Nonetheless, the 1990s saw little progress, as Beijing set preconditions for talks that the Dalai Lama give up his alleged views on Tibet independence and his alleged separatist activities, and also publicly admit that Tibet is part of China, that Taiwan is part of China, and that the PRC is only lawful government of China (Jiang 1998b). Nonetheless, discussions were restarted with visits led by the Dalai Lama's envoy Lodi Gyari in 2002–8. However, these were held under the auspices of the Communist Party of China's (CPC) United Front Work Department, signaling their "non-governmental" character and potentially limiting their political impact.

China's military occupation of Tibet has left a legacy of tension and resistance (Wang 2009; Xu 1999). China's national integration program for Tibet is pursued through local development programs combined with ongoing criticism of the Dalai Lama's "government in exile" (SCIO 1998). During the past several years, public airing of policy perspectives and the convening of direct discussions between China and the Tibet government in exile suggest possibilities for change in the relationship. But China has also moved aggressively to curb local dissent, control religious activities that challenge Beijing's dominance, and promote urbanization and infrastructure development under its "Western Development Program" (Fischer 2002). And so restiveness remains, as China's migration policies have brought large numbers of Han Chinese into Tibet Autonomous Region, and tensions between goals of assimilation and accommodation continue to challenge Beijing's policies. Violent riots in Lhasa and in Tibetan areas in Sichuan, Gansu, and Qinghai outside the Tibet Autonomous Region in spring 2008 further complicated matters (CECC 2009; Barnett 2008a; Smith 2008). On the one hand, these events seemed to harden China's negotiating position, while the unrest also created an opportunity for Beijing to recognize the limitations of its policies.

Xinjiang Uighur Autonomous Region

China's relationship with Xinjiang reflects historical factors of conflict between successive Chinese dynasties and the vigorous cultures of the Silk Road (Millward 2007; Millward and Tursun 2004; Perdue 2005; Whitfield 1999). The commercial importance of the Silk Road invited socio-cultural discourse but also raised the possibility of conflicts over control. The emergence of ocean trade routes from Arabia, expansion of the Tibetan empire into the Tarim basin in the seventh to eight centuries, and the gradual displacement of local Buddhist cultures by Islam all contributed to the decline of the Silk Road. The rise of the Mongols linked the Yuan dynasty with the Tarim region, although the succeeding Ming focused dynastic interests inward to China proper. The Manchus reasserted China's control over the Tarim and Dzungerian Basins, defeating or co-opting Dzunger and Khoja competitors and retaining suzerainty through the Qing reign of Qianlong (Millward 2007: 83–97). The story of the "Fragrant Concubine" whose tomb still graces the outskirts of Kashgar epitomizes the exoticism that Imperial China associated with the Western Frontier of Xinjiang (Millward 1994; Tyler 2004: 57–87). The Qing nomenclature for the territory labeled *Xinjiang* ("new frontier") reflected an effort to entrench a perspective on Xinjiang as a western borderland of China rather than an eastern dominion of the Turkic socio-cultural world (Starr 2004b: 6; Bovington 2004b).

Qing decline in the nineteenth century, coupled with the "Great Game" of resurgent British and Russian imperialism saw Xinjiang dominated by local satraps such as Yakub Beg (Millward and Tursun 2004). Although he died facing nearly certain defeat at the hands of Qing general Zuo Zongtang, Beg's kingdom of Eastern Turkestan was recognized by Russia and several central Asia states and continues as a powerful image in the minds of Chinese and Uighurs alike. Under the Nationalists, China continued to assert its interests in Xinjiang, although the stability promised by Chinese dominion was often undermined by a combination of venal administration, the resiliency of local warlord armies, and a series of localized Islamic and Turkic rebellions. By the time of the Anti-Japanese War, Nationalist government control was tenuous at best and came to depend on an alliance with the first Uighur and Kazakh-dominated Eastern Turkistan Republic (ETR) (1933–34), which in turn was overturned by the Chinese warlord Sheng Shicai in 1934. A second ETR was established in 1944 in what is now the Yili Kazakh Autonomous Prefecture, but it was overcome by the PLA in 1949 (Millward and Tursun 2004: 82–85).

China's policies in Xinjiang reflect the importance of the region to Beijing's conception of national interest (Gladney 2004b; Ma D. 2003). Xinjiang has multiple riches of natural resources including oil and natural gas, which are seen as essential to China's economic development. Xinjiang's strategic location in central Asia has lent particular importance to the local development policies of the PRC central government (Becquelin 2000; Schichor 2004). Like Tibet, Xinjiang has seen a significant influx of Han Chinese migrants, as well as efforts by Chinese officials to restrict local religious practice and language usage (Ford 2008; Weston 2008). Yet Xinjiang remains a highly contested region whose multiple ethnic groups and largely Islamic culture are wholly distinct from Han China (Gladney 1991; Chang 1997). Denouncing purported terrorist agendas and activities by Islamic separatists in Xinjiang, the Chinese government has attempted to ally itself with US-led anti-terrorism efforts (SCIO 2002c, "True Colors … "; Chan 2001a; Liu and Du), even as it sees Xinjiang as an important bastion against expanding US interests (Zhang Z. 2005: 268–80). Chinese immigration has changed the face of the Autonomous Region capital Urumqi, while local nationalities—particularly Uighurs and Kazakhs—remain dominant elsewhere in the Autonomous Region. The south of Xinjiang (*Jiangnan*) remains a center of Uighur nationalism—the Idhkah Mosque near the center of Kashgar standing as the symbolic center of anti-Han sentiment. This mixing of religion and national identity is also evident in privately funded mosques established in such places as Artush despite the denial of state funding. China's policy-makers seem acutely aware of the power of these local religious and nationalist sentiments (Ma D. 2005), although efforts to impose social control in the service of national integration often seem ineffective.

The tensions inherent in the blend of religion and local identity are evident in signs throughout the interior of the mosque (evident in mosques across the *Jiangnan* area and in Urumqi as well) extolling in Chinese, Uighur, and English the virtues of ethnic unity and prohibiting "separatist" (*fenlie*) activities. While the only readers of such mosque postings denouncing *fenlie zhuyi* seem to be Chinese and foreign tourists, the postings seem curiously maladroit—a clumsy effort to insert governmental imperatives into what otherwise would be sanctuaries of local culture and identity. The term "*fenlie zhuyi*" is variously translated as "splittism," "separatism," and "secessionism." Each of these translations is inadequate to convey the deep opprobrium which the PRC regime attaches to activities seen as threatening to divide its claimed geographic territory. What the regime fears most perhaps is "secessionism" to the extent that this involves potentially lawful and legitimate steps toward separation of a particular region from PRC jurisdiction. Separatism suggests unilateral and extralegal removal by a regional political authority of a given

8 Overview

territory from PRC jurisdiction. The practical difficulties of such separation locally, and the long-standing principle of international law granting sovereign states the right to use force to suppress separatism, work in favor of the Chinese government's resistance to this sort of *fenlie zhuyi*. "Splittism" is a more literal translation but has few if any equivalents in the political–legal discourses on sovereignty.

Inner Mongolia Autonomous Region

The Great Wall of China is mute but powerful testimony to China's historical insecurities about its Northern Frontier in the face of more or less constant threat of incursion by nomadic tribes from the north. Peoples from the north, including the Xiongnu of the Han Period, the Mongols, who defeated the Song and established the Yuan Dynasty, and the Manchus, who collaborated with Mongols and defecting Chinese generals to overthrow the Ming and found the Qing dynasty, frequently challenged the integrity and security of traditional China (Elvin 1973). The establishment of the Inner Mongolian Autonomous Region (IMAR) in 1947 bears the imprint of a historical legacy that included the Qing division of Inner from Outer Mongolia; Nationalist efforts to integrate Inner Mongolia; and the alliance of the Tumed Mongols under Ulanhu with the Chinese communist revolutionary base at Yan'an (Bulag 2004, 2002a; Reardon-Anderson 2005). China's policies toward Inner Mongolia have reflected broad tensions between Chinese imperatives of national integration and security and local concerns with identity and place. The Mongols themselves are distinguished by tribe and locale, among for example the so-called "Western" Mongols (mostly Tumed Communists associated with Ulanhu) and their Ordos Mongol affiliates, and the "Eastern" Mongols (mostly returned from Japanese colonialism in Manchuria). China's efforts at co-optation and control have been carried out through Mongol cadres such as Ulanhu, who professed loyalty to Beijing. Indeed it was reaction to the period of Mongol dominance in IMAR in the 1950s and early 1960s that contributed to the Han backlash during the Cultural Revolution when local culture was violently suppressed. Security dimensions also have played an important role—particularly during periods of tension in Sino-Russian relations.

Conflicts between the nomadic culture of the Steppe and the settled culture of the Han Chinese also play an important role in areas such as social and economic development policy. But for its bilingual signs and billboards, the IMAR capital Huhehaote (Hohhot) looks much like other Chinese provincial capitals. The pride with which local elites speak of inter-marriage between Mongols and Han, and the apparent absence of Mongol communities and Buddhist lamaseries contrasts with the vibrant insularity of the Hui district with its Muslim hospital and great mosque and madrassa, and speaks to the assimilation of local cultures into the greater China. More recently, questions of desertification and degradation of the grasslands, competition for control of the lucrative cashmere industry, and urbanization have all come to dominate China's relations with Inner Mongolia. Against these broad themes of identity, environment, economy, and security, tensions remain over the meaning and extent of autonomy in local governance.

The Outer Periphery: challenges of internationalization

China's relations with the Outer Periphery are colored less by factors of ethnicity, than by internationalization, colonialism, and local identity. For Taiwan, colonial practices by Japan played an important role in relations with the Mainland, while more recently cross-strait relations have been affected by relations with the United States and the international political economy. The colonial legacy of Britain and Portugal determined much of China's approach to the recovery of Hong Kong and Macao. China's relations with Hong Kong set the tone for its relationship with Macao, even to the point of parallel provisions in the Basic Laws for these two "Special Administrative Regions" (Xiao 1993, 1990). In Hong Kong and Taiwan, local identities also play a significant role, along with historical isolation from China proper, language differences, and changing economic conditions. This study will focus on Hong Kong and Taiwan as examples of China's post-colonial policies in the Outer Periphery.

Hong Kong Special Administrative Region

Hong Kong occupies a special place in China's self-awareness and its perception about relations with the world at large. The legacies of European colonialism and imperialism are particularly poignant in Hong Kong, and often overshadow the reality of historical tensions in social, economic, and political relations between Northern and Southern China in general, and between Beijing and Guangdong in particular (Goodman and Segal 1994; Lau and Kuan 1989). Yet these internal tensions are powerful. Mongol and later Manchu domination of North China contributed to Southern Chinese identities of cultural purity and contempt for the rustics of the North China Plain. Northerners on the other hand hold to their identities as descendants of the Yellow Emperor and often view their southern compatriots with ambivalence. The multiple southern dialects of Chinese—particularly the *Guangdonghua* spoken in Hong Kong—are dismissed as nearly unintelligible by many northerners, who prize their own dialects as "standard." North–south relations in China are complicated by ethnic disparities as well. Purported to be of northern, possibly Xiongnu, origins, the Hakka were driven south at the time of the Mongol invasion in the thirteenth century and have been seen by the local Han as displaced "guests" (*kejia*) and marginalized since at least the Yuan Dynasty (Hattaway 2000). Thus, China's relationships around Hong Kong are complicated by internal factors unrelated to the colonial legacy.

10 *Overview*

Yet, China's view of Hong Kong is inextricably linked with the colonial experience. The story of Britain's wresting of Hong Kong and Kowloon from Qing control is well known (Fairbank 1953). What is often overlooked, however, is that relations between two great empires were driven by cultural representatives drawn not from national elites but rather from local frontier society. Neither the British nor the Qing merchants whose actions led ultimately to British rule in Hong Kong could be considered the socio-cultural elite of either country—both the Jardines and Mathesons and the clans of Mowqua and Howqua were rather tawdry standard bearers for their respective cultures (Collis 1946). Neither did the local government officials of either country command significant political authority, as each state was dismissive of the other's claims to status and prestige. Chinese nationalist sentiment over Hong Kong has itself been historically conflicted. While anti-Manchu nationalism called for "overthrowing the Qing and restoring the Ming" (*fan Qing fu Ming*), the prospect of a foreign bourgeois empire defeating the militant literati culture of the Central Kingdom even under Manchu rule was particularly galling to China's sense of itself.

The process by which the British colonial territory of Hong Kong reverted to PRC sovereignty is well known and has been well told (Roberti 1996). Issues over the intentions and expectations underlying the deal negotiated between Britain and China; questions about the legitimacy of the process by which colonial authority over Hong Kong was passed from one sovereign state to another, and debates over the implications for Hong Kong's future will no doubt continue to dominate the academic and policy discourse around the application of Deng Xiaoping's "one country–two systems" model for governance in Hong Kong. At the end of the day, the combination of a nationalist commitment to retaking control of Hong Kong from imperialist Europeans and a general sense of northern chauvinist disdain for the south works to ensure that Beijing retains a strong hand over Hong Kong, even while striving to ensure that Hong Kong has little influence in China proper. More recently, the power of Shanghai political interests in the PRC, both during the period of Jiang Zemin's presidency and afterward, has worked to marginalize Hong Kong's status and influence yet further.

The result is a contested society in which local and global values are embedded. On the one hand, Hong Kong retains its international character. Despite challenges from resurgent Shanghai (and also Singapore and Tokyo), Hong Kong remains an important financial center. With its manufacturing enterprises moving into the Pearl River Delta, Hong Kong has attempted to expand its financial and professional service sectors and to present itself as an essential gateway to China. The continued (albeit somewhat diluted) commitment to the rule of law has persuaded many international private and public actors to base their China activities in the Hong Kong Special Administrative Region, while the generally high level of human resource development remains an important impetus for local post-industrial development.

Yet Hong Kong's socio-economic and political conditions increasingly reflect its subordination to the PRC. China's control over Hong Kong's political system is exercised through a range of Party and government units, including the Leading Small Group on Hong Kong Affairs (*Xianggang shiwu lingdao xiaozu*) and the State Council's Hong Kong–Macao Affairs Office (*Xianggang Aomen shiwu banggongshi*), which have worked to ensure that PRC interests are protected and promoted. Hong Kong's practical dependence on good will from the PRC remains an important factor—for just as Kowloon–Canton Railway (KCR) cars carrying daily supplies of pork, the water pipeline running alongside the railroad, and the lorries loaded with agricultural produce that fill the highway from the Hong Kong–PRC border crossing into Kowloon embody Hong Kong's dependence, so too does the daily influx of PRC tourists affirm Hong Kong's economic dependency on the Mainland. Mainland influences in Hong Kong are everywhere evident, from commercial real estate investments by Mainland companies, the expanded use of Mandarin, the increased presence of Mainland-produced goods in shops and street stalls, to the increasingly evident patterns of pedestrians exiting the MTR subway walking on the right (as on Mainland) rather than the left as the traffic management system and its British colonial designers expected.

This conflict between internationalism and national subjugation is reflected in much of the political history of the post-handover period, where conflicts have arisen between Beijing's policy preferences and those of local interests (Lau 2002). Political questions over such issues as the right of abode for children of Hong Kong residents, protections for political dissent, the structure and process for Legislative Council elections, public security policy and practice, and the appointment of the Chief Executive, have generally been resolved in favor of Beijing. As with areas of the Inner Periphery, Hong Kong has seen significant levels of migration from China. For Chinese whose personal or professional prospects in the Mainland are limited, Hong Kong offers considerable opportunities. As well, China has actively promoted commercial and institutional linkages that would ensure a pro-PRC voice among the population. Elite circulation has played an important role in this regard, as the colonial elite whose status depended on ties with and loyalty to Britain has largely been replaced by a new elite with closer ties and loyalty to China.

Taiwan

Taiwan's contested position in the contemporary world may be appreciated by reference to its historical place on the periphery of China (Eskildsen 2005). Still a frontier of sorts, Taiwan has undergone far-reaching social, economic, and political changes over the past two decades that affect its relationship with Mainland China (Gold 1986; Edmonds and Goldstein 2001; Simon and Kau 1992). While implications for Sino-American relations are never far from Beijing's policy-making calculus on Taiwan (Tucker 2005), local factors play a more dominant role. Driven by relative parallels in the timing and focus of economic reform policies in the two regions, as well as factors of shared language and culture, close economic relations between Taiwan and the Mainland represent a foundation for cooperation (and possible conflict) (Tung 2004). However, while there are aspects of shared history and culture upon which reconciliation might be based (Johnston 1993), important socio-economic and political changes in Taiwan have stimulated systemic divergence with China and encourage local claims to autonomy and possibly independence (Bellows 2000; Rigger 1999–2000). Ever-widening differences in legal and political culture reflect contrasts in institutional performance driven by different degrees of commitment to reform. Taiwan's legal system has become more institutionalized and internationalized than China's (Wang 2002; Lo 2006). Political reforms in Taiwan have seen the voluntary ceding of power by the ruling KMT (Kuomintang) following its electoral defeat in 2000, and contrast directly with the continued refusal by Beijing to permit non-Communist parties and politicians any meaningful role in governance. Thus, Taiwan's experience with a transformative democratizing economy where political and economic reforms coexist presents a direct contrast with policies of the PRC government and a challenge to the legitimacy of the Chinese Party/state (Bellows 2000). Paradoxically, as the recently elected government of Ma Ying-jeou has moved to improve relations with Beijing, legal institutions in Taiwan appear to have become more compliant with PRC priorities ("Mentor Urges"; Hirsch 2009). While disturbing to many foreign observers, this trend may work to facilitate easier harmonization of Taiwan and PRC policies and legal culture.

The election of President Chen Shui-bian in 2000 and his reelection in 2004 seemed to be watershed events for Taiwan's relations with the Mainland (Corson 2004; Henderson *et al.* 2004; Tan 2004). During his first term, Chen succeeded in steadily pushing China to accept new dimensions of acceptable discourse on Taiwanese autonomy. On one hand, Chen sought to expand links with China, without making further concessions to China's claims to sovereignty over Taiwan. Acknowledging the principle of "one China," Chen declined to accept China's interpretation of its meaning and implications, adopting instead a principle of "agreeing to disagree" (*bu gongshi de gongshi*) (Zhang 2003). An inter-party (*kuadang*) small group articulated a dictum of "three acknowledgements, four recommendations" (*sange renzhi sige jianyi*) in 2000 that implied the possibilities of further coordination with the Mainland but nonetheless underscored the separateness of Taiwan's constitutional and legal systems and its claim to distinct international status (Xingzheng yuan dalu weiyuanhui 2003: 21). Chen's discourse of "political integration" (*zhengzhi tonghe*) implied a degree of separation significantly greater than that contemplated under Beijing's preferred "reunification" (*tongyi*) language ("President Chen's Cross-century Remarks"; Zhang 2003: 90). Chen's statement in 2002 that there was a state on each side of the Taiwan Strait ("*yibian yiguo*") seemed finally to cross the line of what Beijing considered acceptable discourse ("Guowuyuan Taiwan Bangongshi").

However, through much of 2002–3, economic problems and uncertainties about the China relationship had diluted Chen's popular support. Despite, or perhaps because of, his increasingly vigorous challenge to Beijing's claims of sovereignty over Taiwan, Chen seemed unable to build significant popular support for a second term. The "Pan-Blue" team, comprising an alliance between the KMT and the People First Party (PFP), seemed to be capitalizing effectively on popular dissatisfaction with corruption and mismanagement by Chen's DPP government. The alliance of the KMT's Lien Chan with the PFP's James Soong offered a potentially powerful alliance of traditionalist, mainlander based political organizations. The apparent popularity of local KMT candidates like Taipei Mayor Ma Ying-jeou suggested potential depth in the opposition to Chen's presidency. While Taipei and Northern Taiwan remained a center of KMT support, Chen Shui-bian's support in southern Taiwan (including Kaohsiung and Tainan) seemed to be growing northward along class lines. Deep-seated resentment of KMT privilege and entitlement among working people in Taipei raises open questions about the KMT's willingness to help Taiwan's workers who had been buffeted by economic decline and increased unemployment. However, Chen's razor-thin victory in the presidential election and his loss in the local elections of December 2004 and subsequent resignation as chair of the DPP revealed the divisiveness of his China policies and particularly his localization policies in Taiwan. The visit to China by KMT chief Lien Chan in April 2005 underscored the importance of Mainland relations for Chen's political opponents.

Ma Ying-jeou's victory in the presidential elections of March 2008 signaled the potential for new policies on closer ties with China. Ma campaigned in part against the economic failures and alleged corruption of the Chen Shuibian government but also called for a new approach to China that would depart from Chen's policies of separation. Soon after the election, plans were under way for exchanges of high-level visits and acceleration of negotiations over direct travel and commercial links between Taiwan and the Mainland. The potential for disappointment remains, however, as differences in expectation and capacity of Mainland and Taiwan leadership groups as well as domestic political conflict are likely to continue to impede full reconciliation. Nonetheless, a process seems under way of structural adjustment that reflects acceptance of a core dynamic of center–periphery relations.

Perspectives on China's policies of legalization and governance

A key element in China's relations with the areas of the Inner and Outer Periphery is the increasingly central role that law plays in governance in China generally and also the extent to which law remains an instrument of policy. China's legal reform efforts have been linked closely with issues of national integration (Hewitt 1999). China's governance in Inner and Outer Peripheries is based formally on their classification as sub-national entities under the PRC Constitution. In the Inner Periphery, constitutional arrangements for local governance in Autonomous Regions such as Tibet, Xinjiang, and Inner Mongolia remain subject to the unitary state model applied elsewhere. In the Inner Periphery, the Chinese government has attempted to lend greater authority to its rule through references to programs of "legalization" (*fazhihua*), by which the rule of law serves as an expression of state policy and an instrument for its enforcement (State Council Information Office 2004a). Yet legalization discourses also constitute a contested domain as rule of law principles are deployed to challenge the policies and practices of the Party/state (Zhang 2008; "Chen Daojun").

In the Outer Periphery, China's practices of governance in Hong Kong and its proposals for unification with Taiwan reflect continued tensions between Beijing's perspectives on national integration and local concerns with autonomy. Hong Kong and Taiwan are objects of Beijing's effort to establish the "Special Administrative Region" as yet another constitutional model for governance (Wang 2002). Yet China's commitment to the rule of law remains contested. In Taiwan, for example, despite tightening of economic relations with the Mainland (Cheng 2005), the government has on several occasions suggested that reunification will depend on China completing its efforts to build a rule of law system (Chiu 1993). Hong Kong's relations with China have repeatedly involved disputes over constitutional questions about jurisdiction, political authority, and the rule of law (Ghai 1997; Chen 1997). Thus, China's law and policy on national integration with its peripheral areas reveal tensions around the orthodoxy of official legal culture on such questions as institutional jurisdiction and process, the role of law in policy enforcement, and legal restraints on state action. These tensions may be understood in light of international perspectives on local governance, society, and economy evident elsewhere.

Perspectives on governance, society, and economy

International discourses on governance of political, socio-cultural, and economic relations offer useful contexts for examining China's governance policies and practices in the regions of the Inner and Outer Periphery. Discussion of political dimensions of China's relations with the Inner Periphery can draw usefully on policy discourses of federalism, which offer insights to the dilemmas of central–local relations that inform national integration programs. In China generally, central–local relations have been an important dynamic in economic, legal, and political reform processes (White). While the PRC Constitution provides that China is a unitary rather than a federal state, in practice the interplay of power and politics between the central and sub-national governments echoes practices of federalism (Davis 1999; Dougherty and McGuckin 2002; Dougherty, McGuckin, and Radzin 2002). While policy and scholarly discourses in China have come increasingly to accept the need for federalist principles (Huang Yafeng 2001; Song 2000), the discourse of federalism has often has been associated with writings by political dissidents (Yan 1998, 1996), and hence has had little official traction.

Socio-cultural relations in China's Inner Periphery may be examined by reference to scholarly discourses of multiculturalism in areas such as policy process (Brown 1997), legal institutions (Backhouse 1999), minority relations (Sunahara 1999), and jurisdictional issues (Bartlett 1990; Tennant 1990). While the PRC Constitution and various laws and regulations affirm the rights of China's national minorities, existing work on China's minority policies raises important questions of whether these empower or marginalize non-Han cultural groups (Sautman 1998; Karmel 1995–96; Mackerras 1999; Wang 1998). Han privilege has often led to marginalization of local cultures (Dreyer 1976; Mackerras 1994, 1999), even as the result has been further fracturing of the mythology of a unified Chinese state (Gladney 2004a).

Socio-cultural relations also intersect with human rights questions in areas of suppression of dissent (Amnesty International 1992a,b; HRW 2006b, 2000), economic exploitation (Fischer 2002, but see Sautman 2000), and social marginalization and Han chauvinism (Bulag 2004). As an advocate for the 1993 Bangkok Declaration on Human Rights ("Final Declaration"), China has embraced a "dynamic and evolving process of international norm-setting" as an opportunity to articulate and justify new standards for human rights that comport with policy priorities of the Chinese government. The privileging of collective over individual rights remains a key element in China's rights discourse (Xu and Qu 2001; He 2006). China also supports principles of the Bangkok Declaration on intrinsic hierarchies of rights, conditionality of political and civil rights on socio-economic development, contingency of rights on local conditions, and other issues that depart from the principles established at the UN World Conference on Human Rights (compare "Final Declaration" with "UN World Conference"). Despite criticisms of the so-called "Asian Values" discourse (Kelly and Reid 1998), such alternative views on human rights have come to challenge liberal rights models (Van Ness 1999). These perspectives on international law standards play an important role in official justifications of China's policies in the Inner Periphery (SCIO 2004a). Indeed, Chinese policy statements embracing greater participation in the international system are predicated on the extent to which the system comports with China's systemic and substantive requirements (Gao 2006). Such positions reveal the extent to which China's compliance with international standards remains contingent on the interests of the Party/state.

Economic dimensions of China's governance in the Inner Periphery operate in the context of social changes that have taken place across China in the wake of the economic growth policies of the past 20 years (Perry and Selden 2000; Dirlik and Meisner 1989). The quest for economic growth and the simultaneous reduction of the role of the state in social and economic life has brought on what might be termed a condition of "post-Socialism" where the Party/state continues to wield significant political and administrative control but chooses to remain uninvolved in the social and economic welfare of the people (Zhang 2008). Yet economic conditions in the Inner Periphery, are vastly different from China proper where dramatic economic growth rates have transformed social conditions. While the Western Development Program (WDP) announced in 1999 purported to raise living standards and expand opportunities for prosperity, the benefits for local minorities remain uncertain.

In the Outer Periphery, China's policies and practices may similarly be understood by reference to a range of international policy discourses. Federalist issues of center-local relations are central to the discourse of local autonomy (Chu 1999–2000). Issues of democratization (Tsang and Tien 1999; Weller 1999; Ghai 1999), sovereignty (Lee 1998), strategic and security relations (Tucker 2005; Zhao 1999–2000; Job, Laliberte and Wallace 1999–2000), economic interdependence (Hsing 1996), and international legal relations (Charney and Prescott 2000) have stimulated greater interest in building federalist-type relationships between China and its Outer Periphery.

Discourses of multiculturalism can assist in understanding PRC law and policy on socio-cultural dimensions of national integration with Hong Kong and Taiwan. While the areas of Hong Kong and Taiwan embody many elements of Han society in China proper, the greater internationalization of these areas has created social conditions that are quite distinct. These variations present significant challenges for China's programs of management and control. as differences between China and its Outer Periphery invite appreciation of cultural diversity, even within the broader ambit of Han societies. As debate continues over the potential for cultural affinity (Johnston 1993; Rigger 1999), the resurgence of local traditional customs and perspectives, particularly around religion (Leung and Chan 2003; Laliberte 2006; Brown 2006), suggests potentially significant differences between Hong Kong and Taiwan and China that warrant analysis through discourses of multiculturalism. Language too plays a role, as the local languages of Hong Kong (Guangdong dialect) and Taiwan (Min-nan dialect) present opportunities to express and validate local identity.

Economic relations between China and the Outer Periphery may also be understood in part by reference to discourses of globalization, which emphasize minimal state intrusion in economic affairs, prioritize issues of market access and trade liberalization, and in general subordinate political authority to the needs of economic growth (Held *et al.* 1999; Lechner *et al.* 2000; Stiglitz 2002). With discourses of globalization as backdrop, Hong Kong and Taiwan have boasted significant economic achievements, supported by greater integration with the world political economy and with uncertain implications for closer ties with the Mainland. While China's efforts to target investment to Hong Kong and to attract investment from Hong Kong and Taiwan have created opportunities for integration, questions continue about the politicization of economic relations.

Reception of norms: the role of Selective Adaptation

While interdisciplinary perspectives are useful to illuminate particular issues and processes relevant to PRC governance in the Inner and Outer Peripheries, specific Chinese policies and practices must still be examined in light of their own particular purposes and content. This unavoidably involves analysis of standards and norms (Etzioni 2000). China's policies and practices of governance in the Inner and Outer Periphery are influenced unavoidably by normative perspectives on political, social, and economic relations. The normative dimensions of China's policies and practices of governance in the peripheries may be understood by reference to the process of *Selective Adaptation*. In contrast to perspectives suggesting the inevitability of convergence of local socio-economic and political arrangements with a global ideal informed largely by values of liberalism (Friedman 1999; Landes 1998), selective adaptation involves a process by which non-local institutional practices and organizational forms are mediated by local norms (Potter 2001; cf. Kennedy 1994). Selective adaptation is made possible by ways in which governments, elites, and other interpretive communities express their own normative preferences in the course of interpretation and application of practice rules (Fish 1980). These interpretive communities comprise government officials, socio-economic and professional elites, and other privileged groups exercising authority borne of political and/or professional position, specialized knowledge, and/or socio-economic status (Miller and Liu 2001; Fewsmith and Rosen 2001). Interpretive communities act as intermediaries who serve as conduits for norms by interpreting non-local (often international) standards for application locally (Dezalay and Garth 2001). With regard to China's relationships with the Inner and Outer Peripheries, the interpretive communities of particular importance naturally include the formal organs of state governance such as State Council Ministries, commissions such as the National Development and Reform Commission (NDRC), and specialized offices such as the Hong Kong and Macao Affairs Office and the Religious Affairs Bureau. Of particular importance is the CPC's United Front regime, which has responsibility for relations with minority nationalities and overseas Chinese groups as well as matters of religion and culture. As well, Party-led leading small groups (*lingdao xiaozu*) on policy issues such as the Western Development Program, minority nationality affairs, and relations with Taiwan and Hong Kong are also part of the interpretive communities that affect policies and practices in the Periphery. The influence of training and education on the perspectives of graduates who go on to make up China's interpretive communities in policy and law is acknowledged in debates over the relative importance given local and international perspectives in curriculum development. Selective adaptation depends on a number of factors, including *Perception*, *Complementarity*, and *Legitimacy*.

Applied to China, selective adaptation analysis permits understanding of local responses to non-local standards at both the conscious and subliminal levels. Intentional or not, interpretation and implementation of international agreements in trade and human rights will depend on normative perspectives of interpretive communities. Thus, the effect of local approaches to governance will depend in part on the extent to which local interpretative communities assimilate the norms underlying particular governance standards. At a consensus level, this means intentional assessment of particular governance standards in light of perspectives on local needs and conditions. Equally important is the prospect that local interpretive communities subject various governance standards to a less conscious process of reception in light of interpretive community norms.

Perception influences understanding about particular governance standards and rule regimes (Unger 1975; Etzioni 2000: 157–78). *Perceptions* about factors such as the purpose, content, and effect of foreign and local institutional arrangements affect the reception and interpretation of these arrangements. For example, in the process of considering international standards while also addressing local institutional arrangements for political, economic, and socio-cultural relations, local interpretation of international perspectives on federalism and local governance, development and local economic relations, and multiculturalism and local society will likely hinge on the content and accuracy of perceptions about non-local institutional rules and practices and about the norms that inform local systems. The interpretation and possible application of non-local standards in light of local systems and norms thus depends on perceptions about both. Factors of perception also play a role in the ways that members of China's interpretive communities, influenced by their training and education, bring to bear personal perspectives about international law and relations in responding to the requirements of international rule regimes (Zeng 2001; Xiao 2003). Thus, perception affects the reception of international legal standards by local interpretative communities, and ultimately influences China's responses to implementation.

Drawn from principles of nuclear physics, complementarity describes a circumstance by which apparently contradictory phenomena can be combined in ways that preserve essential characteristics of each component and yet allow for them to operate together in a mutually reinforcing and effective manner (Bohr 1963; Rhodes 1986; Seliktar 1986). Complementarity may influence the extent to which norms and practices of local cultural communities can engage in mutually effective ways with institutional rules and processes associated with outside systems. For example, local interpretation of international perspectives on federalism and local governance, multiculturalism and local society, and development and local economic relations may depend on complementarity between international and local forms and processes (Kennedy 1994; Potter 2002). Factors of complementarity also arise around questions of compliance with international standards. Local analyses of China's engagement with globalization tend to emphasize the need for compatibility with China's systemic and substantive requirements (Li *et al.* 2005; Gao 2006). Thus, complementarity informs the relationship between local accommodation and resistance to international standards on sustainability in light of local conditions and needs.

Legitimacy is a key factor in the processes by which interpretive communities receive, assess, and transmit institutional and normative arrangements. Certainly legitimacy concerns the extent to which members of local communities support the purposes and consequences of selective adaptation (Weber 1978; Wilson 1992; Rose 2000; Scharpf 2000). As well, legitimacy affects the ways that interpretive communities interpret international perspectives on issues such as federalism and local governance, development and local economic relations, and multiculturalism and local society. Whereas the forms and requirements of legitimacy may vary, it remains essential to the effectiveness of selectively adapted governance practices. Legitimacy may derive from any variety of factors, including patterns of socio-cultural relations, ideology, or local socio-economic or political interest. Whether viewed in terms of pragmatic assessments of the benefits conferred by particular institutional systems; conformity with moral values; or the rational acceptance of the authority of specific regulatory arrangements, legitimacy is an essential element of compliance (Suchman 1995).

Dynamics of legitimacy are evident in China's academic and policy discourses as well as its governance behavior on political, social, and economic relations, where efforts to build legitimacy domestically and internationally are prominent (Jiang 2005). China's engagement with international trade and human rights institutions and standards reveals similarly contested dynamics of legitimacy building. The often informal process by which PRC policies are negotiated with and implemented through local political officials, whether in Han China or in the periphery regions of Tibet, Xinjiang, and Inner Mongolia, reflects contested dynamics over how legitimacy is sought for specific policies and for the governing regime more broadly, and under what terms. China's continued insistence that discussions with the Dalai Lama be confined to informal discussions under the auspices of the CPC's United Front Work Department seems clearly an effort to deny legitimacy to whatever political aspirations the Dalai Lama might hold and ensure that the only legitimate discourse is one confined to cultural and religious issues. Across the Inner Periphery different identity perspectives can be seen to affect issues of legitimacy of policies ranging from education and health to economic and social policies, even to geographic boundaries. Ethnic nationalism has been identified as a key element of identity that may determine the legitimacy and thereby the effectiveness of minority nationality policies (Gladney 2004a) or the potential for capitalist economic growth (Greenfeld 2001). While the requirements of legitimacy may vary with time, space, and context, the effectiveness of selectively adapted regulatory forms depends to an important degree on legitimacy of the content and process of selection.

China's increased participation in the international legal system invites appreciation of issues of normative engagement, as international standards are selectively adapted by interpretive communities influenced by factors of perception, complementarity, and legitimacy. While participation in the world political economy has brought exposure to liberal governance regimes, the dynamics of selective adaptation continue to adjust these to China's official norms of centralized governance (Potter 2003b). The continued influence of norms of Confucian patrimonial sovereignty along with concerns over national unity, wealth, and power have supported orthodox ideals and practices of governance that remain hierarchical and authoritarian (Potter 2004). To a very great extent, as an emerging power with the capacity to impose its own interpretations of international law, China couples the privileges of sovereignty with the practicalities of self-interest to create new norms of international law (Han 1990). While unable for political and economic reasons to reject openly the norms, institutions, and processes of globalization, many Chinese government leaders and policy-makers remain apprehensive about the socio-economic costs of close interconnection with global systems (Heer 2000; Lung 1999). As well, China's relative size and importance allow it to limit the imposition of foreign regulatory norms. Faced with challenges to comply with human rights agreements, for example, the Chinese government often rejoins that it has adopted foreign (mostly Western) rule of law principles (SCIO 2000). Selective adaptation suggests that this involves more than simply issues of political will. Supplementing analysis of willful resistance to reception of international governance standards, selective adaptation helps explain how engagement with international standards of governance is mediated by local cultural and material conditions. Selective adaptation also assists us to understand the origins and implications of local interpretations of imported legal standards, thus illuminating distinctions between local contextualization of familiar institutional arrangements, and truly innovative local approaches that depart from the confines of imported legal forms.

Organizational perspectives: Institutional Capacity

Normative analysis of China's relations with the Inner and Outer Periphery may be supplemented by organizational analysis examining the structural dimensions of policy and practice. This study deploys the paradigm of institutional capacity as an organizational approach to understanding policies and practices of the Party/state on governance in the periphery.

Institutional capacity refers to the ability of institutions to perform their assigned tasks. Institutional capacity has been examined from relational perspectives that focus on issues of responsibility between organizations and their constituencies, efficiency in performance and the use of resources, and accountability to varying sources of authority (Savitch 1998). Functional perspectives have also been applied to the question of institutional capacity, in such areas as access to information, effectiveness, and methods of communication, organizational symmetry, and ability to enforce rules and directives (Blomquist and Ostrom 1999). However, as institutional performance remains contingent on domestic political and socio-economic conditions (Healey 1998;

Martin and Simmons 1998), local conditions of rapid socio-economic and political transformation in China pose particular challenges for institutional capacity. Regulatory institutions operate in an environment of changing contexts and priorities where policy consensus over socio-economic and political transformation in post-Socialist China remains uncertain. Hence institutional capacity in China may be seen to depend on more fundamental conditions of identity, purpose, and perspective (Betancourt 1997; Desveaux 1995; Zweig 2000). Accordingly, institutional capacity in China may usefully be examined by reference to issues of *Institutional Purpose*, location, orientation, and cohesion.

Institutional purpose concerns the extent of consensus around institutional goals. Thus, the capacity of China's government institutions to implement policies and programs of governance for the Inner and Outer Peripheral areas depends on the extent of clarity and consensus regarding policy objectives. Just as China's political reform has been driven by policy goals of social stability and the need to preserve the Communist Party's monopoly on power, so too has legal reform been driven largely by policy imperatives centered on economic growth. The prerogatives of the Party/state remain dominant as neither the imperative of hegemony nor the pursuit of legitimacy are dependent on meaningful accountability to the popular will. Nonetheless, while there is little impetus to imbue China's legal institutions with the "relative autonomy" from state control ascribed to legal institutions in the European and North American traditions (Balbus 1977), there remains significant potential for disagreement and conflict within the government over policy issues affecting the Periphery.

Institutional capacity also depends on factors of geographic *Location*, particularly the question of balancing central authority with decentralization of social and economic development initiatives (Wunsch 1999). China has a long tradition of tension between local and central authorities, and among the regions, and this is particularly pronounced in the periphery. The practical divisions of power and authority between local and central government departments permit an interplay of power and politics between the central and sub-national governments that echoes practices of federalism (Dougherty and McGuckin 2002; Dougherty, McGuckin, and Radzin 2002). Yet the PRC Constitution provides that China is a unitary rather than a federal state which, while nominally encouraging local initiative, still subjects local authorities to unified leadership of the central government. In the process of bargaining that accompanies the allocation of resources and the distribution of costs and benefits of policy initiative (Shirk 1993), formalistic requirements of submission to the unified state limit the flexibility of local officials. Rigid adherence to contested ideals of unitary authority also limits the ability of legal institutions at both local and national levels to exercise even limited autonomy in support of predictability and stability in socio-economic and political relations.

Institutional capacity also depends on *Institutional Orientation*. Orientation refers to the priorities and habitual practices that inform institutional performance. For governance institutions in China, orientation involves

22 *Overview*

particularly the tension between formal and informal modes of operation. This is particularly sensitive in the Inner Periphery, where local social norms may privilege non-formal mechanisms for decision-making, dispute resolution, and resource allocation. Much has been written on the role of informal networks as vehicles for socio-economic regulation (Gold *et al.* 2002). *Guanxi* in China is often seen as operating in juxtaposition to the role of law and legal institutions (Arias 1998; Hui and Graen 1997), reflecting perceptions about the weakness of institutions for managing social, economic, and political relations and allocating resources (Xin and Pearce 1996). Thus, *guanxi* may serve as a substitute for the norms and processes associated with formal institutions, allowing more flexible responses to increasingly complex social, economic, and political relations. Thus the negotiated process of policy implementation is critically dependent on *guanxi* relations. But *guanxi* is not unique to Han culture and may well be shared by local cultures of the periphery. The resiliency of informal relational networks has called attention to the potential re-emergence of civil society dynamics in China. However, the potential role of informal institutions is challenged by the regime's continued insistence on maintaining formal organizational systems to defend ideological orthodoxy and enforce political loyalty. The tension between statist ethics of formal institutionalism and the pervasive local informal arrangements that it strives to control tends to divert resources from institutional performance and undermines institutional capacity.

Finally, institutional capacity depends on issues of *Institutional cohesion*, involving the willingness of individual officials within institutions to comply with edicts from organizational and extra-organizational leaders and enforce institutional goals. Conflicts arise when the goals of particular organizations differ from those of the individuals within these organizations—such as where goals of public policy that drive organizational priorities require subordination of parochial interests of individual officials within the organization. Instances where local minority cadres distort or delay policy implementation would be one example of challenges of institutional cohesion. China's anti-corruption campaigns may be seen as attempts to promote bureaucratic reform by disciplining and subordinating individual goals of officials to organizational goals of institutions (Kwong 1997). Ongoing efforts at bureaucratic reform have faced continuing difficulties in subordinating individual interests of officials to organizational norms of institutions. In the peripheral areas, issues of institutional coherence are particularly important, because of the overlapping influences of economic opportunity and bureaucratic dominion over local social groups.

Summary

China's relations with its Inner and Outer Peripheries reflect factors of history, cultural and geographical perspectives, and changing material conditions. While the particularities of the interplay among these factors vary depending on the context, law and policy remain a constant feature. Factors of selective adaptation and institutional capacity offer useful vectors by which to understand China's policies and practices of governance in these areas. Applied to China's policies and practices on managing local political, social, and economic relations in the Peripheries, these paradigms will generate a comprehensive approach to understanding China's approach to governance in the context of local conditions and the influences of globalization. The discussion that follows concerning political authority, socio-cultural relations, and economic development reveals elements of commonality and difference among the regions of the Inner Periphery and between the Inner and Outer Periphery areas.

2 Political authority in the Inner Periphery[1]

China's governance of the Inner Periphery has generally focused on priorities of political control, socialist transformation, and economic development. While Chinese and foreign observers frequently point to the extent of local resistance to central government rule (Perry and Selden 2000), and to local manifestations of the central state (Diamant *et al.* 2005; Tanner 1998), governance regimes for the Inner Periphery continue to reflect the policy priorities of the Communist Party of China (CPC). In particular, the Party/state has come to emphasize statist legal forms to formalize and lend legitimacy to policy preferences, while attempting to justify its policies and practices by reference to formal law, particularly the PRC Constitution, the Law on Autonomy in Nationality Areas, and ancillary laws and regulations.

Legal provisions for governance in the Inner Periphery

The legal framework for governance in the Inner Periphery derives primarily from the PRC Constitution, the Nationality Regional Autonomy Law (NRAL), and ancillary regulations. In light of China's formal Constitutional and legislative provisions for governance in the Inner Periphery, much attention has also been paid to problematic enforcement of international human rights standards espousing rule of law ideals (Amnesty International 1992a,b; HRW 2006); disparities of economic and social wellbeing (MacKerras 2003); and troubling practices in the regulation of religion (Potter 2003a). While such problems may be taken as evidence of an unwillingness by the PRC government to accept international standards of governance, China's behavior can also be understood in light of normative and organizational factors that influence the content and enforcement of China's own laws.

Constitution of the PRC

The Chinese Constitution addresses governance in the Inner Periphery under Section VI concerning governance in autonomous regions (as well as prefectures and counties). Particular attention is given to formal representation in organs of government. Article 113 provides for appropriate representation at the local People's Congresses by nationalities inhabiting a minority autonomous area region, prefecture or county other than the nationality(ies) in whose name the area is designated. While aimed ostensibly to ensure that non-titular minorities such as Kazakhs and Tajiks in Xinjiang, or Tibetans and Daurs in Inner Mongolia are included in local People's Congresses representation, this provision also has the effect of ensuring representation of Han Chinese resident in minority nationality areas. As well, such provisions tend to reinforce local perceptions that China aims to rule local non-Han minorities by promoting traditional rivalries and political competition among them, thus weakening factors of commonality in relation to the Han (Gladney 2004b: 110–12). Articles 113 and 114 require that among the Chair and Vice-Chairs of the autonomous area People's Congress Standing Committee, as well as the administrative head of the area, be members of the local titular nationality. In fact the chairs of China's five autonomous regions People's Congresses are Han CPC Secretaries, calling into question China's adherence to its own constitutional requirements.

While these provisions allow the appearance of local minority participation in local governance, no parallel provisions govern Party organs. The pervasive influence of the CPC is well known, such that local minority administrative leaders are often perceived as impotent followers of the Han-dominated CPC (Rudelson and Jankowiak 2004: 309). Indeed, authoritative government directives confirm that the Party considers itself to be the final arbiter of minority nationality interests (SNAC 2002: 155). In minority nationality areas, this has the potential to weaken the legitimacy and influence of the local minority administrative heads. While minority officials at operational levels in the bureaucracy are reported as trying to ensure fairness and justice for local minorities—their limited political influence affects the ongoing process of negotiation that comprises local governance and policy-making. While appointment of local minority officials by Han-dominated CPC organs attempts to ensure their malleability in favor of Han-dominated policy positions, tensions remain over political position and personal nationality and identity among minority cadres and People's Congress representatives.

Article 115 affirms the functions and powers of local governance organs, but qualifies these by the limitations of the Constitution, the NRAL, and other laws. This provision affords a rough parallel with the powers granted provincial governments under Constitution Chapter V, including the power of local People's Congresses to enact local regulations subject to reporting to the National People's Congress (NPC) Standing Committee "for the record" (not for approval) (see Constitution: Art. 100). Nonetheless, the imperative to obey the Constitution and the laws (Constitution: Art. 100) includes the requirement under NRAL Art. 7 to "place the interests of the state as a whole above all else." This effectively prohibits local governments from directly opposing policy controls from higher levels, thus diminishing the effect of provisions granting local governance departments authority to adapt state laws and policies to local conditions. Proponents of greater democratic and legal development in China concede that principles of local adaptation should extend beyond the limits of the national minority autonomy system (Zeng 2002: 43–47). The tension between a formal autonomy that is subject to higher-level direction, and local adaptability in the course of enforcing state law and policy means that the extent of local autonomy in practice is unclear. Thus, local officials whether of Han or minority origin hoping to adapt state law and policy to local conditions are restrained by the content of the very laws and policies they are attempting to interpret. The issue becomes more acute with Party officials appointed from outside the region, who may have little incentive to attempt to strengthen local autonomy.

Article 116 reveals similar tensions with respect to the authority of Autonomous Region People's Congresses to enact local autonomy regulations (*zizhi tiaoli*) and specific regulations (*danxing tiaoli*) in light of local characteristics. Such regulations are distinguished from the ordinary regulations covered in Article 115, which are presumably subject to the simple reporting requirement imposed on provinces and centrally administered cities. People's Congresses in the various Autonomous Regions must submit local autonomy regulations and specific regulations to the NPC Standing Committee for approval. Despite the nominal parallelism concerning ordinary regulations, the expansive scope of autonomy regulations and specific regulations suggests that Autonomous Region People's Congresses face approval requirements for local rule-making that are not imposed on provincial People's Congresses (compare Constitution: Arts. 100 and 116). Yet Autonomous Region People's Congresses may approve on their own authority regulations enacted at lower autonomous prefecture and county levels and then simply report to the NPCSC for the record. This creates incentives for Autonomous Region governments to avoid the necessity for NPC approval by coordinating regulatory decisions at lower levels, which in turn can be explained by reference to building local political relationships (Liu and Wang 1998: 229 *et seq.*) This has the potential to undermine local initiative and flexibility at the sub-autonomous region level, as the scope for local government action remains constrained by the terms of AR-level governance initiatives. Indeed so far none of China's autonomous regions has adopted specific regulations, due largely to disputes within particular regions over priorities and policy content.

Articles 117–19 extend significant authority to local Autonomous Region governments in areas of financial management, local economic development, education, science, culture, public health, and physical culture. These provisions underscore the dependency of local government initiatives on central Party and government priorities. Financial autonomy is generally limited to autonomy in the management of local financial resources, but must still adhere to centrally directed policies and plans (Song 2003: 213–16). While similar restrictions exist at the provincial level, the balance of power in the ongoing negotiations between the provinces and the central government over finances seems more balanced (Fischer 2002). Local development plans must also operate under the guidance of state plans. Thus, state initiatives like the Western Development Program (*Xibu da kaifa*) remain outside the purview of local autonomy, while local development efforts must continually defer to priorities issued from the Center. Constitutional grants of local autonomy over administration of education, science, and culture are qualified by the requirement of protecting and putting in order (*zhengli*) cultural heritage and promoting cultural development. These normative standards are then interpreted to mean conformity with Han educational, scientific, and cultural criteria, even as these are portrayed in non-ethnic terms of socialism, modernization, development, and opening up (Wu 1998: 65–167).

Article 120 addresses local security matters, allowing local governments to organize local public security forces to response to concrete local needs, in accordance with the state military system and subject to State Council approval. This provision allows for state direction of local security activities—particularly in peripheral areas where border security and perceived threats of separatism and terrorism have been used to justify expanded national security initiatives (Ma D 2003). Responses to unrest in Tibet and Xinjiang in 2008 and 2009 revealed the operation of this provision in practice.

Article 121 addresses the key governance issue of local language usage in governance activities (Bovington 2004a: 133–37). Direct interaction between government and administrative officials and local residents often involves teams of Han and local minority officials whereby the Han cadre makes the decisions and the minority cadre simply translates, insulating the Han official from direct contact with local minority people. Poor relations between minority and Han cadres are described as increasingly serious, worse even than the period of the 1950s and 60s (Sun Yi 2006: 309–10). In light of the extent of Han domination in places like Xinjiang and Tibet during the first two decades of PRC rule (Millward and Tursun 2004: 87–98), this is a gloomy assessment indeed. While the enactment in 2000 of a law on simultaneous language usage was heralded as an example of the government's commitment to protecting local minority languages, challenges to its full implementation suggest that minority language usage remains marginalized ("Xuexiao shi guanche"; "Renda jiao-ke-wen-wei").

Article 122 depicts the central government as providing financial, material, and technical assistance to autonomous areas and assisting with training local minority cadres. This provision tends to undermine local autonomy as the assistance and training are expressly intended to strengthen central control and ensure policy compliance with central level policy priorities, many of which are not supported locally (Wu 1998: 47–49, 181–82).

Nationality Region Autonomy Law

The NRAL summarizes China's national policies and historical experience in managing relations with its minority nationalities. Enacted initially in 1984, the law was amended in 2001 to account primarily for inclusion of issues related to economic development. The 2001 amendments also reflected the policy orientation of a 1998 Report by the fifteenth CPC National Congress ("China: On CPC Report") and the State Council's 1999 White Paper on

National Minority Policies (SCIO 1999), which called for further formalizing the content and boundaries of autonomy of nationality areas (*minzu quyu*) as essential to national unity and development. The tasks associated with autonomy of national areas include implementation of national laws and regulations, training of minority nationality cadres, self-reliance and contribution to national development, national assistance to the economic and cultural development of nationality areas.

The NRAL is aimed expressly at resolving contradictions in the relationships between central and local authority (Song 2003: 29). Interestingly the joining of terms "nationality" and "region" speaks to questions about which nationalities are included (tellingly the law's title does not mention "minority nationalities"). China's official designation of 56 nationality groups ignores the existence of hundreds more that have not received official designation. Official designations of nationalities also overlook the diversity within designated ethnic groups—in Xinjiang for example the designated Uighur nationality overlooks significant ethnic diversity within the designated group and also ignores religious, linguistic, and political differences among Uighurs themselves (Gladney 2004b: 108–10). Moreover, the all-inclusive term "nationalities" establishes an artificial equality between the dominant Han Chinese and minority population—a particular problem in regions where Han migration has increasingly outpaced local population growth, making local nationality groups minorities in their own homelands. Much of this turns on the effort to entrench principles of unification and centralism, through requirements that nationality autonomy must be subject to state leadership and safeguard national unity (State Council 1999, "Xinjiang zhonggong xuanchuan bu"). The law formalizes policies repudiating notions of "ethnic autonomy" (*minzu zizhi*), "local autonomy" (*difang zizhi*), and "federalism" (*lianbang zhuyi*), and instead confers limited administrative autonomy to areas defined in terms of nationality groups and subject to central leadership (Song 2003: 37). Authoritative statements by NPC deputies from Inner Periphery areas of Xinjiang and Inner Mongolia rejecting principles on "seeking regional and departmental interests at the expense of state interests" ("NPC Mulls Law") exemplify the limits to autonomy contemplated under the NRAL.

At root, the NRAL is aimed at delegating to Autonomous Region Governments limited autonomy to handle civic affairs that are deemed by the Party/state to be a legitimate focus of local governance. Under the label "masters of their own house," minority nationalities are granted authority to manage matters such as cultural expression, heritage and tradition, family relations, etc., as long as this does not intrude on the policy priorities of the central Party/state. And it is the apprehension of the Party/state that issues of minority identity, religion, language, and culture will serve as alternate sources of legitimacy and focal points for loyalty that drives the central government to supervise and restrict such exercises of autonomy as might emerge from minority areas. Thus, the NRAL exemplifies the basic quandary faced by the Han-dominated regime—how to gain legitimacy by appearing to grant autonomy, while at the same time restricting that autonomy so that it does not pose a threat to the power of the Party/state. The contradictions of the NRAL reflect this more fundamental contradiction of China's policies toward governance in the Inner Periphery.

The underlying principles informing the NRAL underscore the dominance of central control. Thus, nationality policy is subordinated to the "four basic principles," namely the imperatives of Marxism–Leninism Mao Zedong Thought, the socialist road, CPC leadership, and the dictatorship of the proletariat (Song 2003: 51–57). This reinforces policy efforts aimed at safeguarding national unity and preserving national interests, while also ensuring that policies on equality and unity of nationalities prevent local resistance to central control. Regulations issued by the Nationalities Affairs Commission and the State Secrets Bureau classified under three levels of secrecy restriction (a) nationalities work on topics such as analysis of conditions potentially harmful to national unity or social stability as well as anti-separatist policies and measures (highest restriction); (b) nationalities policies and measures still under discussion as well as measures for resolving disputes among nationalities and issues in Taiwan, Hong Kong, Macao and other areas abroad that relate to nationalities work in China (middle level restriction); and (c) important issues related to implementing nationalities policies, nationality autonomy work, and international and language matters (basic restriction) ("Minzu gongzuo zhong": Art. 3). By controlling dissemination of information about nationalities policies, the regulations add yet another layer of protection for central state interests. In many ways, the very objectives of the NRAL are in conflict with the reasons for its enactment—namely in the course of defining what nationality autonomy means and what are its limitations, the law works to diminish the very ideal it is intended to celebrate.

Revisions to the NRAL in 2001 were made in part to conform to the expanded role accorded socialist legality (*shehui zhuyi yifa zhiguo*), to support increased investment and development in minority areas, and ensure coordination with other regulatory regimes in China (Dai 2002: 34–42). While the effort to formalize central policies on governance in the periphery is part of a broader program of legalization (Bu 1993; Liu 2003: 275–78), it has particular significance in light of the strong cultural and social resistance to expressions of Han domination in minority areas such as Xinjiang and Tibet (Sun *et al*. 2001: Chapter 2). The NRAL regime for local legislation and rulemaking is essential to controlling such local impulses while still conferring limited governance powers ("NPC Mulls Law").

The unitary state principle dictates that local laws and regulations conform to central Party policies, conform to the limits on jurisdiction conferred to the localities, and confirm to laws enacted at the national level (Zhao 2004: 18–19; "China: On CPC Report"). Thus, the NRAL reiterates constitutional provisions on securing NPC Standing Committee approval for local autonomy regulations and special regulations before they go into effect (NRAL: Art. 19). Moreover, while the NRAL Art. 46 parallels Constitutional provisions (Constitution: Arts. 127 and 128) on courts being responsible to local representative congresses and that judicial decisions are subject to supervision from higher level courts and from the Supreme People's Court, the NRAL omits constitutional provisions on judicial autonomy from administrative interference (Constitution: Art. 126). Hence ideals to bring "legalization" to the conduct of judicial institutions remain constrained by the imperative to preserve the power of the central Party/state.

Under the terms of the unitary state, the PRC Constitution emphasizes socio-economic unity with communities in the periphery. In the Inner Periphery, this is reflected in calls for equality, unity, and mutual assistance with China's minority nationalities (Xin 2004: 226–27). Uncertainties over the relative balance of authority between local and central political and legal authorities are compounded by the particularities of nationality autonomy rules. While local specialists argue persuasively for expanded autonomy to implement national policies such as the Western Development Program, the requirement that local measures conform to national policies and interests tends to marginalize local initiative—even to the point where national level officials fail to take local conditions and suggestions into account (Liu and Shi 2003: 26). This tension between Han officials at the local and central level further complicates governance in the nationality minority areas.

The relationship between central and local political authority can be understood in light of the distinction between "autonomy" (*zizhi*) and the broader term *zizhu*, which can mean "autonomy" as well as "sovereignty." Autonomy as expressed through the term *zizhi* means essentially "self-government," a discretionary jurisdictional status conferred by the Constitution on selected geographic regions in China (Constitution: Arts. 30–31; Wang 2002). Thus, the NRAL specifies the sectors in which local autonomy may be exercised (economic development, education, culture, etc.), subject to broad state planning and approvals. This perspective on autonomy may be compared with the autonomy conferred to foreign investment enterprises under the term "*zizhu*," by which these business are granted a wider scope of independence over matters such as enterprise management, labor, finance, etc. ("Guowuyuan guanyu guli": Art. 15; "Provisions of the State Council": Art. 15; "ZRG Taiwan tongbao touzi baohu fa": Art. 9). The key distinction lies in the nature of conferred authority. Under nationality autonomy (*zizhi*) principles, the authority of local governments is conferred as a discretionary delegation of power from the central government and is qualified by continued central powers of leadership and approval. Under business autonomy (*zizhu*) principles, enterprises are insulated from government interference.

While the NRAL purportedly recognizes local autonomy, requirements for central approvals and the subordination of local economic programs to national supervision suggest that autonomy remains highly constrained (Moneyhon 2002). Thus, Article 15 of the NRAL requires submission to central government leadership and central legal and regulatory provisions. NRAL Article 19 specifies central approval for such local regulatory measures. Decisions and edicts enacted by "higher state organs" (*shangji guojia jiguan*) deemed inappropriate to local conditions may be adjusted or suspended, but this requires local autonomy area organs to seek prior approval from the issuing bodies (NRAL: Art. 20). Economic and financial policies enacted by nationality autonomous areas, while supposedly based on local conditions and requirements, remain subject to the leadership of state planning (NRAL: Art. 25).

State Council White Paper on regional autonomy

The principles of the NRAL were reiterated in the State Council's 2005 White Paper on regional autonomy (SCIO 2005b). The White Paper reiterated principles of autonomy set forth in the original NRAL, although each is subject to considerable interpretation and debate.

(a) "Independently Managing the Ethnic Group's Internal Affairs in Its Autonomous Area"
This ideal is explained solely in terms of the ability of minority nationalities to stand for and vote in elections, which in turn are closely controlled by government and Party processes. The wide gaps between policy preferences of elected deputies and the policy decisions that are ultimately passed and approved by the Party/state speak to the limited influence and effect of the formal capacity to participate in elections. The regulatory controls imposed by the central government and Party leadership often leave little room for adjustment by "elected" representatives at the local level. Hence the limited notion of an ethnic group's internal affairs has significance for the meaning and scope of autonomy more broadly.
(b) "Ethnic Autonomous Areas Enjoy the Right to Formulate Self-Government Regulations and Separate Regulations"
The levels of approvals needed for local self-government regulations to take effect diminishes their functional autonomy. The limitations on permissible interpretations of local legislative authority affect the meaning and scope of autonomy. Moreover, since no Autonomous Region has managed to pass so-called "specific regulations" or "autonomy regulations" that might give meaningful operation to the ideal of self-governance, claims and assertions about rights to self-government remain highly abstract and formalistic.
(c) "Using and Developing the Spoken and Written Languages of the Ethnic Groups"
Bilingual language policies have been problematic in practice, resulting in implicit and often overt suggestions that minority nationalities learn Mandarin, rather that continue to insist on managing socio-economic

and political relations in local languages. Once again, a right purportedly recognized for local minorities remains formalistic and unrealized.

(d) "Respecting and Guaranteeing the Freedom of Religious Belief of Ethnic Minorities"

As discussed in Chapter 3, China's law and policy on freedom of religious belief is strictly limited, distinguishing between belief and behavior and sharply limiting the latter. In essence, people are free to believe what they wish as long as their actions conform to the expectations and policies of the government.

(e) "Retaining or Altering the Folkways and Customs of Ethnic Groups"

China's nationality policies discussed in Chapter 3 reveal assumptions about the fading away of ethnic diversity in the face of a state-wide national culture (largely Han dominated). As a result, preservation of local culture tends to diminish recognition of local ethnic diversity—even to the extent of encouraging simplistic portrayals of minority nationality cultures (even by Han clad in nationality costume) as occurred during the opening ceremony to the Beijing Olympics August 8 2008. Efforts to "preserve" traditional cultural works to essentialize Han preconceptions about minorities and impede recognition of diverse patterns of change in minority communities.

(f) "Independently Arranging, Managing and Developing Economic Construction"

As discussed permissible levels of local adaptation are confined by the imperative of submission to national development goals. As exemplified by the Western Development Program discussed in Chapter 4, central directives on economic policy sharply constrain local initiatives.

(g) "Independently Developing Educational, Scientific, Technological and Cultural Undertakings"

As discussed permissible levels of local adaptation are confined by the imperative of submission to national development goals. The continued influence of the CPC United Front units in the management of education, science, and culture continues to underscore the continued dominance of Han-centered prerogatives of the central Party/state.

Aside from questions about the meaning and implementation of ideals about autonomy, broader governance norms of the Party/state operate to undermine local autonomy. For example, orthodox expressions of Party ideals in "governance capacity" (*zhizheng nengli*) subordinate nationality autonomy areas to central authority:

China's ability to sustain national stability and unity is inseparable from our Party's correct nationalities policies. ... Autonomy of nationality areas is a precondition for national unity and nationality autonomy areas are inseparable parts of the PRC. Their autonomous institutions do not enjoy the same powers as sovereign countries, but operate only as political authority in particular areas. The basic spirit of the autonomy of nationality areas is to oppose secession of nationalities and safeguard national unity.

(Yao 2005: 129–30)

As well, governance norms articulated through institutions of the state insist on the sanctity of the unitary state model (Constitution: Art. 3; SCIO 2005b). Under this approach, nationality autonomous regions and provinces are subject to central dictates. This affects national autonomous regions more than provinces, as their capacity to negotiate spaces of insulation from central fiat are free from the distortions of Han-minority relations, claims about separatism and ethnic nationalism, and the national security dimensions of existing along China's Inner Periphery with bordering and potentially hostile nations.

Taken together, the Constitution, the NRAL, and the State Council White Paper on Regional Autonomy formalize policy preferences of the Party/state on political dimensions of governance in the Inner Periphery. These establish benchmarks for governance practices in the region.

Policies and practices of governance in the Inner Periphery

The application of China's laws and policies on governance in the Inner Periphery is revealed through governance practices in the Nationality Autonomous Regions of Tibet, Xinjiang, and Inner Mongolia.

Tibet

Perspectives on China's governance in Tibet have unavoidably been influenced by questions about the historical bases for Chinese sovereignty (Grunfeld 1996; Norbu 2001; Shakya 1999; Smith 2008). While the legal justifications for Chinese sovereignty and for Tibet independence remain subject to debate (Sautman 2001), China's policies in Tibet have widely been cast in colonial terms (*"China's Tibet"*). In contrast to central government assertions about "peaceful liberation" (*Heping jiefang Xizang*) and the "quelling of armed rebellion" (*Pingxi Xizang panluan*) to justify the imposition of Chinese rule, many in the international scholarly community have suggested that China's assertion of political control represented an exercise in invasion and annexation (International Commission of Jurists). Other issues arise concerning the right to self-determination of the Tibetan people (ICLT 1997; McCorquodale and Orosz 1993; Sloane 2002; Harris 2008b). Without retracing the arguments surrounding these important issues, China's policies of governance in Tibet remain worthy of inquiry nonetheless, and can usefully be examined by reference to the official reporting on Tibet work as well as particular perspectives of the ruling CPC.

As with other areas of the Inner Periphery, China's rule in Tibet has been cast in terms of formal law and regulation, subject to the dominance of

Party policy (Sorensen and Phillips 2004; ICLT 1997). During the period following the 1992 Minority Nationalities Work Conference, governance priorities for Tibet involved three major issues: (a) economic development; (b) religion policies; and (c) structures of autonomy. Following the Work Conference the government accepted marginally wider accommodation of minority aspirations. With the exception of particularly sensitive issues like civil and political rights, the government permitted a wider range of local opinion and expression, allowed establishment of local NGOs for social development and poverty reduction, and permitted an increased number of Tibetans to study abroad (Shakya 2008: 11). As revealed in the official record of the CPC Tibet Committee on governance activities in Tibet (Zhonggong xizang zizhiqu weiyuanhui, hereafter "RMET"), each of these policy discourses began with initiatives by the Party Center in Beijing, which were then transmitted through the Party committee system to the local governance administration. Important policy initiatives emerge from the processes of Party committees and then are disseminated to government administrative departments for implementation. Tibet Autonomous Region (TAR) Party congresses are held to finalize local policy initiatives that are then formally enacted by TAR government and People's Congresses ("Xizang jiakuai").

The consistent pattern reported in the RMET reveals that TAR governance decisions, representative congress meetings, legislative and regulatory initiatives, and other governance initiatives were preceded by meetings of the TAR Party Committee at which the process and content of local administration are discussed and approved. For example, following the 1992 Minority Nationalities Work Conference, the TAR Party Committee oversaw dissemination of General Secretary Jiang Zemin's January 14 speech to all levels in the government and distributed edicts on local programs for economic development later in January (RMET 2005: 607). This was followed in March by publication of TAR government policies on economic development (RMET 2005: 615). Similarly, throughout 1993–94, the TAR Party Committee can be seen directing government initiatives in areas of education policy, health policy, and economic development (including foreign investment) (RMET 2005: 667–72). The reassignment of Chen Kuiyuan from Inner Mongolia to succeed Hu Jintao as Tibet Party Secretary in 1992 saw increased attention to reliance on economic development policies to quell local unrest. Premier Li Peng's speech to the Third Tibet Work Conference noted that Ren Jianxin (Supreme People's Court), Luo Gan (Politburo member in charge of the *Zhengfa*— law and politics—system), and Wang Yaoguo (CPC United Front Work Department) would be responsible for implementation of Tibet development policies, thus revealing the combined role of Party political organs and punitive legal institutions in carrying out government programs (Li Peng 1994: 474).

Following the Third National Tibet Work Conference in July 1994, the TAR Party Committee oversaw distribution of conference materials and directed policy formulation to implement work conference directives

(RMET 2005: 681–92). Following a Beijing CPC meeting on recruiting Tibetan cadres, the TAR Party Committee convened working sessions in Tibet to oversee cadre recruitment efforts in the local government administration (RMET 2005: 701–27). In December 1995, the TAR Party Committee convened to approve the Fifth Five Year Plan for Tibet (RMET 2005: 733). In 1995, following the death of the Panchen Lama, the delicate issue of selection of a successor presented major challenges for the central government. The CPC United Front Work Department and the State Council Religious Affairs Committee prepared the final political reports on the selection process and results (RMET 2005: 730). After the selection was finalized in November, the TAR Party Committee provided direction to the TAR government on information and propaganda efforts on this highly sensitive issue (RMET 2005: 730–38). Party security chief Luo Gan played a central role in the selection and in the preparations for implementation, indicating CPC appreciation of the extreme sensitivity of the Chinese government's decision to thwart the selection made by the Dalai Lama in favor of its own preferences (RMET 2005: 730).

The dominance of the TAR Party Committee in coordinating local government processes of policy-making and implementation continued in evidence through the late 1990s on issues of economic development, education, environment, and religion (RMET 2005: 796, 817, 833, 859, 866, 871). This pattern of dominance by the TAR Party Committee suggests how the Party seeks to retain nearly complete control over government decision-making on issues of governance in Tibet. While this pattern is generally consistent with provincial governance in Han areas of China proper, it is particularly noteworthy in areas such as the TAR which are nominally classified as "autonomous" areas. Moreover it appears that control by the Han-dominated CPC is greater in the TAR because patterns of patronage and mutual restraint that affect governance in the provinces of Han China (Goodman 1997) are not as evenly balanced between local and central power in minority nationality areas where Han-minority relations are inherently skewed in favor of Han dominance.

Of particular importance to structures of governance were the revision to the Nationality Region Autonomy Law in 2001 and the issuance of the State Council White Paper on Tibet (SCIO 2004b). As applied to Tibet, the NRAL's provisions on local autonomy (*zizhi*) are constricted by requirements of fealty to national policy goals and institutional requirements of achieving central-level approvals for local legislative and policy initiatives. When interpreted in light of Party policy imperatives, the limited autonomy provisions of the NRAL are further confined to the limits of national development and security goals. As discussed in the State Council White Paper, autonomy for Tibet's minority nationalities depends on upholding principles of national unity and opposing separatism—thus inserting central political imperatives as criteria for determining the acceptability of local assertions about autonomy. The White Paper forcefully distinguishes the situation in Tibet from that in

Hong Kong, where greater grants of autonomy are in place (SCIO 2004b). China's claim to long-standing sovereignty over Tibet is interpreted to mean that concessions about local conditions, evident in the one country–two systems approach applied to Hong Kong (and Taiwan) do not apply in Tibet ("Dalai Lama urged"). Instead, Tibet's autonomy depends on fealty to China's CPC-led socialist system while local autonomy is confined to matters of implementation of national policy directives.

As with other issues, the leadership role of the TAR Party Committee has been critical. Following the national work conference on Tibet cadres in September 2003 (RMET 2005: 1030), TAR Governor Re Di gave an important speech to the Central Party School on Tibet, addressing issues of cadre recruitment as well as broader questions of governance (RMET 2005: 1032). A TAR cadre meeting in October was followed by the expanded session of the TAR Party Committee in November (RMET 2005: 1034–36). These laid the groundwork for the TAR representative congress held the following May and the distribution of the State Council's White Paper on Tibet in May (RMET 2005: 1053–54). Tibet Governor Re Di's speech on nationalities autonomy set the tone for these meetings (RMET 2005: 1055), and offered a preview of the campaign to increase recruitment of Tibetan cadres by central and local CPC units (RMET 2005: 1062–63) and the ongoing efforts to implement the Nationality Region Autonomy Law (RMET 2005: 1068). The inspection tour of Tibet by the CPC United Front Work Department in November suggested the extent of Party attention to local implementation of autonomy policies as well as local reactions (RMET 2005: 1076). As with other policy initiatives, autonomy policies for Tibet were pursued through careful preparation through the CPC system and particularly the use of the TAR Party Committee as a vehicle for local dissemination. The transfer of Zhang Qingli from Xinjiang to be Tibet Party Secretary in 2005 suggested that the Party center remained committed to political repression of local aspirations for greater autonomy.

Yet, as indicated by the violence that broke out in Tibet and in Tibetan regions in Gansu, Sichuan, and Qinghai in March 2008, Party and government policies aimed at building stability and development have resulted in ongoing resentment (Yardley 2008a; York 2008). The extent to which the central authorities seemed unaware of the extent of the resentment was evident in a pair of widely publicized interviews with TAR Party Secretary Zhang Qingli that appeared only a week before the first protests, in which Zhang sought to highlight the successes of CPC nationality policies in Tibet even while attacking the Dalai Lama ("Zhang Qingli zuoke").

Reports appear to agree that the unrest began as a non-violent demonstration outside the Jokhang Temple in Lhasa on March 10 2008 to mark the forty-ninth anniversary of an unsuccessful Tibetan uprising against Chinese rule (CECC 2009a; Congressional Research Service: 1–4; Barnett 2008a). Arrests followed, which were then protested by monks from the Drepung, Sera, and Ganden monasteries, who were then also contained by security forces.

Protests expanded across the TAR and into Tibetan areas of neighboring provinces of Sichuan, Gansu, and Qinghai. On March 14, in the face of apparent inaction by Chinese public security forces, Tibetan crowds began attacking Chinese businesses and individuals in Lhasa, resulting in violent suppression by the People's Armed Police and Public Security organs and the arrest of demonstrators and sympathizers, under the rubric of "people's war" against supporters of the Dalai Lama and so-called "nationalist separatism."

The central government's response to the unrest revealed the extent to which stated policy priorities of security and development are enforced through the threefold organs of public security, procuracy, and judiciary (*gong-jian-fa*). Detention of hundreds of demonstrators was followed by prosecution and sentencing of upwards of 55 people to imprisonment ranging from three years to life (Wong 2008b). Lawyers who offered legal assistance to Tibetan protesters were summoned for questioning and told to avoid such sensitive cases, and warned that their licenses would be suspended (UN Committee Against Torture 2008a: para. 2(b); Chinese Human Rights Defenders 2008; Drew 2008a). At least two lawyers who defended Tibetans arrested after the uprising actually were denied renewal of their licenses (Cody 2008). In an ironic twist, such repression in the TAR has expanded to areas of environment and labor in Han China, suggesting that models of repression developed for the nationality autonomous regions have subsequently been applied in Han areas of China proper. The tools of dominion in the Inner Periphery are thus used to establish Party/state dominance in the core.

In a pattern of repression reminiscent of the martial law period following the 1989 protests, the government has targeted the Tibetan population as a whole, imposing self-criticism and political education campaigns not just in the monasteries where the 2008 protests began, but at virtually all levels of civil society (Shakya 2008: 23). Under the leadership of a "110 Command Center" including the PLA, People's Armed Police, Ministry of Public Security, and the CPC's United Front Work Department, a wide-ranging campaign of education, suppression, and intimidation has been launched to bring Tibet under control (Rajan 2008). TAR Party Secretary Zhang Qingli has instituted a series of administrative committees in monasteries to control religious activities associated with alleged ethnic nationalism and to wage long-term education and propaganda efforts against the Dalai Lama ("Olympic crackdown"). An aggressive security presence across the TAR has seen expanded use of security checkpoints, spontaneous arrests, and violent attacks on Buddhist monks (ICT 2008b).

The government's crackdown in the TAR and neighboring areas was coupled with strident denunciations of the Dalai Lama. In a coordinated series of editorials issued March 17, the government accused the Dalai Lama of instigating the violence ("Dalai jituan"; "Zhenfeng xiangdui"; Lague 2008; Barboza 2008), even as he denied involvement and threatened to resign if the violence continued ("Dalai Lama threatens"). Labeling the Dalai Lama as a "terrorist," Party and government security organs intensified efforts to arrest and intimidate Tibetans in the TAR under the rubric of "people's war" (Lam 2008b; ICT 2008b). Even as discussions were under way to recommence a seventh round of talks with the Dalai Lama, the government kept up its personal attacks, labeling him a "jackal clad in monk's robes and an evil spirit with a human face and the heart of a beast" (Singh 2008).

Following the violent suppression of Tibetan demonstrators, China faced significant international pressure to continue dialogue with the Dalai Lama as an implied condition for support for the Beijing Olympics. Premier Wen Jiabao's public assertion of a willingness for dialogue made the talks unavoidable ("Chinese Leader") and in late April, the government announced it would meet with envoys from the Dalai Lama (Yardley 2008b). Yet on the eve of the May 4 talks with the Dalai Lama's representatives, who called for a reassessment of China's Tibet policy (Gyari 2008a) the government labeled him a criminal ("China Condemns") and accused him of "spewing lies" ("Beijing Commentary"). The Chinese government treated the one-day talks with caution—terming them "only a beginning" and denying that further discussions were scheduled, insisting that the Dalai Lama meet preconditions including stopping separatist activities ("China lays out ground rules"). The Dalai Lama's envoy by contrast termed the session useful and indicated that the two sides had agreed to meet again (Pomfret 2008).

A seventh round of talks was scheduled for early June, but then postponed due to the Sichuan earthquake ("Beijing–Dalai Lama Talks"). Even so, the Dalai Lama expressed a sense of uncertainty as to whether the current approach to dialogue was having any effect on China's policies in Tibet ("Gloom descends"). Nonetheless, the talks resumed July 1 (Yardley 2008c), involving Du Qinglin, Director of the CPC United Front Work Department and Lodi Gyari and Kelsang Gyaltsen, envoys of the Dalai Lama ("Chinese central"). The talks ended without agreement, as the Dalai Lama's representative termed the session "one of the most difficult sessions" ("Tibet envoy"). Although agreement was had for an eighth round of talks to begin at the end of August, there is emerging a palpable sense of frustration from the Dalai Lama's side, questioning the sincerity of the Chinese commitment to resolution of the Tibet question and challenging Beijing's characterization of claims raised by the Dalai Lama (Gyari 2008b). The Chinese government has proposed a new round of talks, but once again insisted on preconditions, including acceptance of the "three adherences" (CPC leadership, socialism with Chinese characteristics, and the existing regional autonomy system set forth in Chinese constitution and laws) ("Dalai Lama urged"). In a major change of position, the Dalai Lama apparently indicated a willingness to accept the socialist system insisted on by the Chinese side: "The main thing is preserve our culture, to preserve the character of Tibet ... that is what is important, not politics" (Kristof 2008).

Yet the Chinese preconditions extend to other issues as well. According to Du Qinglin, implementing the regional autonomy system included four requirements:

1   The interests of the country and the Chinese nation should be put above all else. National unification and ethnic solidarity must be resolutely safeguarded;
2   The regional ethnic autonomy system is exercised under China's unitary system and is difference from the federal system or confederation as implemented in some countries;
3   The regional ethnic autonomy system is a basic policy for solving ethnic issues in China and a fundamental political system in the country. It is different from the "one country–two systems" system implemented in Hong Kong and Macao;
4   The regional ethnic autonomy system is a combination of ethnic autonomy and regional autonomy and will never allow ethnic splitting in the name of "true ethnic autonomy" to undermine ethnic solidarity ("Dalai Lama Urged").

Du Qinglin's articulation of the components of China's nationality regional autonomy system underscored the government's limited vision of local autonomy. Requirements on such matters as the primacy of national interest, rejection of federal and quasi-federal arrangements, and distinguishing between nationality autonomy and the autonomy extended to Hong Kong and Macao (and by implication Taiwan) underscore familiar orthodoxies on the primacy of central over local interests, priorities, and power. The critique of autonomy based on ethnic identity echoes provisions of the NRAL discussed above, and yet raises doubts about the very ideal of autonomy for minority nationalities. The emphasis on regional autonomy combined with the reality of increased Han dominance in Tibet suggests that few if any provisions are made or expected to safeguard meaningful autonomy for minority nationalities in general and Tibetans in particular. Despite the Dalai Lama's overture on the issue of socialism, the Chinese government representatives claimed the talks had failed and charged continuing perfidy by the Dalai Lama, claiming not only that he had violated the so-called "four not-to-supports" (*si bu zhi*: activities disturbing the 2008 Oympics; supporting violence or terrorist activities; and seeking Tibetan independence), but went on to allege collusion with Falungong and Xinjiang separatists ("China says").

Du's assertions also offered a context of political control and subjugation of Tibet that is glossed over in the 2008 State Council White Paper on Protection of Tibetan Culture (SCIO 2008b). But even as the White Paper extols government efforts to protect Tibetan language and cultural artifacts, it echoes provisions of the NRAL and reiterates conventional policy mantras on equality of all nationalities; claims of Han influences on local nationality cultures; and a formalistic recitation of policy ideals and legislative enactments on social and economic development as if they were evidence of actual conditions. Significant attention is given to preservation of the Tibetan language—a laudable expression of policy intention, but which has been uncertain in practice. The White Paper also offers praise for protection of achievements in Tibetan medicine, without acknowledging that the systems for preparing, marketing, and protecting intellectual property in Tibetan medicine privilege the Han Chinese investors and companies which dominate the field. Religious belief is also seen as an area that has been protected under benign Chinese rule, while omitting that the very Chinese laws that are presented as protecting religious beliefs also impose limits on religious behavior, emphasizing requirements of "normalcy," adherence to political orthodoxy, and compliance with ever more stringent rules on religious organizations and activities. The White Paper was issued in an apparent effort to counter charges of "cultural genocide" associated with the Dalai Lama, in response not only to Chinese policies in Tibet generally, but also following the government's harsh crackdown following unrest in March 2008. While the Dalai Lama's acceptance of the socialist system suggested significant movement in his position, whether he will be able to accept ever-escalating Chinese demands remains uncertain—and, indeed, the Dalai Lama has suggested that the talks are not headed in a productive direction and that he may withdraw.

The Chinese government's efforts involve audiences beyond the Dalai Lama and the international community. The White Paper also seemed aimed at responding to a growing cohort of Han Chinese intellectuals who have called for reform in China's Tibet policies. Shortly after the unrest in March 2008, a group of leading Chinese intellectuals, including Wang Lixiong and Liu Xiaobo, published an open letter offering 12 suggestions for dealing with the Tibetan situation ("Twelve Suggestions"). These included calling for an end to Chinese propaganda attacks on the Dalai Lama; investigating the causes of the March unrest; moderation of political investigations and revenge against Tibetan people; opening Tibet to international media; more fulsome implementation of rights to religious belief and freedom of speech in Tibetan areas; and a call for dialogue with the Dalai Lama. While some of these suggestions (e.g., media access; dialogue) have been met at least in a limited way, the call for reassessment of political policies preoccupied with security and suppression of belief and expression remains unsatisfied.

Subsequent proposals for political reform contained in the 2008 Charter 08 document associated with Liu Xiaobo reiterate the need for new policies supporting "dignity, freedom and human rights for minorities" (Link 2009). Liu was subsequently arrested, tried, and sentenced to 11 years in prison (Watts 2009). Wang Lixiong went further to suggest that the solution to the Tibet question lay neither in the Dalai Lama's "middle way" nor in the CPC's policies of control but rather in a system of "progressive democracy" that would combine limited local level elections with provisions for continued political leadership by higher levels (Wang 2008: 33–34). Wang presented this approach as more effective in limiting the possibility of separation and also in restraining the role of religion as a basis for political action.

While such efforts may be dismissed by the government as idealistic efforts by dissidents, other policy proposals are less easy to ignore. Dr. Zhang Boshu, a former scholar at the prestigious Chinese Academy of Social Sciences (CASS), offered similar suggestions including halting demonizing attacks on the Dalai Lama and engaging in dialogue instead (Zhang 2008). Zhang called for expanded protection of human rights including rights in religion, and more effective reliance on a constitutional democratic system—by implication an approach analogous to that applicable for Taiwan (ibid.). Whether such proposals or others will induce the Chinese government to engage seriously in dialogue over reforms in Tibet remains uncertain. To the contrary, repression seems the order of the day, as Zhang Boshu for example was dismissed from his CASS position ("Vocal government critic").

In spite of ongoing debates over the meaning of autonomy and the rights of Tibetans to self-determination ("Time to reconsider"; Harris 2008b), political concessions to the reality of Chinese control continue. The British government decided in October 2008 to formally recognize China's sovereignty over Tibet ("Miliband clears up"; Barnett 2008b) after decades of nuanced ambiguity. The prominent professional journal *Hong Kong Lawyer* apparently decided to reverse its decision favoring publication and instead to suppress an article raising questions about the application of the right of self-determination for Tibet (Harris 2008a). The decision by the US President and fellow Nobel Laureate to avoid meeting with the Dalai Lama in late 2009 was interpreted widely as an effort to appease Beijing and induce cooperation on a range of economic, environmental, and security issues (McCabe 2009). By conforming to Beijing's preferred stance on foreign governmental relationships with the Dalai Lama and by extension affirming disinterest in China's policies and practices in Tibet, such actions may well embolden the Chinese government to resist further compromise.

Chinese policies of repression in Tibet following the unrest of March 2008 (e.g., UN Committee against Torture 2008b: 8–9; Buchung Tsering 2008a,b; Magnier 2008; "Disappearances continue") and the government's belligerent demeanor concerning the dialogue discussions that have taken place offer little cause for optimism. China's continued vilification of the Dalai Lama and its denunciation coupled with obvious distortions of negotiating points submitted at China's request by the Dalai Lama envoys Lodi Gyari and Kelsang Gyaltsen may well undermine the central government's effectiveness in building reconciliation on Tibet issues (compare "Memorandum on Genuine Autonomy" with "Address at the Press Conference"). Indeed, the Dalai Lama's call for a "special Meeting" at Dharamsala in November 2008 suggested a realization that the Chinese government never had a serious intention of negotiating a reasonable accommodation on Tibet (Stewart 2008; "Special Message"). Although the Dharamsala meeting affirmed a commitment to the "Middle Way," significant voices urged a return to former policies advocating full independence for Tibet (Sperling 2008). The Dalai Lama's suggestions that he has "given up" on talks with China ("Dalai Lama says") and the prospect that he will appoint a regent to lead Tibetan Buddhism ("Dalai Lama may appoint") underscore the possibility that his mediating influence on the Tibetan community may diminish. The prospect looms large that the Dalai Lama's peaceful "Middle Way" approach seeking a measure of autonomy for Tibet within the context of Chinese law and subject to Chinese sovereignty will give way to more confrontational approaches.

Patterns and practices of China's governance of Tibet reflect imperatives of central policies on security and development imposed through organizational and procedural mechanisms of Party control. Autonomy is carefully managed to ensure fealty to PRC rule. While China's governance policies have changed over time to accommodate local conditions more fully and even to attempt inclusion of local nationalities in limited areas of governance and decision-making, these are the result of central-level Party decisions. To the extent that local autonomy is recognized, it is not an autonomy aimed at safeguarding the cultures and aspirations of minority nationalities, but rather one that allows limited local administration in a region increasingly dominated by Han Chinese. Such an approach remains consistent with the "unitary state" ideals of the PRC Constitution and the Nationality Region Autonomy Law, and reveals the ways in which autonomy in the Inner Periphery remains constrained by imperatives of Party/state sovereignty and control.

Xinjiang[2]

In Xinjiang, China faces geographic, ethnic, and religious barriers to unified governance and national security (Ding 2004: 15–16). While Jiang Zemin had noted during his first inspection tour of Xinjiang in September 1990 that economic development in the region required political stability, there appeared to be little agreement among leading cadres in Xinjiang as to what were the main obstacles to stability. Governance in Xinjiang has focused to a significant extent on implementation of centrally directed campaigns to attack alleged separatism and terrorism among Xinjiang's local populace (Saiget 2000b; Amnesty International 1992). Local courts were praised for "100% rate in apprehension sanction, hearing approval, case-closing, and legitimacy" signaling the importance of judicial compliance with the higher level directions on the criminal processes of arrest, trial, and sentencing ("Legal System Publicity"). Even after the Central Minority Nationalities Work Conference of 1992 and its policy focus on promoting economic development and combining political control with improved local living conditions (Jiang 1992a), the local government remained focused on cracking down against separatism and counter-revolutionary crimes ("Xinjiang Regional Law").

Inspection visits by Li Ruihuan in August 1994 and Zhu Rongji in September 1995 revealed the extent of local concerns with socio-economic issues such as water treatment and health, although these did not seem to receive as much attention as political factors (Zhu *et al.* 2004: 263–64). The appointment of Wang Lequan as Party Secretary for Xinjiang in 1995 suggested the range of policy priorities that would inform the Party/state's practices in Xinjiang. Formerly Vice-Chair of the XUAR People's Government and Acting Secretary for the region, Wang had long-standing links with Hu Jintao through their shared careers in the Communist Youth League and is said to have Hu's patronage ("Wang Lequan"). Hu's record in Tibet during his 1988–92 tenure there of combining the rhetoric of minority unity with policies of repressive political rule appears to have influenced Wang's similar approach in Xinjiang. Wang had developed a reputation for combining strict fealty to central Party directives with harsh repression of dissent in the regions under his authority. Empowered to address local development concerns while also containing alleged separatism and religious extremism, Wang came to embody the main contours of central policy.

Party Document No. 7 (March 19 1996) issued by the Politburo Standing Committee based on reporting from its Politics and Law Committee on conditions in Xinjiang, concluded that the basic threats to stability in Xinjiang derived from nationalist separatism (*fenlie zhuyi*) and unlawful religious activities (Zhu *et al.* 2004: 259). Acknowledging the complexity and long-term character of these challenges, the report called for all levels of Party and government to wage unremitting struggle against separatist activities. Jiang Zemin echoed these themes on his return visit to Xinjiang in 1998, and expanded the potential reach of China's nationalities policies to focus not simply on socio-political issues within the XUAR but on their impact for the region as a whole—underscoring an expanded appreciation of Xinjiang's strategic importance for China's relations and interests in Central Asia (Zhu *et al.* 2004: 258–60). Thus issues of ethnic nationalism and religion took on significance not just for local social stability but for China's national interests.

Outbreaks of violence in Yining and Urumqi in February 1997 called to mind a lengthy history of local resistance (Wang 1999) and inspired the central government to further efforts at repression. Local campaigns in Aksu and Yili saw alleged separatists punished with execution and life imprisonment ("China Said to Arrest", "Xinjiang Daily"). In March the NPC amended the Criminal Law of the PRC to increase the severity of criminal sentences for "terrorism" and permitting persons alleged to be "taking advantage of national or religious problems to instigate the splitting of the state or undermine the unity of the state" to be charged under the harsh provisions on endangering state security ("Xinjiang Secretary"). In April, the Xinjiang Party Committee and People's Government began a security campaign based on the spirit of the Politburo Document No. 7 and its "Opinion on the work of correcting security and seriously attacking violent crime" (Zhu *et al.* 2004: 260). Upon returning from a trip to Europe where he pressured governments to support China's stand on ethnic separatism, NPC Chair Qiao Shi noted, "We must always guard against and strike hard at activities to split the unification of the motherland and undermine unity among people of various ethnic groups—it will be our top priority work at present and a task for a long time to come" ("Qiao Shi Stresses Efforts").

During the years following the Yining events, the government oversaw continued severe punishments imposed on alleged separatists. During 1997 through 1999, upwards of 30,000 cadres were assigned to security work, including local level rectification and establishment of basic level security organs (Zhu et al. 2004: 260–61). The tasks for the campaign revealed the extent of alienation of local communities and the challenges faced by the Party in building local support. Combined with imposing avowedly harsh measures to punish alleged separatism and religious extremism, the rectification also aimed to induce local level cadres and communities to expose national separatists and to conduct face-to-face education to raise ideological and political awareness ("Teams sent")—all of which seemed an admission of the gulf that separated central government imperatives from local perspectives and interests, and Han-dominated Party perspectives from those of local minority communities. Beijing has articulated themes of "anti-separatism" and used the rubric of "anti-terrorism" to crack down against local dissidents (You 2004). General Secretary Jiang Zemin's return visit to Xinjiang in July 1998 following attendance in Hong Kong of first anniversary celebrations on the handover and attendance of a meeting of Shanghai Cooperation Organization members in Kazakstan, embodied themes of national unity and security ("China: Jiang"). Noting the importance of Party policy restricting religious adherents to normal and lawful activities, Jiang also emphasized the role of the PLA, People's Armed Police (*Wujing*), and Public Security organs in ensuring unity and stability (ibid.).

In February 1999, two alleged terrorists were subject to a public trial and execution in Yili and eight others sentenced to lengthy imprisonment ("AFP: PRC Executes"), while in August 1999, alleged separatists in Nongsishi (within Yili Prefecture) were executed or imprisoned, while death sentences were imposed on ten other defendants in Yili ("AFP: PRC Sentences"; "APF: 10 Moslem"). In the Autonomous Region capital of Urumqi 10 people were executed in March 1999 and another 45 given suspended death sentences for crimes of provoking unrest (Abulkhatin 1999), while in October separatist defendants were subject to a public sentencing rally followed by execution ("Muslim Terrorists"). These efforts served notice to local communities of the central government's intent to suppress religious proselytism as a separatist activity.

Compounding the intensity and duration of judicial punishments against alleged separatism, the central government directed a renewed "Strike Hard" campaign following a Central Public Order Work Conference April 2–3, 2001. At this meeting, Jiang Zemin, Zhu Rongji and other state and Party leaders emphasized the use of local political and legal institutions to crack down on serious crime including activities of separatists ("National Public Order Work Conference"). Zhu's speech set the tone and revealed much about the policy priorities of the central Party/state. His reference to bringing local thinking into line with central priorities avers to the ongoing challenge of enforcing central directives through local officials. While policy enforcement often involves complex and informal processes of adjustment to local interests and conditions, Zhu reveals impatience with outcomes that do not conform to judgments and policy-making arrangements of the Center. This is underscored by Zhu's directive that local officials "resolutely act in accordance with central demand." While acknowledging that the "strike hard campaign" should address economic crime, the sequencing in Zhu's references to economic crime and then public order (noted twice) indicates the priority given to the latter, and in the context where public order is conflated with control over alleged ethnic separatism and religious extremism (through the reference to "current outstanding problems"), conveys the importance placed on control of local minorities. Zhu's reference to the "practical results" suggests that the time-honored practices of pro forma and short-term compliance with the directives of central campaigns would not be acceptable.

Attendance at the Central Work Conference by government and party officials from Xinjiang, including from the Xinjiang Production and Construction Corps (*Bingtuan*), signaled the extent to which the Strike Hard campaign would be aimed at alleged separatism in Xinjiang and would deploy a wide range of political and security organs (ibid., "Agence France Presse"). Shortly thereafter, Xinjiang Party Secretary Wang Lequan convened a regional public order conference in Urumqi April 14–15, at which the strike hard campaign was announced for Xinjiang, to be implemented by the local Party Politics and Law Commission ("Xinjiang Party Secretary"). More than 500 officials, including Party secretaries at all localities as well as chief judges and prosecutors were instructed to direct the campaign against separatism and terrorism (ibid.). Courts in particular were called upon to use model cases as examples of the Party/state's resolve to punish alleged "splittists". Whatever protections might be afforded in theory by China's criminal procedure system seemed secondary to the need for courts to:

> ... conscientiously clean up the cases on trial and ensure promptness in handling cases and making court decisions. ... In the near future all localities must select a group of major cases which have influence on society, hold public trials, hand out severe punishments to a group of criminals, execute a group of criminals, and swiftly form a powerful momentum for the "strike hard" drive throughout the region.
>
> (ibid.)

Following this meeting, the Xinjiang Autonomous Region High Court took the lead in carrying out instructions to accelerate public trials and punishments of alleged separatists ("PRC to Intensify"). Notices issued to local courts in Xinjiang directed specific punishments for separatist activities (ibid.; "Xinjiang Prefecture"). The Strike Hard effort was aimed not only at alleged separatists, as local public security organs and the courts seemed to direct significant efforts toward non-political crimes of murder and robbery, rounding up some 6,000 criminal elements and law violators in May ("PRC's Urumqi"). Nonetheless the campaign was an important example of the deployment of political–legal institutions in the service of policy goals of the Party/state. "Legalization" of governance still meant subservience to the imperatives of the Center.

The extent to which the Party found itself struggling with alleged separatist and religious sentiments among its own local cadres was evidenced by the Xinjiang CPC Committee's "Interim Provisions on Disciplinary Punishments for Party Members and Organs that Violate Discipline in Fighting Separatism and Safeguarding Unity" ("Xinjiang Regulations on Party Discipline"). These regulations acknowledged "violations of Party discipline committed by Communist Party members and Party organizations," and specified a wide range of punishable activities, including:

(a) Planning and organizing national separatist activities and engage in illegal activities under the cover of religion both as "core members" and less involved "participants".

The tacit admission that local Party officials were engaging in separatist activities and participating in religious activities underscored not only failed enforcement of provisions of the Party Constitution and the various Party discipline measures, but also raised questions as to whether such provisions would ever be enforceable through local minority cadres. The conflict between the imperatives of the Han-centered Party/state and the local perspectives of minority cadres was coming into sharp relief.

(b) Sheltering and giving financial and material assistance for separatist and religious activities.

This reference likely alludes to local minority cadres contributing to local mosque-led fund raising efforts. Interpreted through the lens of local minority cultures, funds acquired through such efforts went to supporting a variety of Muslim causes, including construction and maintenance of mosques, support for community organizations, and relief for destitute Muslims (expressing fealty to the third pillar of Islam—the "*zakat*") (Makris 2007: Chapter 4). However, interpreted through the lens of central Party/state policies, such contributions to minority community causes constituted impermissible support for separatism and religion.

(c) Failing to check or report on separatist and religious activities.

This suggests that local minority cadres were essentially turning a blind eye to behavior of local nationalities which, while possibly violating central directives, was understood by local cadres as an unavoidable expression of local identity.

(d) Tolerating religious services, scripture studies, and Ramadan observations that disrupt study and work.

This underscored the tension in PRC policy on religion that distinguishes between freedom of belief and sharp limits on religious conduct. Under the provisions that freedom of religion not intrude on state and social interests, or interfere with the educational activities of the state (Constitution: Art. 36), virtually all religious activity could be essentially banned. The matter is compounded by the Muslim requirements of regular prayer throughout the day (the second pillar of Islam) and the observance of Ramadan (the fourth pillar of Islam).

(e) Acquitting separatist and religious criminals or otherwise "obstructing the case-handling process".

This provision reveals once again, the dilemmas facing local minority cadres in enforcing central policies. Certainly part of the problem is that local cadres are directly complicit in separatist and extremist activities. However, in many cases local minority cadres are deeply mistrusted by local communities. So it seems unlikely that direct complicity is a core problem. More likely is that, through the ongoing process of negotiated enforcement, local cadres make regular judgment calls on enforcement of government edicts on control of local minorities, which run counter to the orthodoxy of the Party/state. Whereas the Han-dominated Party views all local minorities as potentially separatists and all local religion as hostile to Party rule, local minority cadres obvious have a more nuanced view that constrains enforcement against separatism and religious extremism to only the most serious and obvious cases.

(f) Printing and publishing written separatist or religious materials or viewing audio-visual materials.

Here again the listed "violation" reflects a tension between the expectations of the Party/state that all cadres be strictly isolated from local community and religious activities and the reality that minority cadres remain part of the local community (indeed this is one reason for their recruitment to the services of the Party/state). Pamphlets and hand-bills are widely used in local communities to disseminate information on community events and religious observances. As well, religious DVDs are widespread. Assistance from minority cadres in printing and photocopying community notices is common, as is their joining community groups in viewing religious videos.

(g) Linking with international religious organizations (including participating in pilgrimages).

While pilgrimage to Mecca (the Haj) is the fifth pillar of Islam expected of all Muslims, minority cadres are prohibited from participation by the prohibition against Party members participating in any religion ("Party warns"; "Zonggong zhongyang zuzhibu guanyu tuoshan"). The Chinese government has permitted Hui Muslims to journey on the Haj, but has severely restricted pilgrimage activities by Uighurs (CECC 2009b: 130). The citation here reflects an admission that such controls are enforced with great difficulty.

(h) Approving construction of religious sites.

Under the regulations on the maintenance of religious sites, the state prohibits construction of new mosques except at locations where a mosque had existed previously. While the state continues to deny any funding for such activities, private donors and communities remain a major source of support for construction and refurbishment of mosques. However, government approvals are still required. The "violation" listed here admits the extent of minority cadres approving mosque construction either in direct contravention of state regulations, or more likely with a rather flexible interpretation of what is meant by the exception for pre-existing facilities.

(i) Sending their children to religious schools.

China's restrictions on religion continue to ignore the close relationship between religion and community identity. Thus "religious schools" often combine religious education with standard school subjects. Attendance at religious schools is thus not only a matter of religious observation but also an expression of commitment to a local community. As well, in light of the general deterioration of educational resources in China generally, and especially in remote areas, decisions by minority cadres to place their children in religious schools reflect imperatives of community participation and responsible child-rearing at least as much as commitment to religious faith.

(j) Failing to take a clear-cut stand against separatism and religion.

Herein lies the fundamental dilemma of local minority cadres. On the one hand the Party/state recruits minority cadres from local communities in an effort to build governance capacity in those communities. However, the regime also expects local minority cadres to adhere to a clear and complete separation from the values of minority cultures and faith practices. The tension reflects not only the extent of idealistic expectations about the transformation of individuals through their service to the Party/state, but also raises the question of whether such expectations will ultimately make deployment of local minority cadres impossible.

The sheer range of offenses suggests not only the intensity of the campaign to enforce orthodoxy, but also the kinds of activities already detected among Party cadres in Xinjiang. The Xinjiang's CPC Committee's "Interim Provisions" revealed the extent to which government and Party programs were undermined by a general lack of understanding of local conditions and resentments. If the offenses listed were being committed by Party members, what then to expect of the local populace? Nonetheless, while its response remained largely reactive, the local CPC committee could portray itself as active in implementing Beijing's policies of suppressing separatism.

These efforts paved the way for Hu Jintao's "Inspection Tour" of Xinjiang June 8–16, 2001. While the April work conference and the enactment of the local Party discipline measures emphasized punitive efforts at control, Hu's remarks focused on the longer-term need for ideological training. Approving the "remarkable achievements" associated with the Xinjiang CPC Committee, Hu emphasized the importance of cadre training and affirmed that "strengthening ideological education with maintaining ethnic solidarity and the motherland's unity as the main contents is a fundamental policy for maintaining Xinjiang's stability" ("Hu Jintao stresses"). Ideological education for local cadres ("Xinjiang Party Committee") and the education system more broadly ("China: Xinjiang To Bolster") remained a central theme for the anti-separatist campaign over the following year, as a lead up to the sixteenth National CPC Congress. Hu's emphasis on education and training seemed to fit a broader pattern of CPC political campaigns—namely that early phases of harsh repression against selected outliers is followed by education of the survivors who are encouraged by the fate of the punished to learn the virtues of political compliance. Thus is found the application of the mantra "kill the chicken to scare the monkey" (*sha ji xia hou*) in the context of control over minority areas.

The Party/state's responses to local resistance have not only taken the form of formal repression. While the focus on political dimensions of stability remained a dominant theme, the central government has acknowledged the importance of indirect causes of local dissention. With support from government policy departments, Chinese scholars have begun examining the link between social wellbeing and political stability (Wang *et al.*, 1998). Specialists have called for field research on local social groups to support policy recommendations on economic and social development policies (Na La) As well, public education campaigns aimed at popularizing Xinjiang as a business and tourism destination have emerged (Pu *et al.*, 2000) Nonetheless, the focus of official analysis of conditions of stability and development in Xinjiang remain focused on the fight against separatism, and particularly with vigorous suppression of alleged terrorism by the East Turkestan Liberation Movement (Liu and Du). Considerable efforts have been devoted to indoctrinating local cadres on "correct" views about Xinjiang's history and society. These efforts are aimed to ensure political cohesion within governance organizations—recognizing the extent to which local cadres have often retained their ethnic and religious identities. Official "cadre readers" (*ganbu xuexi duben*) on ethnicity and religion note the need to accommodate local traditions and religious practices even while emphasizing China's sovereignty over Xinjiang:

> In order to progressively strengthen great unity among various nationalities in Xinjiang and promote Xinjiang's sustainable and healthy development of Xinjiang's economy, all our cadres and masses must correctly understand the issues of Xinjiang's history, ethnic and religious issues.
> (Tian *et al.* 2001: 2; Tian 2001: 2)

Education and action are combined through the XUAR government's efforts to enforce state claims against high profile human rights defendants, such as Nobel Prize nominee Rebiya Kadeer ("China Rejects"). Following Kadeer's release and exile to the United States, her son Ablikim Abdiriyim was sentenced to nine years imprisonment for separatist activities and two other sons were also sentenced to imprisonment and charged US$ millions in fines ("China sentences"). Kadeer herself was blamed for alleged incidents of terrorism in March 2008, including an alleged plot to crash an airliner headed for Beijing ("Rebiya Is Major Culprit"). The alleged plot was said to involve an effort by Uighur nationalists to smuggle explosive liquids aboard an airliner bound from Urumqi to Beijing (Chang 2008; Van Wie Davis 2008). Although neither the charges nor Ms. Kadeer's denials have been substantiated ("Uighur Leader"), the pattern of accusation reflects the central government's continued preoccupation with conflating ethnic dissent with terrorism. Other government charges associating terrorism with alleged separatist activities immediately prior to the 2008 Beijing Olympics included the claims of a grenade attack on August 4 killing 16 police officials in Kashgar ("Police station raided"); suicide bombings August 10 in Kuqa in the northern part of Xinjiang killing 11 people (Parry); the murder of 3 Chinese security officials August 12 in Yamanya (Shule county east of Kashgar) ("Three murdered"); a knife attack killing 2 Uighur police officers in Peyzawat (Jiashi county, east of Kashgar and Liufu) August 27 ("Chinese Police Killed"; Drew 2008a).

While uncertainties have arisen concerning the official Chinese account of the first and most violent of the attacks (Wong 2008a), the cumulative effect of the unrest was to lend yet more urgency to the government's campaign against local dissent. In response, Xinjiang Party Secretary Wang Lequan warned of a "life and death" struggle against terrorism, separatism, and religious extremism ("Xinjiang boss warns"). The XUAR government convened a cadres conference in early September to address issues of national stability and the struggle against terrorism, directives from which were then disseminated to Urumqi and other levels across Xinjiang calling for increased vigilance and resistance to splittism and Westernization encouraged by the United States and other hostile forces ("Wulumuqi shi zhaokai"). Even before the attacks, Xinjiang authorities had begun cracking down on travel by Uighurs—restricting travel to Mecca for the Hajj (D.T. 2007: 97–98) and curtailing access to Beijing during the Olympics (Cody 2008b).

The outbreak of violence in Urumqi in July 2009 signaled further failures of China's policies of control (CECC 2009b: 243–45). Governmental claims that the unrest was fomented by outside agitators echo the position taken in 2008 concerning protests by ethnic Tibetans, and rang just as hollow. The overwhelming evidence from eyewitnesses and people with first-hand knowledge is that the unrest in Urumqi erupted as a result of local police mishandling what started as peaceful demonstrations, combined with deep simmering frustration over China's policies on minority nationalities. Frustrated with official silence and delay in investigating and punishing Han Chinese complicity in the beating and death of a Uighur worker at a toy factory in Shaoguan, Guangdong, demonstrators in Urumqi called for an investigation of the events at Shaoguan, as well as better treatment of migrant Uighur workers in China and more even-handed treatment of Uighurs more broadly. Conflicts between migrant Uighurs and local Han workers in Guangdong and between migrant Han laborers and local minority workers in Xinjiang suggests that whatever class solidarity might be espoused by the ideals of Chinese socialism remains compromised by ethnic tensions. Following police attacks on the demonstrators, many Uighurs turned against local Han residents resulting in nearly 200 dead and hundreds more injured. Questions arise as to the delayed response of the local security forces. While local police claimed fear of inciting more violence, the possibility that the authorities cynically permitted the violence to escalate in order to mobilize public opinion against the Uighurs cannot be discounted. This interpretation seems to find support in the government's decision to broadcast widely and frequently the violence perpetrated against Han Chinese with little parallel coverage of violence against Uighurs. The government's depiction of a subsequent spate of incidents of syringe stabbings as "violent terrorist crimes" contributed to a culture of fear ("More suspects prosecuted"). Following the inevitable crackdown, death sentences were imposed on at least six Uighurs (Wong 2009b) while many more are reported to have disappeared with no official procedures and process against them (HRW 2009).

While the dismissal in September 2009 of Urumqi Party Secretary Li Zhi and Urumqi Public Security chief Liu Yaohua, suggests a degree of rethinking by senior leaders concerning policy and practice in Xinjiang, significant changes do not seem forthcoming, although there was speculation that XUAR Party Secretary Wang Lequan would be reassigned. The State Council White Paper on Xinjiang issued in September 2009 reflected the perceived need to disseminate official orthodoxy on the region in the wake of the July violence, but also revealed the extent to which little had changed in the policies of the Party/state. The White Paper gave primary attention to issues of economic development, while providing little information on the extent to which aggregate development figures such as gross domestic product increases for XUAR had benefitted local minority populations (SCIO 2009a). The White Paper depicts preservation of local minority cultures in terms of support for music, dance, literature, and art, but says nothing about preservation of language and religion as integral elements of local minority culture. Reiterating orthodox discourses on ethnic equality and unity, the White Paper conceded that the Han constitute nearly half the population, but attempts to make the case that Xinjiang had long been a multicultural region that included a significant Han presence. The White Paper presents the English translation of *minzu* as ethnic, departing from long-standing practice to translate *minzu* as "nationality," which suggests continued intense concern over issues of identity and self-determination for local minority nationalities. In addressing issues of religion, the White Paper reiterates official doctrine on freedom of religious belief while retaining limits on religious behavior—only "normal" religious activities are permitted and significant restrictions are articulated against religious practice, including ensuring ethnic unity and social stability and prohibited interference in state affairs and education. The White Paper devotes considerable attention to issues of national unity and social stability, using the rhetoric of anti-terrorism to denounce so-called

"East Turkestan" forces, a catch-all term not limited to the specific East Turkestan Islamic Movement but rather seeming to include anyone resisting policies and practices subordinating Xinjiang to the dictates of the Party/state.

The prominence given to repression of alleged separatist activities, terrorism, and religious extremism casts something of a pall on government efforts to institutionalize state policies of nationality autonomy. Under the local legislation provisions of the NRAL, Xinjiang XUAR has authority to enact local laws and regulations in areas of social and economic development (Tiemuer 2001a: 525). Indeed, both the Central and the XUAR governments portray local economic development as the solution to problems of separatism (Saiget 2000a). Comparing the scope and content of local legislation and rule-making with local regulations implementing national law reveals limits on the extent of local autonomy actually conferred to the local government. In areas related to natural resources, national sovereignty is paramount and local rule-making is confined to adopting measures for implementation of national legislation. Thus, Xinjiang's regulatory regime on (a) water rights ("XUAR shixing ... Shuifa"); (b) energy ("XUAR shixing ... Jieyue"), and (c) nature conservation ("XUAR shixing ... Yesheng"), for example, are confined to measures for local implementation of national legislation. Socio-economic sectors such as consumer law and workers' compensation are similarly outside the reach of autonomous local legislation ("XUAR shixing ... baoxian"; "XUAR shixing ... xiaofeizhe").

Locally enacted regulations on social and economic issues remain subject to the guidance of national law. Local regulations on economic development authorized under the NRAL remain subject to national priorities. Xinjiang's regulatory regime for encouraging foreign investment, for example, is confined by provisions of national law and regulation and by the policy requirements of the Western Development Program ("XUAR Guli"). Xinjiang's collective contract rules ("XUAR jiti") address issues of employment and labor conditions subject to the provisions of national labor contract and trade union legislation (Art. 1). Even rather mundane local regulations, in areas of staff maternity insurance, for example, provide benefits for costs of delivery and maternity care according to standards set forth in national regulations as interpreted according to local conditions ("XUAR cheng zhen"). These limitations on local initiative to enact legislation and regulations that are autonomous from the policy norms that inform national legislation reveal much about the meaning of autonomy in the context of the NRAL. Such limitations take on even greater import in light of the overwhelming policy priority of suppressing separatism.

China's policies and practices of governance in Xinjiang bear many similarities to those in Tibet. This should come as no surprise in light of Tibet Party Secretary Zhang Qingli's experience as commander of the Xinjiang Production and Construction Corps (*bingtuan*) and Vice Party Secretary of Xinjiang until his reposting to Tibet in 2005. Political imperatives of sovereignty and security result in policies of suppression of local activities that might suggest resistance to central control. This has an impact on efforts to formalize governance, either through institutions like the courts or through local legislation. As a result, official rhetoric on local autonomy rings hollow, as the scope for local initiative remains sharply constrained. This in turn has the potential to undermine efforts by the central government to build community with local society and imperils aspirations about autonomy for China's westernmost regions.

Inner Mongolia

The exercise of political authority in Inner Mongolia Autonomous Region is conditioned by official claims about assimilation with China proper. Building on the "Inner Mongolia Autonomous Government" recognized by the CPC in May 1947, the Inner Mongolia Autonomous Region (NMAR) was established as the first minority autonomous region in the PRC. Under the leadership of Ulanhu, the NMAR enjoyed model status in the PRC (Hao 1991, 1997; Xu and Wang 1999). While Ulanhu ensured that the NMAR remained under the ambit of central Party and government control, his own stature also ensured that Inner Mongolia received higher levels of central investment and a measure of functional autonomy.

The NMAR administration has attempted to preserve a modicum of autonomy by entrenching local rule-making powers even while affirming submission to central level law and policy. The distinction between autonomous region laws and regulations that must undergo scrutiny by the National People's Congress, and laws and regulations enacted by Autonomous Region political subdivisions which do not (Constitution: Art. 116) was underscored in NMAR measures enacted in 1989 and 1993 ("NMAR ... zhiding difangxing fagui" and "NMAR ... pizhun difangxing fagui"). Consistent with efforts by provincial governments in China proper to bolster their autonomy, but most unusual for administrations of minority nationality "autonomous regions," the NMAR regulations suggest an effort to protect local initiative. An expansive interpretation of the provision that local laws and regulations enacted by political subdivisions within various autonomous regions need only be submitted to the National People's Congress for the record (in contrast to enactments of autonomous region people's congresses themselves, which must undergo central level approval), appeared in a 1998 edict that classified autonomous region government laws and regulations enactments as *local* enactments ("NMAR renmin zhengfu yiding difangxing"). This reflected a nuanced use of nomenclature and definition of government enactments in the context of the NRAL's distinction between local measures and autonomous region regulations, to expand local autonomy. This suggests in turn that the NMAR administration has successfully used a balance of submission and legality to expand local political authority in ways not apparent in the NRAL.

Certain sectors such as Taiwan investment ("NMAR guli Taiwan") and Trade Union organization ("NMAR ... Lianxi huiyi") remain subject to national legislative purview. Similarly with natural resources such as water rights ("NMAR ... Shuifa"), although in the related area of water conservation, the NMAR government has pursued "local regulations" on water conservation ("Woguo shoubu"). Yet local autonomy is asserted through expanded claims to rule making authority on local issues of development and through measures on local supervision of enforcement of central policies and laws. Various regulations enacted in 1994 and 1995 gave the local representative congress standing committee authority to supervise enforcement of central level edicts—on the one hand expressing formal submission to central authority while clarifying local power to oversee the exercise of that authority locally ("NMAR ... zhifa jiancha"; "NMAR ... jiandu gongzuo").

Local regulatory responses to the Western Development Program are further evidence of efforts by the Inner Mongolia government to assert autonomy from Beijing (Liu and Shi 2003) The NMAR regulations implementing the Western Development Program accord nominal fealty to the central policy program, but devote nearly exclusive attention to substantive rules and standards for local implementation, frequently referencing existing regulations already in place dictating local priorities ("NMAR shishi xibu daikaifa"). Reflecting a nuanced balance of accommodation and resistance, the regulations acknowledge that existing national provisions will take precedence where they are preferable (*youyu*) to local measures, but in all cases local implementation is subject to approval by the local government (Art. 42).

Assertion of local autonomy is evident in other areas as well. Thus, regulations on economic incentives for enterprises in Huhehaote are to be interpreted in light of Inner Mongolia Autonomous Region rules as well as national laws, and according to local conditions ("Huhehaote shi"). IMAR regulations on encouragement of foreign investment emphasize autonomy for local planning approvals in areas outside those controlled by national regulations and interpretation of these issues is done by the local government development office ("NMAR guanyu guli waishang"). Local policies on integration of development and investment efforts are similarly couched in terms that acknowledge national development programs but leave the details of local implementation relatively free from central control, on matters of both substantive rules and interpretation procedures ("Guanyu jinyibu kuangda").

The balance between national and local priorities is illustrated in part through the legal regime for environmental protection of the grasslands. While national economic development interests focus on expanding growth rates and reducing dependence of local political subdivisions on the central budget, local concerns tend to focus more directly on sustainability, preservation of local traditions, and ensuring local control over resources. Under the Grasslands Law (1984, rev. 2002), the grasslands are specifically described as national resources except where law and regulation ascribe collective ownership (Art. 9), suggesting priority for state ownership. By contrast, the

Inner Mongolia Administrative Measures for the Grasslands (1984, rev. 1991, rev. 2004) place state and collective ownership on an equal footing ("NMAR caoyuan"). Moreover, local regulations attempt to expand provisions in national law for local use rights (*shiying quan*) and local production contracting (*chengbao jingying quan*), enabling individual villages and households significant leeway to manage land, once two-thirds of the village committee members have agreed. The proportional voting requirement is aimed in part to limit conflicts over conversion of pastureland to farming forestry—which combines cultural conflicts between migrant Han and local Mongolians with issues over obtaining the highest economic return from particular forms of land use (Bai 2001).

Uncertainties over the extent of collective ownership and contracted management underscore differences of interest and perspective between national and local land use standards (Zhou 2005). While national ownership is aimed in part to ensure unified national management and also to prevent local parochial interests from disrupting efforts at environmental protection and sustainability, collective ownership and local use rights enable grassland use to respond to local needs. At the root of the problem is the sad reality that existing changes in land use patterns have made it all but impossible for grazers to retain their traditional way of life, as agricultural and industrial uses have already impinged significantly on the amount of pastureland available. The NMAR administration combined enactment of "local regulations" with differing levels of potential encroachment on national policy priorities. In an apparent effort to underscore its autonomy on grasslands policy, the NMAR administration combined enactment of the revised draft of the Mongolia grasslands law with promulgation of rules on nominally local issues of Mongolian language work and investigation and theft of electricity ("NMAR ... tongguo sanxiang").

Thus, the NMAR has attempted to preserve significant levels of autonomy, not only in the implementation of central laws and policies but also in the interpretation and enforcement of these locally. In contrast with conditions in Tibet and Xinjiang, the NMAR has managed to achieve higher levels of operational autonomy in a range of policy areas. One reason for NMAR's success in all this seems to be that the region is more closely assimilated with the central government. The personal ties between Ulanhu and the central Party establishment put NMAR on a good footing initially, and this has been reinforced through an inexorable process of assimilation, through Han in-migration, intermarriage, and local political accommodation. These efforts are combined with vigorous repression of political dissent, including harsh imprisonment regimes ("Hada in Prison") and alleged torture of prisoners ("Jailed Inner Mongolian"). While the reality of Inner Mongolia's autonomy remains somewhat less that official rhetoric might suggest, NMAR practices of compliant resistance have had some effect on building space for local aspirations, even when these are not fully consonant with central imperatives.

Normative and organizational perspectives

Political dimensions of China's governance in the Inner Periphery can be understood in light of normative and organizational features. The dynamic of selective adaptation helps explain some of the normative preferences evident in China's governance policies while many of the structural and organizational elements can be understood in light of institutional capacity.

Selective Adaptation

While China purports to integrate international law standards into its minority policies (SCIO 2004a), China's governance policies reveal normative preferences that help to explain tensions with international standards. In particular, China has resisted efforts by advocates of greater autonomy for Tibet and Xinjiang to use Chinese and international law to support their claims for self-determination (Davis 2008). For example, members of the "Dalai Lama clique" are claimed to "stress the need to wage a "legal struggle" against the Chinese government" while in Xinjiang "national separatists" are alleged to be "supported by outside hostile and religious forces, they have adopted a method that combines "armed struggle" and "peaceful and legal struggle" to conduct their national separatist activities" (Ai 1999). China has used its diplomatic resources to pressure neighboring countries into supporting its positions on alleged separatism by local nationalities in the Periphery. Speaking in Ankara, for example, NPC Chair Qiao Shi praised the Turkish government for imposing restrictions on nationalist separatist activities conducted in Turkey by Xinjiang Uighurs (who share ethnic affinity with the Turks), but also cautioned that any dilution of Turkey's respect for China's sovereign and territorial integrity would harm friendly relations ("Qiao Shi Stresses Xinjiang").

Nonetheless, there remain important differences of normative viewpoint that affect the ways that China pursues governance in the Periphery. The government has articulated its preferred political standards for governance through the regulatory regime and also through periodic White Papers on issues such as autonomy for minority nationalities and local governance in Tibet (SCIO 1999, 2004b, 2009b). As well, government responses to reports by the UN and member states such as the United States, and through statements to the UN Human Rights Commission (and later the Human Rights Council) reflect a commitment to further the "process of international norm-setting" referred to in the Bangkok Declaration on human rights ("Final Declaration"). China's reliance on the right to development discourse to justify development programs and also marginalize universality principles regarding civil and political rights represents a normative response to international norms.

Thus, political dimensions of governance in China's Inner Periphery may be understood in terms of selective adaptation. This process of mediating international standards by reference to local norms is affected by factors of perception, complementarity and legitimacy.

Perception

Political dimensions of governance in the Inner Periphery are subject to limitations on perception. Perception affects understanding on many issues, but three are crucial—sovereignty, alienation, and security. Despite the authority of international law discourses supporting themes of self-determination for ethnic minorities (ICESCR: Art. 1; ICCPR: Art. 1), limiting state sovereignty through themes of collective responsibility and human rights ("UN human rights chief"), and asserting the possibility of supra-national governance (Buergenthal *et al.* 2002: 27–70; Helfer and Slaughter 1997; Ramcharan 2005), orthodox expressions of the policy preferences of the central Party/state reveal quite different perceptions about sovereignty. Perceptions among interpretive communities in China about international law standards generally are strongly oriented toward the inherent sovereignty of the nation-state and its freedom from outside interference (Rao and Huang 2002; Liu 2003).

As well, perceptions about China's alienation from the international system remain powerful. Textbook references contrasting China's colonial past and resulting weakness in foreign relations with its current strengths tend to encourage a sense of both grievance and opportunities for correction and redress that influence attitudes toward the international system (Li 1999; Wang 2003). The status of international law as a source of Chinese domestic law remains unclear (Chen: 129–30; Zhang 2001), while the willingness and ability of Chinese governance institutions to implement international legal standards are uncertain (CECC 2004). Perceptions that criticisms of China's governance in national minority areas is driven by US or international power politics for example suggest important conditions for China's engagement (Liu 2004). These factors contribute to a sense of alienation from the international system.

Factors of perception about both local and international security also affect China's policies toward the Inner Periphery. The primacy of domestic security priorities was evident in the role of the PLA and People's Armed Police (*Wujing*) in preserving social stability, as noted by Hu Jintao in his speech on the fiftieth anniversary of the "peaceful liberation" of Tibet (Hu 2001a). These roles were noted once again in the official government statements on the fiftieth anniversary (Zhonggong zhongyang ... wushi zhounian hedian"). Perceptions about the strategic designs of NATO and the United States in Central Asia have contributed to China's efforts to build economic and security relationships with Russia and the Central Asian republics (Zhao 2001). China has linked this effort directly with the effort to resist international (or perceived US-led) support for nationalist separatist activity in Xinjiang ("Strategic Direction"). Participation in the Shanghai Cooperation

Organization represents China's first foray into multilateral organizations not exclusively economic in scope (Chun 2004). The organization is centered around security concerns in Central Asia, giving particular attention to issues of "terrorism, separatism and extremism." Perceptions about security in central Asia are matters of particular concern to China in light of the complexities of its governance in Xinjiang (Gladney 2004b; Ma 2003). Much as the "Western Development Program" is predicated on the assumptions that economic development will reduce minority unrest, the SCO's inclusion of economic dimensions to regional cooperation reflects perceptions about the deployment of economic policies to further pursue its security interests.

Complementarity

Selective adaptation of international governance standards also involves complementarity between international standards and the preferences of the Chinese government. Complementarity plays a significant role in the relationship between China's doctrine of autonomy as self-rule (*zizhi*) and international discourses on autonomy, self-determination, and sovereignty. International law standards on autonomy place significant emphasis on factors of legislative and judicial independence; political leadership by local people, and grants of autonomy consistent with powers exercised and shared by other political subdivisions (Moneyhon 2002: 142). Specialists on China's nationality autonomy system interpret "self-rule" (*zizhi*) as a subset of the broader concepts of sovereignty (*zhuquan*), autonomy (*zizhuquan*), self-determination (*zijuequan*) that attach to the nation-state (Zhang 2005: 15–28). While not as expansive as autonomy rights attached to sovereign states, self-administration (*zizhi*) is both dependent on them for its authority and effectiveness and also a local complement to their international exercise. However, conflicts over the scope of autonomy conferred to nationality regions involve more than semantics—to the point where proposals to avoid interpretive conflicts over self-rule (*zizhi*) and autonomy (*zizhu*) invite reliance on the alternative rubric of common administration (*gongzhi*) (Miao 2005: 335–37). In light of the potential problems inherent in the "equality of nationalities" principles entrenched in the Constitution and the NRAL, the limitations that self-administration, let alone "common administration," imply for participation by China's minority nationalities in setting content for Party policy and government rule are significant.

Alarmed by the potential precedent set by international action to protect minority Muslims in Kosovo and suggestions that China's Inner Periphery areas have similarly legitimate claims (e.g., Harris 2008b), China has rejected application of international collective security principles aimed at protecting self-determination for minorities to its own minority nationalities in Xinjiang and Tibet ("Article on Kosovo Crisis"). China has relied on expansive interpretations on national sovereignty to resist comparisons of Tibet and

Xinjiang with ethnic crises in Kosovo and Chechnya (Ai 1999). Efforts by international critics to draw on the internationally recognized right of self-determination, so often used by China in the past, come under particular attack. The right of self-determination (*zijuequan*) is considered a principle of international relations that is not applicable to nationality relations within particular states (He 2005: 263–64; "Statement by Ms. Che Ying").

Thus, the governing orthodoxy of the Party/state reveals particular priorities around notions of state sovereignty. In China's multi-cultural environment subject to the dominion of a Han-dominated ruling Party, assertions about self-determination for minorities are quite predictably rejected because they raise the possibility of legitimate minority resistance to Han domination. Hence, the discourse of self-determination is confined the realm of resistance to foreign intrusion, consistent perhaps with China's past use of the rhetoric of self-determination to justify Cold War policies of resistance to both US and Soviet hegemony but largely inconsistent with internationally accepted doctrine (Steiner and Alston 2000: 1248–1305). To the extent that the legal discourse on "self-determination" does not support China's limited views, the integrity of those who suggest the relevance of the discourse for critiquing China's policies and practices in the Inner Periphery are dismissed as driven by "ulterior motives." Thus, official orthodoxy distorts international law doctrines and discourse to ensure complementarity with the policy imperatives of the Party/state.

The influence of complementarity is also evident in China's pursuit of security through participation in the Shanghai Cooperation Organization (SCO) (Chung 2004). While adopting much of the rhetoric of the US-led anti-terrorism campaign as justification for suppression of Islamic separatists (Chung 2002; Chan 2001a; Bao 2001; Si 2001a; "PRC Xinjiang"; "Apparent Text of PRC"), China has embraced the SCO as a counterweight to US influence in Central Asia (Gladney 2003; Ma 2005; Si 2001b). No doubt prompted by Beijing ("PRC: Li Peng joins"), the XUAR administration proposed to the National People's Congress a bill on religious affairs management that would specifically link efforts against terrorism with suppression of alleged religious extremism through China's participation in the SCO ("Xinjiang Chairman").

Legitimacy

Legitimacy is an important factor in the selective adaptation of international standards on governance in the Inner Periphery. To an important degree, legitimacy of official policy depends on legitimacy of leading officials. The personal and political affiliations of Xinjiang Party Secretary Wang Lequan and Tibet Party Secretary Zhang Qingli with CPC chief Hu Jintao (Lam 2008a), tend to construct local leaders' views of their own legitimacy and authority in terms of their political loyalties to Hu and his hard-line policies that saw Tibet erupt in violence in 1987 and 1989. Rather than attending to legitimacy from local communities of national minority inhabitants of the Inner Periphery, these leaders interpret their political legitimacy in terms of service to their patron(s) at the top of the CPC hierarchy. This has a marked effect on the policies and perspectives they bring to their work in Xinjiang and Tibet.

The tensions of legitimacy for China's engagement with international governance standards in connection with the Inner Periphery are also evident in the disparate expressions of central policies concerning minority nationalities. White Papers on Tibet and on ethnic autonomy generally are aimed at an international audience. Interviews given to the international press by officials of local nationalities are intended to affirm local support for China's sovereignty over minority areas ("Urumqi Mayor," "Xinjiang Dispatches," "Xinjiang Leaders Denounce"). While such efforts reveal efforts by local officials to build legitimacy with their superiors, little attention is paid to building legitimacy locally. Perhaps the effectiveness of local officials in mediating central directives and negotiating their application locally depends more on legitimacy with superiors than subjects, but the general inattentiveness to local legitimacy is striking. Viewed in comparison with the enumerated offenses by local minority cadres in the "Xinjiang Regulations on Party Discipline," the positions of compliance taken by leading officials in Xinjiang underscore inconsistencies of discourse and behavior between leading and local cadres in the region.

As well, China has devoted considerable efforts to managing international expectations about its governance of minority nationality areas. Thus, the CPC opinion on foreign propaganda work issues in November 2004 reveals a commitment to trying to control foreign information and understanding about governance in the Inner Periphery (RMET 2005: 1080). This is coupled with efforts to influence public opinion in North America (RMET 2005: 1058–59). The PRC State Council's report on separatism in Xinjiang recounts details of alleged Islamic terrorist activities in an effort to build common ground with US attitudes in the wake of the September 11, 2001 attacks ("Apparent Text of PRC"), while public responses to US Congressional support for Rebiya Kadeer suggest further concern with protecting the legitimacy of China's policies of control in Xinjiang ("AFP: PRC FM"). China's public portrayal of civil unrest in Tibet and Xinjiang has appropriated language associated with US anti-terrorism policy. Thus deployment of institutions and processes of social control, public security, criminal prosecution against demonstrators seeking greater fairness and lawful treatment of minorities is couched in terms of suppression of terrorism. Here again is evident the effort to build international legitimacy for policies of control over minority nationalities.

Although the legitimacy dimension in China's policy and academic discourses on international law may in some respects concern local audiences, by and large the audience whose legitimacy is sought is the international community. China's record of attempts to lead particular groupings of international actors ("the international socialist movement," "the non-aligned movement," "the community of developing economies," etc.) has been driven in part by the quest for legitimacy, not only from these groups but also from the rest of the international community before whom China's stature might be secured by reference to its leadership of particular coalitions (Han 1990: Chapters XI, XX, XXIV). Recent official statements explaining policies of greater participation in the international system seem aimed to build legitimacy in the broader international community (Jiang 2005). The importance of legitimacy is demonstrated throughout, as China strives to present its legal and political system as compatible with international human rights standards. Acceptance of international human rights standards depends in part on their compatibility with existing priorities. Thus, international human rights norms of state responsibility are cited to support the primacy of Chinese government control in human rights enforcement (Zhou and Xie 2001; Sun 2001). As well, the attention paid to China's historical claims to sovereignty over Tibet and Xinjiang and to purported assimilation of local nationalities in Inner Mongolia speak to the importance China attaches to achieving legitimacy for its governance programs, both domestically and internationally.

Institutional Capacity

China's exercise of political authority in the Inner Periphery can also be understood in light of institutional capacity. In particular issues of institutional purpose and location, as well as institutional orientation and cohesion affect the outcomes of Beijing's policies toward the Inner Periphery.

Institutional Purpose: expectations about political authority

China's governance in the Inner Periphery reflects factors of institutional purpose. Recalling the potential significance of policy changes following the 1992 National Work Conference on Nationality Policy, governance practices in the Inner Periphery have remained wedded to priorities of stability, economic growth, and CPC dominance. The over arching preoccupation with social stability has tended to dominate all other concerns such that issues of economic and social development, policies on religion, international affairs, and many other issues are viewed through the lens of security and stability. Harsh repression of local ethnic leaders seeking improved conditions for minority nationality peoples has become something of a norm that, instead of succeeding in building security and stability, has attempted to reinforce local feelings of alienation and frustration with the Chinese rule. Economic development, while potentially important to improving the lives of local people, has been manipulated primarily to suit the national interests of resource and energy security and to provide employment and opportunity for migrating Han from elsewhere in China. As well, economic development is treated from an instrumentalist point of view, as a mechanism for building passivity amongst local minority nationalities. Policies of political authority have also continued to underscore the primacy of the CPC, and by extension the preservation of Han dominance. The prominence given to policy statements from the Party Secretaries of the Autonomous Regions of Inner Mongolia, Xinjiang, and Tibet over those of the government heads of these areas speaks volumes both to local people and to the nation as a whole as to where political authority ultimately rests. In the contentious climate of the Inner Periphery, where Han-minority relations are a fundamental context for the exercise of political authority, the primacy of the CPC in policy-making tends to reinforce patterns of domination. Finally, the preoccupation with preserving the power of the Party's political authority in the Inner Periphery speaks to an approach to governance that almost by definition cannot take adequate account of the views and aspirations of local people. Exacerbated by the ethnic tensions that are intimately intertwined with it, the preoccupation with Party supremacy tends to accentuate the gulf between rulers and ruled in the Inner Periphery.

These general features of institutional purpose pose significant obstacles to institutional capacity in the Inner Periphery. First of all, they engender significant policy disagreement, not only in Beijing, but in the Inner Periphery itself. Contesting voices over the handling of the latest unrest in Tibet and Xinjiang, for example, revealed the depth of disagreement over China's policies there (Sisci 2009; Wei 2009; Wang 2007, 2008). Establishment intellectuals also weighed in, calling for the release of Uighur economist Ilham Tohti, who had been detailed following the July 2009 outbreak of violence in Xinjiang (Wong 2009a). As well, the preoccupation with security tends to create self-fulfilling prophecies about local resentment and unrest, as the ever-more intrusive security state embarrasses supporters, alienates moderates, and further enrages those already resistant to Chinese rule.

Institutional Location: tensions between central and local perspectives

China's regulation of the periphery reflects important tensions between local perspectives and views from the Center. Aside from the obvious issues present in the interpretation of a national statute concerned with local governance, particular *Institutional Location* questions arise over issues about local knowledge. China's governance of the Inner Periphery has traditionally exhibited features of internal colonialism, with significant Han-dominated oppression of local culture (Bulag 2004; McCarthy 2002; Dreyer 1976). Calls for more research on local conditions in the periphery suggest continued concerns over central government ignorance and inattention to local conditions (Ma 2003: 28–29). In Xinjiang, for example, case studies on underground religious, economic, and political relationships reveal the extent to which central policies on minority affairs, economic development, and national security are often based on inadequate or incorrect information about local conditions (Tiemuer and Mao 2003; Ma 2003). The violent outbreak in February 1997 at Yining and the bus explosions the same month in Urumqi, while relatively minor and an infrequent departure from a pattern of mostly passive resistance, revealed the extent of local dissatisfaction with central government policies and practices in Xinjiang, and revealed serious shortcomings in the government's level of knowledge about local conditions (Ma 2003: 92–100).

Similarly, the government's failure to foresee and forestall demonstrations and violence in Xinjiang and Tibet in Spring 2008 spoke to a significant failure of intelligence and analysis at the local level. Reporting on perceived social stability problems in the periphery also suggests significant differences of perspective between Beijing and local units. From Beijing's perspective, building stronger local knowledge is linked specifically to more effective propaganda efforts that in turn are aimed at protecting social stability (Ling 2003). The NRAL's provisions on local public security also reflect the central government preoccupation with issues of ethnic separatism and anti-terrorism, even as local governments are focused on local issues of standard policing (Song 2003: 291–95).

Factors of institutional location are also evident in comparisons between central and local views on development. Thus, central government reporting on Tibet emphasizes quantitative factors such as economic accumulation and output; numbers of graduates from educational institutions; and population and land use statistics ("Xizang de xiandaihua"). Local perspectives, however, tend to focus instead on qualitative questions about cultural and religious identity and social wellbeing (Wang 2009: 372–74). Similarly in Xinjiang, central reporting tends to emphasize quantitative measurements of development (Wang et al. 2003: 7–18), in contrast to perspectives of local people who tend to focus on qualitative indicators of wellbeing (Tyler 2004: 214–21).

Institutional location issues also arise in the context of internationalization and globalization. In both minority policy and religion policy, official interpretations focus on the extent to which international human rights movements have challenged central policies (Wang 2002: Chapter 14; MacKerras 2003). Economic development too is subject to the influences of globalization, which affects both development goals and approaches to achieving them. Thus, the central government occupies a location between international observers and critics – internal sources go so far as to identify these as "Western hostile forces" (*xifang didui shili*) (XUAR Minzu Shiwu: 191–93), and sub-national locales where minority and religion policies are carried out. International religious movements such as Islamic fundamentalism and Christian evangelism are seen to exert influence on religious activities in China. This is also seen as challenging the authority of the central government to implement policy, and affects its approach toward conferring autonomy through the NRAL. Qualifying as it does the authority of local governments to limit application of central priorities and policies, the NRAL works to ensure that local autonomy does not challenge the prerogatives and power of central government agencies. The respective locations of international, state, and local institutional perspectives exert influence over this process, thus affecting institutional capacity.

A useful example of the effect of location on institutional capacity questions surrounding the NRAL lies in the question of language policy. Drawing on the Constitution, the NRAL provides that government activity is conducted in the local minority language. Yet case studies from the periphery suggest that local language usage remains a difficult problem (Sun 2006). On one hand, the Han authorities contend that use of Chinese language is essential for development ("Putonghua taken as Key Factor"). In response, urban elites in peripheral areas of Inner Mongolia, Xinjiang, and Tibet see mastery of Mandarin Chinese as a prerequisite for career success, and so arrange training for themselves and education for their children accordingly. Use of Mandarin in government departments remains fairly standard, while local minority cadres use their own language as a means of protecting their cultural identity from Chinese overseers. Chinese cadres assigned to the periphery have shown little interest in learning local languages, while the masses of migrant Chinese entering these areas are even less interested (Bovington 2004). The result is a significant gap in local knowledge for Han officials. And since generally Han remain in privileged positions of power within local government units, their continued isolation from local social discourse has a direct impact on government administration. As it affects the internal dynamics and operational performance of local governance institutions, the question of institutional location contributes importantly to institutional capacity in the process of balancing local autonomy with central oversight under the NRAL.

Institutional Orientation and cohesion: qualities of local governance

Institutional orientation is also a factor, as the exercise of political authority remains couched in formalistic terms of legalization and Party rule. As indicated through its White Papers on Tibet and Xinjiang, the government has devoted considerable energy and resources to promulgating a wide range of legal and regulatory enactments aimed at establishing a legal foundation for its rule. Disparities between responses of leading cadres in Inner Periphery and local minority cadres highlight the tensions of institutional orientations that focus respectively on relationships with superiors or with communities. These disparities come particularly to the fore in the context of the negotiated processes of policy enforcement.

Yet the interpretation of these measures and their implementation at the local level tend to be distorted in order to further the purposes of security and stability even as the local conditions that might promote these aims are ignored. Thus, outbreaks of unrest in Tibet and Xinjiang reflect underlying resentments that cannot be legislated away, and show few signs of being controllable through the current regulatory scheme. The government's persistent efforts to demonize figures of local esteem, such as Rebeiya Kadeer and the Dalai Lama, have had quite the opposite effect locally, as public respect for these individuals continues to rise. Formalistic recitations of principles, such as those dictated to the envoys of the Dalai Lama by Director Du Qinglin of the Party's United Front Work Department, embody disjunctions between official government statements and local interests and perspectives. The focus on national interests evident in State Council White Papers on Tibet and Xinjiang and in official commentaries on recent crises there, offer little support for localized perspectives suggesting that China's national interest is served by promoting social justice and development locally. The persistent orientation toward centralized, top-down rule coupled with expectations about compliance through forceable compulsion suggests an orientation of political authority that has little chance of succeeding amongst local people.

Issues of institutional cohesion are also evident. The listing of offenses by local minority cadres in the "Xinjiang Regulations on Party Discipline" reflect the extent of conflict between the orthodoxy of the Party/state and the reality of local cadre values and behavior. While the embeddedness of local minority cadres in local communities is taken as a major reason for their recruitment and deployment, such local integration would seem to render unachievable the organizational goal of adherence to Party/state orthodoxy on governance. As well, harsh repression of local people in the aftermath of social unrest in Tibet in Spring 2008 and in Xinjiang a year later; persistently ineffective efforts to preserve local language use; and the continued dominance of a Party hierarchy dominated by Han officials all work to discourage local minority nationalities to take seriously their potential as agents of change. The willingness of local minority nationalities to support official government policies for reasons other than political or career expediency remains limited. While levels of corruption do not appear significantly different from levels reported elsewhere in China, the potential for privateering and abuse in the wake of state-funded economic development programs remains to be considered.

Summary

Official law and policy on governance in areas of the Inner Periphery reveal basic priorities on issues of local autonomy, security, and political control. As applied to the framework of law and policy on governance autonomy in the Inner Periphery, selective adaptation analysis suggests that factors of perception, complementarity, and legitimacy all have significant effects on the content and implementation of standards of governance. Institutional capacity analysis reveals the extent to which factors of purpose, location, orientation, and cohesion also affect the interpretation and application of legal regimes. Such normative and organizational perspectives offer a clearer understanding of the likely futures for China's governance in the Inner Periphery.

The dynamics of selective adaptation and institutional capacity will continue to be useful in understanding future policies and programmatic responses as the PRC Party/state continues to engage with local and international normative standards in constructing regimes for political authority in the Inner Periphery.

3 Socio-cultural relations in the Inner Periphery

Governance of socio-cultural relations in the Inner Periphery reflects combined influences of accommodation and assimilation. Regulatory and policy pronouncements extolling the virtues of diversity are combined with practices and policies emphasizing the importance of the unitary state. Even while recognizing the excesses of the Cultural Revolution, in terms of both radicalization of cultural activities and the privileging of Han chauvinism, current Party policies on society and culture evince a preoccupation with control.

China's laws and policies on relations with minority nationalities evince a tension between orthodox approaches to diversity and conformity that is linked in varying ways depending on behavior. Cultural diversity in areas such as costume and consumption is seen as acceptable, and, local variations in dress, food, and housing are touted as exemplars of China's policies of multiculturalism. Diversity in areas of social relations such as marriage and family are treated with greater concern, although local practices are given limited exception from national policies on population control and gender equality. Issues of education, language, and religion give rise to sensitive questions as local preferences are often seen as in conflict with national policy priorities. China's policies and law on regulation of minority nationalities offer a particularly useful glimpse on perspectives of the Party/state on the societal dimensions of governance in the Inner Periphery.

Minority nationality affairs

The central government's regulation of social relations in the Inner Periphery is inextricably intertwined with state policies on minority nationalities. As with other aspects of PRC governance, documentary texts are an invaluable source for expressions of official orthodoxy. The Constitution and the Nationality Region Autonomy Law (NRAL) provide basic principles on minority nationality matters, reflecting Party policy imperatives. More specific regulatory treatment emerges on specific issues such as education and culture.

Constitution and law

Constitutional provisions on minority affairs form the legal basis for other legislation such as NRAL. Related to this are issues of regulation of religion, to which the NRAL and related minority governance laws and policies frequently refer. Article 4 of the PRC Constitution articulates norms about equality, unity, autonomy, and development in minority affairs. Existing work on China's minority policies raises important questions of whether these empower or marginalize non-Han cultural groups (Sautman 1998; Karmel 1995; Mackerras 2003; Wang 1998). Each of the provisions in Article 4 is laden with meaning, based on China's policy record and current policy documents.

Article 4.1 provides that all nationalities in China are equal. This provision suggests a formalistic approach to equality, connoting equality of status rather than equality of actual conditions (Sautman 1999). While this provision apparently stands as a prohibition against discrimination against minority groups and individuals, its reliance on formal equality norms also raises the possibility of entrenching substantive socio-economic inequalities through removal of regulatory accommodation for special needs of marginalized groups (Bulag 2002a: 123–24; Sun *et al.* 2001).

Article 4.2 affirms that the state protects the lawful rights and interests of minorities and upholds and develops relationships of equality, unity, and mutual assistance among all nationalities. The rights and interests referred to in this provision must be lawful in order to be protected, meaning that these may not contravene provisions for Party supremacy, the socialist system, state interests and other privileged domains, whose protection is the prerequisite to "lawfulness." As with other areas of constitutional rights, this imposes significant limits on rights enforcement. Moreover, the state is accorded the dominant if not the sole role in protecting lawful rights and interests. The state's monopoly on stewardship over matters of equality, unity, and mutual assistance has the potential to deprive minority groups of authority to determine the substantive or procedural dimensions of these ideals. The rubric of the unity of nationalities essentially prohibits minorities from challenging inequality in relations with the Han Chinese. The formalism which informs interpretation of Chinese law generally allows the constitutional declaration of equality between nationalities to be taken as a reflection of reality. Under conditions where all nationalities are presumed equal, challenges to inequality are deemed not only in conflict with actual conditions, but also a challenge to the authority of the Constitution and the ideals of unity. Official statements on minority policy direct Party and state leadership over issues of equality, unity, and mutual assistance, thereby privileging central objectives of the Party/state over priorities of local minorities and by extension Han over minority perspectives. By asserting the Party/state's monopoly on power to effect change, the Constitution also denies civic groups—particularly those associated with non-Han communities—any authority for action (SNAC 2002: Chapter 3).

Constitutional Article 4.3 prohibits discrimination against and oppression of any nationality, and prohibits acts undermining the unity of nationalities or instigating their secession. This provision's use of the term "any nationality" (*renhe minzu*) includes Han within the protected category, thus undermining provisions restricting Han Chinese activities (Wu 1998: 6–8). This has resulted in increased Han dominance of economic and political life in minority areas (Tyler 2004: 211–21). The proscription against undermining the unity of nationalities works to prohibit expressions of anti-Han sentiment in minority areas, and has been applied against peaceful demonstrations, literary and media reporting, and policy debates that are seen to challenge Party policy (XUAR Minzu Shiwu Weiyuan Hui; Ma 2003: 103–5). This doctrine also is aimed to deny minorities lawful access to discourses on self-determination as justification for expanded rights to justice and fair treatment. The prohibition against secession is clear on its face, but it also clearly linked to the broader theme of unity of nationalities.

Article 4.4 provides for state assistance to areas inhabited by minority nationalities. This provision's reference to state aid in development invites imposition of particular models of development that tend to emphasize urbanization, capital-intensive infrastructure development, and socialist market forces (Weiler 2004). While these approaches are understood by government policy specialists to contradict local practices and aspirations, the solution tends to lie in intensified education and cultural assistance that will make such approaches to development more palatable locally (Ma Z. 2003: 12–17).

Article 4.5 provides for the carrying out of regional autonomy and the establishment of organs of self-government in areas where people of minority nationalities live in compact communities (*juju*), but affirms that all national autonomous areas are inalienable parts of China. This provision's reference to autonomy in national minority areas is limited to administration over purely local issues, which remains subject to central state and Party leadership, and does not nominally at least include autonomy to depart from legal and regulatory provisions of higher levels (Song 2003: 51–57). As well, the phraseology defining minority areas, particularly the use of the term compact communities, indicates areas occupied nearly exclusively by minorities. Migration programs increasing Han populations in areas of Inner Mongolia, Xinjiang, and Tibet present significant challenges to minority-oriented governance in these areas. The reference to minority areas being inalienable from China underscores the government's continuing concern with separatism and the ongoing effort to refute doctrines on self-determination for national minorities (Ma D. 2003: 177–90).

Article 4.6 provides for local language usage and protection of local cultures. In 1991, State Council Document 32 acknowledged a positive linkage between support for minority nationality languages and ethnic unity, progress, and prosperity (Zhou 2001). Yet systematic implementation of multilingualism in minority nationality areas has been problematic. Particularly in light of the increasing size of the Han populations in minority areas, constitutional references to language rights for people of "all nationalities" works to augment and legitimate social and political factors that impede use of local minority languages at government and educational institutions in minority areas. In the face of the diversity of language usage by "all nationalities," Mandarin Chinese becomes a common default language choice (Wu 1998: 263–66). As well the suggestion that nationalities may choose to reform their own ways has been interpreted as justification for government-sponsored education and cultural "reform" programs aimed at improving the quality (*suzhi*) of minority populations and the potential for their assimilation into the dominant culture (SNAC 2002: 196–98).

Thus, constitutional provisions on nationality affairs provide significant justification for state-centric governance and for gradual diminution of local ethnic identity. Efforts at the Ministry of Culture to draft national legislation on protection of popular culture (*minjian wenhua*) of minority nationalities, along the lines of local measures in Yunnan and Guizhou, remain incomplete (Zhang and Bao 2004: I. 5.) When viewed in light of related discourses on the conditionality of constitutional rights and the national unity imperatives of minority policy, the provisions of the PRC Constitution serve to entrench policy ideals and approaches that have potential to marginalize minority nationalities.

The NRAL affirms the importance of the basic constitutional structure for implementing policies of the CPC on ethnic issues. The NRAL affirms its grounding in the PRC Constitution (NRAL: Art. 1), and affirms the importance of ensuring compliance with the PRC Constitution (NRAL: Art. 5). This necessarily involves obedience to the four basic principles of fealty to socialism; Marxism–Leninism Mao Zedong Thought; the people's democratic dictatorship; and the supremacy of Party rule—which are listed specifically along with other rubrics including socialist democracy and legal system as bases for managing local autonomy in nationality areas (NRAL Preface). This in turn involves Party policy as the basis for legal norms and behavior. Thus, the centrality of the unified state is therefore entrenched in the NRAL (NRAL: Art. 5). Administrative regulations for minority affairs in villages and cities were enacted in 1993 to augment provisions of the original NRAL allowing local adaptation of nationally mandated programs in areas such as education and culture, health and family planning, and economic development, tax, and finance ("Minzu xiang," "Chengshi minzu"). Yet these remained focused on local implementation questions, rather than issues of the substantive content, goals, and direction of central policy. National goals remain paramount.

Policies on minority nationalities

Just as China's Constitution and laws are embodiments of Party policy, their interpretation and application are also dependent on changing policy imperatives. The National Work Conference on Nationalities Policy of January 1992 was an important watershed for Party policy on minority affairs. Mindful of the depth of alienation of local minorities that erupted in violence in Lhasa in 1989 and Xinjiang in 1990 (not to mention the disaster of the violent suppression of the 1989 student democracy movement in China proper), the Work Conference themes included enforcement of political orthodoxy and suppression of local resistance. However, the conference also echoed themes of unity and equality incorporated in the original 1984 NRAL, and acknowledged the importance, complexity, and general importance of nationalities policy (Jiang 1992b). Recognition of these seemingly obvious elements of conflicted relationship between China's Han-dominated government and the conditions of its minority areas signaled a belated acceptance of the failures of past efforts at assimilation of minorities to Han culture.

Under the 1992 Work Conference, key tasks for nationalities work— deemed essential despite formalized achievements in political equality and idealized rhetoric about commonality of interests among nationalities— included resolving continued disparities in economic and cultural development between nationality areas and China proper; redressing conflicts of rights and interests particularly in the economic sphere; building mutual understanding about social habits and language use; addressing the role of religion in local minority nationalities relations; and building unity among nationalities (Jiang 1992b; Li 1992). Specific initiatives were mandated for economic and social development in minority nationality regions, including increased investment, development of educational, scientific, culture and health programs, and granting greater leeway for local initiative and self-rule (*zizhi*) in implementing national policies under the NRAL, but subject to overriding principles of national unity and Party leadership.

The 1992 Nationalities Work Conference targeted socio-economic development as a key element for nationality policy in the near-term, laying the ground for the application of the Ninth Five Year Plan and later the Western Development Program as vehicles for building stability, curbing unrest and strengthening submission of minority nationalities to PRC governance under the limited autonomy principles of the NRAL (ibid.; Li 1992). In hindsight, such confidence seems misplaced in light of the challenges discussed in connection with the Western Development Program. Nonetheless at the time, the approach was a marked departure from the policies of less than benign neglect that had characterized minority nationalities relations in China previously. The new policies were also a response to perceived efforts by "international hostile forces" to use nationalities and religion to "Westernize and divide China" (Jiang 1993a: 278). Thus, China's nationalities policies during the 1990s were driven by recognition of the needs of domestic reforms as well as the effects of international conditions of globalization.

Building on the directives from the national work conference, the CPC United Front Work Department incorporated nationalities work into its program of work for the 1990s, focusing specifically on "accelerating development of economic, technological, educational and cultural affairs in nationality areas" ("Gonggu he fazhan"). However, under the rubric of "opposing ethnic chauvinism" (*fandui da minzu zhuyi*), these initiatives were to be implemented in conformity with national priorities and the needs of the entire country ("Gonggu he fazhan": 54). This attention to subordination of local interests to national priorities would inform interpretation and implementation of nationalities policy in such areas as economic and social development, self-rule under the NRAL, and minority cadre training.

To the extent that the 1992 Work Conference committed central government departments to pay increased attention to protecting minority culture, this tended to focus on strategies and plans for linking culture work with economic development through cultural performances, museum exhibits, arts and crafts, and the construction of "culture halls" (*wenhua gong*) ("Wenhuabu, Guojia minwei"). While such efforts may have resulted in preservation of some traditional cultural forms, they also reveal stylized conceptions of tradition that do little to support the more complex processes by which local cultures and communities would interact with increasingly forceful manifestations of Han culture. Thus, while the new policies of engagement suggested themes of accommodation to needs of minority nationalities that marked a departure from past practices that alternated between neglect and assimilation, the terms of the new approach betrayed assumptions about China's normative expectations and operational capacity to engage with its minority nationalities productively and effectively.

While the 1992 Work Conference proposed a range of initiatives in response to a complex array of social–economic needs, the focus of implementation was soon directed more specifically toward economic development. The State Planning Commission adopted similar measures although these seemed to focus primarily on capital investment with only nominal attention paid to conditions of local socio-economic production (Guojia jihua: 62–63).

The priority given to economic development as a basis for resolving minority problems was reiterated at a 1994 national conference (Jiang 1994b). The potential for economic development initiatives to disrupt local nationality communities became clear in the strategy to establish economic and technical cooperation links between the minority areas of China's west with other areas in China proper (Li 1994). Matching the resource wealth of western China with the productive and technical capacities of China proper would require integration of local development goals and processes in the Inner Periphery with national conditions and objectives. In the first round of co-operation initiatives, poverty alleviation linkages were established between Inner Periphery regions of Xinjiang, and Inner Mongolia with Shandong, and Beijing respectively, while Tibet was notably omitted ("Guowuyuan fupin") Economic investment linkages of Beijing and Jiangsu with Lhasa, Shanghai and Shandong with Shigatse, and Tianjin and Sichuan with Chamdo have been noted however (Ng and Zhou 2004: 560).

Thus, within a few years following the 1992 Nationalities Work Conference and its nominal appreciation of the multi-faceted dimensions of nationalities issues and particularly the appreciation of local realities and implications of social and economic inequality, China's nationalities policy had come to focus on the dimension of economic development. Although such a plan made eminent sense viewed from the standpoint of planners in Beijing, the potential for further disruption and alienation of Han-minority relations remained strong. By 1999, the subordination of nationalities policy to economic development initiative was relatively complete, as the Western Development Program came to embrace virtually the entire range of policy initiatives. In addition to economic development programs themselves, the WDP and its market-oriented development priorities were to serve as the basis for cadre training, building national integrity and unity of nationalities, and the exercise of Party leadership (Jiang 1999; Zhu 1999).

While economic development remained the basic priority for nationalities policy, changing conditions in Central Asia and in the international political climate on China's policies in Tibet and concerning the Dalai Lama leant greater importance to political dimensions. Thus the policy outcomes from the 2001 Central Nationalities Work Conference linked local social and economic development with national goals of stability and unity (Zhu et al. 2004: 248). Once again official texts are instructive, as the 2001 Central Nationalities Work Conference asserted several key points, including:

(a) Production, development, and withering away of nationalities is conceded to be a long-term process such that differences among nationalities will remain for a long time.

Drawing on Marxist discourses about the withering away of political institutions in light of changing material conditions (particularly the erosion of class struggle), the notion of nationalities withering away suggest as well that changing material conditions (in this case economic growth) will diminish ethnic distinctions between different economic actors. However, in acknowledging that differences among nationalities will exist for a long time, the provision empowers organs of the Party/state to ensure continued stability and resist ethnic nationalism.

(b) Nationalities issues can only be resolved as part of China's program of socialism with Chinese characteristics.

This nod to the centrality of state-led social and economic change also suggests diminished potential for local autonomy. To the extent that socialism with Chinese characteristics entrenches socio-cultural values associated with Han society, including state-led development, local autonomy is undermined.

(c) Various nationalities have a duty to uphold national unity as their paramount interest.

These explicit standards of national unity further undermine efforts to access meaningful autonomy for local minorities, even as they formalize requirements of minority subordination to Han-dominated conceptions of national unity. These standards effectively prohibit efforts legal or otherwise to assert distinctive minority perspectives on policy and governance.

(d) State protection of nationalities rights and interests focuses primarily on principles of equality of nationalities.

As with Constitutional principles on formal equality, the policy discourse on "equality of nationalities" works to privilege Han dominance and to undermine efforts to redress discriminatory effects of policies of the Han-centered Party/state on a wide variety of issues including economic development, education, and culture. While such efforts may well be justified in order to secure meaningful equality, presumptions about formal equality effectively prohibit efforts to secure preferential treatment for minority nationalities necessary to safeguard their identity.

(e) Unity among nationalities requires mutual respect.

The emphasis on mutual respect may encourage greater efforts by representatives of the dominant Han culture to engage more fully with minority nationalities. When juxtaposed with legal provisions on equality, however, such calls remain simply hortative in nature. Moreover, there is also the implication that minority nationalities need to grant more respect to the Han, thus challenging perceptions of local minorities that the Han are nothing more than intruders into local homelands.

(f) Nationalities have a duty to cooperate with each other.

Similarly with the principle on mutual respect, the duty to cooperate may be of little practical import, when viewed in light of legal provisions on equality. In PRC political vernacular, cooperation (*hezuo*) involves doing things together, but does not imply shared political authority. Hence Han cooperation with minority nationalities need not be accompanied by concessions on material or political conditions. As well, cooperation by nationalities with Han may well be interpreted as a duty to assist in Party/state policies and programs, many of which aim to subordinate local minority autonomy.

(g) The major tasks for nationality work involve economic development and production, which are the basis for resolving other issues.

This clear affirmation that economic development is the foundation for nationality work underscores the government's assumptions that economic growth will resolve other nationalities issues. Whether such assumptions will be borne out remains to be seen.

(h) The nationality autonomy system is the basis for resolving China's nationalities issues.

This affirms the terms of the nationality autonomy system as set forth in the Constitution, the NRAL, and associated laws and regulations, and underscores the limitations on local autonomy permitted by the regime. As with other examples of formalism in Chinese law and policy, the emphasis on formally articulated policies tends to diminish attention to substantive performance and consequences.

(i) Nationality policy includes the task of continuing to building a corps of minority nationality cadres with high ideological and moral quality and technical and cultural quality.

The linkage of "quality" with minority nationality cadre recruitment expresses presumptions that "quality" is measured by reference to compliance with Han-dominated Party orthodoxy. This also tends to underscore assumptions about the low "quality" of minorities generally in comparison with Han Chinese. The emphasis on ideology and morality point to the need for programs of indoctrination in Party/state ideals, while the reference to technical and cultural matters focuses attention on formal education according to Chinese standards.

Each of these provisions reveals assumptions and expectation about conditions in minority areas that raise significant challenges for operational effectiveness. Assumptions about the withering away of nationalities reveal a historical-materialist vision about the transitory nature of ethnicity, and tend to diminish the inherent worth of local nationality cultures. This explains much about China's past policies, and also opens the way for continued Han cultural dominance. References to "socialism with Chinese characteristics," privilege PRC policy priorities in place since 1992 emphasizing economic accumulation and a concomitant disregard for state intervention to correct disparities of income and opportunity. This suggests that development efforts in the Inner Periphery are less likely to attend to disparities of economic opportunity and competitiveness between Han and minority communities, which bodes ill for prospects of marginalized groups—particularly in light of the challenges posed by Han in-migration for local participation in economic development.

The imperative of preserving national unity speaks once again about China's continued preoccupation with national security concerns in its nationalities policy. Unity among China's nationalities is presented as an historical task for the Party in the twenty-first century and one that is now a major emphasis of the "3rd generation leadership" (State Nationalities Commission 2002: 64). While some attention is given to relations among nationality groups, particular emphasis is given to opposition to separatism, particularly in Xinjiang and Tibet (contrast Wu 1998: 8–9 with SNAC 2002: 65). As revealed across the Inner Periphery, this tends to build a culture of mistrust and to distract attention from local community and social development efforts, once again privileging themes of assimilation over accommodation of minority nationality perspectives and concerns.

Recitation of the principle of equality among all nationalities underscores the extent to which ideals of formal equality displace attention to realities of socio-economic inequality between Han and minority nationalities. Principles of formal equality are grounded in idealized characterizations of China as a unified multi-ethnic state (*tongyi de duominzu guojia*), comprising Han as well as minority nationalities (NRAL Preface; SCIO 1999). Principles of formal equality raise the possibility for continued marginalization of local minority communities in the face of continued Han in-migration to the Inner Periphery, as policy and legal processes and institutions are guided by norms of formal equality (Dai 2002: 13–25), rather than needs of local conditions. This may work to diminish efforts to accommodate particular social conditions of minority nationalities. Exhortatory language about mutual respect and cooperation suggest appreciation of the gaps between formal equality and realities of socio-economic and political inequality, and reveal the extent to which dynamics of Han-chauvinism continue to plague relations with minority nationalities. Yet remedial measures are left in the realm of abstract ideals, even as expectations about local cooperation between nationalities are used to subordinate local minority communities to the preferences of Han business and economic interests, and also to induce local communities to cooperate in political campaigns against separatism.

Party and government measures to achieve equality among national ethnic groups are pursued through improving material conditions through education and culture (SNAC 2002: 71–73), and suggest the government's withdrawal from preferential programs for minority nationalities, such as exceptions to population control measures, allowances for local language usage, incentives for economic activities, and preferences in local access to education. Thus the State Council's 2002 decision on minority nationality education recited principles of self-reliance and tailoring education to the limits of local conditions as the basis upon which to proceed with basic goals of providing nine years of basic education and eliminating childhood illiteracy, and also influence the implementation of operational measures such as increasing investment in education, and pursuing bilingual education at the elementary and middle school levels ("Guowuyuan guanyu shenhua gaige"). While education of minority nationalities is considered essential to achieving economic development and combating separatism, frank assessments of minority education acknowledged serious shortcomings. Continuing problems of teaching attitudes and methods (ranging from lack of commitment to inadequate bilingual teaching), resources (lack of investment and facilities), and staffing plagued minority education such that in comparison to national achievements in the two basic policies (*liang ji*) on basic education and childhood illiteracy, only half of minority areas had achieved the nine-year basic education goal (Li L. 2003).

China's minority nationalities policies were revisited once again at a 2005 national work conference, from which emerged a new government White Paper (SCIO 2004a, 2005b). The 2009 White Paper on Ethnic Policy (SCIO 2009) affirms the basic policy priorities of central control voiced through discourses of equality, unity, autonomy, and development. Yet the White Paper also endeavors to respond to some of expanding criticism from the international community to which China's aspirations of greater stature and legitimacy are aimed (e.g., CECC 2009b). The shift in nomenclature from "nationalities" to "ethnic" as a descriptor for minority policy suggests an effort to undermine the claims to national identity of Tibetans, Uighurs, and other minority groups, and to appropriate language from minorities policies in countries like the United States and the UK, which have criticized China's treatment of minorities. The fact that the Chinese term "*minzu*" remained unchanged suggests as well the extent to which the White Paper is aimed at China's international audience—supporters and critics alike. Further, in a tacit acknowledgement of the contested sovereignty held by China in minority areas such as Tibet and Xinjiang, the White Paper admits the historical record of "short-term separations and local divisions in Chinese history." Yet the White Paper claims that "unification has always been the mainstream and trend in the development of the country," asserting that central governments of Han or minority origin considered themselves "orthodox reigns of China"—in effect conflating the national aspirations of Mongols and Manchus with those of the Han Chinese. The White Paper also claims that the long-standing existence of a unified ethnic country by different ethnic groups reinforced their allegiance to the central governance and their identification with Chinese culture. These claims, while perhaps illuminating the increased awareness of the central Party/state that claims to sovereignty over minority nationality areas is far from settled, also indulge in selective reading of history to reassert such claims.

The White Paper reasserts the principle of equality among ethnic groups (SCIO 2009a: Section II). The White Paper provides that all ethnic groups have equal status regardless of their population, size, history, and level of social and economic development. Despite formal rhetoric allowing for "special rights and interests" for minority communities, the White Paper devotes hardly any attention to specific examples or efforts that might redress historical imbalances of prosperity and political and economic opportunity that characterize Han-minority relations. The doctrine of formal equality essentially prohibits efforts to overcome disparities of wealth and development between Han and local minorities, thus undermining efforts to provide structural benefits and preferences for marginalized groups. Such a principle of formal equality continues to entrench the operational inequalities that stem from disparities of education and economic opportunity that characterize China's development policies. Thus, even as the White Paper extols increases in industrial output and characterizes the traditional socio-economic patterns of minority communities as "a life full of misery," the development programs adopted by the state such as transportation, water conservancy, construction, and natural resource exploitation are precisely the ones that have alienated local minorities not least because they have not improved opportunities for employment and prosperity for local minorities (CECC 2009b).

While the White Paper acknowledges the importance of poverty alleviation and improved health care in minority areas, and claims vigorous support for balanced development, yet all such efforts are subject to central leadership thus privileging central policy concerns over alleged separatism and minority nationalism rather than local concerns around community development (SCIO 2009a, Sections III, V). Measures of economic development cited in the White Paper give primary attention to aggregate growth indicators with scant attention to the ongoing disparities between Han migrants and local nationality groups. In light of the continued influx of Han migrants—encouraged under policies of equality and unity of ethnic groups—aggregate growth figures tend to reflect the distortion of economic benefits toward Han and away from local minority groups.

The White Paper emphasizes principles of ethnic unity, which are linked closely with the doctrines associated with autonomy for minority nationality areas (SCIO 2009a, Section III). Yet such provisions work mainly to entrench central political authority over local autonomy. Ethnic unity is also attached to the economic development policies of the Party/state—in particular the Western Development Program. Yet the WDP is driven by central government objectives about development and coupled with political imperatives around suppressing alleged minority separatism and nationalism. Perhaps most tellingly, the White Paper emphasizes the efforts by the Party/state to mete out criminal punishment against local minorities for violations of law. As revealed by the official reaction to demonstrations in Tibet (2008) and Xinjiang (2009) that began peacefully only to descend into violence in the wake of state repression, orthodox views extend the notion of unlawful behavior to include expressing virtually any views with which the Party/state disagrees on matters of minority policy or human rights and governance in minority areas. The White Paper emphasizes the need to establish permanent mechanisms and emergency response plans for ensuring unity and stability. In the face of Han dominance of the institutions of Party/state power, increased Han migration and economic dominance in minority areas, and the general absence of meaningful opportunities for redress of grievances by minority populations, such measures are tantamount to official admission that repression will be used to ensure Han control of minority communities in minority areas.

Minority cadre policy

Minority cadre policy is an important benchmark for China's management of social relations in the Inner Periphery. While minority cadre training has long been a formal component of nationalities policy, dating back to the PRC People's Government's 1950 "Provisional methods on minority cadre training," the purpose and implementation focused largely on indoctrination into Han-dominated CPC political norms (Li H. 2004: 93–95). Following the Cultural Revolution, with its Han-chauvinist excesses that saw widespread destruction of minority cultural expressions and artifacts, efforts resumed during the 1970s to rebuild relations with minority nationality cadres (e.g., *Zhonggong zhongyang zuzhibu*; *Guowuyuan guanyu minzu*). By the 1980s efforts to legalize minority cadre training were evident in the NRAL's requirements that local governments achieve an appropriate balance in their operational units between local minority cadres and cadres of other nationalities (Art. 18). While local governments are given responsibility for education, the NRAL charges "higher level organs" with responsibility for assisting with cadre recruitment and training (NRAL: Arts. 71–72). Implementation of Party policies and state laws and regulations would seem heavily dependent on the role of local cadres, whose local knowledge—including cultural affinity, local language fluency, and social linkages with local communities—is essential to the institutional interface between China's rulers and local society. However, this has been officially acknowledged only belatedly and with considerable misgivings arising from lingering uncertainties as to what would be the role for minority cadres and by extension what would be the prospects for building loyalty and patriotism within a newly created minority cadre elite (He 2005: 273–74).

The 1992 Nationalities Work Conference resulted in renewed attention to minority cadre training as a vehicle for dissemination of central Party and government policy. In contrast to previous practices of less-than-benign neglect, appointment of minority nationality cadres has been given greater attention since the 1992 National Minority Nationalities Work Conference. Speaking to the meeting, Jiang Zemin termed creation of a corps of minority nationality cadres with ability and political integrity essential to resolving China's minority nationalities question (Jiang 1992b: 40). Li Peng offered a more instrumentalist formula for training, selecting, and using (*peiyang, xuanba he shiyong*) minority nationality cadres, suggesting that minority cadres could not be selected for use until they had been property trained—i.e., indoctrinated in the orthodoxies of the Party/state. Li also called for increases in the number of minority cadres and for improving their composition (*jiegou*) structure and quality (*suzhi*): "all departments, systems, and professions (*bumen, xitong, hangye*) should positively and actively adopt multiple methods and forms to assist nationality regions to train specialists for needs of the job" (Li P. 1992: 49–50). Hence the focus is on training first, through which political reliability as well as technical knowledge can be instilled and "quality" of minority cadres ensured. Selection is then based on the success of the training process, and finally deployment is made in the service of the broader national goals articulated by the Party and government.

Following the 1992 meeting, the Nationalities Affairs Commission considered minority cadres training essential to achieving goals of training minorities for local administration; countering separatism, and furthering economic development (SNAC 2002: 190–93). Each of these goals reveals priorities of central policy. Autonomy for nationality regions is limited to administration of local issues; minority cadres are seen as useful mainly as an interface to persuade or coerce local compliance with Han-dominated Party directives; and minority cadre involvement in development would be implementational rather than deliberative—carrying out central Party and government policies and imperatives in the course of their work, but having little impact on policy design. Minority cadres are thus seen as a useful conduit through which China's policy programs for the Inner Periphery will be implemented, although questions remain whether local minority nationality concerns will be incorporated effectively into central initiatives.

While the operational climate suggested a greater willingness to accommodate local minority nationality conditions, internal debates continued over the precise content and program for minority cadre training. A national work conference on the topic was convened in June 1993, and emphasized broad goals on the need to raise political reliability; train cadres for middle and higher levels; establish minority cadre corps for the basic levels of village and township; and strengthening cooperation between Han and minority cadres (Hu J. 1993). Each of these areas focused on ensuring effectiveness of minority cadres in carrying out central Party and government policies was paramount.

Yet the formal "Opinion" summarizing the results of the meeting was not issued until December, reflecting continued debate on the specific content and program for minority cadre training. In particular, questions arose over placement of minority cadres in basic level cadre corps or at high level policy positions. The policy goals for minority cadre training highlighted in the "Opinion" reflected a series of compromises on this issue, but also echoed underlying concerns about the political reliability ("quality") of minority cadres. Thus the Opinion called specifically for raising the quality of minority cadres—particularly on issues of political reliability and acceptance of Party policy on nationality affairs and religion; establishing basic level minority cadre corps where minority cadres could use their local knowledge and relationships in agricultural and husbandry production; establishing minority cadre corps in selected technical areas—including emerging areas of finance and management, but also in politics and law; paying attention to selection of leading cadres; and training a younger generation of minority cadres ("Zhonggong zhongyang zuzhi bu, Zhonggong zhongyang tongzhanbu"; Sun Y. 2006: 136–37).

Following the 1993 work conference, cadre training classes linked the question of "quality" with the need to integrate local development efforts with national goals. Thus, minority cadre training would incorporate requirements to build a socialist material cultural and spiritual civilization among minority cadres along with the requirement to integrate regional economic development with national priorities (Wang Zhaoguo 1996: 162 *et seq.*). Cadre quality was thus measured according to factors of political loyalty and subordination to national imperatives of the Han-dominated Party/state. Accordingly, policies of separation are imposed that remove minority cadres from their home towns ("to temper them") and assign them for two years of training or for longer appointments to temporary posts elsewhere (Liu and Wang 2001). This echo of the traditional Chinese "policy of avoidance" seems aimed less at curbing corruption and more at isolating minority cadres from cultural support networks that might work to preserve vestiges of local identity and sensibility.

Yet Chinese analysts continue to claim that local governments in China's Inner Periphery are characterized by the "low quality" (*suzhi di*) of minority cadre personnel (Lai 2002: 30 *et seq.*). The focus on improving the "quality" of minorities generally and minority cadres in particular relates not only to issues of political reliability but also a more generalized sense of assimilation into Han cultural values (Sun Yi *et al.* 2003; Wu 1998: 162, 252–53). Minority cadre education is focused on raising the "quality" of minority cadres by elevating their scientific and cultural level ("National Forum Held"). The content and purpose of minority cadres training has focused largely on displacing traditional cultural norms with norms of socialism and cultural civilization associated with Han China (SNAC 2002: 169–71). Improving scientific and cultural "quality" of minority cadres involves basic education but more importantly focuses on instilling loyalty to notions of national unity and Party supremacy (SNAC 2002: 191–92). To the extent that cadre "quality" involves assimilation of PRC norms of political orthodoxy and Han cultural norms (Kipnis 2006), minority cadre recruitment and training programs will continue to face obstacles and resistance. Implicit in this is the imperative to "modernize" minority nationalities so as to raise the "quality" (*suzhi*) of non-Han groups and improve their economic and cultural lives (Wu 1998: 162).

Dilemmas of minority cadre recruitment come into sharp relief in the State Nationalities Commission's own regulations on the staff complement (*bianzhi*) for minority nationalities ("Guojia minzu shiwu weiyuanhui zhineng"). Based on the State Council's general notice on staff complements in state institutions, the Nationalities Commission notice outlines the Commission's functions, organization, and staff numbers. While the Commission's functions include coordination of minority cadre training under the aegis of its personnel department, no mention is made of the Commission's authority and activity to promote hiring of minority cadres to administrative positions of meaningful importance. The staff complement for the Commission does not include reference to a proportion of minority cadres.

At the June 26–27, 2000 National Forum on Cultivating and Selecting Ethnic Minority Cadres, local Party committees were charged to "strengthen leadership" ("National Forum Held"). Principal leading comrades of Party and government were directed to take direct control over policy direction and content. The "Opinion" issued following the Forum focused on linking cadre education with economic development and the particular needs of nationality areas—opening the way for practical training programs that would be necessary to implement state development programs ("Guojia minwei, jiaoyubu"). Thus, minority cadre recruitment is used increasingly as a mechanism to "educate" selected representatives of local society on the virtues of China's policies and practices. Minority cadre training is a key component in efforts to build social stability and counter perceived threats of minority nationality separatism (Sun Yi 2006, *et al.*).

However, despite suggestions of possibly benign intentions in theory, the practice of minority cadre recruitment, training, and work assignment has served to further alienate local minority peoples and even the cadres themselves. In many instances, immediately upon retirement, minority cadres often discard permanently the clothes, language, and customs of Chinese bureaucratic life in favor of their own national forms. To the extent that minority cadre training is linked to economic development programs of the Western Development Program, this too works to entrench state-centric governance norms that tend to marginalize local cultural perspectives ("Guowuyuan guanyu shishi"). While the numbers of minority cadres continue to rise, both in aggregate and as a proportion of local Party cadres generally, questions remain of whether this contributes to stability and the diminution of strained relations between local nationalities and the Han, or between local society and the central Party/state.

The 2009 White Paper on Ethnic Policy addresses the dilemma of cadre training (SCIO 2009a, Section VII), although the bulk of the discussion simply reiterates previous policy positions articulated in the Constitution and the NRAL on cultivation of minority cadres—by implication re-affirming existing policy priorities. While the White Paper omits the language of "quality" (*suzhi*), and acknowledges the need for inclusion of minority cadres in government, the language used is one of paternalism that speaks of "lowering the standards"; establishing quotas despite the "open selection and competition" for appointment of cadres to leading positions; and "preferential treatment." Absent is an acknowledgement that local minority cadres may be actually better suited than Han cadres to design and implement local policy. Instead the White Paper emphasizes the government's practices of assigning cadres (by implication, Han cadres) to promote the development of minority areas. Thus, the White Paper reaffirms a typology by which the Han are depicted as making "arduous efforts and selfless contributions" for minority areas and local minority cadres are recruited and trained for such efforts through processes that deny the quality and effectiveness of local minorities to be stewards of their own communities.

Practices in the Inner Periphery

The application of China's nationalities law and policy in the Inner Periphery reveals notable variation based on local conditions. Political concerns about resistance in Tibet and Xinjiang tend to dominate interpretation of nationalities policy and law, whereas application in Inner Mongolia tends to reflect a higher degree of assimilation of China's national priorities.

Tibet

While the Central Nationalities Work Conference of January 1992 may be seen as a watershed of sorts, after which PRC policy on Tibet began to include themes of economic development and improved living standards, the shift from themes of minority assimilation and Han dominance was slow in coming. Emerging from an era where policy goals of assimilation were coupled with undisguised Han chauvinism, the Central Nationalities Work Conference followed on the heels of a landmark inspection visit to Tibet that revealed startling depths of poverty and alienation among the local populace. The Tibetan protests of 1989 were powerful evidence of the extent of discontent. President and Party General Secretary Jiang Zemin's speech to the 1992 Work Conference emphasized themes of equality of all nationalities and committing the central government to assist in Tibet's socio-economic development (Jiang 1992a). This stood in marked contrast to the summary of Tibet policy issued by the central government in May the previous year that focused on the need for Tibet to assimilate the advanced scientific culture of its big brother nationalities (*xiongdi minzu*, i.e. the Han) and emphasized military enforcement of national unity and suppression of "separatist" (*fenlie zhuyi*) forces ("Zonggong zhongyang, Quanguo renda changweihui, Guowuyuan, Zhongyang junwei qingzhu Xizang heping jifang sishi zhounian hedian"). Driven by such a limited vision, government responses to local efforts to preserve Tibetan identity and language had focused on suppression of nationalism and separatism rather than accommodation of local concerns (Shakya 2008: 20). While Jiang's 1992 speech vigorously attacked errors of "separatism and ethnic nationalism" as well as criticizing related policy challenges of Taiwan independence and pan-Islamism (a reference to separatism in Xinjiang), Jiang also linked improved conditions in Tibet with China's broader national interests. While minority nationalities policy would come generally to be subject to stiffer central control, Jiang's speech also suggested principles for more engaged and flexible policies on Tibet.

The Third Tibet Work Conference in July 1994 stressed equality of nationalities and the need to remove discrimination against minorities ("Zhonggong zhongyang, Guowuyuan guanyu jiakuai"). Under the rubric of the "two inseparables" (*liangge "li bu kai"*) in place at the time (to which was added a third inseparable, concerning relations between minorities), government policy on nationality relationships—among cadres and in society—stressed an ideal of common interests and commitment by Han and Tibetan nationalities (ibid.; Wu 1995; "Zhonggong zhongyang", "Sanshi zhounian hedian"). While themes of accommodation were evident, themes of assimilation continued as Jiang's speech to the Work Conference noted the need for Tibet to assimilate the cultures of other nationalities (Jiang 1994a). As well, Jiang stressed themes of national unity and resistance to separatism. Insisting that stability was an essential precondition for development in Tibet, Jiang attacked calls associated with the Dalai Lama for broader autonomy for Tibet. Jiang termed the struggle against the Dalai Lama clique (*Dalai jituan*) to be a continuation of "the struggle of the Chinese people against plots by foreign interventionist forces to split China," denying that this was an issue of autonomy but rather was a matter of national unity (Jiang 1994a: 459).

Jiang condemned purported calls for Tibet independence, or recognition of a "Greater Tibet" that would include other provinces of China such as Qinghai and Gansu that have large and traditionally resident Tibetan populations (ibid.). The Central Committee and State Council "Opinion" emerging from the Third Tibet Work Conference emphasized linkages between economic development and political stability, calling specifically for renewed efforts to ensure national and ethnic unity, opposition to separatist activities by the Dalai Lama and international forces ("Zhonggong zhongyang, Guowuyuan guanyu jiakuai").

In the area of minority cadre policy, Jiang Zemin claimed in his speech to the Third Tibet Work Conference that over 70 percent of the approximately 60,000 cadres working in Tibet were of Tibetan nationality (Jiang 1994: 462). Wu Bangguo's speech to the Third Tibet Work Conference in 1994 emphasized the *"libukai"* principles and called for efforts to unify cadres of different nationalities (Wu 1995). Citing the model of Kong Fansen,[1] Wu extolled ideals of unity with the local nationalities masses and called for establishing basic level Party organizations and political authority; unifying development and stability; and training local cadre corps. Each of these elements required a high degree of integration between transplanted Han and local Tibetan nationality cadres. Yet selection of Tibetan cadres has remained contentious. Speaking to the Tibet delegation to the ninth National People's Congress (NPC), Hu Jintao suggested that selection of Tibetan cadres should be premised on their political quality and proper views on nationality and religion policies, emphasizing once again that selection could take place only after proper inculcation in the political imperatives of the Party/state (Hu 1998). Speaking to the Central Party School on the twentieth anniversary of the Tibet cadre training program, Hu Jintao reiterated the theme of raising the quality of Tibet nationality cadres through political training and indoctrination in Party policy on nationalities and religion (Hu 2000).

The Central Committee and State Council "Opinion" on Tibet development issued following the Fourth Tibet Work Conference in 2001 gave particular attention to cadre policy ("Zhonggong zhongyang, guowuyuan guanyu zuohao"). The "Opinion" seemed to draw back on previous statements emphasizing the need to increase recruitment of local Tibetan cadres. Noting the need to attend to actual conditions and attending to the needs of the job (*dui kou zhi ai*) it suggested that the needs of economic development would require technically trained cadres, which might be in short supply locally and which might require more attention to the role of Han cadres. While the importance of opposing separatism was noted along with the role of the "basic cadre corps," more attention was given to the importance of establishing a corps of leading cadres and to bringing in excellent cadres through rotation—a clear allusion to bringing in Han cadres from elsewhere in China.

In his speech on the fiftieth anniversary of the "peaceful liberation" of Tibet, Hu Jintao returned to the theme of ensuring a correct political orientation and point of view among Tibet cadres, as an essential component in resistance to separatism (Hu 2001b). Linked with a critique of the Dalai Lama's alleged use of issues of ethnicity and religion to harm relations between Tibetans and Han, this suggested a growing disquiet over the political reliability of Tibetan cadres. While the need to recruit minority cadres remains, this has increasingly become subordinated to the policy of promoting scientific development and human resources in nationality autonomy areas—even if these are not oriented toward minority recruitment (Hu 2005b).

Xinjiang

China's nationalities policies applied in Xinjiang during the 1990s and beyond are generally viewed as placing a premium on resistance to separatism and the assertion of central government control (HRW 2005; Gladney 2003; Becquelin 2000). Particular attention has been given to the role of Party leadership over interpretation of the role of "autonomy" (*zizhi quan*) under the NRAL and its implications for balancing regional development goals with conditions and interests of local minority communities (Liu Jun 2003 *et al.*: 256–60). Although economic development has been a recurring theme of nationalities policy in Xinjiang, the subordination of local nationalities to the imperatives of the Han-centered Party/state (often conflicted with the "national interest") has worked to undermine the effectiveness of economic development as a basis for local community support. Basic nationalities policy in Xinjiang holds to the ideal that economic development will contribute to (and also requires) stability and will be effective as a counter to separatism (Qing *et al.* 2003). Economic development has come to be considered the "pre-condition and guarantee" for resolving issues of strengthening unity of nationalities and ensuring social stability ("Guojia Minwei Zhengfa Si": 231). Conversely, delays in achieving goals of establishing the political and legal systems needed to implement China's nationalities policies in Xinjiang are attributed to the region's general condition of lagging behind in economic development (Liu *et al.* 2003: 271).

Official analyses of nationality policy in Xinjiang tend to address questions about unity of nationalities nearly exclusively in terms of opposition to separatism (Ma D. 2003: 177–84; Re and Tie 2003). Jiang Zemin's 1990 inspection visit saw the doctrine of "two inseparables" (*liangge "li bu kai"*) expanded to include a third, concerning the inseparability of minorities nationalities from each other—likely a recognition that in multicultural regions such as Xinjiang where not only Uighurs are ethnically and culturally diverse, but where interaction with other minorities such as Kazakhs and Tajiks is not only common but also fraught with potential conflict (He 2005: 280–82).

The separatism issue was given particular prominence at a Politburo Standing Committee meeting convened in March 1996 by Jiang Zemin to hear reporting from the Political-Legal Committee on conditions in Xinjiang (Li and Liu 2003; Zhu *et al.* 2004: 259–61). The summary of the meeting was issued as Central Document No. 7 (1996), which concluded that problems of social stability in Xinjiang were the result of separatism and unlawful religious activities ("Record of the Meeting"). Distributed to XUAR CPC Committee, Lanzhou Military District CPC Committee, and to local units of Central Committee and State Council departments and ministries, military committees and united front organizations, the document focused on the need to build a stable economic development zone in Xinjiang. The main threats to stability were identified as national separatism and illegal religious activity, where "the main problem is that international counter-revolutionary forces led by the United States of America are openly supporting the separatist activities inside and outside of Xinjiang." The document called for increased vigilance and action by "every level of Party and government leadership," including People's Armed Police (PAP) and People's Liberation Army (PLA). This conjoined reference to Party and government leadership with the PAP and PLA underscored the dominant role of the Party in what would nominally be considered state security organs, illuminating the basic identity and orientation of the Party/state. Moreover, the call for vigilance and action at "every level" alluded to challenges in enforcing Party policies at local levels.

Document No. 7 also called for strengthening of security organs (including police and state security units) to fight separatism—particularly in Southern Xinjiang (*jiangnan*), where the central Party/state saw Han–Uighur relations as the main challenge of China's management of identity and culture in Xinjiang. While the influx of Han to Urumqi has meant that the balance of ethnic populations has shifted in favor of Han dominance, in the south, Uighurs remain dominant and Han migration is limited, not least by the generally forbidding and hostile terrain. That the political–legal apparatus would emphasize the *Jiangnan* area spoke to the deep levels of apprehension and distrust of local Uighur people.

Under the directives of Document No. 7, the Xinjiang Production and Construction Corps (*bingtuan*) was to be strengthened as a basis for defending social stability. The *binguan* remains a key instrument in the governance strategies and practices of the Party/state. Echoing the Han-centered nature of the Party/state, the *bingtuan* serves as an economic as well as social vehicle for local dominance. Document No. 7 also called for strengthening the PLA and closer cooperation with Public Security, State Security, and People's Armed Police units. Here again is evident the importance attached to military and security organs as vehicles for exercise of power by the Party/state. To a significant extent, the professionalism of the PLA and its hard-earned reputation for serving the people (in Han China at least) make it unsuited to local public security tasks. The Tiananmen crisis of 1989 gave ample evidence of the PLA's reluctance to participate in suppressing social action. Hence the call for closer cooperation between PLA and local security units reveals appreciation of the depth of the PLA resistance to social control mandates while also expressing calls to overcome such reluctance.

Document No. 7 called for the use of international diplomacy to isolate Xinjiang separatist organizations calling for recognition of "East Turkestan." References to diplomatic efforts against particularly the "East Turkestan Liberation Movement" seem in local context to be a call for more fulsome promotion of the regional security agenda of the Shanghai Cooperation Organization. While most international diplomacy activities are concentrated with the Ministry of Foreign Affairs, Xinjiang's location offers multiple opportunities for interaction with neighboring states on regional development policies and programs. The policy on diplomatic isolation of Uighur independence supporters is thus inserted into local economic development agendas.

Finally, the document called for accelerated economic development and improved living standards—particularly in the context of the Ninth Five Year Plan. Here again, the emphasis is on economic development as a mechanism for resolving problems in local minority relations. Yet even as the effort to raise living standards is asserted, the potential for further alienation of local communities remains, as economic development policies privilege Han over minority interests.

The breadth of proposed Party and government participation in anti-separatism efforts was nearly unprecedented, revealing the depth of concerns about the problems addressed and in particular the recognition that central Party edicts and policies were not being enforced at the local level. Following the outbreaks of violence in February 1997, the XUAR launched a wide-reaching rectification campaign based on the findings of Document No. 7 (Zhu et al. 2004: 260–72). The initiative focused on inspections and political work at local levels, extending to 1008 villages spread across 383 villages and towns and five regions, districts, and cities. Some 101 departments and 18,000 cadres were sent from XUAR units to the district, township, and village level to conduct investigations and rectification. In 1998, 15,000 cadres across the XUAR were implementing the campaign in the localities—nearly 17,000 by 1999.

In contrast to classical cadre rectification campaigns where work-styles and operational effectiveness were to be reviewed and corrected, the 1998 campaign was essentially an exercise in enforcement and punishment. Linked to the "strike hard" anti-crime campaign, it represented an attempt to extend Party power from the urban centers of XUAR to the rural areas and to the heavily minority-populated regions of western and southern Xinjiang. Despite recognition of ongoing problems with relations between Han and minority cadres (Tiemuer 1996: 460–61) and the implications this raised for effective management of nationality policy, the 1998 campaign seemed to rely on familiar themes of subjugation and control.

Thus, the application in Xinjiang of China's nationalities policy has been unavoidably dependent upon enforcement of policy imperatives of national unity, stability, and repression of alleged separatism. According to an investigation report on social stability issued by the Politics and Law Department of the State Nationalities Affairs Commission in mid-2001 on the Document 7 campaign, outstanding problems included the lingering effects of Han chauvinism and nepotism among leading Han cadres, while among minority cadres were problems of parochialism—including failure to develop a Chinese nationalities identity (*Zhonghua minzu rentong*) (Guojia minwei zhengfa si: 228–29.) Continuous ongoing education and rectification campaigns followed, culminating in a January 2002 anti-separatism meeting calling for essentially a state of ongoing vigilance and suppression (Zhu *et al.* 2004: 272). By mid-year, Party secretaries at the district, *zhou* and municipal levels, leaders of government divisions (*ting*) and bureaux (*ju*) as well as enterprises and schools were brought into the campaign. By 2004 some 11,000 units and 490,000 cadres had participated in re-education activities.

The issue of minority cadre training in Xinjiang appeared to receive scant attention prior to the 1992 Central Nationalities Work Conference, leaving a sense of complacency over the purported achievements of minority cadres in areas of political economy, technology, culture and education and health (Tiemuer 1990: 272). Following the 1999 State Council "Notice" on training of minority nationality cadres, efforts accelerated in Xinjiang through various Party and cadre schools with annual trainee intake rising from 1,000 per year to 3,500 over the following three years, with primary attention paid to linking cadre training to the needs of economic development (Liu *et al.* 2003: 258). While significant attention has been paid to use of local languages in minority cadre training, educational curricula have tended to focus mainly on political and policy issues around religion, social stability, and development. Recurring problems with minority cadres lacking enthusiasm for the Party's nationality autonomy policies and instead simply using their positions to pursue self-interest remain unresolved. Proposed solutions include scientific cadre evaluation programs, supervision and inspection systems, and expanded formalization and "legalization" of nationality policy. Enhancing political loyalty and reliability has come to be the foundation upon which to build professional qualifications for minority cadres (Sun *et al.* 2003: 298–300)

Enactment of the revised NRAL in 2001 brought renewed attention to minority cadre training, although the content of training and the placement of minority cadres continue to receive little attention (Tiemuer 2001b: 541). Reports on minority nationality training and recruitment in peripheral areas of Xinjiang (Sun *et al.* 2003) and Tibet (Zeng 2002: 415) suggest that these remain focused at the basic level and have limited effect on the Autonomous Region governance. Statistics published in 2003 indicated that of the 329,000 minority nationality cadres in Xinjiang, 420 were assigned to the division (*ting*) and bureau (*ju*) levels in XUAR Party organs, 3,700 to the county (*xian*) and office (*chu*) level, and 21,300 to the township (*xiang*) and village (*zhen*) and section (*ke*) levels, while the assignment of technical cadres in areas of political, economic, culture, education, technical, and health work had increased nearly eight-fold since 1978 to 229,000 ("XUAR minzu shiwu weiyuan hui" 2003: 186).

Issues of language use are particularly important for practices of nationality policy in Xinjiang. The dominance of Mandarin for Han-dominated governance frequently conflicts with issues of Uighur identity and culture that are intimately linked with local language use (Dwyer 2005). While nominal attention has been paid through Party policy and law to bilingualism and use of local languages, practice has been inconsistent. Despite enactment of regulations in 1988, 1993, and 2002 ("XUAR minzu yuwen"; "XUAR yuwen wenzi gongzuo tiaoli" 1993, rev. 2002) calling for greater use of local minority languages, use of Mandarin continues to dominate official government activities. Mandarin use by local cadres is seen as a sign of loyalty to Beijing (Magnier 2006)—as well as a vehicle through which they are intended to become more receptive to indoctrination in China's political norms. Preferences available to minority applicants for university and job placements are more favorable for those with Mandarin fluency (cf. Sautman 1998: 93). Despite the ideals expressed in NRAL Article 10 about protecting use and development of local nationality languages, scarcely a year after the revised law went into force, instruction in Uighur was banned at Xinjiang University ("Uyghur language banned from university"). As education is a key factor in socio-economic mobility for local nationalities (Hannum and Yu 1998), increased reliance on Mandarin seems virtually certain to increase among Xinjiang'a minority nationalities, with inevitable potential for disruption of socio-cultural identity.

The 2009 White Paper on Xinjiang (SCIO 2009a) addresses the issue of recruitment of minority cadres. However, the policy summary continues to emphasize issues of "quality" of minority cadres that can only be resolved through training in Han-centered education and fostering in the orthodoxies of the Party/state. The White Paper notes that heads of numerous government subdivisions and departments are drawn from local ethnic groups, but says little to counter long-standing complaints that minority cadres are marginalized from core decision-making. The White Paper says nothing about the role of minority cadres in leading Party organizations.

Inner Mongolia

PRC nationalities policies applied in Inner Mongolia reflect historical conditions of China's expansive assertions of political control and contemporary practicalities of maintaining that control. Han migration into northern border regions of Inner Mongolia began well before the founding of the PRC. Similarly with the pattern in neighboring Manchuria (Reardon-Anderson 2005: 143–46), Han migrants in Inner Mongolia settled during the spring–fall agricultural season, often then returning to China proper for the winter (Yan 2004: 134 *et seq.*). Although these "wild geese" (*yangxing ren*) did not consider themselves more than temporary denizens of the local frontier, their constant and expanding presence established patterns of interaction with local Mongol nationalities that would continue to influence perceptions and practices under the PRC.

Informed by often idealized historical interpretations of revolutionary relations between Mongol and Chinese opponents to KMT rule and Japanese invasion in the 1930s and 1940s, forced collaboration imposed on local Mongol communities resulted in cultures of accommodation that undermined local foundations for identity such as language, religion, and community (Bulag 2003, 2006). While opportunities for resistance remained (Borchigud 1995), preservation of local languages in education and training seems essential to protection of local cultural identity. Ever-expanding Han population figures are testament to patterns of in-migration from China proper, although exceptions for local minorities under China's population control policies begun in the 1980s have seen proportional population growth slightly in favor of Mongol over Han nationalities (MacKerras 1994: 440). Nonetheless, the effects of migration and assimilation have privileged Han socio-cultural norms on dynamics of urbanization and administrative organization (Bulag 2002b).

Minority cadre training in Inner Mongolia builds on policy and regulation on education for minorities generally. For example, building on national laws on education and nationality region autonomy, Huhehaote municipal regulations require the people's governments at all levels to prioritize education for minority nationalities ("Education Regulations": Art. 2). Political indoctrination (patriotism, socialism and Marxist views on nationalities) is combined with attention to work–study programs and vocational teaching ("Education Regulations": Arts. 4, 13, 18). The emphasis on residential and subsidized schools combines imperatives of social control with appreciation of the social realities of providing education to nomadic communities ("Education Regulations": Art. 2).

Education backgrounds provide essential context for the methods and content of minority cadre training (Yuan J. 2001). Educational background is scrutinized, beginning with recruitment to training units such as the Party school and administrative institutes and the preparation of training curricula that include not only culture and specialized knowledge but also political and Party orthodoxy. As well, cadre training is offered in decentralized locales as well as concentrated locales such as the Party school, while attention to raising the quality of recruits extends to issues of technology, culture, and the ability to function in China's socialist market economy. Classroom curricula include Marxism, economics and law, and modern management, with roughly equal student time devoted to in-class and vocational study. Specialized classes are offered on topics such as finance, macro-economics, agricultural and husbandry economics, village and township enterprise management, and marketing, with a rough balance of in-class and vocational training. A final range of classes on related topics such as Mandarin, document drafting, and written Mongolian are linked with specialized topics in science and technology, finance, and public administration. In addition to combining in-class and field training, minority-cadre training classes emphasize analytical methods, heavy reliance on written course materials, and combined use of Mandarin and Mongolian as the languages of instruction. Facing declining usage of Mongolian, the IMAR government has attempted to expand its use by government officials and in education ("Moves to save Mongolian language").

Minority cadre training in Inner Mongolia is associated with a range of policy imperatives linked to China's nationalities policy more broadly, including equality of nationalities; implementation of the official autonomy system; resisting separatism; and promoting economic development (Li H. 2004: 90–93; Bu 2003: 104–5). Yet these were given significantly different sub-texts than those evident in Tibet and Xinjiang. Ideals of equality of nationalities was linked specifically to more effective minority participation in Party and government departments. The pursuit of opportunities for effective participation in party and government departments in IMAR speaks more to issues of partnership and collaboration than the notions of "quality" and control associated with minority cadre policy in Xinjiang and Tibet. Implementation of local autonomy was linked directly with goals to ensure that local governance institutions include cadres who express concerns and aspirations of local minority nationalities. While the emphasis on regional autonomy echoes similar provisions in Xinjiang and Tibet, the express call for cadres who represent local minority interests is distinctive. While calls for national unity are familiar, the linkage of separatism with "Western hostile forces" (*xifang didui shili*) suggests that the issue is one of external subversion rather than internal dissent—a noteworthy distinction from the discourse of separatism and religious extremism in Xinjiang and Tibet. Economic development was couched in terms of specific benefits to minority nationalities. The specific reference to the need to ensure development for minority nationalities addresses directly the need to correct fundamental flaws in development policies in Xinjiang and Tibet, namely that state-driven policies coupled with formalistic assertions of equality of nationalities work to prejudice minority interests and aspiration. Thus, as with other dimensions of Inner Mongolia governance, the extent of integration with China proper as well as the history of relative passivity and compliance seem to enable more pronounced efforts to safeguard local minorities.

With these ends in mind, minority cadre training has focused on providing technical training to an expanding proportion of minority trainees. Figures compiled by the Chinese Academy of Social Sciences through 2001 indicate that local minority cadres made up 24.8 percent of the total cadre corps (n = 189,400/763,500)—a greater percentage than the Mongol–Han nationality ratio generally (Sun Y. 2006: 140). In comparison with Tibet and Xinjiang, minority cadre training in Inner Mongolia has focused more closely on technical than political education as 35.16 percent of trainees participated in junior college (*da zhuan*) training and an additional 32.88 percent received technical (*zhong zhuan*) training. Small percentages received full university-level education.

While these are noteworthy achievements, the pattern of employment for cadres who have completed training (16.94 in government departments; 46.71 percent in non-governmental departments; and 12.6 percent in enterprises) suggests that the role for minority cadres in policy decision-making and implementation remains limited. This is compounded by official perceptions about inadequate educational and political preparation, the effects of poor economic conditions; and habitual attitudes of egalitarianism and disdain for commerce continuing to impede the "quality" of recruits (Sun Z. 2001: 77–78), and may contribute to ongoing difficulties in increasing overall numbers for minority cadres. Local nationalities who appreciate the limitations on their participation in politics and government units, where cadre corps are growing faster than in sectors such as economics, technology, health and agricultural science (Sun Y. 2006: 143), are less likely to participate enthusiastically in minority training efforts where the personal and social costs of being co-opted to Chinese rule are not compensated by access to meaningful influence and status. A paradoxical corollary seems to be that access for local minorities to Party and government postings remains dependent on their political reliability, which Han governance officials often assume to be lacking.

While academic and policy initiatives on preserving Mongolian culture dispense with traditionalist approaches to preservation of culture as artifact in favor of acknowledging the importance of a lived and dynamic culture operating in response to changing conditions—even asserting the need for true local autonomy (*zizhuquan*) under the NRAL over notions of local administrative initiative (*zizhiquan*) (compare Zhang and Bao 2003: 6 with Du 2006: 195–203), such views are in a sense made possible by the very domination by which local minority culture is threatened. Important attention is paid to the need to strengthen formal legal institutions and to ensure effectiveness of laws and regulations protecting local nationalities culture (Zhang and Bao 2003: 8), although the dependency of these efforts on China's Han-dominated legal and administrative systems tends to marginalize local nationality voices in the processes and outcomes of protection. These in turn challenge the prospects for preserving local autonomy of identity, even if such autonomy can be seen to be present in areas of political governance and economic development policy. Local protests over perceived mistreatment of the legacy of Genghis Khan reflect tensions over issues of agenda-setting and implementation on policies of protection of local culture ("Mongols resist"; "Genghis Khan's tribe").

Religion

PRC law and policy on socio-cultural relations in the Inner Periphery are intimately linked with the regulation of religion.[2] Tensions over diversity and unity in cultural relations come into sharp relief, as religion involves perhaps most directly the potential for conflicts of loyalty. China's most senior leaders have acknowledged the links between religion policy and minority policy, which in turn intersect with issues of national unification, social stability, economic development, and national defense in the frontier areas of the Inner Periphery ("Jiang Meets"). China's preoccupation with subordinating minority identity to national policy imperatives involves placing limits on religious activity through law, policy, and practice.

Constitution and law

As with many features of social regulation in China, the regulation of religion proceeds essentially from the policy dictates of the CPC, which are then expressed and enforced in part through law and administrative regulation. The foundational legal principles for religious rights in China are contained in Article 36 of the PRC Constitution (1982), which provides for freedom of religious belief; freedom from coercion to believe or not believe in religion; freedom from religious discrimination; and protection of "normal" religious activities coupled with proscriptions against disruption of social order, impairment of citizens' health, or interference with state education; and freedom from foreign domination in affirming the freedom of religious belief. The Constitution also makes clear that such freedom does not extend to behavior, which remains subject to Constitutional limitations and the constraints of Party/state policy. The parallelism used to link belief and unbelief underscores the Party's basic policies supporting atheism. While this provision is an important statement of principle that Party and state organs may not intrude on matters of belief, it also leaves aside issues of religious behavior that are subject to existing and expanding restrictions. Normal religious activities are those connected with the five recognized religions of Buddhism, Daoism, Islamism, Catholicism, and Protestantism, which conform to Party/state policies and regulations. Expansive references to public order, health, and education provide further justification for Party and state limitations on religious behavior. The reservation against foreign religious organizations or individuals operating in China originally involved reactions to Christian missionary activities in China, although more recently the focus has been on international Islam.

In explaining the meaning of Constitutional provisions on religious freedom, Peng Zhen noted that from a political perspective the common elements of patriotism and adherence to socialism bind those who believe in religion and those who do not (Peng 1982b). This underscored the imperative of submission to Party/state control as a condition for enjoyment of religious freedom. Protection of freedom of religion was qualified as well by provisions of the PRC Constitution Article 33 conditioning the exercise of citizens' rights on their performance of duties: "Every citizen enjoys the rights and at the same time must perform the duties prescribed by the Constitution and the law." These duties included upholding the four basic principles (Peng 1980), which impose a duty to uphold the socialist road, the dictatorship of the proletariat, leadership of the Party, and Marxism–Leninism Mao Zedong Thought (Deng 1983: 150–51). Thus, the granting of free religious belief remained conditional not only on compliance with law and regulation, but more fundamentally on submission to the policies and edicts of the Party/state.

The Constitution provides authority for specific legislation on the matter of religion. National regulations on religious affairs enacted March 1 2005 embody the State's reliance on formalized legal measures to control religion ("Zongjiao shiwu tiaoli"). Article 2 depicts a right to freedom of religious belief and prohibits discrimination on grounds of religion. Yet the regulatory regime also contains numerous limitations on rights, including prohibitions on infringing the interests of the state, society and the collective and affirmative duties to safeguard the security, honor, and interests of China and uphold the socialist system (and by extension Party rule) (Constitution: Arts. 1, 51, 52).

In light of continued Party policy on control of religion in minority areas (and elsewhere), the reference to religion in the CPC Constitution amended at the Seventeenth CPC National Congress in October 2007 did not suggest liberalization but rather underscored the need to enforce Party policies of control: "The Party strives to fully implement its basic principle for its work related to religious affairs, and rallies religious believers in making contributions to economic and social development" ("CPC Constitution: General Program"). The provision was linked to policies on "socialist ethnic relations" revealing once again the assumed linkages between minority nationalities and religion.

While the national regulations affirm in Article 3 the government's protection of normal religious activities, the use of the term "normal" (*zhengchang*) leaves to the state discretion to limit protection of human rights in religion. The Provisions also prohibit in Article 3 undermining social order, state education, or state and social interests, allowing yet further limitations on the exercise of human rights in religion. Religious groups (*tuanti*) are tightly regulated and are effectively insulated from international and local co-religionists through principles of "independence, self-determination, and self-operation" ("Zongjiao shiwu tiaoli": Arts. 4, 6). Dissemination of religious ideas is restricted through prohibition of publications (*chubanwu*) that "undermine" peaceful co-existence and amity between religious and non-religious citizens, discriminate or insult religious or non-religious citizens, publicize religious extremism, or violate principles of independence, self-determination, and self-operation ("Zongjiao shiwu tiaoli": Art. 7). Criminal responsibility attaches to those who sabotage state security and public safety, interfere with public order, or trespass on public or private property ("Zongjiao shiwu tiaoli": Art. 40). The national regulations displace previous measures regulating places of worship ("Guowuyuan guanyu zongjiao huodong changsuo guanli tiaoli"), expanding upon their provisions for application, registration, and annual reporting on management of religious sites.

In addition, specific regulations apply to control various types of religious activity, including registration of religious organizations and places of worship and conduct of foreigners (RAB-PRD 2002). Religious organizations must apply to register with the local People's Government following inspection and agreement from the State Council Religious Affairs Bureau (RAB), affirming their compliance with the requirements of the PRC Constitution and laws ("Zongjiao shehui tuanti dengji guanli shishi banfa"). Religious education academies must implement CPC policy and submit to Party leadership, and their curricula, programs and personnel are subject to approval by the Religious Affairs Bureau (RAB 1988). The officially approved curricula incorporate state policy into religious instruction ("Excerpts"). Activities such as recruiting believers among primary and secondary school students, propagating religious ideology in schools, establishing illegal (i.e., not properly approved and registered) religious schools, enrolling young people, and traveling abroad to attend seminary are all considered in violation of the provision that religion may not obstruct state education ("Notice"; RAB 1988). As well, measures have been enacted attacking so-called "illegal sects," particularly the now-famous *Falun Gong* movement (Ownby 2008).

Party policy

Interpretation and application of constitutional and legal provisions on regulation of religion continue to depend on Party policy. Recent Party policy on religion has reflected a marked departure from the policies of the Maoist period, when imperatives of socialist transformation led generally to repression of religious belief and practice. At the outset of the post-Mao reform period, the official summary of CPC policy on religion issued in 1982 as "Document 19" signaled a relaxation of restrictions against religion, and stated the basic policy as one of respect for and protection of the freedom of religious belief, pending such future time when religion itself will disappear ("Guanyu woguo shehui": 59–60). Party policy recognized five basic characteristics of religion including its long-term character, mass base, national and international aspects, and complexity (Ye 2001). The long-term character of religion militated in favor of patient persistence in Party policies of co-optation and control. The mass character served as a cautionary note that the Party could not easily ignore or control the some 100 million people believed to participate in religion. The links between religion and national and international questions called for attention to the interplay between ethnicity in such areas as Tibet and Xinjiang and the imported religions of Buddhism and Islam. The complexity of religion was seen to require careful analysis of the processes of popular belief as a prerequisite for effective policy.

In 1991, the CPC Central Committee/State Council's "Document No. 6" expressed the regime's policy response that attempted to co-opt religious adherents while also repressing challenges to Party power ("Zhonggong Zhongyang Guowuyuan guanyu jinyibu"; "Document 6"). The document emphasized increased regulatory control over all religious activities while claiming to avoid interference with normal religious activities. While the reference to non-interference seemed benign on its face, the qualification that this extended only to "normal" activities suggested an overarching purpose to confine religion to the limits of law and policy.

Document No. 6 grew out of the State Council's National Work Conference on Religion December 5–9, 1990, at which there was relatively frank discussion on the number of religious adherents in China and a recognition of the need for limited tolerance (Luo 2001: 428–32). Document No. 6 claimed to protect freedom of religious belief, while requiring believers to comply with imperatives of Party leadership, social stability, and social interests. The document reiterated the foundational importance of the 1982 Document No. 19, but called for expanded efforts to implement Party policy on religion, using legal and policy measures to control religious activities. Document No. 6 directed public security organs to take forceful measures to curb those who use religious activities to "engage in disruptive activities," "stir up trouble, endanger public safety, and weaken the unification of the country and national unity," or "collude with hostile forces outside the country to endanger China's security." Such provisions were used to justify restrictions on religious activities in Inner Periphery areas such as Tibet and Xinjiang ("Zhongyang Danxiao": 412–15), and also limited proselytization, recruitment, fund-raising, and other activities in support of organized religion (Spiegel 1992: 8–13). As well, the CPC Organization Department issued measures to address the problem of Party members ("particularly those in areas inhabited by minority nationalities and areas where the influence of religious forces is relatively great"), including submission to Party discipline inspection proceedings and potential relinquishment of Party membership ("Zhonggong zhongyang zuzhi bu" 1991).

Responding to conditions in the minority nationality areas—including alleged efforts by "international hostile forces" to "Westernize" and "divide" China—CPC General Secretary Jiang Zemin articulated three principles of all round and correct implementation of Party policy: reliance on law to manage religious affairs, and positively encouraging mutual adaptation of religion and socialist society (*jiji yindao zongjiao yu shehui zhuyi shehui xiang shiying*) (Jiang 1993a). These three principles (*san juhua*) would come to represent the foundation for Party and government policy on religion (He H. 2004: 245–47). The primacy of Party policy encouraged general flexibility in content and application of norms for regulation of religion—allowing the Party to adopt specific measures in response to changing conditions and to preserve Party leadership as the basis for control of religious rights. The emphasis on legal regulation expressed recognition of the need to formalize standards and procedures for administration of religious affairs, although as with all other aspects of law in the PRC, this is ultimately dependent on the needs and priorities of Party policy. The reference to mutual adaptation (*xiang shiying*) remains contested. Although it recognizes to some degree the need for socialist society to acknowledge and permit limited religious activities, the primary emphasis has been on religious communities and activities deferring to the needs of socialism, which by extension include the national political and development imperatives of the Party/state.

The State Council's 1997 White Paper on "Freedom of Religious Belief in China" reiterated the point that "religion should be adapted to the society where it is prevalent" and that religions must "conduct their activities within the sphere prescribed by law and adapt to social and cultural progress" ("Freedom": 246–247). The White Paper reiterated the distinction between religious beliefs which the state purports to protect, and "illegal and criminal activities being carried out under the banner of religion." ("Freedom": 247). The distinction between protected belief and unlawful behavior is made according to CPC policies, as expressed in the provisions of the Constitution and specific laws and regulations. In his speech to the December 2001 National Work Conference on Religious Affairs, Jiang Zemin called once again for adaptation between religion and socialism ("Jiang Zemin, Zhu Rongji"). However, the December 2001 work conference also expressed the more conventional aspects of Party policies on control of religion ("Quanguo zongjiao"). Jiang Zemin called for the Party and state to guide religion to conform to the needs of socialism, and to prevent religious adherents from interfering with the socialist system, the interests of the state, and the requirements of social progress ("Jiang Zemin, Zhu Rongji").

Politburo Politics and Law Chair Luo Gan's speech on tasks for 2002, given just prior to the work conference, stressed the need for suppression of disruptive religious activity in minority areas under the rubric of "religious extremism and terrorism" ("At National Meeting"). Following the work conference, idealized depictions of religious adherents as eager to subordinate their religious convictions to the needs of national unity revealed efforts at norm-building. At a meeting of representatives to the Chinese People's Political Consultative Congress (CPPC), religious and nationality identities were subsumed under ideals of patriotism (Meng 2002).

Thus, despite apparent changes in religion policy suggested at the 2001 national religion work conference through the rubric of mutual adaptation (*xiang shiying*) (Jiang Zemin 2001), subsequent interpretations made it clear that it was religion that would have to do most of the adapting. Ongoing repression of religious activities in minority nationality areas continued;

> The government's crackdown on religious activity in the Xinjiang Uighur Autonomous Region has increased in intensity since 2001. New central government legal provisions and local measures from the Tibet Autonomous Region (TAR) government intensify an already repressive environment for the practice of Tibetan Buddhism.
> (CECC 2007: 90–91)

Practices in the Inner Periphery

China's legal and regulatory provisions are also aimed at specific religions in the Inner Periphery. Ever apprehensive about potential links between religious belief and ethnic tension, the government regulates religious activities of minority nationalities in Tibet and Xinjiang closely to ensure repression of nationalist separatism (Madsen 2000). Echoing Constitutional provisions and Party policy, the Nationality Region Autonomy Law provides in Article 11 that "normal" religious activities are protected, but prohibits use of religion to "disrupt social order, impair the health of citizens, or interfere with the educational system of the state." The Western Development Program remains a key component in Beijing's efforts to still ethnic and religious tension in the Inner Periphery ("PRC's Wang"). Speaking about the WDP, Hu Jintao emphasized the need to ensure that religious belief did not conflict with state law and policy, noting in particular efforts to control selection of patriotic temple priests and resisting foreign forces that seek to use religion to transform China's socialist society (Hu Jintao 2004).

Tibet

Prior to the 1992, Party policy on religion in Tibet emphasized the requirements of CPC Central Committee Documents No. 19 (1982) and No. 6 (1991) prohibiting interference with state administration and education under the guise of religion. In effect this allowed the TAR government to intrude at will on religious activities and organizations, as any resistance was interpreted as a violation of Party policy. The TAR government has also relied on the ever-expanding inventory of laws and regulations limiting religious freedoms to matters of individual faith and proscribing actions under the guise of religion that challenged national and ethnic unity and other policy imperatives of the socialist Party/state ("Zhonggong zhongyang tongzhanbu").

Regulation of religion has aimed at control of a religious revival in Buddhism and of political questions surrounding the authority of the Dalai Lama (Goldstein and Kapstein 1998; MacInnis 1989). Reacting to an outbreak of anti-government unrest in 1988–89 in Lhasa, the government imposed martial law and stepped up efforts at securing political control (Karmel 1995; Amnesty International 1992b). Provisional regulations issued by the TAR People's Government in 1991 expressly link goals of national integrity, unity of nationalities, and social stability with protecting freedom of religious belief and safeguarding rights and interests of religious groups and organizations, and places of worship ("Xizang zizhiqu zongjiao"). Such qualifications are absent in similar regulations of the same period issued elsewhere in China (e.g., in Gansu, Hubei, Guangxi Zhuang Autonomous Region, and Ningxia Hui Autonomous Region), indicating the importance attached to them in Tibet specifically ("Xizang zizhiqu zongjiao": Art. 1; "Gansu sheng zongjiao"; "Hubei sheng zongjiao"; "Guangxi zhuang zizhiqu zongjiao";

"Ningxia hui zizhiqu zongjiao"). Recitations on legal protection of religion are coupled with requirements to accept Party leadership and uphold the socialist system, and proscriptions against use of religion or feudal religious privileges to interfere with government administration, judicial work or education ("Xizang zizhiqu zongjiao": Art. 3). Limitations on numbers of monks and their activities are coupled with restrictions on linkages with monasteries outside the TAR, while prohibitions on use of religious activities to foment separatism (including promoting Tibet independence), harm the unity of nationalities, disrupt social order, or commit other crimes are coupled with threats of "education and rectification" (*jiaoyu yu zhengdun*) ("Xizang zizhiqu zongjiao": Arts 7, 9, 25).

Commenting on the struggle with Dalai Lama in his speech at the Third Tibet Work Conference in July 1994, Jiang Zemin insisted that this was not an issue of religious freedom but rather a question of national unity and the need to resist separatism (Jiang Zemin, 1994: 459). Jiang reiterated Party policy positions that the legal protections for religious freedoms were to be limited to "normal religious activities" and that religious activity must be kept separate from political activities—"we must heighten our vigilance in attacking the minority of people who use the guise of religion to carry out harmful activities" (ibid: 461). Following the Dalai Lama's demurral to China's offer of negotiations, government regulation of religion in Tibet since 1994 has focused on a political agenda of attacking elements associated with the Dalai Lama (Human Rights Watch/Asia). Aside from refusal of negotiations with the Dalai Lama and the ban against display or possession of his photograph, the government's campaign included ensuring that civic education curricula denounced religion ("Education for ethnic") and imposing re-education and in some cases dismissal of monks over their loyalty to the Dalai Lama ("Excerpts"; Chan 2001b), and the subversion of the Dalai Lama's selection of a new Panchen Lama (Liao 1995; Mirsky 2000; RMET: 708–10). Expulsion of nuns and the demolition of Buddhist institutes and monasteries reflect an ongoing commitment to ensuring control over religious education and instruction in Tibetan Buddhism (TIN 2001). The government's commitment to controlling those who challenge it was evident as well in efforts to persuade India to return the Karmapa Lama, whose flight from Lhasa shocked Beijing in early 2000 ("PRC Spokesman").

The central government used its control over the selection of the reincarnated Panchen Lama to articulate core policies on religion and to reiterate themes of opposing separatism and struggle against the Dalai Lama in the interests of national and ethnic unity (Li Ruihuan 1995: 504). Jiang Zemin's speech to the Tibet delegation to the First Session of ninth NPC focused on the religion dimensions of Tibet work, including the successful process for selection of the Panchen Lama in 1995 and the expanded patriotic education in temples and legal management during 1996–97 (Jiang Zemin, 1998).

Consistent with the tone of the December 2001 central work conference on religion, the theme of control was reiterated in a December 13 commentary in the *Tibet Daily* on a Central Committee outline concerning implementing citizens' moral construction, which focused on "strengthening unity with the broad masses of people who do not believe in religion," supporting "normal and orderly religious activities," and strengthening Party leadership ("Xizang Ribao Commentator"). Meeting with the Chinese-controlled Panchen Lama, Hu encouraged the recently selected youth to continue his religious and cultural studies in order to understand properly the mutual adaptation of religion and socialist society while also respecting national law and promoting social stability, ethnic unity, and national unity (Hu Jintao 2005).

Echoing official statements requiring Tibetan reincarnation rituals and practices to comply with state law that accompanied the government's insertion of its own choice as the recognized reincarnation of the Panchen Lama (Li R. 1995: 504), the Religious Affairs Bureau's Document No. 5 of 2007 asserted government power to approve the selection of living Buddhas ("Reincarnation of living Buddha"; Spencer 2009). Permission would be granted upon a showing that the majority of local religious followers and temple administrative organizations require the reincarnation—in effect allowing the RAB which approves the appointment of temple staff to control the process. The system used to determine the reincarnation system and the temple where the Buddha is to be located must also receive state approval—initial approval from the local RAB department and possible examination and approval by the government of the autonomous region or province, or by the RAB and State Council. Reincarnations claimed without such approvals are declared invalid and illegal. Aside from the potential to limit selection of a new Dalai Lama, the new regulation reveals much about the government's policy views on permissible scope of religious activities. The RAB's suggestion that it would intervene in selections of living Buddhas only where national and societal rather than purely religious interests are involved reveals the extremely limited perspective on what are the permissible boundaries of religious belief. Expansive interpretations of national and social interest have in the past attempted to insulate religious belief and conduct from any connection outside purely abstract faith—undermining any potential relevance to actual social life. The recent RAB regulation seems consistent with this approach. The RAB is also active in ensuring that Tibetan members of the CPC comply with Party policy against believing in or being members of any religion (RAB Doc: Oct. 2007 on political purity of Tibetan Party members).

Xinjiang

Control over religious activity in Xinjiang reflects Chinese government fears about the potential for subversive convergence between religion and ethnic nationalism (MacInnis 1989). This tends to be reinforced by policies classifying the Uighurs as a single ethnic group implied to have unified socio-religious sensibilities, even though this runs counter to an empirical reality that reveals considerable diversity of religious and ethnic loyalties (Gladney 2004a: 193–95, 218–19). Provisional regulations on administration of religious activities were issued in 1990 ("XUAR zongjiao huodong"). The measures prohibited individuals and organizations from using religious activities to oppose the leadership of the Party, the socialist system, and the people's democratic dictatorship (Art. 5). More specifically the regulations prohibited religion from interfering with state activities in administration, judiciary, culture, education, marriage, population control, or health matters, and from interference with social order, production, work, or the order of people's lives (*minzhong shenghuo zhixu*) (Art. 9). Religious personnel are restricted to the localities where they are registered, and religious teaching and the preparation and distribution of religious materials are subject to state supervision. Regulation of religious staff was expanded yet further by specific measures enacted in 1990 requiring fealty to state law and policy and support for Party leadership and the socialist system and other PRC political imperatives ("XUAR zongjiao zhiye"). Beijing seems particularly concerned about the capacity of global Islam to lend influence and legitimacy to local Islamic movements in Xinjiang.

Policy priorities underlying the 1990 regulations presaged some of the terms of CPC Central Committee Document No. 6 that was issued the following year (Tiemuer 1990: 287–91). Party policy on religion was to be the central operational imperative—especially the limits to belief and the restrictions on behavior, and the proscriptions against Party members believing in religion (although Party members who took part in religious rituals could do so to "benefit their links with the masses"). Cadres were to win over, unite with, and educate religious people—especially to build their observance of state law, support for national unity, and patriotism. The regulation called for stricter enforcement of Xinjiang regulations limiting registration and approval of religious sites. Attention was to be given to training a younger generation of religious workers while sectarian conflicts were to be resolved—particularly the conflict between belief and unbelief, working to ensure that retired CPC cadres do not participate in religious activities and upholding the Four Basic Principles. The document called for building friendly international linkages and resisting penetration by hostile international religious forces—relying on Party policy on religious organizations being free from outside interference, applied by reference to the Four Basic Principles.

These provisional regulations reflected focus on education, propaganda, and United Front work in responding to a complex range of challenges facing implementation of religion policy in Xinjiang. As well, the measures echo the underlying principles of Document No. 6 of 1991, particularly the conclusions that religion is deeply embedded in the societies where it is present, that religion will remain influential for a significant period of time, and the importance of "legalization" of measures to control religion. The local provisional regulations were augmented in 1994 with a broader set of rules on administration of religious affairs which reiterated prior limitations on religious activities but also included new references to the principle of submission to Party leadership, support for the socialist system, and proscriptions against harming national integrity, unity of nationalities, and social stability ("XUAR zongjiao shiwu guanli tiaoli": Art. 4). The regulations require approval and registration of religious organizations and places of worship, imposing control mechanisms for inspections and annual reporting, and requiring approved identity cards for religious staff. Ominously, the regulations provide that violations would be dealt with under China's notorious "Security Administration Punishment Regulations," whose flexible provisions offer not even that scant protection available to defendants under China's criminal law (Art. 29). Following the issuance of Document No. 7 in 1996, a propaganda education campaign was launched in 1996 by the XUAR CPC Committee and government to publicize the directives of the document on fighting separatism and religion (Tiemuer 1996: 460–61).

Party Document No. 7 (1996) noted that village level organizations had fallen into the hands of religious powers, and called for strengthening government institution building at the basic levels of government, and to creating a dependable cohort of cadres—especially to train a large number of Han cadres loyal to Party policy ("Record of the meeting"). The recognition of challenges in local policy implementation is echoed here with particular attention to the need to recruit Han cadres, who by implication will be more "dependable" than local minority cadres. The reference to "religious powers" suggests continuing inability to accept the intertwining of religion and local identity and reveals an assumption that local cadres are incapable of separating religious faith from government responsibilities. The answer seems to be to turn away from minority recruitment and return to policies of reliance on Han cadres.

The document called for implementation of Party nationality policy and policy on religion—focusing particularly on ethnic separatism and unlawful religious activity. Even as nationality policies are conflated with management of religion, the priority given to separatism and unlawful activities reveals the priorities in Party policy on religion. Propaganda and education were to be conducted in schools opposing separatism and religion and strictly enforcing rules against CPC members believing in religion. The apparent difficulty faced by the Party/state in enforcing rules against Party members participating in religion is apparent. Here again, a major source of the problem is the inability to distinguish between religion as a matter of day-to-day identity and culture, and religion as an inspiration and instrument of minority resistance to Han dominance. While the Party might well be correct in assuming that religious faith unavoidably undermines faith in other normative systems such as Party ideology (He H. 2004: 232–34), the matter is complicated by the overlay of ethnic resistance to Han rule and the concomitant (albeit diminished) expectations that Han rule should offer improved conditions for local people. For Party officials, acceptance of the ideology is essential, hence the prohibition against participation in religion. Yet the expectation that propaganda and education will succeed in transforming the perspectives of local people seems increasingly unrealistic.

The emphasis on stability and related suppression campaigns against separatism and unlawful religious activities continued to dominate the agenda for nationality work in Xinjiang (Tiemuer 1997). The XUAR CPC Propaganda Department's 1997 campaign on atheism education for Party cadres in Turpan ("Xinjiang region sees") revealed not only the extent of the Party's commitment to enforce its prohibition against Party members believing in religion but also how deeply entrenched religious belief and identity remains for minority cadres. Indeed, local cadres are alleged to have leant support to separatist and illegal religious activities (Ma D. 2003: 80).

Pursuant to these directives, education and training of religious personnel is permitted only by approved patriotic religious groups, while people in charge of scripture classes must support the leadership of the Party and the socialist system, and safeguard unity of all nationalities and unification of the motherland. Led by the Party's United Front Work Department, the RAB, and the China Islamic Association, education for Imams and staff in Xinjiang's mosques has emphasized CPC policy on religion—particularly the emphasis on "normal" religious activities and the need to adapt to requirements of socialism ("China conducts training courses"). Training of religious leaders focuses on political training that includes patriotism and national unity, Party policy and law on religion, ideology, and social stability ("Xinjiang Educates"; "PRC: Xinjiang's Hotan Prefecture"; "Xinjiang Party Official") National interests of patriotism, loyalty to Party and government, and support for social and economic development must take precedence in religious affairs ("Xinjiang's Official"). Nine-month compulsory training sessions for mosque leaders were instituted in late 2001, as part of an "Imam political re-education campaign" under the Central CPC United Front Work Department and the RAB to tighten controls and religion and sever ties between mosques and alleged separatist activities (Chan 2001b). As indicated in the 2001 Central Nationalities Work Conference (Zhu *et al.* 2004: 248), religion policy is a key element of local governance, as resolving nationalities issues was seen to require enforcement of Party policy on religion. This linkage between policies on nationalities and religion has been widely acknowledged, and tends to suggest an acceptance of the linkage between religious belief and ethnic identity. Yet this principle also tends to essentialize both nationality and religion, thus overlooking much of the diversity that characterizes both.

Informed by these priorities, local interpretation of the national regulations on religious affairs has given particular attention to their application to halt the so-called three forces (ethnic splittist forces; violent terrorist forces; and religious extremist forces) said to dominate religious activities in Xinjiang ("Xinjiang Leaders, NPC Delegates"). Prefectures are empowered to issue their own regulations aimed at strengthening state control over local religious activities ("AFP: Circular Urges Scrutiny"). Yet tensions over local efforts to adapt central policies to local conditions are also evident. The XUAR's July 2002 forum on religion work, convened to implement decisions flowing from the 2001 national work conferences on religion and united front work, focused on the three dimensions articulated by Jiang Zemin of legalization, adaptation, and education ("Xinjiang United"; Jiang Zemin 2001b). In contrast to the stridency of speeches at the national work conference by Luo Gan and Zhu Rongji, however, the XUAR forum emphasized a softer approach of accommodation, albeit still in the service of national policy priorities:

> The basic guideline of current religious work is to correctly understand the objective reality that religion will last for a long time during a socialist period, actively guide religion to conform to socialism, and politically guide religious people to love our country, support our socialist system, and support the leadership of the Community Party of China. At the same time, we should reform some religious rules and religious doctrines that do not confirm to the socialist system, let some active elements of religious virtue serve socialism, and adapt to the new situation and new tasks of socialist modernization construction.
>
> ("Xinjiang United")

Not three months later, however, XUAR Party Secretary Wang Lequan issued a corrective. Speaking in October to an Autonomous Region Religion Work Conference convened by the XUAR Party Committee and People's Government, Wang noted that the imperative of stability required greater attention in religion work be paid to issues of national unity, unification of the motherland, and safeguarding national security ("PRC: Wang"). Wang offered a sharper interpretation of the three-fold approach emerging from the December 2001 national work conference. Legalization included imposing discipline on religious believers and activities, controlling the political qualifications of religious leaders to ensure "ardent love of the motherland, support for the Communist Party leaders and the socialist system, opposition to national splittism and illegal religious activities, and defense of national unity and the unification of the motherland," and banning establishment of new religious sites ("at this time the places for religious activities throughout the Autonomous Region are adequate to meet the needs of normal religious activities of religious believers" (ibid.). Adaptation required that religious believers subordinate themselves to and serve the higher interests of the country and overall national interests, while education required greater efforts to reinforce Marxist religious views and the Party's religion policy (ibid.). While Wang's interpretation seemed authoritative, debate continued over methods. At the time of the XUAR religious work conference, Xinjiang Daily's editorial echoes themes from the July meeting ("Xinjiang Ribao Editorial"). Local discourses emerging after the October meeting returned to themes of accommodation and patience ("PRC to Maintain").

Reporting on human rights in Xinjiang provides many examples of harassment and repression of Islamic teachers, mosques, schools, and practitioners who might contribute to secessionist sentiment (HRW 2005: Section 7; Amnesty International 1992a). Draft amendments to the 1996 XUAR regulations on religious affairs impose further restrictions on religious activities ("Record of the Meeting"). Recently, Beijing has used the US-led war against terrorism to justify repression of Islamic activities in Xinjiang, through a concerted campaign of arrests and executions of alleged separatists (Information Office 2002; Lam 2001; "China claims"; Smith 2001). Even the *bingtuan* has been drawn in to efforts to control religious behavior labeled as religious extremism and splittism ("At National Meeting").

Examples of local efforts to control religion emerge from Hetian (Hotan), through policies of "five supports, five safeguards, six impermissibles, and three restrictions" (*wu zhichi, wu baohu, liu buzhun, san xianzhi*) (Zhu et al. 2004: 269).

FIVE SUPPORTS

(i) Support religious personnel and staff in carrying out Party policy on religion and propaganda education on law and regulation.
(ii) Support religious personnel and staff in voluntarily resisting the intrusion and spread of extremist religious thinking with harmful results.
(iii) Support religious personnel and staff in making positive contributions to marital customs and practices of believers.
(iv) Support religious personnel and staff in enriching the study and use of science by believers.
(v) Support religious personnel and staff in managing religious sites and activities according to law.

FIVE SAFEGUARDS

(i) Safeguard observance of state law and normal religious behavior by religious staff and believers.
(ii) Safeguard compliance with Party policy on religion and implementation of the right to belief and unbelief.
(iii) Safeguard religious staff and believers abiding by their own beliefs, rituals, and customs.
(iv) Safeguard believers studying the right to freedom of belief according to law.
(v) Safeguard religious staff and believers against unlawful interference.

SIX IMPERMISSIBLES

(i) No distribution of religious texts.
(ii) No stirring up hostility among nationalities.

(iii) No distribution of treatises promoting separatism or harming unity of nationalities.
(iv) No propagandizing of texts or books and audio visual materials containing fanatic religious views.
(v) No use of hot social issues to interfere with administrative affairs.
(vi) No carrying out of religious activities in broken down areas.

THREE RESTRICTIONS

(i) Friday teachings restricted to half an hour.
(ii) Ramadan restricted to traditional ritual activities.
(iii) Teaching Ramadan activities restricted to mosque grounds.

These measures are striking not only for what they reveal about the depth of religious practices in Hotan, but also the efforts to extend principles such as legalization, mutual adaptation, and the priority given to CPC United Front initiatives in co-opting and containing existing religious activities. Yet these faint echoes of the modestly accommodating policies of the 2001 National Work Conference on religion are combined with severe restraints on religious education, places of worship, and particular religious practices, such as Ramadan, where religion and local minority nationalism often intersect. Not surprisingly perhaps Hotan was the site of protests in March 2008, apparently sparked by official policies banning Islamic scarves and head coverings (French 2008a,b). Periodic crackdowns to limit religious observances across Xinjiang during the Islamic holy month of Ramadan in September were aimed primarily at government and Party officials, although generalized proscriptions against religious practices of men wearing beards, women wearing veils, and group prayer music have also been reported ("Xinjiang crackdown").

Thus, at both the regional and local levels within XUAR and in the context of a wide range of socio-cultural and economic contexts, control over the behavior of religious believers is a key element of nationalities policy in Xinjiang. While mutual adaptation may continue to describe the perspective of tolerance adopted publicly by the Party and government, the practical operation involves ongoing restraint on religious behavior. Ranging from restrictions over places of worship, education, and rituals followed by religious leaders and believers to suppression of links between religion and social and economic relationships, China's policy and law and religion in Xinjiang remains a forceful reminder of the intensity of central government efforts at control.

Inner Mongolia

Policy practice on religion in Inner Mongolia reflects the influence of political and security concerns, in part because the dominant religion is Tibetan Buddhism and Islam exerts significant influences through the local Hui community. Party policy tenets on religion on such issues as separation of education and religion; non-support for religious organizations, prohibitions on belief by Party members; and suppression of cults are applied to Inner Mongolia, with particular attention given to programs to manage religion while it retains a "short-term foothold" (*lizu jieduanxing*) in society (Bu He 2003: 153–54). This attention to short-term management is more prevalent in Inner Mongolia than in Tibet and Xinjiang, where religion and national identity are more closely aligned. In Inner Mongolia by contrast, local identity tends to be driven more by issues of ethnicity, community, and language.

As a result, management of religion appears to focus on institutional measures for control. Representative Congress Standing Committees at the Banner and County level are required to attend to state law and policy in their handling of religious affairs (Art. 12.12). But at lower levels (e.g., *Sumu*, Township, and Nationality Autonomous Townships), it is the People's Governments rather than the Representative Congresses that are authorized to address issues of religion, "safeguarding the rights of minority nationalities and respecting their customs" (compare "Working Regulations of the People's Governments" Art. 3.12 with "Working Regulations of the People's Congress" Art. 12:12). Since local governments are not subject to the minority nationality representation requirements imposed under the NRAL on representative congresses, expanded governmental authority may also diminish the potential for local community input on religious affairs.

Under local measures paralleling the national regulations on registration of places of religious activity (*zongjiao huodong changsuo*), places of worship in Inner Mongolia must be registered with the religious affairs office of the people's government at the Banner and County level and above ("NMAR zongjiao"). As with the national registration regime, recognition of enumerated rights to limited autonomy in management, religious activity, finances, and materials is conditioned by requirements of compliance with constitutional and legal provisions on control of religion, support for national integrity, the unity of nationalities, and social stability, and the separation of religion and education. Religious education is confined to approved sites and must be strictly separated from the state subsidized education system: "no organs or individuals shall make use of religion to hinder the education activities of nationality schools." ("Education Regulations": Art. 5). Administrative and criminal penalties may be imposed where religion or superstition is used to interfere with education in nationality school (ibid.).

Normative and organizational perspectives

As with other dimensions of China's governance of the periphery, management of nationalities policy can be understood in light of selective adaptation and institutional capacity. China's reception of international human rights standards on minorities and religion reveal the normative dynamics of selective adaptation analysis while implementation suggests functional elements of institutional capacity.

Selective Adaptation

Chinese policy and practice on socio-cultural relations in the Inner Periphery reflect the influences of selective adaptation on reception of international human rights standards on management of minority and religious affairs. Under conditions where international human rights standards are not informed by a uniform set of normative principles (Kelly and Reid 1998; Steiner and Alston 2000; Van Ness 1999) China's interpretation of international standards and norms reflects the importance of normative perspectives as a basis for local reception of non-local standards. Thus, the selective adaptation paradigm seems particularly appropriate to further understanding of China's engagement with international legal regimes in human rights.

China has long been a party to the International Convention on the Elimination of All Forms of Racial Discrimination (ICERD), which prohibits denying human rights and socio-cultural, economic, and political freedoms based on ethnicity or race. China has signed both the International Covenant on Economic, Social and Cultural Rights (ICESCR) and the International Covenant on Civil and Political Rights (ICCPR). China's ratification of the ICESCR reflected a limited willingness to acknowledge international human rights standards, subject to reservations that preserve China's policy preferences on labor rights. Most recently, China appears to be preparing to ratify the ICCPR, starting the policy review process (Shi Jiangtao 2005), and sending delegations to North America and Europe to collect information on expectations about the needs for compliance.

Yet China continues to face criticism over its limited performance of international human rights standards on minority affairs (Bulag 2002a; MacKerras 2003). China's performance of substantive human rights standards on minority affairs is often criticized as ineffective (CECC 2006), while procedural problems in institutional enforcement and reporting are also evident (Choukroune 2005). Conflicts between Chinese law and policy and the principles articulated in the ICCPR on matters of minority rights raise questions whether ratification will bring about meaningful change in China's law and policy. In the areas of ethnic minority rights, China's human rights perspectives are closely linked with normative assertions about the inherent superiority and desirability of development models that assume the need to modernize minority groups while marginalizing their cultural and religious distinctiveness. Thus, China's 2004 Minority Nationality White Paper depicts rights of minority nationalities in terms of achieving assimilation with Han social and economic standards and norms (SCIO 2004a). The 2009 White Paper on Ethnic Policy reiterates that national imperatives of stability, national unity, and economic development take precedence over local concerns over identity and preservation of socio-cultural norms (SCIO 2009b).

In the area of religion, while China appears nominally responsive to international law standards, practices of the Party/state seem to conflict with nominal commitments to international standards. While Chinese orthodoxy on freedom of religious belief is presented as consistent with international agreements, such as the Universal Declaration of Human Rights Article 18 and the ICCPR Article 18, which recognize the right to freedom of thought, conscience, and religion, legal restrictions on religious practice appear to depart from international standards. The ICCPR, which China has signed and is currently contemplating ratification, includes protections not only for religious belief but also for the right to "either individually or in community with others and in public or private, to manifest his religion or belief in worship, observance, practice and teaching" (ICCPR: Art. 18). Article 18 permits only such "limitations as are prescribed by law and are necessary to protect public safety, order, health, or morals or the fundamental rights and freedoms of others" (ibid.).

While China purports to rely on the language of international law about the freedom of religious belief, PRC law, policy, and practice impose strict limits on religious behavior (SCIO 1997). China's 1996 White Paper on religion emphasizes freedom of belief but imposes strict limits on behavior (SCIO 1996), while the 2004 nationalities White Paper (SCIO 2004a) and the 2009 ethnic policy White Paper (SCIO 2009b) both emphasize China's claim to respect freedoms of belief while retaining the right to suppress activities deemed threatening to state interests. This reveals a limited reading of the provisions. China's restrictive approach reflects a perception that the necessity provision can be satisfied by formalistic definitions of necessity that are not necessarily empirically based.

Selective adaptation factors of perception, complementarity, and legitimacy are also in evidence. Perceptions about the origins and implications of international standards on minority rights have a significant effect on their reception in China. Academic and policy arguments linking discourses on minority rights with conditions of economic and political globalization underscore China's historical exclusion from the processes of international norm setting, and invite increased assertiveness in articulating standards more favorable to China's national policy goals (Miao 2005: 300–301). Perceptions that human rights criticism of China is driven by US or international power politics, for example, suggests important conditions for China's engagement (Liu J. 2004).

Factors of perception are evident in China's official interpretations emphasizing the character of religion as limited to individual faith rather than individual or collective behavior. While this may reveal a certain degree of political convenience, genuine issues of perception can be identified as informed by Chinese historical and literary distinctions between individual religious figures of passive contemplation such as the Buddhist monk painters of the Song (such as Liang Kai) and Qing (such as Badashanren) dynasties (Wang Z. 1985; cf. Bush 1971), and the problematic consequences of the many religiously inspired rebellions against imperial governance (Perry 1980). Perceptions that organized religion represents a threat to Party power inform much of China's normative perspective on freedom of religion in the Inner

Periphery. As well, perceptions that international hostile forces use religion as a way to challenge China's political authority are well entrenched among political and policy leaders. Perceptions that religious organizations are essentially hostile to the nominally atheist CPC are also in evidence. Such perceptions do much to explain China's normative position on freedom of religion in the Outer Periphery.

Complementarity is also evident in the normative engagement that underlies China's policies on sovereignty and security in the Inner Periphery. Embracing the US government's "war on terror," the PRC government has resorted anti-terror discourses to justify increasingly repressive policies against national minorities (Pao Wenwei 2001). China's subordination of consular treaty requirements and the international citizenship doctrines incorporated into PRC Nationality Law to an anti-terror agenda in the case of Huseyin Celil ("MacKay") suggest a selective approach to international law compliance that is conditioned by domestic security imperatives. The Celil matter has taken on greater prominence as the United Nations Committee Against Torture raised allegations that Celil had been held incommunicado in China for a long period, and allegedly tortured before being sentenced to life imprisonment (UN Committee Against Torture 2008a, paragraph 8). The Celil case reveals the extent to which the operational reality of China's implementation of international legal standards on minority rights is subject to security imperatives where there is normative complementarity with international practices.

Dynamics of complementarity are evident in assertions that compliance with international human rights standards requires support for China's sovereignty imperatives (Li Wanqiang 2006); acceptance of the limits of local conditions (Tang Tianri 2003); and preservation of China's governance priorities (Wang Guangxian 2002). Perceptions about the primacy purportedly given state security and sovereignty under international law remain fundamental to responses to criticisms of China's practices in Tibet and Xinjiang (Miao Jiafu 2005: 315). Acceptance of limitations imposed by local conditions and the use of law and regulation to ensure local policy priorities remain conditions for China's acceptance of ICCPR standards (Liu and Hao 2001). Patterns of complementarity are also evident in the ways that China's policies on religion give primacy to control over alleged religious extremism and terrorism and echo principles underlying the US government's war on terror. The PRC government has resorted anti-terror discourses to justify increasingly repressive policies against national minorities and their religious practices (Pao Wenwei 2001).

The importance of legitimacy is evident in virtually all aspects of nationality policy. Certainly the legitimacy of the government and the CPC depend in part on the extent to which claims to territorial integrity and social harmony are supported by the dominant Han culture and are exercised in the Inner Periphery with sufficient grace as to generate some measure of legitimacy among the minority nationalities resident there (MacKerras 2004).

As well, China strives to demonstrate to international as well as domestic audiences that its legal and political system on nationality rights is consistent with international standards. Thus, international human rights norms of state responsibility are cited to support the primacy of Chinese government control in human rights enforcement (Zhou and Xie 2001). The legitimacy dimension is also evident in official discourses on protection of human rights as constructed by China's constitutional system, limited to those expressly granted by the Party/state, and qualified by duties to uphold Party rule and prevent ethnic separatism (Constitution: Arts. 1, 51; Zhang J. 2004). Legitimacy dynamics are also evident in China's rebuttals to annual reports from the United States criticizing China's human rights record and its counter-reports on American human rights abuses, which seem aimed to establish a legitimate moral equivalent between China and the United States on human rights issues ("Human Rights Accusations"; SCIO 2002b; Cody 2005).

Factors of legitimacy are also evident in the government's issue of a series of State Council White Papers on Nationalities Policy aimed to address international audiences. Thus, the 1999 White Paper recited principles of equality and autonomy for nationalities under the Constitution and the NRAL, while extolling achievements in social and economic development (SCIO 1999), even as local realities are often at odds with these assertions. Similarly, State Council White Papers on Tibet (SCIO 1998, 2002a, 2004b) and Xinjiang (SCIO 2003a) aimed at explaining and justifying China's claims to sovereignty and defending its policies on nationalities. Semi-official bilingual reporting on achievements in minority nationality development is also used to legitimate China's policies and practices in Tibet (Lian 2006). Official denunciations of US criticisms on Tibet (Zhang Z. 2005: 241–53) and Xinjiang ("China: Raidi") are also part of China's effort to build legitimacy both domestically and abroad for its nationalities policies. When China was listed as a country for "special concern" in the 1999 US State Department Annual Report on Religious Freedom, the RAB responded with indignation at what it termed rudeness and naiveté in US intervention in China's internal affairs ("US Charges").

Aside from debates as to whether China is in compliance with its international obligations on the human right to religious freedom, the government also faces significant domestic challenges to the legitimacy of its policies on religion. As suggested by Lyman Miller (1996) in the context of the scientific community, when members of Chinese society owe their loyalty to norms more powerful than those articulated by the Chinese government, regime legitimacy becomes a critical problem. Just as scientists owe a higher loyalty to the norms of science and as a result have often been sources of resistance and dissent, so too do religious believers owe a higher loyalty to their own religious norms that may force a choice between loyalty to the regime and faithfulness to belief. To the extent that policies on regulation of religion require a degree of subservience that is inconsistent with religious conviction, compliance will be elusive. And if enforcement of these policies can be achieved only through repression, the distinction between compliance and resistance may fade as religious believers find compliance unworkable and are driven even further underground.

Institutional Capacity

China's policies on minorities and religion may also be viewed in light of the paradigm of institutional capacity. Factors of institutional purpose, location, orientation, and cohesion affect institutional capacity in areas of minority nationality policy.

Policy and law on nationalities affairs reveal the influence of institutional purpose, which affects the capacity of state organs charged with implementation. Institutional purpose is characterized by conflicting themes of accommodation and control of local minority nationalities and religion. Party policy on minority affairs has shifted gradually from themes of assimilation to a combination of accommodation and increased sensitivity to the local conditions of minority nationalities (MacKerras 2003; Sautman 1999; "Hu Jintao Addresses"; "New historic chapter"). However, the specifics of Party policy remain heavily weighted in favor of state-centric governance. National unity remains the fundamental priority of the Party and government to which minority nationalities must owe fealty (SNAC 2002: 46). NRAL provisions subjecting local autonomy to the leadership of the state are supplemented by requirements of central Party leadership (NRAL Preface; Wu 1998: 43). At the local levels, state unity is seen as an overriding priority. For Tibet, unity of the Chinese state is presented as the primary policy goal, to which issues of development are subordinated (SNAC 2002: 53). For Xinjiang, State interests are presented as paramount, subordinating local social and economic relations to national unity goals (Miao 2003). In Inner Mongolia, where issues of separatism are somewhat more remote and where the historical legacy of local accommodation to Han migration, national imperatives on national unity have not been as intrusive as in Xinjiang and Tibet (Zhang Z.: 56–57; Bai 2001; Zhang W. 2005; Zhang Y. 2005; "Zhong Na di yi jie").

Factors of institutional location are obviously important in tensions over the formation in Beijing and application in the region of nationality policies. Perspectives from Beijing on Han-minority relations differ widely from those of local nationality communities. As well, factors of institutional orientation play a key role in the communication of central policies. The "legalization" program by which China's nationalities policies have been gradually codified into formal law and regulation satisfies China's goals of modernization and regularization (Zeng X. 2002; Zhang W. 2005: 99–116; He: 283–84, 300–304)—a welcome contrast perhaps to perceived abuses of political authority in earlier periods of PRC rule. But in the Inner Periphery, such formal regulatory models of state governance often appear to local officials and communities as rather alien creations imposed at the local level with little attention to local needs and conditions.

The capacity for implementation of local autonomy under the NRAL will depend significantly on factors of institutional cohesion. Minority cadre policy is an important indicator of the dynamic of institutional cohesion, for it is both the need for and apprehension about an increased substantive role for officials from minority nationality communities that characterizes current Chinese efforts. Formalized efforts to establish quotas for minority nationality representation at national meetings suggest the effects of formalism in establishing numerical representation (e.g., 17 Mongolians from IMAR; 22 Uighurs from XUAR; 12 Tibetans from the TAR) and invite questions as to the relationship between form and substance in ensuring representation for and from minority nationality cadres (e.g., "Apparent Text of Plan").

Institutional cohesion is potentially undermined by minority cadre training approaches focused on establishing basic level cadre corps (*jiceng gangbu duiwu*) ("Zhonggong zhongyang zuzhi bu": 138–39). While these allow local minority cadres to work at local levels and possibly to be effective agents of governance in the decentralized context of the Inner Periphery, they may also work to block minority cadres from participation in government administration at higher levels. This certainly influences the dynamic of negotiation that often characterizes implementation of central policies at local levels in the Inner Periphery. This also tends to underscore a perception about the role of local minority cadres as essentially translators and implementers of governance programs, rather than interpreters and designers of policy. Despite its utility in terms of program implementation, this has the potential to undermine institutional cohesion more broadly.

Attitudes of Han cadres toward minority counterparts remain divisive. Hu Jintao's address to a Politburo Study Session underscored that training in minority policy, particularly its socialist theoretical justifications, must be focused not only on minority cadres but on Han cadres: "We should educate not only the masses, but also cadres; educate not only cadres of minority nationalities, but also cadres of the Han nationality and educate not only ordinary cadres, but also leading cadres" ("Hu Jintao Addresses"). Hu's focus on leading cadres suggests problems with ensuring consistent attention by local Chinese officials to minority policies—a key dimension of which is recruitment and training of minority cadres.

Across the Inner Periphery, recruitment and training of minority cadres has not resulted in their rejection of local loyalties, but rather has created a sense of intense conflict between central government policy goals associated with Han China and the perspectives and values of local society. Thus, while the NRAL provides for expanded recruitment and training of minority nationality cadres, the ways in which these goals are conceived and implemented poses problems for institutional cohesion that may undermine the capacity of the NRAL to achieve its desired balance between central control and local autonomy.

Policy and law on religion reveal dynamics of institutional capacity as well. The influence of institutional purpose is evident in the ways that the Minority Autonomy Law addresses issues of religion. Government policies on religion are inextricably intertwined with policies on national minorities (Jiang 1993; Li R. 1994; SNAC 2002: 206–7). Yet differences arise over the extent to which religious belief constitutes an integral part of ethnic identity. Where religious identity is separated from ethnic identity, this leaves open the potential for Party policies challenging religious activities to be insulated from criticism that they are inconsistent with preservation of minority identity (Wang et al. 1995: 136–46). On the other hand, where religious belief is treated as an inseparable part of minority identity (SNAC 2002: 211–15), coordinated approaches are possible that incorporate religion policy with minority nationality policy. Differences between these approaches have an impact on the state's regulation of religion. Particularly in the context of perceived threats to national security, separatism, and terrorism (Ma D. 2003: 13–15), contradictions over relations between minority and religious identity have a direct impact on state policy.

One major difference in view concerns the very nature of religion itself—as an artifact of cultural customs, or a central element of local identity. Some participants in the policy discourse in China treat religion as a particular reflection of minority nationality culture, thus suggesting it remains a legacy of pre-modern, backward minority nationality culture and is therefore subject to modernization and reform (campaigns) (Wu Shimin 1998: 313–19; Wang Zuoan 2002: 33–44, 69–81). On the other hand, where it is considered a contemporary social phenomenon, grounded in current social conditions (Song Caifa 2003: 327–33), longer-term approaches focused on mutual accommodation (*xiangshiying*) *of* religion and society are possible (Jiang 1993a; compare Wang Zuoan, Chapter 7, with Zhongyang Dangxiao: 399 et seq.). Even the ways that policy analysts include religion as a component of cultural customs, or as an independent category, suggests approaches to religion as an artifact of tradition or of contemporary life (contrast Song 2003 with Tianjin 2004 and Wu S. 1998).

As well, issues over institutional purpose arise in addressing the relationship between religion and national interest. Religion is often treated as an alternate focus of loyalty that competes with the state for popular support (Wang Zuoan: 8–10). Thus, issues of separatism and social unrest in peripheral areas are attributed to activities by religious groups (Ma D. 2003: 146–51). This construction of religion as a competitor with the state for popular affiliation works to support unidimensional approaches that interpret religious identity as either patriotic or not. Alternate approaches acknowledging separation of religion and politics (Liu et al. 2003: 265–67) appear to allow for policy responses that are more accommodating, although expansive interpretations of the scope of political activity may in the end constrain the permissible range of religious activities yet further. As with the regulation of nationalities policy, dynamics of institutional location and institutional orientation are clearly evident in the relationship between center and locality on religion policy.

Summary

China's laws and policies on minorities and religion reflect the central government's preoccupation with matters of national integrity, unity of nationalities, and resistance to separatism. In the realm of minority policy, normative perspectives drawn from analysis of selective adaptation suggest that China's policy process is heavily influenced by perceptions about international and domestic threats, the use of imprecise international standards to support state policy and the concern for establishing legitimacy domestically and internationally. Organizational perspectives drawn from institutional capacity analysis suggest that conflicting purposes, varying perspectives based on location, uncertain applicability of central government policies at the local level, and difficulties with building community support for nationality and religion policy suggest that there is still much to be learned in China's efforts to address issues of nationalities effectively. China's policies and law on regulation of religion are presented as consistent with international human rights standards, but appear inconsistent with requirements to protect not only the freedom of religious belief but also the freedom to practice religion. These issues are particularly evident in Tibet and Xinjiang, where ethnic identity and religion are so closely intermingled. Questions arise as to whether the central government's approach reflects an accurate understanding of this relationship, as national identity and sensibilities of separatist nationalism need not be the same. Nonetheless, the embedded nature of religion in local culture and identity continues to pose significant challenges for regime control.

4 Economy and development in the Inner Periphery

Economic relations are a core element in China's policies and practices of governance in the Inner Periphery. China's economic reforms are tied closely to legal reform—particularly in areas of contract and property law, and in foreign economic relations, where the central government asserts primacy in legal and regulatory articulation of Party policy initiatives (Potter 2001). Constitutional provisions on local government in the nationality autonomous regions empower local People's Congresses to implement central policies through examination and approval of economic and social development plans, local administrative budgets, and implementation reports (Constitution: Art. 115). The Constitution also directs People's Congresses in nationality autonomous regions to adopt regulatory measures consistent with national law and subject to approval by the National People's Congress Standing Committee (Constitution: Art. 116). While autonomous region governments have nominal autonomy to oversee local financial administration and to administer local economic development arrangements, these are subject to the broad guidance of state systems and plans (Constitution: Art. 117, 118).

These limitations are reiterated in the Nationality Region Autonomy Law (NRAL), which subjects local economic construction programs, policies, and plans to the requirements of state planning, while leaving implementation up to local governments (NRAL: Art. 25). While general supervision of economic policy performance falls to the local People's Congresses, this role is limited and remains subject to central state authority. The local People's Congresses, nominally charged with oversight of local People's Government, the People's Courts and the People's Procuracy (so-called "one mansion, two compounds"—*yi fu liang yuan*), but exercise only indirect supervision subject to the overall principles of ensuring compliance with Party and state policies, ensuring stability of the socialist market economy, and ensuring overall benefit to the national economy (Zhou 2001). In the Inner Periphery, the Western Development Program is central to the government's efforts to promote integration and curb dissident and separatist sentiments.

China's Western Development Program

The central government's priorities for economic relations and development in the Inner Periphery reflect a tension between the broad priorities of the Western Development Program (WDP) and local development needs. Priorities of the Western Development Program include attracting foreign investment, financial reforms, tax incentives, market-based bank lending, policy lending to support capital projects, securities investments, expanded insurance provisions, and development of natural resources (Zeng 2003). Policy goals for Western development focus on enterprise-based growth, market-centered economic performance, foreign investment, government oversight of competition and trade, and market stabilization programs (Li Shantong 2003). Yet the WDP also purports to embody the central government's regional priorities and expectations for economic relations and development in the Inner Periphery. These have particular importance for the areas of Inner Mongolia, Xinjiang, and Tibet.

China's WDP echoes historical themes and aspirations of Chinese governments dating back at least to the Qianlong period (Perdue 2005; Lary 2007). The Maoist period saw the establishment of the Xinjiang Production and Construction Corps (XPCC, or *bingtuan*) using decommissioned military personnel and prison populations both during and after incarceration to facilitate development. During the post-Mao reform period, the central government recognized the importance of border development and began to develop regional planning processes to facilitate internal and external trade through the Inner Periphery (Xie 1999). Nonetheless, despite the impressive economic growth rates achieved in China's coastal areas, the Inner Periphery areas continued to lag. A 1999 report by the National Conditions (*guoqing*) Research Institute in the Chinese Academy of Sciences indicated that the development gap between ethnic minority regions and the coastal areas had widened, attributing this to steady population increases coupled with inadequate educational facilities, poor infrastructure, poverty, slow progress in developing foreign trade and investment relations, and lingering effects of the planned economy (Yu 1999; Sheng and Tao 2002). This was a major agenda item on the 1999 Central Nationalities Work Conference, whose priorities included bringing all nationalities onto the socialist road, and accelerating economic and social development for all nationalities, especially ethnic minorities (Li Dezhu 2000). In operational terms, this meant diminishing preferences for minorities under the theme of socialist equality of all nationalities (including Han) and relying on economic development as the basis for assimilation of minorities in the broader Chinese state. Not surprisingly, this combination of political and economic factors became a salient feature of the WDP (Yeung and Shen 2004; Goodman 2004; Sines 2002; Lai 2002; Onishi 2001).

The WDP was announced in 1999, and the Leading Small Group responsible for coordinating policy development established early in 2000. Informed by criticisms that the policy-centered nature of the WDP, particularly its initial shortage of legal provisions and restrictions, invited abuse by unaccountable regulators and by economic actors engaging in extra-legal or unlawful activities (Xie and Ma 2002: 134–35), the State Council gradually formalized the WDP regulatory regime through a series of edicts that took on the form and implied authority of administrative regulations articulating economic development priorities and processes ("Guowuyuan guanyu shishi"; "PRC State Council Notice"; "Guowuyuan Xibu Kaifa Ban 2000"; "Opinion on the Implementation"; "PRC State Council Opinions"). Premier Zhu Rongji's summary instruction on the tasks for the WDP focused on

(a) infrastructure investment—particularly transportation (road, rail, air); resource development—particularly oil and natural gas; and telecommunications;
(b) environmental protection and construction—emphasizing investment in forestry, land, and other unused environmental resources;
(c) coordination of local development in China's western regions with economic and development conditions and priorities elsewhere; and
(d) expanding reliance on technology and education as the basic condition for development (Zhu 2000).

While the State Council's WDP Leading Small Group held nominal authority over WDP programming, the State Council's regulatory efforts were issued through the Party Center, thus opening the door for ongoing policy debate with agencies such as the State Planning Commission over development priorities ("Zai 16"). The State Development and Reform Commission's power to dictate foreign investment incentive schedules, albeit subject to State Council approval, allowed expanded participation in the WDP policy process and eroded further the regulatory authority of the State Council WDP Office ("ZRG Fazhan"). Incorporation of WDP policy programming with the Tenth Five-Year Plan ensured subordination of the infrastructure and construction development goals of western development to national economic development goals ("Guowuyuan Xibu Diqu").

The Sixteenth Party Congress affirmed commitments to increase support for Western Development through investment in fixed assets (primarily infrastructure projects), tax incentives, and financial transfer payments ("Party Congress"). Goals of "ecology protection and construction" (*shengtai huanjing baohu he jianshe*) seemed oriented toward local sustainability goals but in fact focused on infrastructure building, consistent with more explicit objectives of "accelerating basic infrastructure engineering and construction" (*jiakuai jichu sheshi zhongdian gongcheng jianshe*) and "accelerating rural infrastructure construction" (*jiakuai nongcun jichu sheshi jianshe*) ("Zai 16"). The emphasis on national priorities was clear:

> Implementing the Western Development Program is an important program for promoting unity and enrichment of various nationalities;

and a necessary measure for ensuring consolidation of frontier areas and national security. Western development is a strategic adjustment that benefits development of a unified national market, perfects the socialist market economy, stimulates economic integration and promotes integration of regional economies.

("Zai 16"; "Guowuyuan Xibu Kaifa Ban 2003")

Energy development is a key priority in the WDP, reflecting China's growing energy needs and Beijing's drive to secure foreign capital and technology (Ogutcu). The central government has also aimed to induce foreign investment into the areas covered by the WDP, in part through tax incentives that reduce by up to 50 percent the business income tax otherwise assessable against foreign businesses (Pun). While the State Council's 2000 notice on WDP implementation offered a range of development priorities, including infrastructure; ecology and environment; agriculture; industry; tourism; and technology, education, culture and public health, priority was attached to key areas of transportation infrastructure that will "make the most of central cities" so that development of the West can be an "engine of growth for other areas" ("PRC State Council Notice").

Interpretation and application of WDP priorities reveal policy choices that tend to diminish attention to local social and cultural conditions. While WDP authorities seem aware of local cultural systems rooted in nomadic pastoralism and that small-scale economies might be threatened by the policy orientation of the WDP (Ni 1998), these challenges were generally overlooked. Conventional price mechanisms designed and implemented by the State Planning Commission were to be established as the basis for development programs and resource allocation ("Guojia Jiwei chutai") while infrastructure development programs targeted urbanized areas already linked with China's transport grid rather than pastoral and migrant communities ("Chinese Official Outlines"). Chinese planners at the central and local levels seem committed to the securing national benefits of economic growth regardless of local cultural conditions:

> Xinjiang Uygur Autonomous Region ... has decided to do away with its traditional economic pattern encompassing mainly agriculture and livestock as major parts. It aims to take development opportunity to transform itself into an international trade center in west China.
>
> ("Development of West China")

Official interpretations of WDP programs tend to give priority to national rather than local outcomes. The State Council's 2001 WDP policy priorities ("Opinion") gave particular attention to central investment in construction; basic infrastructure (transportation and telecommunications); centrally administered financial transfers credit and tax policies; land use and natural resource development; foreign investment; technology transfer; recruitment of technical and professional personnel; and science and technology development. Each of these priorities underscored the reliance on central policy priorities as well as the transfer of capital and human resources from Han China to the Inner Periphery. While nominal attention was paid to local education and social services, these were listed last and clearly accorded secondary importance. In its 2003 circular on progress and tasks, the State Council's WDP Office formally affirmed the priority of national policy goals of "national development, unity of nationalities, and frontier stability" ("Guowuyuan Xibu Kaifa Ban 2003"). The WDP's emphasis on infrastructure development in areas such as rail and road transportation and distribution of energy supplies also supported national rather than local development objectives (Zhao and Han 2002). Capital construction investment programs and associated land use rules were aimed at supporting transfers of Western energy supplies from the coast and inland areas of China proper, while the WDP's foreign investment inducement measures were aimed primarily at resource extraction for the benefit of national economic growth ("PRC State Council Opinions," paras. 2, 5, 24, 31, 34). Human resource development under the WDP emphasized recruiting and transfer of "talents and intellectuals" from China proper to the Western regions, more so than education and training of local minorities ("PRC State Council Opinions," compare paras. 56–58 with para. 54).

Environmental restrictions on WDP programs also gave priority to ensuring local submission to state policies and regulations, recognizing the challenges posed by local conditions but giving little attention to the possibility that local environmental management goals and methods might offer effective alternatives to national imperatives (Guojia huanjing baohu ju). This has the potential to marginalize a wider range of local socio-cultural norms that constitute foundations of pastoral identity, particularly relationships with the land and resources (Adger 2000). While allowances for local initiative were made in the early years of the WDP, national coordination under the rubric of "macro-economic control" has become a cornerstone of the WDP ("Speech by Li Zhibin"). While some national planners have noted the importance of sustainability and balanced development that raises local living standards (Li S. 2003; "Guojia Minwei Zhengfa Si"; Yang 2000), the measure of living standards tends to focus on consumption and accumulation rather than qualitative measures of social wellbeing. In any case, the obstacles to substantially revising national planning to accommodate for local identities and cultural perspectives make it unlikely these will be included as measures of development under the "Go West" program. Moreover, the goals of the program itself seem centered on assimilation and integration of minority nationalities in the broader national society of China. Grounded in principles of equality of all nationalities, Western Development serves as a vehicle to strengthen integration of China as a multi-ethnic society through assimilation of minorities, and ensure that legal protections of minority nationality identity remain subject to overall national unity goals (Li D. 2000).

Reflecting the broad relationship between national legal and economic reform programs in the post-Mao period, the WDP was an important factor in efforts to establish legal regulatory regimes for the nationality autonomous regions (Yang 2004). The WDP provided impetus for efforts to strengthen civil and economic law regimes on issues such as contracts, property, and administrative process to support economic development. Yet this was primarily an effort to extend to the Inner Periphery existing norms and practices on legalization of governance in Han China. Thus, support for legal development under the WDP is the responsibility of state organs and departments, while enterprises in nationalities areas are accorded the lawful rights and responsibilities of legal persons under the national legal system, and members of minority nationalities themselves are to be protected as consumers under fair competition regimes and to receive special accommodations for the cultural requirements of their nationality status (Li Z. 2003). This bespeaks notions of formalism in authority and equality rights, such that legal provisions entrenching the authority of government agencies and the legal rights of economic actors serve as foundational principles against which are made nominal adjustments for local conditions of nationality culture. Few provisions are made responding to local concerns on such issues as targeted employment and economic opportunity for local communities, conditions on business competition that empower local nationalities, and adjustment of legal and regulatory regimes to account for local socio-cultural norms. To the contrary, reliance on formal legal institutions to ensure compliance by members of local ethnic groups with state development policies has tended to underscore the disengagement of law from local socio-cultural practices and expectations (Wang 2002: 303–12).

Economic development has been a key element in the central government's efforts to "resolve the nationalities problem" (*jiejue minzu wenti*). Specific incentives have focused on preferential financial and monetary programs, tax incentives, "trickle down" approaches to wealth building under the rubric of "the first to become wealthy assist others to become wealthy" (*xianfu bang houfu*), support for village and township enterprises, trade in ethnic products, linkage programs between the coastal developed areas and the interior, poverty alleviation through financial and tax inducements, resource development, and border trade (Jin and Gong 2004: 146–50). Under the provisions for the NRAL requiring central level support for minority areas, national support programs have provided for cooperative linkages among coastal cities and provinces with particular minority areas. In Inner Mongolia, linkages with Shanghai have been expanded as part of the WDP (Chen and Qian 2000). In Tibet linkages have been established between Beijing and Jiangsu with Lhasa, Shanghai and Shandong with Shigatse, and Tianjin and Sichuan with Chamdo (Ng and Zhou 2004: 560). These relationships and the general reach of central government support for WDP initiatives are emblematic of perceptions about the linkage between local interests in economic development in minority areas and national interest in resolving the challenge of assimilating minorities into Chinese society more broadly (Shi 2007: 366–67). Although the principles of the NRAL suggest that the policies and programs of Western Development will be adjusted to suit local needs, the interests of the central Party/state are given priority through the focus on national economic development and the assimilation (rather than accommodation) of minority nationalities into the national polity (Su 2001). And while the absence of clear policy guidelines may be an invitation to provincial level adaptation and intervention (Holbig 2004), national policy imperatives continue to dominate discussions of implementation.

Central development policies emphasizing market-oriented entrepreneurship, service industries, and linkages with China's developed coastal areas have often resulted in marginalization of local ethnic minorities. Disadvantaged by lack of educational opportunities, capital, and access to market networks elsewhere, local ethnic minorities are also generally unaccustomed to the commercial orientation called for by Western Development policies. As a result, Han businesses often displace local community economic interests in taking advantage of state preferences. To the extent that the WDP offers all entrepreneurial firms equal opportunities to compete in an increasingly commercialized environment, Han Chinese firms are privileged by virtue of culture, education, and economic resources. To the extent that a Han-dominated officialdom acts more intentionally to assist related Chinese firms and individuals, local ethnic minorities are disadvantaged further.

Practices in the Inner Periphery

China's practices on economic development in the Inner Periphery reflect the application of centrally conceived policies to minority nationality areas where local conditions are more often than not quite distinct from the conditions of China proper. This has a significant effect on policy implementation, but also on the ancillary effects that economic development might bring for social change.

Tibet

Central government programs on economy and development in Tibet have traditionally confronted obstacles of geographic isolation and local cultural conditions, which often conflict with Beijing's economic development objectives (Ng and Zhou 2004). Years of central government policies imposing economic production initiatives unsuited to the region did little to combat widespread poverty and resentment in Tibet. The First National Tibet Work Conference in March 1980 coupled with Hu Yaobang's inspection visit in May signaled renewed attention to local economy and development issues (Goldstein 1997: 63 *et seq.*). The results of Hu's inspection tour were incorporated in a flexible program announced by the Second National Tibet Work Conference in February 1984 allowing agricultural and animal husbandry policies to be based on local conditions (Wu Jianli). This was consistent with the provisions of the newly enacted NRAL. Under the ideals of regional ethnic autonomy, the Tibet Autonomous Region (TAR) was to have greater authority to manage economic development locally (SCIO 2004b).

Yet central government directives remained powerful, as central economic policy decisions as well as resolutions of central work conferences on Tibet in 1980, 1984, 1994 were dutifully incorporated in edicts issued by the TAR CPC Committee. Thus, 1984 policies on price supports decided based on the inspection tour of Hu Qili and Tian Jiyun were adopted by the TAR CPC Committee, which revised its own decision on economic structural reform to comply with central edicts on the issue (Wu J. 2001). Following the Central Committee's decision in September 1988 on economic retrenchment, the TAR CPC Committee enacted parallel measures on economic order. In the wake of the Lhasa riots of 1989 and the national political crisis associated with the 1989 student democracy movement, the TAR CPC Committee adopted the ten-point Politburo decision on Tibet, focusing on political unity and opposition to alleged separatist activities of the Dalai Lama. Central policy decisions on enterprise restructuring associated with Deng Xiaoping's 1992 *Nanxun* were incorporated in the TAR CPC decision on deepening reform, particularly in areas of managerial autonomy for enterprises, allowing cadres to work in enterprises and establishing employment contract systems, relaxing wage and hiring restrictions, establishing production responsibility systems for evaluating factory managers, building linkages with the developed coastal areas, expanding marketization for goods and services (including labor), and protecting social service functions of increasingly autonomous and privatized enterprises ("Zhonggong Xizang ... guanyu shenhua"). In mid-July 1992, the TAR government promulgated provisions encouraging domestic and foreign investment in Tibet, focusing on general investment inducements for joint ventures, securities deals, technical cooperation and real estate development ("Provisions for Encouraging"). Little attention was given to encouraging investments in specific economic sectors with particular benefits for local socio-economic change.

Village and township enterprises were also given considerable autonomy in production and hiring plans ("Xizang ... guanyu dali fazhan"), while tertiary industries in agricultural areas were given tax and financial incentives to pursue trans-departmental and trans-enterprise projects including contracted production, leasing of state-owned enterprises, and formation of integrated group companies ("Xizang ... guanyu jiakuai fazhan"). Central policies and regulations on approval of individual and privately run enterprises were adopted in Tibet, and applied to sectors of schools, kindergartens, private hospitals and clinics, mining, light industrial production of household goods and agricultural by-products, commerce, services (food and beverage, repair work, consulting, transportation), and receiving investment from foreign firms for processing and foreign trade ("Xizang ... guanyu jiakuai geti"). Individual and private enterprises were given prominent roles in developing rural areas by facilitating commercialization of agriculture and animal husbandry through the integration of local markets, establishing facilities for processing transportation and sale of agricultural and livestock products, and building foreign trade linkages ("Xizang Zizhiqu Dangwei").

Central government policy has repeatedly emphasized the relationship between economic development and local political stability (Jiang, 1993b). The July 1994 Third National Tibet Work conference decisions focused on marketization, increased central investment in Tibet infrastructure and improved living standards as methods for building social stability. At the Conference, Jiang Zemin asserted the need for stability as a precondition for economic development and raising of living standards (Jiang, 1994a). Yet economic investment targets remained focused on infrastructure and natural resource development, and the link with increasing local employment and living standards remained unclear. Speaking to the Conference, Premier Li Peng addressed more prosaic questions about specific aspects where Tibet's economic conditions lagged behind the rest of China (Li P. 1994). Li noted that low levels of economic development and living standards meant that the population still struggled to secure basic necessities of food and clothing, that the infrastructure needs of electricity and transportation remained unmet and that culture, education and media continued to lag. Li drew direct linkages between these economic conditions and the potential for separatist activities. As had Jiang Zemin before him, Li Peng called for a combined effort at national assistance and local self-reliance, in effect suggesting that national economic investment in Tibet must be coupled with local government responsibilities to ensure patriotism in education and culture, to support national and ethnic unity, and to suppress separatist activities (Li P. 1994: 475).

The Central Committee and State Council "Opinion" emerging from the Third Tibet Work Conference emphasized the role of economic development in thwarting separatism through improved living conditions ("Zhonggong Zhongyang Guowuyuan guanyu jiakuai"). The Opinion called for a doubling of economic production over ten years and a concerted program of poverty reduction and improving prosperity. Specific sectors for development attention included agriculture and animal husbandry, mining, forestry, natural resource development, construction materials, light industry, textiles, and handicrafts, as well as commerce, services, and infrastructure development (including power generation). Specific economic development targets were augmented by political directions on safeguarding national unity, curbing separatism, and preserving social stability, suggesting the potential for politicization of economic development initiatives—particularly where local minority interests resist competition and dislocation by migrant Han business interests. This potential was underscored by additional directives on linking economic development with Party policy on nationalities and religion work— once again sounding a note of required submission of local to national priorities.

As incorporated in the TAR CPC policy program, the Ninth Five Year Plan priorities included focusing on local development as an element of national modernization, integrating central decisions with local conditions, economic restructuring and expansion, improving production and incomes in agriculture and animal husbandry, implementing enterprise reform, particularly development of secondary industries and expanding marketization, natural resource development, ensuring social stability in the midst of economic growth, and expanding reliance on science and technology (Wu J. 2001: 348–49). The role of science and technology was underscored in local regulations on integrating technology with economic development through prioritizing foreign investment projects involving technology transfer and linking technology-related investment with local product development and infrastructure programs ("Xizang ... guanyu jinyibu").

The TAR government's priorities under the Tenth Five Year Plan focused on implementing the WDP—particularly in integrating economic and social development to building national unity and opposing separatism ("Xizang ... guomin jingji"). Key areas of "economic structural adjustment" (meaning expanding the role of the socialist market economy) included science and technology, industrial production, and urbanization. Other priorities included natural resource production; human resources; foreign economic relations; social and economic development; and the building of socialist spiritual civilization with socialist democracy and legal system. Although articulated by the local TAR government, each of these objectives reflected the priority given to central policy priorities over local needs. While the emphasis on local development as a means of reducing the threat of separatism suggested that the central government might focus its efforts on improving local living standards, the discourse of stability gradually came to dominate policy discussions. Stability came to become a precondition for implementation of local development policy and ultimately for state investment in local living standards. Speaking to the Tibet delegation to the Ninth National People's Congress (NPC), Hu Jintao underscored that the role of the Party and the central government in pursuing economic development programs would be aimed first and foremost at ensuring social stability (Hu 1998). Citing the spirit of the Fifteenth Party Congress, Hu specified four aspects of Tibet work as including (a) promoting unity of nationalities and opposing separatism; (b) building a group/team of politically reliable local cadres; (c) building patriotism; and (d) resolving internal contradictions (which were explained as involving local conflicts over development and economic change—a critical issue of conflict between Han and Tibetan populations). Each of these was tied closely to policies on social stability and suggested increased state intrusion in local socio-economic and political relationships.

As indicated in the rubric (*tifa*) "development, stability, security" (*fazhan, wending, anquan*) ("Zhonggong Zhongyang Guowuyuan zhaokai"), Beijing's economic policies in Tibet are inseparable from the broader dilemmas of

China's rule. Economic development is seen as the key to pacification of the region, as rising living standards are deemed essential aspects of the "leapfrog style development" (*kuayue shi fazhan*). Central investment in fixed assets under the Ninth Five Year Plan was reported at 23 billion yuan, while the Tenth Five Year Plan promised to double the level of supports and subsidies provided under the Ninth Five Year Plan (Tibet Propaganda Department).

The Fourth Tibet Work Conference in 2001 heralded no dramatic policy shifts on the order that characterized its predecessor of 1994. Economic development continued to be the core policy goal, to be coupled with enforcement of the themes of ethnic and national unity expressed in Party policy on nationalities and religion, and continued opposition to the "splittism" of the Dalai Lama and hostile international forces (Jiang 2001). One important initiative was the effort to partner Tibet with specific regions elsewhere in China, a program that would see specific trade and investment links between Lhasa and Beijing and Jiangsu, and other similar partnerships as a component of the WDP (Zhu 2001; Li R. 2001). Emphasis on economic development would also see increased attention to economic structural reform and greater attention to the market economy—all of which tended to privilege the business role of Han immigrants over local Tibetans ("Zhonggong zhongyang, guowuyuan guanyu zuohao"). Hu returned to these themes in his speech to the Tibet delegation to the fifth session of the Ninth NPC, noting the increased importance of economic institutions (as opposed to government functions) in economic development in Tibet (Hu 2002) and in his emphasis on the "scientific development concept" being linked with the WDP (Hu 2004). The conference mandated central investment of 31.2 billion yuan in 117 projects, including 12 billion yuan for the Tibet section of the Qinghai–Tibet Railway—a striking example of a centrally mandated infrastructure project designed and implemented to suit a particular interpretation of local socio-economic needs (*China's Tibet* 2003: 54). Financial commitments for centrally mandated projects were apparently increased to 37.9 billion and ultimately 90 billion yuan in 2002 (Cooke 2003).

Beijing's analysis of Tibet's economy suggests a starting point of virtually zero—"modern industry" is reported as "having grown from nothing," while Tibet is described as historically "having not a single highway," and tertiary industries such as commerce, tourism, postal services, and information technology were "unknown in old Tibet" (SCIO 2002a). China's program to "modernize" Tibet has seen heavy investment in infrastructure—particularly transportation, communications, and energy, with concomitant expansion of urbanization. Yet these programs are widely seen as having limited benefits for human rights conditions for Tibetan people (Tibet: Tracking Dissent 2007). Indeed, expansion of infrastructure has uncertain benefits for local Tibetans (CECC 2009a: 42), although it is welcomed by migrant Han living in the TAR ("From Telephones to Fibre Optics").

Subordination of local policies on economy and development in Tibet to central planning goals appears to entrench privileges for in-migrating

Han Chinese rather than local Tibetan people (Fischer 2002). Official surveys from the TAR suggest that rural poverty remains the highest in China and that in the largely Tibetan province of Qinghai extreme poverty is actually increasing—reflecting a widening gap between urban and rural living standards (TIN 2003a,c; Ma R. 1994). Thus, while economic growth rates in construction and the tertiary sector (particularly transportation, telecommunications, tourism, and trade) suggest significant economic expansion, agriculture has continued to lag—suggesting that activities in which Tibetans are primarily employed remain far behind those staffed by and catering to migrant Hans (TIN 2003b). The Qinghai–Tibet railroad has been severely criticized as a political initiative aimed at increasing Han migration into Tibet, facilitating further militarization of the region, and ignoring the wishes of Tibetan people about development and social wellbeing, while having little commercial value and significant environmental costs ("Controversial"; *Tracking*). The railway is scheduled to include six new lines under a construction plan to be completed by 2020 (Xin 2008). While some progress has been made in environmental protection efforts on the Tibetan Plateau (SCIO 2003b), environmental stewardship continues to be subordinated to economic growth policies. For example, claims that a string of newly planned dams to be constructed in southern Tibet represent an environmentally responsible path toward energy self-sufficiency have been hotly contested by environmental specialists (Branigan 2008).

Xinjiang

While official comparisons between Tibet and Xinjiang attempt to ascribe blame for local poverty to separatist forces (the Dalai clique in Tibet and extremist religious forces in Xinjiang) (Luobu 2001), the record of China's policy behavior suggests otherwise. Xinjiang had long been virtually ignored by central economic policy-makers, being relegated to a subservient role as a supplier of raw materials (Moneyhon 2002). During the 1990s, however, with the fall of the Soviet Union, the increased activism of the United States in the Mid-East and Central Asia, and the rising militancy of local Islamist separatist sentiment, Xinjiang began to receive renewed attention from the Center (Becquelin 2000).

Agricultural policy focused on contributions to the national economy, building irrigation and hydropower resources for agriculture, supporting the household responsibility system by linking household production autonomy with broader systemic reforms in areas of production inputs and marketing, diversification of production through development of secondary and tertiary production, expanding the role of science and technology in agriculture, and improving living standards and strengthening education on national unity as a defense against separatist sentiment (Zhang 2001: 266–67). In animal husbandry, traditional management methods associated with state planning and non-diversified one-dimensional (*danyi de*) economic structures were to be replaced by market-oriented entrepreneurialism, inviting industrialization of traditional cultural economies ("Zhonggong XUAR ... muxu ruogan wenti"). Focusing on production of grain, cotton, animal husbandry, fruits, and sugar, Xinjiang's implementation of CPC Central Committee decisions on marketization of agriculture required abandonment of state supports for peasants under the rubric of "resolving for the thousands of families and tens of thousands of peasants to enter the market unfettered by departments, regions, and ownership systems" ("Zhonggong XUAR ... nongye he nongcun").

Industrial policy in Xinjiang focused on enterprise reform and natural resource development. The importance of resource exploration in Xinjiang was recognized in the Eighth Five Year Plan (1991–95), along with the need to expand foreign economic relations under the rubric of "opening up" (Christoffersen 1994). The 1991 "Decision of the XUAR CPC Committee and People's Government on Expanding the Opening Up Policy" called for revising the "ossified" (*guosi*) structure of the XUAR foreign trade administration so as to support increased exports from Xinjiang ("Zhonggong XUAR ... Guanyu jinyibu"). Among the measures enacted was the distribution of import–export companies to the county level, expanding export rights for enterprise groups and productive enterprises, establishing border trading companies and expanding trade facilities (factories, workshops, and transport stations), and consolidating existing markets and opening new ones.

National laws for foreign economic relations were given particular attention, as the "Decision" called upon foreign trade enterprises to attend to contract performance and to attract foreign investment and technology transfer through the "foreign invested enterprise" (FIE) system envisioned under legal regimes for Joint Ventures, Cooperative Enterprises, and Wholly Foreign-Owned Enterprises. These efforts to extend the reach of the state economic regulatory system were reinforced by policy efforts to encourage transition to the socialist market economy as a way to improve quality and productivity in agriculture and animal husbandry ("Zhonggong XUAR Guanyu jiakuai fazhan nongxuqu"). Changes were slow in coming, however, and the Ninth Five Year Plan (1996–2000) reiterated previous calls for reform. Industrial reform remained a problem, as state-owned enterprises continued to run up big deficits, requiring further state subsidies combined with stern instructions against increasing capital outlays to cover losses ("Zhonggong XUAR Guanyu shenhua gaige").

The central government's 1999 decisions on the Western Development Program recognized that local economic development had potential to support social and ethnic stability (Lu *et al.* 2003: 339–40; Qing *et al.* 2003; Zhu 2004: 313, *et seq.*). Following a conference of provincial and autonomous region Party officials in Ningxia August 16–18 2000 convened to disseminate results of a Central Ideological and Political Work Conference (Zeng 2003: 568), local Xinjiang officials were charged with dissemination of central policies on political and ideological conformity ("guide the cadres and the masses in toeing the line of central policy decisions"), as the foundation for implementation of local development programs ("PRC's Ding Guangen"). The Central Propaganda Department directed local government efforts to disseminate and enforce central policy on national unity as the prerequisite for stability and local economic development. During his August 2000 inspection visit to Xinjiang, Propaganda Director Ding Guangen called on local officials to implement the policies approved at the meeting and noted specially the importance of combining economic development with efforts to build stability and ethnic unity ("Ding Guangen Makes"). Under themes of "macro-economic adjustment," economic and social development, foreign investment, poverty reduction, transition from plan to market, and commonalities of interest in economic development, central economic policies are aimed at resolving tensions among minority nationalities through promoting consumption and accumulation. Thus, the Western Development Policy offered tax preferences for poverty alleviation programs in the primarily Uighur areas of southern Xinjiang (*Jiangnan*) ("Xinjiang jiang chutai").

While Xinjiang's economy and development have emerged as a national priority for China—expressed in part through the elevation of XUAR Party Secretary Wang Lequan to the Politburo in 2002—central economic policies for Xinjiang continued to emphasize the production of raw materials. Central government dominance in economy and development programs in Xinjiang was also evident in the extent of state investment (Sautman 2000)— the Tenth Five Year Plan calls for investments of over 400 billion yuan. Although a central feature of Xinjiang economic policy since the 1990s has been to diversify away from over-reliance on coal and cotton (Zhang 2001: 267), these resources remain central. Agriculture policy continues to support production of cotton, alternatively referred to as "white gold" and as the "white pillar" of the Xinjiang economy (Cau 2004; "China: Report"). The Tenth Five Year Plan also called for strengthening the competition in international markets for Xinjiang cotton (Xinjiang Xuanchuan Bu 2003a).

The other pillar (the so-called "black pillar") of the Xinjiang economy is oil, the 900,000 square kilometers devoted to oil and gas production in Xinjiang purporting to comprise one-fifth of China's total, and the reported 3.5 billion yuan in tax revenues from oil and gas production in 2001 comprising 21.4 percent of Xinjiang's total tax revenue (Xinjiang Xuanchuan Bu 2003b). While production remains a central feature of China's economic program for Xinjiang, processing receives less attention—China's 2003 White Paper on Xinjiang addressed agricultural output and production figures for crude oil, raw coal, and cotton yarn, with little reporting given to processing of value added goods (SCIO 2003a). A five-year study by Xinjiang University suggested that the ongoing problems of agriculture, villages, and peasants (the so-called three problems of *nongye, nongcun, nongmin*) could not be fully resolved without better integration of agricultural production with processing and marketing (Xinjiang Keji 2004). Yet this has also led to efforts to settle nomadic communities through the fixed residency (*ding ju*) policy, often conflicting with nomadic cultures (Li S. 2003).

The WDP's emphasis on urbanization, internationalization, and market-driven growth has opened significant opportunities for inward Han migration to Xinjiang (Becquelin 2004). To an important extent the Western Development Program offers a "safety valve" for unemployment in China proper—thus raising possible tensions between migrant Han laborers and local communities (Marquand 2003a,b). Local Uighurs are widely seen as excluded from the purported benefits of the WDP (Goodman 2006; Lim 2003; Yom 2001). By contrast, the program is seen to benefit local Han administrators and immigrant Han workers, who are not generally well integrated into local society and culture, as patterns of language use, religion and social relations suggest continued isolation of incoming Chinese from local nationalities (Ji and Gao 1994).

Key WDP infrastructure investment programs have focused on transportation, expansion of oil and gas production and the construction of a natural gas pipeline to the east coast, and rehabilitation of the Tarim Basin. Regulations on tax inducements for Western Development investment projects emphasize the application of tax preferences for transportation, electric and hydropower, post and telecommunications, agriculture processing, and tourism ("XUAR guanyu Xibu"). While the measures acknowledge the context for local conditions, the tax preference scheme reveals assumptions about key activities, participants, and beneficiaries of WDP that suggest little attention has been paid to the needs of local communities. The role of tax incentives presumes their effectiveness in directing investment, which in turn indicates expectations about formal documentation of business activities. As well, the participant-beneficiaries of tax preference arrangements are assumed to be of sufficient size and organization so that tax reductions in the range of 10 percent will be effective inducements for economic behavior. Each of these sectors involves financing and management from the center, with the bulk of managerial authority retained by Han Chinese. While the XUAR government has adopted specific regulations to improve the "soft environment" for investment through what are basically anti-corruption measures aimed at simplifying and speeding up of administrative processes, reduction of fees, and greater supervision of officials ("Xinjiang tuichu"), government links with Han controlled businesses in Xinjiang continue to raise the prospect of favoritism and corruption (Buckley 2004). The potential for distortion of benefits in favor of Han businesses is evident in the concentration of Western Development funds in Han-dominated areas such as Urumqi ("Xinjiang zhiding youhui"). Efforts to simplify administrative processes on such matters as taxation suggest efforts by central authorities to respond to local needs ("Yili zhou guoshui"), but also seem woefully out of touch with the realities of local ethnic economies where even simplification of administrative procedure means little in terms of actual economic behavior.

The role of the *bingtuan* remains central to economy and development policies in Xinjiang (SCIO 2003a; Zhang X. 2001: 274–77). Established to provide a production base to support People's Liberation Army (PLA) activities in the newly "liberated" region (Zhu *et al.* 2004: 132–44), the *bingtuan* has come to embody the military's penetration of the local economic and industrial structure (Laogai Research Foundation 1996). With a total population of 2.5 million, the *bingtuan* is nominally subject to joint leadership of the central government and the XUAR government, although its autonomy from local control is well established (Seymour 2000). The status of the *bingtuan* is suggested by the position of Xinjiang Party Secretary and Politburo member Wang Lequan as First Political Commissar of the XPCC ("Xinhua: Bio"). The *bingtuan* was formed under the auspices of the PLA, and it retains a distinctly military character through its role in reclaiming borderlands and protecting remote national boundaries. The *bingtuan* has also served as a venue for administrative punishment—particularly reform and reeducation through labor, underscoring the linkage between military and public security functions.

The *bingtuan* has taken particular responsibility for infrastructure construction, particularly road-building, irrigation, and land conservation. The *bingtuan's* position of relative parity with the XUAR government is underscored in land use regulations adopted in Xinjiang to implement the National Law Use Law ("XUAR shishi ... tudi guanli fa"). While *bingtuan* land administration departments are to accept leadership of the XUAR land departments in their day-to-day activities (Art. 5), *bingtuan* land is classified as state land (Art. 7), effectively removing it from local control. The *bingtuan's* reliance on conscripted labor, its military *cum* policing functions, and its integration with local development projects all contribute to policies discouraging relocation of *bingtuan* residents back to China proper. While the *bingtuan's* responsibility for building local employment represents in part an investment by the central government in improving local economic opportunities ("Xinjiang Party Secretary's Speech"), the preferences extended to it (e.g., "Wujia hui shang") entrench a culture of privilege that tends to operate against empowerment of local producers. *Bingtuan* officials are unapologetic about the potential that predatory procurement and production prices and conditions imposed on local suppliers may actually undermine local development.

As well, the Central Government has tried to establish Xinjiang as a regional economic hub through which to build closer links with the bordering economies of Kazakhstan and Russia. China's support for the Shanghai Cooperation Organization (SCO) furthers policy goals on relations with the central Asian states in a range of economic as well as security issues, including cross-border economic relations (Lanteigne 2005: 133–35; Munro 2006). While given less attention initially, economic issues have come to prominence with a long-term program of multilateral trade and economic cooperation, including establishment of a development fund and business council ("Tashkent Declaration"). Much as China's domestic WDP is predicated on the idea that economic development will reduce opportunities for separatism, so too does the SCO's inclusion of economic dimensions to regional cooperation reflect China's priority of using economic growth to build political stability. China's support included a US$90 million development fund to support SCO efforts at regional cooperation ("Council of Heads").

The transportation infrastructure dimensions of Western Development are aimed in part at linking Xinjiang more closely with China proper (Wang S. 2003: 238–40). President Hu Jintao's lengthy inspection tour in September 2006 underscored the Chinese government's appreciation of the strategic importance of Xinjiang, and the effort to build political compliance through economic development (Gossett 2009). While the strategy seems generally successful in nurturing local attitudes that prize economic links with China over Uighur independence (Magnier 2008), China's political repression of prominent Uighur businesswoman Rebiya Kadeer suggests the political limits on Beijing's support for local economic development ("A Voice"; Seytoff 2006). Having released Ms. Kadeer to exile in the United States, the government then arrested her son on charges of separatism and sentenced him to nine years imprisonment ("China sentences"; "Inherited").

Thus, law and policy on economy and development in Xinjiang reflect tensions between efforts to develop agricultural, petroleum, and mineral resources on the one hand, and security programs aimed at suppressing local dissident and separatist movements. As with China's development programs in Tibet, the interplay of political and economic influences the content and direction of economic policy. Claims by central government officials that stability is a prerequisite for development inform the interplay between political and economic priorities in China's policies for Xinjiang. The depiction of material conditions favorable to development such as climate, geography and resources is combined with attention to human conditions of which commitment to national unity is paramount ("Li Peng Stresses"). Yet the priorities of local officials focus less on the dimension of political control than on practicalities of economic growth, displacing attention to national unity with calls for action on issues such as resolving employment issues; social security; reforming administration inspection and fee structures; clarifying economic rights in law and regulation; and implementing investment incentives (Wang H. 2002). Sustained economic change will depend in large part on how these tensions between central and local priorities are resolved.

Inner Mongolia

In Inner Mongolia Autonomous Region (IMAR), the 20 years following the beginning of China's economic reform program in 1978 saw a somewhat halting and uncertain process of local adaptation (sometime compliant, often resisting) of central programs on agriculture and production responsibility, economic system reform, and opening to the outside world (Yuan 2001). IMAR is often perceived as a model of compliance with state economic policies and development priorities. In contrast to other areas of the Inner Periphery, Inner Mongolia's levels of economic development are generally compared with other developed areas in China in orthodox reporting. Although the IMAR is still seen as lagging behind other developed areas in China, the comparison itself reveals much about the central government's perspectives on conditions in the IMAR (Zou 1997). While animal husbandry has traditionally been the mainstay of the Inner Mongolia economy, efforts to rationalize production and introduce market mechanisms have been characterized by strong governmental leadership (Li J. 2001). Under the "double responsibility system" (*shuang chengbao*) reforms, ownership of livestock and usage rights to land were allocated to households in exchange for contracted terms of debt and tax payments (Sneath 2000: 129–33). Central policies for economy and development in Inner Mongolia have focused generally on expanding existing economic resources in agriculture, animal husbandry, energy resources (particularly coal), and border trade (Wang and Yang 2004). However, local cultural structures have often resisted widespread acceptance of state economic policies aimed at marketization and privatization (Humphrey and Sneath 1999: 54–58, 103–9; Williams 1996), as different cultural attributes of Mongols and incoming Han migrants resulted in different levels of receptivity to economic reform policies (Ma and Pan 1994: 120–24).

An additional element involves environmental conservation, particularly stewardship of the sensitive grasslands. The Ninth Five Year Plan (1996–2000) saw state investment in four local "economic pillars" of coal mining, building materials, chemicals, and animal husbandry ("China: Inner Mongolia Viewed"). Natural resource development was subject to basic principles of integrated development and economic benefit, increased use of science and technology in transformation of natural resources, integration of foreign economic relations with local development, focus on marketization, and pursuit of sustainable development and environmental protection ("NMAR 'jiu wu' ziyuan"). Under the environmental protection program, water conservancy efforts under the 9th FYP saw increased grain yields, but also underscored the urgency of the lowering water table (Liu L. 1997). Rational land use planning was aimed to target agricultural and animal husbandry activities where they could be most productive, while also rebuilding denuded forest and grassland areas and rehabilitating waterways ("Zonggong Neimenggu zizhiqu"). Implicit in this discourse is blame placed on local ethnic minorities for irrational land use and environmental degradation (Williams 2002: Chapter 2). Local allocation of grazing rights without concomitant land ownership rights has reportedly contributed to degradation of grassland areas, as herders engage in common access grazing with insufficient attention to long-term sustainability (Thwaites *et al.* 1998: 333–35). Common agricultural use unrestricted by localized ownership and usage rights is also seen to contribute to land degradation (Brogaard and Zhao 2002: 223).

Despite evidence supporting the need for localized management, the policy and regulatory framework centered on the authority of the central government. Land use in Inner Mongolia is heavily dependent on interpretation of the Grasslands Law of the PRC (1985), which provides that grasslands belong to the state, unless collective ownership is specified. This raises the possibility of conflicting interpretations when compared with the general constitutional provision that rural land belongs to the collective. Grasslands may be requisitioned for state construction. Disputes over ownership are to be resolved by the People's Government, raising further potential of interpretation in favor of state rather than local interests. Central control is underscored by the authority over grasslands use accorded to central government departments for farming and animal husbandry. Central policies on forest preservation are driven by national rather than local environmental concerns (Li J. 2001).

The Ninth Five Year Plan also gave significant attention to expanding Inner Mongolia's foreign trade posture ("NMAR 'jiu wu' dui wai"). As NPC delegate and CPC Secretary for Inner Mongolia Liu Mingzu put it, economic development was a political issue, necessary to ensure political stability in this border area—suggesting a pattern of responding to political concerns of minority nationalities with economic efforts aimed at raising living standards of urban and rural residents (the so-called "two increases"—*liang jia*) (Liu M. 1996). Coupled with this was the so-called "two-shifts" (*liang bian*) calling for transition from planned to market economy and from extensive economic growth to intensive—an attempt to draw back from comprehensive large-scale state investment in across-the-board economic growth targets, and to focus instead on support for tertiary agricultural and animal husbandry-related industries and an expanded role for foreign trade.

Under the Ninth Five Year Plan, economic development goals included natural resource development, opening up to foreign economic relations, expanding science and education, building human resources through training programs, and promoting brand-name products (especially cashmere), all of which were aimed at strengthening Inner Mongolia's self-reliance under market economy policies ("China: Zou"). As Jiang Zemin noted during his 1999 inspection tour of Inner Mongolia, natural resource development included particular attention to mining and processing of rare minerals, which Deng Xiaoping had labeled China's equivalent to mid-East oil (Liu M. 1996). China's entry to the World Trade Organization would present Inner Mongolia opportunities to expand the market share of its cashmere industry (Chu 2002), driving the local government to assert the need to integrate rural producers and urban processes ("PRC: Inner Mongolian Chairwoman"). Expansion of the border ports such as Manzhouli (whose trade volume reportedly increased some 20 percent annually beginning in 1999) underscored Beijing's effort to build on Inner Mongolia's significance as an entrepot for Sino-Russian commerce and ultimately Asia–Europe trade (Xibu 2003; "Sino-Russian Border Port"; "CPC Political Bureau Alternate"). The emphasis on branding was intensely politicized, as leading management offices (*qiye lingdao banzi*) were established to approve particular brands and corps of leading enterprise managers (*youxiu qiye duiwu*) offered the prospect of political and economic patronage ("NMAR 'jiu wu' mingpai").

Opposition to reform of state-owned industries was particularly intense in Inner Mongolia, drawing the attention of Premier Zhu Rongji, whose inspection visit in July 1998 was focused on expediting reform, scrapping insolvent enterprises and seeing to the unemployment problems caused by lay-offs of state workers (Chi *et al.* 1998). The entrenched relationship between Party organs and commercial enterprises was underscored by training programs that treated Party cadres and enterprise managers as essentially interchangeable—through integrated training, policies emphasizing general knowledge as opposed to specialized skills, and Party-led initiatives to establish human resource markets ("NMAR 'jiu wu' rencai"). Measures enacted by the Autonomous Region government on circulation of Party cadres were aimed at preventing entrenchment of local officials, but met with limited success, as indicated by the need to repeatedly issue new regulations directing continued circulation of Party officials (Zhang D. 2001: 402). The intransigence of the unemployment problem was underscored by the fact that five years later Hu Jintao was forced to revisit the issue and promise specific government initiatives ("Hu Jintao inspects").

With the Tenth Five Year Plan (2000–5), increased attention was paid to service industries such as tourism ("Qian Qichen Inspects"). Environmental conservation and ecological construction were given particular attention, as the steady erosion of Inner Mongolia's grasslands and water resources heralded looming economic problems. In keeping with the WDP, the newly appointed Chairwoman of the IMAR emphasized continued reform of the industrial structure, agricultural development, urbanization and coordinated development of small cities and towns, and reforming the system of public ownership ("Inner Mongolia's Uyunqimg"). Under the WDP, Inner Mongolia projects focused on transportation infrastructure, "ecological building (*shengtai jianshe*) and environmental production," and reform of the state-owned industrial structure ("Leaders").

Yet such projects remained subject to central policy priorities under the rubric of "macroeconomic control" ("Vice Premier Huang Ju"). Nonetheless, the IMAR government has attempted to tailor the WDP to suit local needs, as evident in regulatory language limiting its application and projects to local conditions ("NMAR shishi xibu"). While foreign investment is encouraged for infrastructure projects such as telecommunications, power generation, energy, and public facilities, local investment is directed toward expanding production and export in local agriculture and animal husbandry (ibid. Art. 1, 6). Support for expanded border trade reflects recognition of this longstanding socio-economic reality for nomadic communities, although the effort to concentrate development in fixed locations such as Manzhouli echoes elements of Han-oriented settlement policies (ibid. Art. 8–10). While efforts to build up professional services in areas of trade facilitation, accounting, and law reflect trends toward professionalization evident in Han China (ibid. Art. 2), local measures also recognize the importance of directing financial resources to local producers (ibid. Art. 21). Other barriers to local economic initiative such as administrative fees are also restricted (ibid. Art. 24). Although not entirely free of policy orientations drawn from development priorities and experience in Han China, programs for implementing the WDP in the IMAR seem more attuned to the importance of local conditions than is the case in Xinjiang and Tibet.

Political dimensions of development continue, as Inner Mongolia's economic and social development programs retain a focus on pacifying local ethnic minorities through imposed social stability and increased living standards ("Hui Liangyu Inspects"). However, local Mongols have become even more restive, as economic opportunities are seen to go disproportionately to Han immigrants ("Genghis Khan's tribe"). To the extent that economic development policies may conflict with efforts to build local autonomy in resistance to Han intrusion, central policy priorities continue to rest with programs of marketization and urbanization and may force local society to adapt, even to the detriment of traditional socio-cultural arrangements (Bulag 2002b).

Normative and organizational perspectives

China's policies and practices on economic development in the Inner Periphery reveal dynamics of selective adaptation and institutional capacity. In the Inner Periphery areas of Inner Mongolia, Xinjiang, and Tibet, global discourses on development and globalization have encountered normative preferences of the Chinese government, while organizational and relational dynamics have affected the management of economic relations.

Selective Adaptation

China's governance policies for economic development in the Inner Periphery reveal the influence of a global modernist paradigm toward economic development. As suggested by the contours of the WDP, development is interpreted by China's economic policy makers and regulators as emphasizing capital accumulation and infrastructure development. As well, the foreign investment and trade programs of the WDP emphasize the importance of export-led growth, revealing the influence of the economic development experience of other economies in Asia (Haggard 1990). China has also sought quite consciously to replicate the experience of North American economic transformation in directing investment to its western regions. Drawing on models that emphasize wage stability, low inflation monetary policy, enforced savings, and direct state investment in infrastructure, China's WDP seems modeled on many neo-classical economic development theories associated with the World Bank and the International Monetary Fund (Stiglitz 2002; Ocampo and Martin 2003; Potter 2003b). The foreign trade and investment strategy also draws heavily on neo-classical economic approaches, attempting to build on what are perceived as natural comparative advantages (e.g., cashmere and rare earths for Inner Mongolia, oil, gas, and cotton for Xinjiang, and mining for Tibet). An explicit implication of these strategies is transformation of local societies through increased personal income and business opportunity.

Yet the assimilation of development strategies and models is mediated by normative preferences of central and local officials and interpretive communities. Thus, factors of perception play a significant role in the largely uncritical acceptance of capital accumulation and infrastructure development as the foundations for economic growth. Perceptions about economic success stories elsewhere in Asia (especially Taiwan, Korea and Japan) are perceived as justification for neo-classical economic modeling on development. Perceptions about local conditions also play a role, as expectations that economic accumulation, rising incomes, and business opportunity will generate political stability and cultural assimilation serve to reinforce the commitment to neo-classical economic development policies.

Complementarity also plays a role—particularly to the extent that neo-classical development models that emphasize wage and price stability and state investment are consummate with China's political and economic policy preferences. A key element of this is the extent to which state-guided development as practiced elsewhere in Asia fits quite well within the governance model of "patrimonial sovereignty"—a not unexpected result given the dominance of Confucian cultural values across Asia generally. Nonetheless, many of the open market norms of neo-classical development models suggest conditions that would be too decentralized and autonomous for China's central planners to accept. Thus complementarity between certain factors of the international neo-classical development model and China's approach to the WDP result in reception of norms and policies that emphasize the continued role of a strong central government in guiding local development.

Legitimacy is also a key factor, as expectations about links between economic growth and political stability are grounded in assumptions about the legitimacy of the regime. While often contradicted by local sentiments that ascribe legitimacy based on ethnicity and cultural-religious values, the Chinese government places much faith in the capacity of economic growth to build legitimacy for the ruling regime.

Institutional Capacity

In the Inner Periphery, institutional capacity has a significant impact on implementation of China's economic development policies. Factors of Institutional Purpose are evident in economic growth strategies aimed at building political stability even while extracting natural resources that support central economic interests (notably oil and gas and minerals) often operate in conflict with local economic development purposes centered on employment stability for local minority peoples. Factors of institutional purpose also arise when economic development in the periphery is seen as a possible solution to issues of ethnic unrest (Qing *et al.* 2003; Ma Da. 2003: 138–42). Thus, restive minorities in the Inner Periphery are constructed as driven by a yearning for materialist comforts that will gradually displace their ambivalence about Chinese rule. This materialist approach ignores the very cultural dimensions that are at the core of minority nationality identities. And since it is largely these identities, rather than material conditions that are the source of hostility to Han rule, it seems unlikely that material wellbeing alone will suffice to resolve problems of Han-minority relations. There seems to be an element of desperation to the economic growth strategy for resolving ethnic conflict. Having seen military occupation, cultural repression, and attempted co-optation of local elites fail to bring minority nationalities into the fold of the greater multi-ethnic China, economic development seems like the last best effort. Yet the very approach to economic development threatens to alienate further those minority nationalities that Beijing needs most to accommodate.

Factors of institutional location are also present, as disparities between centralized economic development strategies (most notably the WDP) and local perspectives are frequently noted by local academic observers. Issues of institutional location are also evident in the challenges presented to autonomy in local governance by state-centered development policies that subordinate the authority, status, and ultimately the legitimacy of local officials. Even as the central government has adopted economic development as a strategy for resolving inter-ethnic conflict, capital-intensive approaches to economic development threaten to alienate further local minority communities. Dynamics of institutional location are evident in ways that the Nationality Region Autonomy Law addresses purposes and indicators of local development in minority areas. The NRAL confers on local government authority to administer economic development programs, subject to national planning (NRAL: Arts. 15–16). However, "higher level organs" are accorded considerable authority and responsibility to assist and direct local development (NRAL: Chapter 6). The Western Development Program exemplifies the tensions between local autonomy and state oversight on issues of development. On one hand, the program has seen significant state investment in local infrastructure in the periphery (Sautman 2000). Yet, basic decisions on resource allocation, project approvals, and regulatory arrangements are made by a central leading group and its subordinate local committees. Autonomous area governments have representation but little control over the resulting economic activity. The Western Development Program reveals the continued dominance of state-directed economic development models ("Quanguo minwei 'shi wu'"; Yeung 2004). The dominant role of central Party and state supervision remains a central feature of State Council decisions on Western Development (Shi 2001a: Chapter 2). In peripheral areas such as Xinjiang, local economic development organs such as the *bingtuan* are themselves still beholden to centralized development models (Ma D. 2003: 212–40;

Seymour 2000). Privileging of central perspectives on development is evident in policy papers that present modernization of the periphery as essential to China's future (Ni 1998). Local cultures are considered as relevant to performance arts, social customs, and literature, but not to forms for economic change (Ma Z. 2003).

Dynamics of institutional orientation are evident in programs associated with the Western Development Program that construct notions of development around priorities of capital-intensive investment, infrastructure, and urbanization (Yeung and Shen 2004; Dreyer 2000; Gao Zhaoping et al. 2000). Each of these priorities relies on formal institutions and a concentration of decision-making among urban educated elites. While these may ultimately be necessary and desirable, the priorities of the Western Development Program suggest a rather authoritarian approach to directing economic behavior by local people. The role of local culture and tradition in economic decision making is marginalized, as development priorities reflect increasingly the centralized approaches to development that characterize Han China. Even when coordination with local conditions is acknowledged, basic policy goals still privilege formalization of economic organizations and regulatory institutions. The orientation of the WDP remains focused on formal processes of project approvals, licenses, formalized regulation and the "legalization" of economic relations. In the societies of the Inner Periphery, however, much economic activity is conducted through informal family networks, while local merchants often resist formal requirements of licensing as intrusive mechanisms for state control. Even as attention is paid to the need to facilitate economic growth for the decentralized communities of farmers and herders that characterize much of the Inner Periphery, development is constructed primarily in terms that conflict with traditional social arrangements (Wang et al. 2003: Chapter 13). Explicitly rejecting "post-modern" viewpoints that extol the virtues of local identity and tradition, authoritative treatments of the Western Development Program call for development to be achieved through reform in local practices (Ni 1998: Introduction).

While poverty alleviation remains an important component of Western Development, solutions are seen to lie primarily in neo-liberal economic approaches centered on accumulation, institutionalization, and urbanization, with little attention to preserving local cultures and traditions ("Guanyu shenru guanche": 158; Zeng Peiyan 2003: Chapter 1; Lan 1999). Local studies have highlighted concerns over the need for sustainability, balanced development, fairness and effectiveness in distribution of benefits (Wang N. 2002), yet official reporting tends to emphasize conventional economic indicators of enterprise reform, market expansion, foreign investment, and unified government regulation (Li S. 2003). Where official reporting on Western Development does acknowledge the importance of local social support for the program, the failure to appreciate linkages between economic and social development results in development programs that have little relevance or support in local non-Han communities (Zeng 2003). Even in environmental

140 *Economy and development in the Inner Periphery*

policy areas, the focus on using technology and engineering to build (*"jianshe"*) the natural environment (Shi 2001b) seems quite distanced from the experience and expectations of local people. Institutional cohesion is also a critical factor, as issues of corruption among Han cadres, Han exclusion of minority nationalities from economic opportunity, and repression of minority businesses on arbitrary charges of separatism and disloyalty continue.

Taken together, these dynamics of institutional capacity raise significant questions about the long-term sustainability of China's economic growth policies for the Inner Periphery. Indeed, considerable debate is now under way in Beijing as to the continued wisdom of the WDP and there is significant likelihood that the resources devoted to the program will be diverted to resolving rural social conflict in China proper.

Summary

Economic development policy dimensions of China's governance in the Inner Periphery reveal continued patterns of central domination. Despite provisions in the NRAL espousing local autonomy over economic development programs, Beijing's control over policy direction and implementation of Western Development Program in the Inner Periphery is quite overt in both doctrine and practice. While formalized rhetoric on local autonomy on matters of economic development in the Inner Periphery appears to permit local governments to exercise influence over economic policy content and process, the realities of central policy implementation through funding controls limit local political initiative. In Tibet and Xinjiang, nominal concessions to local autonomy are trumped by national development imperatives under the Western Development Program, and particularly by the linkage of economic development with central priorities on suppression of ethnic nationalism. In Inner Mongolia by contrast, local strategies of compliant resistance have tended to expand local influence over interpretation and application of WDP goals. In all three regions, the normative dynamics of selective adaptation and the organizational patterns of institutional capacity permit better understanding of the formulation and application of central policies.

5 Implications for the Outer Periphery

China's laws, policies, and practices in the Inner Periphery on political authority, socio-cultural relations, and the economy have implications for the Outer Periphery areas of Hong Kong and Taiwan. While differences exist between the nationality autonomy system established under the Nationality Region Autonomy Law (NRAL) and the provisions accepted by China for the Hong Kong Special Administrative Region (SAR), the PRC Constitution authorizes both systems and both are therefore dependent on constitutional interpretation by the Party/state. The Special Administrative Region system currently applicable to Hong Kong and proposed for Taiwan is a constitutional arrangement for local governance that is structurally analogous to the nationalities autonomy system applicable to the Inner Periphery. In keeping with China's effort to legalize relationships within and among its political subdivisions (Liu 2003; Wang 2002), constitutional interpretation reflects the policy instrumentalism that characterizes the Chinese legal system generally. Just as legislative initiatives proceed first from the Political–Legal Committee of the CPC Politburo, so too does that Committee determine the contours of legislative and constitutional interpretation, working through the Party Committees in the National People's Congress (NPC) Standing Committee's Legislative Affairs Committee (*Fa Gong Wei*), State Council's Legal Affairs Bureau (*Fazhi ju*), and the court system.

China's policy imperatives on issues of governance in the Inner Periphery reveal particular characteristics of the regions involved and differ in many respects from those of the Outer Periphery. Nonetheless, to the extent that China's governance of the Inner Periphery is often preoccupied with issues of national integrity, social stability, economic development, and cultural hegemony, analogous issues arise in the Outer Periphery as well. Thus, with regard to Hong Kong, political questions about the electoral process and enactment of anti-sedition legislation are explained in Beijing as involving issues of national integrity and security. Economic development imperatives are considered the primary criteria for success in the process of reasserting PRC sovereignty over Hong Kong. Socio-cultural questions regarding freedom of religion are linked closely with concerns about stability and control. While the thorny issues of relations between Han and local minorities is not entirely

142 *Implications for the Outer Periphery*

absent in Hong Kong and Taiwan, as complex questions exist of Han relations with minority ethnic groups in Taiwan (China refers to these collectively as *Gaoshan* but the Taiwan authorities have a more nuanced and differentiated approach to such different groups as the Yami and Atayal) and Hong Kong (the Kejia for example) (Hattaway 2000; Hao 2002). But for the most part issues of national integrity, economic prosperity, and social stability are the key issues in China's policy position on reunification. These policy priorities will almost certainly influence constitutional interpretations about the meaning and operation of the Special Administrative Region system that applies currently to Hong Kong and is proposed (with revisions) for Taiwan.

Political authority

PRC law, policy, and practice on political authority in the Outer Periphery are evident in constitutional arrangements and the Party's "united front" practices, as well as legislation aimed at formalizing policy goals. In the Outer Periphery, constitutional provisions on the unitary state and specific legislation aimed at setting the terms for local governance are reinforced by the Communist Party's "united front work" (*tongyi zhanxian gongzuo*) as a basis for building community with the Chinese societies "to include compatriots in Taiwan, Hong Kong, and Macao and overseas Chinese in an alliance that takes patriotism and support for the unity of the motherland as its political basis" (Fang 2004: 180). Under the dictum of "governance capacity" associated with Hu Jintao, the Communist Party's approach to governance in the Outer Periphery is remarkably uniform. Hong Kong and Taiwan are both considered subject to the "one country, two systems" approach. Cadres involved in implementing law and policy on Hong Kong and Taiwan are urged to "uphold policies of 'one country–two systems'" in both areas (Yao 2005: 219–20).

Hong Kong Special Administrative Region

The "one country–two systems" approach applied currently in Hong Kong includes many of the tensions evident in constitutional and NRAL provisions on nationality region autonomy. Article 31 of the Constitution provides for the state to establish special administrative regions subject to legislation enacted by the NPC and in light of specific conditions. Article 62(13) empowers the NPC to decide on the establishment of special administrative regions and the systems to be instituted therein. While no specific autonomy requirements are listed in these constitutional provisions, these were granted to Hong Kong in the course of the Sino-British negotiations and the enactment of the Hong Kong Basic Law. While Hong Kong enjoys considerably more autonomy than is afforded the Inner Periphery under the NRAL,

Chinese analysts depict Hong Kong's legal status as equivalent to that of provinces, autonomous regions, and centrally administered cities of China, particularly in the sense that all local governance authority results from a delegation by the central government (Dai 2003: 44–46). Thus, the relationship between central and local authority, as set forth in the Basic Law, remains a creature of Chinese law (Wang 2002), and therefore is subject to whatever opportunities and restrictions this may entail for future change.

Read in light of the PRC Constitution upon which it is based, the Basic Law of Hong Kong reflects the perspectives of the central government on how the balance between central control and local autonomy should be achieved (Wesley-Smith 1990; Ghai 1999). Article 8 of the Basic Law provides that laws previously in force in Hong Kong, including the common law, rules of equity, and enacted statutes and regulations, along with customary law will remain in effect unless in conflict with the Basic Law and subject to amendment by the Hong Kong legislature. While retention of existing law has given comfort to those who feared the imposition of Chinese law on Hong Kong, the allowance for amendments and the reference to customary law raise the possibility that existing laws and regulations may gradually become diluted by China-based rules. In light of the historical role for customary law in Hong Kong (Coates 1968) and the uncertainties of interpreting customary law (Su 1999), the potential for gradual merging of Hong Kong and Chinese law and custom remains strong.

While the interpretations of the Basic Law text very widely ("Hong Kong's Bill of Rights"; Leung and Zhu 2002), alternatively supporting or challenging conclusions about the potential for meaningful autonomy for Hong Kong SAR, local commentators have suggested that on its face the Basic Law fails to preserve the "two systems" approach (Li Z. 2004: 40–42). Article 2 of the Basic Law confers on Hong Kong a "high degree of autonomy." However, the term autonomy (*zizhi*) as interpreted in light of its usage elsewhere in the Chinese legal system confers a sense of limited local responsibility for self-administration. The Chinese term *zizhi* simply does not connote the sense of insulation from outside authority that is conveyed in the English term "autonomy." In tacit recognition that meaningful autonomy requires local activism, Hong Kong civic leaders have urged broader public participation in the processes of politics and governance (Lu and Siwei 2002, 2003).

Specific provisions of the Hong Kong Basic Law on the relationship between the SAR government and the Central People's Government invite consideration and debate over the meaning of local autonomy. Article 12 provides that the Hong Kong SAR shall enjoy a high degree of autonomy directly under the central government. This provision confirms Hong Kong's status as a political subdivision of the PRC, subject to the conditions set forth in Articles 31 and 62(13) of the PRC constitution. While the promise of a "high degree of autonomy" (*gaodu zizhiquan*) remains significant, it also remains subject to constitutional interpretation. As with language describing autonomy for the Inner Periphery, the use of "*zizhiquan*" to express the idea of autonomy embraces ideals about self-government that are significantly more limited that terms such as "*zizhuquan*" (autonomy) and "*zijuequan*" (self-determination).

Basic Law Articles 13 and 14 provide that the central government shall remain responsible for foreign affairs and defense relating to Hong Kong. This echoes arrangements of the NRAL and the PRC Constitution on the Inner Periphery. By affirming the exclusive authority of the Central People's Government to conduct foreign affairs relating to the Hong Kong SAR, the Basic Law reaffirms the sovereign powers of the PRC and reiterates the subordination of Hong Kong to arrangements on allocation of administrative authority under the PRC constitution. This has significant implications for the meaning of autonomy as applied to Hong Kong, as well as the possibilities for Hong Kong's expanded participation in multilateral arrangements on environment and security, for example (Mushkat 2006). While Hong Kong has enjoyed broader autonomy than "Autonomous Regions" in the Inner Periphery to participate in international organizations such as the World Trade Organization (WTO) and the World Health Organization (WHO), the provisions of Article 13 clarify that such grants of autonomy are discretionary. As with provisions on external affairs, provisions on military defense underscore the ultimate sovereign authority of the PRC government over Hong Kong SAR, echoing provisions of the NRAL and the PRC Constitution governing the Inner Periphery. The Law on the Garrison for Hong Kong Special Administrative Region (1996) links the security of Hong Kong SAR with goals of safeguarding state sovereignty, unity and territorial integrity of China as well as security of Hong Kong SAR ("Zhu jun fa": Art. 1). Despite the proscription against interference in local affairs, the linkage between security of Hong Kong and national policy imperatives allows the central government significant power over the interpretation of local autonomy.

Article 15 empowers the government to appoint the Chief Executive and the principal executive officials for Hong Kong. In contrast to the Inner Periphery where processes for appointment of autonomous region leaders are either concealed or disguised by formalistic allusions to appointment and election, the central government's appointment powers for the SAR are explicit. As the debate over the appointment of the Chief Executive revealed (Lam 2004; Hogg 2005; "Hong Kong lawmaker"), China has taken the view that Chinese law should be a source for interpretations of general rights and processes to be decided "according to law." The central government's resistance to efforts to expand the role of elections for Chief Executive (Chan 2005) tends to affirm its intent to exercise effective control over administrative appointments in Hong Kong. As with the Inner Periphery, this underscores a limited interpretation of the ideal of local autonomy.

Articles 16, 17, and 19 of the Basic Law provide that the Hong Kong SAR shall be vested with executive, legislative, and judicial powers. The distinction between conduct of local administrative affairs and power to appoint the Chief Executive and principal officials reveals limits to the conception of autonomy as primarily an issue of policy implementation rather than an expression of independence in policy formulation. The delegation of legislative authority is broadly consistent with arrangements under the PRC Constitution Article 100 concerning the authority of provinces and centrally-administered cities to enact legislation and report for the record. The general legislative autonomy granted Hong Kong SAR omits provisions for "autonomy regulations" and "specific regulations" enacted in the nationality autonomy regions of the Inner Periphery where NPC Standing Committee approval is needed before such local measures go into effect. Yet the power of the NPC Standing Committee to invalidate local legislation (not contained in Constitution Art. 100 but enshrined in Art. 17 of the Basic Law) underscores the limitations to autonomy contemplated for the Basic Law. China's opposition to general elections by full universal suffrage for legislators ("HK election needs") as well as statements by Chinese officials suggesting that the HK Legislative Council could be dissolved if the democratic opposition were to gain electoral control (Ching 2004), underscore the central government's limited interpretation of local autonomy.

The independent judicial power accorded the courts of Hong Kong parallels provisions on judicial independence in the PRC Constitution Article 126 and does not contain the provisions of NRAL Article 46 on supervision by higher level courts and the Supreme People's Court. Yet the operational limits on judicial independence in China proper should give pause to those who would assume continuing independence of Hong Kong's courts. While the political–legal adjudication committees that guide judicial decisions in the People's Courts of the PRC are not yet present in the Hong Kong courts, the processes for appointment of judges suggests a creeping level of indirect influence from the central Party/state (Hsu 2004). As the "right of abode" cases demonstrated (*Ng Ka Ling* v. *Director of Immigration*; *Chan Kam-nga and Others* v. *Director of Immigration*; Chan *et al.* 2000; Hewitt 1999; Tai 1999), China views final adjudication as limited to application of law rather than final interpretation, which under the Article 67 of the PRC Constitution remains the province of the NPC Standing Committee. Limitations on jurisdiction are consistent with Basic Law provisions granting to the central government exclusive authority over foreign affairs and defense. Perspectives on the meaning of adjudication and the role of the courts in the PRC differ significantly from common law perspectives in Hong Kong. In particular, despite shared doctrines of parliamentary sovereignty, PRC perspectives on judicial independence and judicial authority to interpret legislation are significantly more limited than the common law tradition would suggest, and underscore the potential for political limitations on judicial behavior.

Article 23 of the Basic Law requires the Hong Kong SAR to enact laws on its own to prohibit any act of treason, secession, sedition, or subversion against the Central People's Government, or theft of state secrets, to prohibit foreign political organizations or bodies from conducting political activities in the Region, and to prohibit political organizations or bodies of the Region from establishing ties with foreign political organizations or bodies. As with the linkage between local administration and state security (Basic Law: Art. 14), the authority to enact security ordinances conflates the purported grants of autonomy with the imperative to protect the policy imperatives of the Party/state. This echoes provisions of the NRAL (Art. 7) and the PRC Constitution (Art. 120) governing security initiatives in the nationality autonomy regions of the Inner Periphery. However, in a clear example of the potential for resistance by local communities, efforts by the SAR government to draft a security ordinance under Article 23 gave rise to significant political and social opposition ("Commentary: Miscalculation of public opinion"). The central Party/state's greater tolerance for such political and social resistance in Hong Kong contrasts with suppression of popular sentiment in Tibet and Xinjiang. While factors such as the political and historical background of Hong Kong, its greater international visibility and stature, and its significant populations of foreign expatriates may well have played a role, Beijing's tolerance also seems to reflect a broader willingness to accept dissent from Han communities as opposed to ethnic minority groups.

China's interpretation of constitutional arrangements for Hong Kong, revealed through *inter alia* cases on the "right of abode"; appointment of the Chief Executive; and legislative measures on public security, suggest a continuing commitment to central control. The right of abode cases that emerged shortly after the hand-over led to direct conflict between the SAR government and the Court of Final Appeal. Faced with an adverse judicial decision, the government sought an interpretation of the Basic Law from the NPC Standing Committee, which in effect deprived the court of jurisdiction (Hewitt 1999). The central government's interpretation of Basic Law Article 53 ("Decision") on replacement of the Chief Executive arose as a result of former Chief Executive Tung Chee-hwa's resigning under pressure from Beijing before expiration of his full second term in office (Xianggang wenwei bao; "Beijing formally"). The political and legal disputes surrounding enactment of a securities ordinance under Basic Law Article 23 brought into sharp relief differences of legal and political norms between Hong Kong and PRC communities that called into question the PRC government's perspectives on local autonomy (Fu *et al.* 2005; Tang 2003, 2004).

China's approach to political authority as an element of governance in Hong Kong has echoed themes evident in its policies and practices in the Inner Periphery. Against a backdrop of legal instrumentalism that ensures interpretations of text that satisfy the policy imperatives of the central Party/state, orthodox perspectives on the reach and potential for autonomy in Hong Kong remain limited, as preoccupation with national sovereignty has tended to dominate official discourses on the one country–two systems constitutional model.

Taiwan

Chinese government proposals concerning a Taiwan SAR echo the broad conceptual perspectives of China's constitutionally defined SAR structure and by extension the constitutional arrangements for the nationality minority areas of the Inner Periphery. Discussions and informal negotiations on resolving issues of sovereignty and political authority across the Taiwan Strait intensified following the conclusion of the so-called "1992 consensus" (*1992 gongzhi*) (Xie 2003a: Chapter 3). In 1992, the Taiwan Legislative Yuan enacted a set of measures on people-to-people linkages with the Mainland (Zhu and Wang 2003: 175). While the "consensus" acknowledged the "one-China" principle and accepted the possibility of multiple interpretations, differences in priorities and perspectives between the PRC and Taiwan quickly became evident (Haiyan liang'an guanxi xiehui: Section 3). Whether considered in light of potential for a quasi-commonwealth model (Kuo and Myers 2004) or model of full unification (Tsang 2004b), China's perspectives on Taiwan question can be understood in light of intra-cultural tensions and the contradiction between sovereignty and local identity (Carlson 2005; Callahan 2004). As a "question not subject to debate," China's claim to sovereignty over Taiwan has been grounded in international law principles on statehood (Jiang 2001). Sovereignty claims are also at the heart of China's efforts to deny Taiwan international personality or treaty rights (Yuan 2002). As with efforts at governance in the Inner Periphery, China has endeavored to "legalize" its relationships with Taiwan through a variety of legislative and regulatory measures, many of which are matched by complementary efforts by the Taiwan government (Zhu and Wang 2003; Wang and Chen 2000; Xingzheng Yuan Dalu Weiyuanhui 2002). Yet China's behavior regarding Taiwan illustrates the ways in which PRC's reception of international law remains contingent on assertions of national self interest on matters of sovereignty and security (Chen 2004: Chapters 5 and 6).

China's 2000 White Paper on "The One-China Principle and the Taiwan Issue" (SCIO and State Council Taiwan Affairs Office 2000) expressed a paradoxical commitment to international legal standards of sovereignty while also asserting China's rights to use force against Taiwan. Departing from the principles set forth in the previous 1993 White Paper, the 2000 document added a third condition for China's exercise of its alleged right to the use of force, namely if the Taiwan authorities fail to negotiate a reunification agreement with China promptly and in good faith. The White Paper rejected the "two German states" model associated with German reunification as a basis for cross-strait reconciliation, since this might be taken to support separate sovereignty for Taiwan and the Mainland. Instead, the White Paper reiterated the commitment to "one country–two systems" as a basis for reunification, while allowing for a different application than that of Hong Kong. Whether under China's nominally unified legal regime such an approach will permit the sustained implementation of autonomous regional legal systems remains uncertain (Du 2004).

The 2000 White Paper attempted an international legal argument using theories of state succession to justify claims that China-Taiwan issues are wholly domestic and therefore beyond the reach of international law's general prohibition against the use of force between states. While there is much to disagree with in the content of the argument, the fact that China elected to state its claims in these terms suggests the extent to which China recognizes the need to accommodate the international legal regime in pursuing its sovereignty goals concerning Taiwan. China's perspectives on the application of international law to Taiwan were also evident in the text of a discussion draft (the so-called "Wuhan Draft") on managing reunification with Taiwan (Yu 2002). While those familiar with the drafting process in the National People's Congress have indicated that the Draft was not under formal legislative consideration, the text nonetheless suggested possible approaches to resolving the cross-strait problem. The draft did not renounce the use of force to achieve reunification, but it did suggest several options for peaceful reunification, through establishment of a Taiwan SAR of the PRC, or the establishment of a "Federated Republic of China" (*Zhongguo lianbang gongheguo*). While the first option seemed to draw heavily on the "one country–two systems" approach being applied in Hong Kong (which has been strongly and consistently criticized in Taiwan), the latter offered the possibility of a federation in accordance with the constitutions of both the PRC and the Republic of China. However, the draft stated that if the Taiwan authorities were to delay indefinitely or obstruct peaceful reunification, or in the event of a declaration or substantive steps toward independence (or outside armed intervention or occupation), "non-peaceful reunification" would be imposed.

Despite its non-formal status as an "academic draft," many of the sentiments expressed in the Wuhan Draft appeared in the "Anti-Secession Law" enacted in March 2005 (CCC-OTW and SC-TAO 2005; "Full text of Anti-Secession Law"). Echoing themes from the "one country–two systems" paradigm, the Anti-Secession Law (ASL) provides, "After the country is reunited peacefully, Taiwan may (*keyi*) practice a system different from that on the Mainland, and enjoy a high degree of autonomy." This language underscores that the reach of autonomy anticipated for Taiwan will remain subject to a discretionary grant of permission. By requiring agreement to reunification negotiations first, China seeks to retain a negotiating advantage to determine what will be the "political status of the Taiwan authorities." The Law reiterated that the China–Taiwan relationship will be based in the PRC Constitution (Art. 1), thus extolling principles of national unity and territorial integrity. The ASL suggests that reunification with Taiwan may proceed on the basis of political equality between authorities on both sides of the Taiwan Strait (Art. 7). The political status of the Taiwan government may be a subject for reunification discussions (Art. 7.4). The ASL also allows for discussion of Taiwan's "room for international operations," thus holding out the promise of some sort of international status.

The policy explanations that accompanied enactment of the ASL suggest that the grant of autonomy will remain discretionary and limited. President Hu Jintao's four point opinion focused on (a) the inviolability of the one-China principle and opposition to purported claims about an independent Taiwan; (b) China's "hope" for peaceful reunification remains a matter of state discretion in the exercise of sovereignty; (c) a purported commonality of interest with "Taiwan compatriots" (*Taiwan tongbao*) concerning unification; and (d) China's commitment to preserving its sovereignty and territorial integrity against Taiwan independence ("Hu Jintao tiqu"). NPC Chair Wu Bangguo's review of the legislative process underpinning the ASL focused similarly on the imperative of protecting China's sovereignty and territorial integrity, echoing priorities he had articulated on Tibet ten years earlier ("Wu 2005: 11–12, 1995). In a nod to the expanded attention given to legalization of relations with the Outer Periphery, Wu also affirmed the importance of constitutional principles associated with the one country–two systems model as the "basic policy for resolving the Taiwan question." Taiwan policy coordinator Jia Qinglin focused similarly on the one country–two systems model as basic Party policy governing the Taiwan issue (Jia 2005). United Front Work Department Director Wang Zhaoguo's official "Explanation" of the ASL also emphasized the one country–two systems constitutional model:

> The structure of "one country–two systems" expresses the principle of achieving national unity, safeguards national sovereignty and territorial integrity, adequately accounts for Taiwan's history and reality, and embodies a high degree of flexibility.
>
> (Wang 2005: 37)

Each of these references to constitutional interpretation affirm the authority of central government to adjust the terms of constitutional interpretation on the one country–two systems principle to accommodate China's sovereignty claims and to respond to the needs of resolving the cross-strait issue. When viewed in conjunction with the PRC's 2000 White Paper, such constitutional references underscore the discretionary grant of authority under which local autonomy for Taiwan might be granted by the central government, and asserts rights to forceful unification under principles of national sovereignty and security. The ASL also reserved the PRC's purportedly sovereign right to reunify with Taiwan by force ("Draft Anti-Secession Law Explained"), a point underscored in China's 2004 White Paper on National Defense which reiterated a determination to crush any Taiwan independence attempt at all costs (SCIO 2004c; "Military to crush").

Even as these aspects of the Chinese government's perspective were retained in Hu Jintao's speech to the Seventeenth CPC National Congress in

October 2007, which took a somewhat optimistic tone—to the point of offering a "peace agreement" on the basis of the "one-China principle" ("Full text of Hu Jintao's report, Section X"). Hu refrained from emphasizing "splittism" in Taiwan, and used the term "homeland" (*jiayuan*) to describe the China that both sides of the Strait share. He drew on imagery of shared destiny used by Taiwan leader Lee Teng-hui to suggest potential for a common identity across the Strait, and declined to emphasize the PRC's claim to use force to unify with Taiwan. Hu's approach, while not foreswearing the potential for "non-peaceful reunification," still offered a more moderate approach to the cross-strait problem, seemingly attentive to the domestic politics of Taiwan and the potential for a change away from Chen Shuibian's independence-oriented policies.

The Taiwan parliamentary elections in January 2008 saw the return of the Guomindang (GMD) to power, with immediate expectations about renewed efforts at reconciliation with the PRC (DeLisle 2008). The victory of former Taipei mayor and GMD candidate Ma Ying-jeou in the Presidential election in March signaled a potential transition away from the confrontational cross-strait policies of Chen Shuibian (Dumbaugh 2008a). While China's continued suppression of the March demonstrations in Tibet forced Ma to take increasingly tough public stands against Chinese policy (Bradsher 2006; Hirsch 2008), in his victory speech Ma affirmed his commitment to stronger economic ties with the Mainland and also pledged no war across the Taiwan Strait ("Opposition's Ma"; "Taiwan leader Ma vows"). Ma's inauguration speech echoed themes of normalization, suggesting a framework for improved relations including "no unification, no independence, no use of force" and committing to maintaining the status quo in the Taiwan Strait ("President Ma's").

Following an invitation for Chinese Premier Wen Jiabao to hold "big-issue" talks ("China's premier invites"), Ma Ying-jeou's Vice President-elect Vincent Siew met Chinese President Hu Jintao on Hainan Island April 12 in the highest level contact since 1949 ("Historic China–Taiwan talks"). GMD Party Chair Wu Po-hsiung then met with Hu Jintao May 28 to discuss the potential for weekend charter flights between Taiwan and the Mainland ("Wu-Hu meeting"; "Taiwan's Ruling Party Chief"). Other initiatives by the Taiwan side included expanded "Mini-Three-Links" travel by Taiwanese to the Mainland via the offshore islands of Jinmen and Matsu, expanded cross-strait charter flight operations and eased restrictions on Mainland media visits to Taiwan (ibid.). This set the stage for renewed talks in Beijing June 11–12 between Taiwan's Mainland Affairs Council and the PRC's Association for Relations Across the Taiwan Strait (ARATS) (Ho 2008). The talks resulted in agreements on charter flights, the opening of permanent offices in each others", territories and expanded PRC tourist travel to Taiwan (Mainland Affairs Council 2008a; Hille 2008b; Dumbaugh 2008b). Chinese President Hu Jintao's public praise for the talks signaled the extent of China's support for expanding economic relations as a route to resolving political issues with Taiwan ("Hu meets"). Shortly thereafter, China enacted regulations governing Mainland tourists' travel to Taiwan ("Regulations on mainland"), reflecting the ongoing effort to "legalize" relations in China's Peripheries.

The resumption of MAC-ARATS talks, success in concluding agreements on economic cooperation, and renewed efforts to conclude a broader economic cooperation framework agreement all suggest significant improvement in the cross-Strait relationship. Clearly both sides have concluded that the confrontational approaches associated with Chen Shuibian had been counterproductive, and seem to have agreed that political issues around reunification can be deferred in favor of closer economic ties. Efforts by Ma's administration to suppress anti-unification protesters ("Mentor urges") seem to reflect further efforts to ingratiate the new government with Beijing, while a cooperation agreement on cross-strait judicial assistance suggests that prior Taiwan government doubts about China's legal system have eased considerably (Hirsch 2009). The arrest, conviction, and sentencing of former president Chen Shuibian to life imprisonment for corruption (Lim and Ong 2009) suggested not only the ongoing dilemma of politicized prosecution of corruption (Ma too had been charged with corruption, but cleared, in 2007—Hille 2007), but also revealed the Ma administration's commitment to sidelining Chen and convincing Beijing of Ma's cooperative intentions. Political arrangements are unlikely to be deferred indefinitely however, and much remains to be determined concerning issues such as Taiwan's international status and the constitutional relationship envisioned by the PRC government.

Society: the regulation of religion

China's policies and practices on regulation of religion have important implications for the Outer Periphery, as religious freedoms are central to the socio-cultural and political worlds of Hong Kong and Taiwan where Buddhism and Christianity are prevalent. China's regulatory regime regards Buddhism as one of the five recognized "normal" religions. Buddhism is depicted as the most successful example of a foreign religion coming to China and becoming Sinicized (Wang Z. 2002: 14). Chinese Buddhism is treated with greater tolerance than its Tibetan counterpart, and has generally been co-opted into the social and political orthodoxy. The Chinese Buddhist Association was established in 1953 and has since been actively cultivated as a "united front" exercise in social regulation. On the other hand, restrictions on Tibetan Buddhism (which is followed not only in Tibet Autonomous Region and the Tibetan areas of Sichuan, Gansu, and Qinghai, but also in Inner Mongolia) are more severe and focus on issues of nationality policy ("Zhonggong zhongyang tongzhanbu") and political questions surrounding the authority of the Dalai Lama (Goldstein and Kapstein 1998). As well, the Chinese Party/state imposes restrictions on international Buddhist social service organizations working in China ("Guowuyuan guanyu Zhonghua").

The Chinese regulatory framework on religion gives particular attention to Christianity ("RAB and Ministry of Public Security"; Elegant 1996; Wong

2001). Catholic churches are primarily under the authority of the Chinese Catholic Patriotic Association and the Chinese Conference of Catholic Bishops, while Protestants are subject to the Three-Self Patriotic Movement and the China Christian Council (MacInnis 1989; HRW/Asia 1997; Merwin and Jones 1963). With its longer history of missionary activity in China and its more formalized hierarchy of clergy professing exclusive loyalty to the Vatican, the Catholic Church has posed particular problems for the CPC regime (Madsen 1998; Friedman *et al.* 1991). Catholic clergy associated with the underground church who refuse to renounce the authority of the Vatican have regularly been singled out for criminal prosecution and repression ("What We Learned"). Regulations issued in 1989 called for stepping up control over the Catholic Church, primarily through increased education and indoctrination of state-approved clergy, strengthening the organizational authority of the Catholic Patriotic Association, repression of "Catholic Underground Forces," and strengthening Party leadership (CPC United Front 1998). Tensions with the Catholic Church have been compounded by the Vatican's diplomatic recognition of Taiwan, although normalization of relations with the Mainland remains a possibility, driven by a combination of liberalization and political realism (Liu and Hesse 2001).

The Protestant Church has reportedly received less attention, due in part to its autonomy from the Vatican (Chan 1993: 124). However, the relative fluidity of Protestant organizational structures, particularly the importance of Congregationalist churches and lay clergy, has posed obstacles for Party/state control, leading for calls to repress Protestant evangelical activities under the guise of controlling illegal "sects" (*xiejiao*) (Pomfret 2002; Li and Fu 2002; Amnesty International 2002; HRW/Asia 1997). The charter for the "Three Self" movement underscores its submission to Party leadership, support for the authority of the state and the socialist Motherland, and obedience to the Constitution, laws, regulations, and policies of the state ("Constitution of the National Committee"). The charter for the China Christian Council is less effusive in its support for Party leadership, but still expresses compliance with the Party/state through a commitment to manage its churches according to China's Constitution, laws, regulations, and policies ("Constitution of the China Christian Council").

Christian religious activities by foreigners are subject to particular controls. This is due in part to a historiography that links Christian missionary work with imperialism, and to fears of international subversion through religion (Luo 1997: 65–66). As well, the government strives for control over religion by insulating religious practitioners and activities from their overseas counterparts ("Fourteen Points"). Evangelical Christians from the United States and Korea have been cited as examples of foreign religious interests interfering with China's independence and autonomy in managing religious affairs ("Vigilance Against": 52–54; HRW/Asia 1997: 33–36). Religious broadcasts, Internet information and literature and materials brought into China from abroad are subject to special inspection and confiscation (RAB and Ministry of Public Security 1995). China's regulatory frameworks for controlling Christianity and (to a lesser extent) Buddhism have particular significance for Hong Kong and Taiwan.

Hong Kong Special Administrative Region

In contrast to China's policies and practices of control over social relations in religion, Hong Kong has a long tradition of socio-cultural autonomy. Recognized under the "no change for 50 years" (*wushi nian bu bian*) ideals of the Basic Law and the Sino-British Declaration, Hong Kong's civic society is particularly evident in the right to freedom of religion. Article 32 of the Hong Kong Basic Law affirms the right of religious freedom in both belief and practice. This is consistent with international law standards contained in the International Covenant on Civil and Political Rights, and stands in distinct contrast from the provisions of PRC Constitution Article 36 restricting religious behavior. As discussed in Chapter 3, PRC orthodoxy permits freedom of belief, but imposes significant restrictions on practice, including education, worship, and the construction and maintenance of religious buildings.

Nonetheless, despite implicit and at times open challenge from local interests supporting China's official policies on religion, a consensus on protecting freedom of religion remains strong in Hong Kong (Leung and Chan 2003: Chapter 4). Such freedom extends not only to religious belief but to action as well. Churches and believers continue to work for a continued role for religion in education and political life (Brown 2006). Hong Kong observers view with alarm China's practices of suppressing perceived threats from religion (Fu 2005: 85–89). Under British rule, religious bodies operated and supported many social service and medical facilities in Hong Kong, offering a potential model for a more tolerant and expansive approach to religious work on the Mainland today.

China's 1984 notice on protection of religious freedoms in Hong Kong did little to alleviate fears about the limitations of PRC law and policy ("Xianggang tebie"). The notice limited religious freedoms to matters of belief subject to law and imposed criteria of "independence, non-interference, and mutual respect" on relations between religious organizations and adherents in Hong Kong with other areas in China, and with civic organizations such as schools and hospitals ("Xianggang tebie": 121). While the reference to existing legal provisions for protection of freedom of religion gave some assurance that the limitations of PRC law would not be imposed to restrict religious behavior, the reliance on a rubric of "freedom of religious belief" invited textual and jurisprudential reliance on Chinese law limitations on religious behavior. Under circumstances where Hong Kong law is either absent or unclear, the potential remains for displacement by PRC legal norms on control of religious practice. Stern warnings from Beijing that *Falun Gong* activities would not be permitted in Hong Kong raised further questions about Hong Kong's autonomy to protect religious freedoms ("'Roundup': Falungong Urged"; "Editorial Views").

While the protection of both belief and conduct stands in important contrast to China's limited protection of belief only, as with other human rights recognized under the Basic Law, provisions on freedom of religion remain subject to interpretation by the NPC Standing Committee (Davis 2003). The future of religious freedoms in Hong Kong will depend significantly on continued efforts by civil society to ensure protection for both belief and behavior.

Taiwan

Recognition and protection of religion in Taiwan expanded with the end of martial law and the emergence of democratic institutions (Laliberte 2006; Rubenstein 2004). Article 13 of the Taiwan Constitution provides that "the people shall have freedom of religious belief." While this text appears to parallel the limited protection of belief offered in PRC law, it is augmented by constitutional freedoms of speech, assembly, and association (Art. 11, 14) that are not subject to the political limitations imposed under the PRC Constitution. Religious organizations may register under the Temple Management Law or other legislation for civic organizations, but are not required to do so (USS-DHRL 2000). In practice constitutionally mandated religious freedoms of belief and behavior are generally respected by the Taiwan government and religious communities (particularly Buddhist and Christian groups) remain important participants in Taiwan society and political economy (Qu 1997). While China's proposals on reunification with Taiwan emphasize preservation of many social freedoms, these remain subject to the limitations on local autonomy (*zizhi*) placed by Chinese law. China's willingness to export the effects of its own laws limiting religious freedoms are evident for example in the legal compliance provisions of the "Administrative Methods for Chinese Citizens Travelling To and From Taiwan" ("Zhongguo gongmin"). These regulations govern conduct of both PRC citizens and Taiwan residents, requiring compliance with Chinese laws and regulations, which would include those restraining religious freedoms.

Economy: globalization and development

China's law, policy, and practice on economy and development in the Outer Periphery seem less intrusive than in the Inner Periphery. Indeed, the economies of Hong Kong and Taiwan are seen as models for China's own development. Nonetheless, the central government has attempted to influence the ways in which economy and development activities affect relations with the China Mainland.

Hong Kong Special Administrative Region

During the 1990s, Hong Kong's economic integration with Mainland China has intensified, with increases in direct investment, trade (largely driven by "buy-back" arrangements between Guangdong factories and their Hong Kong owners), and travel (both business and tourism). Ongoing proposals for greater institutional integration have been largely unsuccessful, however, due alternatively to reluctance by the Hong Kong government to become subject to problematic regulatory arrangements on the Mainland and to reticence by the Guangdong provincial government to allow Hong Kong to divert central government economic inducements. The 1997 Asia financial crisis hit Hong Kong hard, resulting in four successive years of stagnation and increasing government deficits. Despite efforts to encourage temporary labor arrangements for PRC nationals to work in Hong Kong ("Regulations Governing Labour"), the steady pattern of manufacturing facilities moving from Hong Kong to Guangdong province since the late 1980s transformed the structure of the Hong Kong economy, such that services now dominate. During Tung Chee-hwa's first term as Chief Executive (1997–2002), the government spent heavily on infrastructure, employment and training programs, and social services (Tung 2004). The subsequent administration of Donald Tsang (2005–) has focused on economic links with the Chinese mainland ("Action Agenda"). Throughout, the government has emphasized the role of professional and technical elites in maintaining Hong Kong's prosperity (Tsang 2005), which raises the prospect of a more politically astute and activist populace, raising challenges for the Hong Kong and Chinese governments.

The Hong Kong Basic Law provides for independent administration of the SAR economy. Interpretations of the Basic Law and its application to the economy will have ongoing significance for governance in Hong Kong (Ma Y. 2003). Property rights are recognized in Article 6 of the Basic Law, while Article 105 provides protection for acquisition, use, disposal and inheritance of property and the right to compensation for lawful deprivation of property. Although these enforcement provisions remain subject to the limitations on existing law, thus raising questions about possible changes, they remain predicated on an accepted right of private property. However, in light of ongoing policy debates in China proper over harmonizing private property rights with the public interest and China's socialist system (Hao 2006; Zhou G. 2006; Dickie 2006; Powell 2007), continuous references to protection by law may potentially work to undermine private property rights in Hong Kong. Even as China has acknowledged Hong Kong's separate social and economic systems, the potential for creeping influence by PRC doctrines on private property remains high.

The Basic Law (BL) requires that the Hong Kong SAR have independent finances, retaining its own revenue and being free from taxation by the Chinese central government (BL: Art. 106). This aims to avoid any implication that the Chinese government will provide local subsidies, and ensure that Hong Kong remains free from Mainland taxes. The SAR government is required to pursue balanced budgets (BL: Art. 107), although as the experience of 1997–2001 indicated, this is a matter of principle rather than practice. The SAR government is directed under the Basic Law to provide an economic and legal environment appropriate to maintain Hong Kong's status as an international financial center (BL: Art. 109). While this may conjure imagery of Hong Kong's heady past status as Asia's leading financial center, those days seem long gone in the wake of the emergence of Tokyo and Singapore as competitors. Moreover PRC policy goals around the establishment of Shanghai as an international financial center raise further prospects of diminishing Hong Kong's leading financial status ("Shanghai outlines"). Whether pursuing status as an international financial center will see Hong Kong continue to protect meaningfully independent legal and policy arrangements for managing finance and the economy remains to be determined. While the Hong Kong government is authorized to maintain independent monetary and financial policies, including foreign exchange, securities markets, and currency policy (BL: Arts. 110–13), such independence might quite easily be interpreted to suit PRC governance norms rather than according to the relatively independent administrative standards associated with Hong Kong under British colonial rule. Hong Kong has maintained its free port status (BL: Arts. 114, 115), and is empowered to retain independent membership in international trade agreements such as the General Agreement on Tariffs and Trade (GATT) and the WTO (BL: Art. 116). Here again the ideals of statutory language may not fully suit the practical realities of China's influence.

The Hong Kong SAR Government is required under the Basic Law to provide economic and legal environments to encourage investment, technology, and new industries, while adopting policies to promote manufacturing, commerce, tourism, real estate, transportation and other services (BL: Arts. 118–19). The Basic Law also provides specific requirements for administration of land leases, maritime transportation, and civil aviation, which in effect retain agreements concluded prior to the 1997 handover and commit the government to maintaining Hong Kong's status as an international transport center. Despite the imagery of Hong Kong as a *laissez-faire* economy, in fact the government retains significant control over socio-economic infrastructure, allocation and regulation of investment opportunities in many economic sectors such as land, telecommunications, and transportation (Overholt 2004). This seems unlikely to change, as it reinforces both the control imperatives of the central PRC government and the interests of an emerging elite of pro-Beijing business and community leaders. Beijing has a strong interest in maintaining control over Hong Kong as an entrepôt to the world economy and ensuring that the SAR's economic strength neither diminishes economic growth prospects for other regions in China nor encourages sensibilities of separatism. Carrying out such efforts indirectly through the SAR government under the context of the Basic Law is consistent with patterns of economic development policy in China's Inner Periphery, where national development interests remain a paramount concern.

Similar strategies would seem to be very much on the agenda of the Hong Kong SAR. The SAR government has worked to incorporate principles of

China's Eleventh Five Year Plan into local development policy programming in areas such as financial reform (particularly on questions about currency exchange rates); transportation infrastructure (including highway development and expanding rail links between Hong Kong's container terminals and ports and depots in China); service sector development (including stronger regulation of legal services and expanding business and information services); and attending to regional coordinated development between Hong Kong SAR and counterpart regions in China (including Shanghai) ("Action Agenda"). Formulated pursuant to conditions of autonomy conferred under the Basic Law, but also keenly mindful of the need to coordinate with other regions and interests in China proper, the Action Agenda reveals an effort to maintain Hong Kong's economic development trajectory through a strategic combination of concessions to potential competitors (Shanghai for example) and assertions of local competitive advantage (such as well-regulated legal and business services).

Hong Kong's economic development agenda remains contingent on the SAR's position as a component of China's Outer Periphery. Hong Kong's traditional status as a global economic hub combines with potential benefits of economic integration driven by socio-cultural and geographic proximity with China. Yet these are also limited by Hong Kong's governance status subject to PRC rule and by associated resistance from competing economic and political interests in China. The long-term dynamic relationship among these factors will determine Hong Kong's economic prospects for the foreseeable future.

Taiwan

Taiwan's "economic miracle" has laid a foundation for local sensibilities about Taiwan's *de facto* independence and influenced expectations about autonomy from the Mainland. Economic links between Taiwan and the PRC offer powerful incentives for peaceful reunification and for meaningful autonomy for Taiwan (Tung 2003; Xiandai xueshu 2002; Cheng 2005). China's efforts to legalize relations with Taiwan through constitutional provisions on Taiwan's unity with the Mainland and supporting the establishment of an SAR for Taiwan extend to economic affairs. The PRC government has sought to build support for its reunification policies among the Taiwan business community through a series of measures to encourage and protect investments, attempting to allay concerns that China's socialist policies would undermine commercial opportunities (Zhang W. 2003). The 1988 "Regulations on Encouraging Investment by Taiwan Compatriots" ("Guanyu guli Taiwan") were part of a broader effort to encourage foreign investment through incentives in matters of taxation, land use fees, and approval preferences. The 1994 "Law on Protecting Investments by Taiwan Investors" ("ZRG Taiwan ... baohu fa," hereafter "TIPL") and their 1999 "Implementing Measures" ("ZRG Taiwan ... shishi xize," hereafter "TIPL-IR") confirmed government commitments to insulate the property and investment rights of Taiwan businesses from political fallout of disputes over cross-strait relations. The TIPL and implementing regulations for protecting Taiwan investment are aimed at creating favorable conditions for investment, assuring Taiwan businesses that their assets in China will not be expropriated or nationalized, insulating Taiwan businesses operating in China from arbitrary fees and bureaucratic intrusion, and generally to further economic and ultimately political integration between Taiwan and China (Zhang W. 2003).

The TIPL contains guarantees that investments, investment interests, and other legal interests of Taiwan nationals will be protected by law (TIPL: Art. 3). The law assures Taiwan investors of their rights to form foreign invested enterprises—including joint ventures, cooperative enterprises, and wholly foreign-owned enterprises—in China, repatriate profits, and exercise managerial autonomy in their Mainland businesses (in contrast to the term "*zizhiquan*" used to denote autonomy on political issues, the broader term "*zizhuquan*" is used to convey autonomy in business terms) (TIPL: Art. 9). The law emphasizes the role of mediation in dispute resolution for Taiwan investments, although it does allow for arbitration and judicial litigation (TIPL: Art. 14). The TIPL-Implementing Regulations (IR) reiterate principles of protection and encouragement for Taiwan investments and provide additional detail for the provisions of the underlying law. As well, the Implementing Regulations affirm the right of Taiwan investors to use the judicial review mechanisms of China's legal regime for administrative reconsideration and administrative litigation to appeal bureaucratic action they believe is unlawful (TIPL-IR: Art. 28). The TIPL-IR clarifies that Taiwan nationals may serve as members of arbitration panels handling disputes involving Taiwan investments (TIPL-IR: Art. 29).

As well, the Taiwan investment protection scheme also imposes on Taiwan investors the obligation to conform to Chinese laws and regulations (TIPL: Art. 3). Taiwan investors are also expected to adapt to national social and economic development plans and conform to the requirements of state industrial policies and directions (TIPL-IR: Art. 6). Investigating issues of implementation in coastal provinces of Fujian and Guangdong (also Jiangsu, Zhejiang, and Shandong), the central government exercised close supervision and monitoring to ensure compliance with the protection provisions for Taiwan investment (Zhang W. 2003: 51). In 1996, the Taiwan Affairs Office of the State Council established a national Taiwan investment coordination office, and issued "Working Methods" for coordinating Taiwan investment (ibid.). By 2003, over 30 provincial and municipal governments, including Fujian, Guangdong, Zhejiang, Jiangsu, Shandong, Beijing, Nanjing, and Chongqing had enacted local measures for protecting Taiwan investments (Zhang W. 2003: 52).

China's Taiwan investment protection regime suggests a somewhat conflicted approach to investment relations with Taiwan. On one hand, most of the investment incentives and protections afforded Taiwan investors under

Chinese law parallel those granted foreign investors from other countries. This is aimed to assure Taiwan investors that they will not be discriminated against formally in China, by virtue of their being from Taiwan. However, the political reality of cross-strait relations introduces elements of informal pressure that are not captured by the legal regime. Thus, in the context of Taiwan elections or other political events, Taiwan business people in China are routinely subjected to special attention from the regulatory and political authorities. As well, the informal understandings that protect foreign business people from the rigid application of Chinese law in matters of civic administration and criminal law are not extended in all cases to Taiwanese, hence the requirement of compliance with Chinese law operates quite differently for Taiwanese as opposed to foreign businesspeople. Thus, China's Taiwan investment regime reflects the complexities of cross-strait relations, even as it attempts to pursue political ends through economic means.

Similarly with trade relations, China's regulatory regime pursues goals of economic integration aimed ultimately at building political accommodation. Promotion of cross-straits trade was given legal expression through measures on small-scale trading, allowing greater business autonomy in import–export trade, and trade administration ("Dui Taiwan diqu xiao'e"; "Guanyu fangkai"; "Dui Taiwan diqu maoyi"). The 2000 "Administrative Measures for Trade with the Region of Taiwan" extends to trade in goods, technology and services ("Dai Taiwan diqu maoyi": Art. 2). The "Measures" require that trade relations not undermine China's national security or public interest (Art. 3). Reflecting increasing political tensions across the strait in 1999–2000 with the election of Chen Shuibian in Taiwan, the "Measures" provided that cross-strait trade contracts may not contain language or diagrams (such as maps) that contradict the "one-China" policy and may not have provisions that obstruct the unification of China (as might occur in contract clauses on matters of choice of law, dispute resolution, or reference to international law and organizations) (Art. 6). Trans-shipment in Hong Kong and Macao is permitted, but subject to Chinese law for these SARs (Art. 9). Disputes are to be handled through mediation, although arbitration and judicial litigation is permitted (Art. 12). Similar provisions are in force for "small scale trading" (*xiao'e maoyi*), to regulate the traditional trade and transport activities of the maritime cultures of the China coast and prevent smuggling ("Dui Taiwan diqu xiao'e").

China's policy on economic linkages with Taiwan as a building block for political unification has supported the so-called "three links" (*san tong*) of transportation, mail services, and telecommunication (Zhang Z. 2003; *Liang'an san tong*). China's regulatory framework for sea and air transport with Taiwan expands infrastructure support for economic integration ("Taiwan haiyan liang'anjian hangyun guanli banfa"; "Guanyu Taiwan haiyan liang'anjian huowu yunshu dailiye guanli banfa"; "Guanyu jiaqiang Taiwan haiyan liang'an jianjie jizhuangxiang banlun yunshu guanli de tongzhi"). While the Taiwan government has sought to narrow the "three links" (*san tong*) through a "mini three links" program that emphasizes ties between Taiwan's offshore islands of Quemoy and Matsu and the Mainland province of Fujian (Tsai 2001), China's entry to the WTO and the effort to build an economic integration zone including Hong Kong suggests the extent to which China sees infrastructural linkages as a first step toward political unification (Wang and Wang 2003; Fu 1999, 2000; Xie 2003a: 478–79, 499–503, 480–81). The initiatives surrounding a proposed cross-straits Economic Cooperation Framework Agreement (ECFA) suggest further efforts to build political integration through regulating cooperation over economic matters. Informal talks on the ECFA were resumed in November 2009, three new Memoranda of Understanding were concluded on cooperation in banking, insurance and securities ("Top Trade Official"; "Taiwan, China sign MOUs").

China's regulatory regime for Taiwan business in the Mainland includes measures on advertising, patent cooperation, technology transfer, and intellectual property protection and expresses the Chinese government's efforts to attract Taiwan-based business to the Mainland ("Guanyu jiaqiang haiyan liang'an guanggao"; "Guanyu dui haiyan liang'an zhuanli"; "Zai zuguo dalu xingban"; "Guanyu chuban Taiwan"; "Guanyu shouli Taibao"). Intellectual property protection for Taiwan business operating on the Mainland proceeds on the basis of equality between Taiwan and Mainland "compatriots" (*tongbao*) and their equal submission to China's intellectual property regulatory bureaucracy, whether for patents, trademarks, or copyrights, thus underscoring China's policy view that Taiwan remains part of the PRC (Zhang W. 2003: 43–50). Yet by their references to the parity of status between Taiwan and other PRC provinces and directly administered cities, by noting that Chinese law (including implied conflicts of law rules) grants recognition of Taiwan law for activities in Taiwan, and by promoting Taiwan business investment in China, these measures formalize Beijing's policy preferences on cross-strait economic relations according to principles of one-China, supremacy of Chinese law, and promotion of cross-straits ties (Zhang W. 2003: 19–22).

As with other aspects of its approach to management of economy and development relations in the Outer Periphery, China's legalization of policy preferences regarding Taiwan remains subject to constraints of the international system. China's membership in the General Agreement on Tariffs and Trade (GATT) has long been complicated by the question about Taiwan's membership (Feinerman 1992). China's accession to the WTO established institutional constraints on trade relations with Taiwan ("Protocol of Accession"; "Report of the Working Party"; Clarke 2009). The Republic of China was a founding member of the GATT, and withdrew after being driven off the Mainland and conceding that it could not uphold its legal obligations concerning GATT compliance. Thus, China's application to rejoin the GATT was inextricably intertwined with questions about Taiwan's political status. As well, economic and political reforms on Taiwan since 1989 brought the Republic of China more closely into compliance with GATT and WTO disciplines than China. This raised delicate questions about the legitimacy of international processes aimed at bringing China into the WTO even though it was not in compliance with GATT disciplines and at the same time excluding the GATT-compliant economic and political system of Taiwan. Ultimately, the compromise reached involved initial entry by China (with concessions and commitments promising to achieve GATT compliance within specified timeframes) and the following day an agreement (from which China abstained) to grant admission to Taiwan as a customs territory of China.

While China's motivations to join the GATT and WTO were many and varied, Taiwan policy was certainly a factor. Chinese policy specialists expect that WTO membership for China and Taiwan will bring on increasing convergence of economic systems, as both China and Taiwan gradually come into full compliance with GATT disciplines on subsidies, dumping, intellectual property and market access (Yan and Zhang 2004). The increasing competitiveness of China in manufacturing and its steady expansion in advanced technology areas has led some observers in Taiwan to worry that China will ultimately displace Taiwan in its comparative advantage technology and consumer goods sectors (Li 2001; Li *et al.* 2001). Others assert that because it is more open and integrated more closely with globalized markets, the Taiwan economy is relatively insulated from Chinese competition or economic aggression (Tung 2003). The linkage of cross-strait economic relations with the broader integration of a greater China economic league (*Da Zhongguo jingji tuan*) or common market (*Da zhonghua gongtong shichang*) including Hong Kong and Macao remains a fond hope of those who seek peaceful and depoliticized relations between Taiwan and the Mainland (Huang 2004). Disparate uses of the GATT "special safeguards provision" and differences in approach to the WTO Dispute Resolution Understanding suggest that the WTO offers as much support for contention as it does for cooperation (Ostry *et al.* 2002). Nonetheless, the potential for increased complementarity between Taiwan and the Mainland economies remains strong, as normalization of cross-strait relations brought on by shared WTO membership accompanied by ongoing efforts to forestall political and security crises allows the two sides to build some degree of mutual accommodation (Gao 2002).

The political victories of the Guomindang and Ma Ying-jeou in 2008 served to heighten the potential for economic integration (Bradsher and Wong 2008). Following the parliamentary elections in January, banking regulators in Beijing and Taiwan agreed to allow Taiwan banks to acquire shares in mainland banks through subsidiaries in Hong Kong (Hille 2008a). Starting with a deal involving Taiwan's Fubon Bank working through its Hong Kong subsidiary to acquire a stake in Xiamen Commercial Bank, the agreement raised the prospect of greater cross-straits financial integration. The second round of "Chiang-Chen" talks of November 2008 saw new arrangements for charter flights—shortening routes, allowing daily flights, and increasing the number of available airports ("Once hostile Taiwan"; Mainland Affairs

Council 2008b). While the Chinese ARATS representative Chen Yunlin faced popular protests and was trapped in his hotel by violent protesters ("Top envoy trapped"), the talks nonetheless resulted in further agreements on direct shipping and flights, postal services, and food safety ("Taiwan leader"; "Beijing–Taipei sign"). Under the agreement, direct flights were begun between eight Taiwan and 21 China cities, including Taipei, Beijing, and Shanghai, while China agreed to open 63 ports and Taiwan 11 to shipping links (Wong 2008d). A new round of talks held in early 2009 to address financial services—an issue made more urgent by the international financial crisis that unfolded in September–October 2008. While negotiations over the CECF appeared to stall in late 2009, reflecting perhaps fundamental differences of expectation—the PRC continuing to aim for political integration through economic cooperation and the Ma government focusing more on building specific protections for Taiwan's economic growth—continuation and the conclusion of a modest agreement seem likely.

China's regulatory approach to relations with Taiwan has been aimed at accommodating closer economic integration as a path to political reunification. China's effort to "legalize" its economic relations with Taiwan fits a pattern already evident in Hong Kong. While Beijing will not countenance economic relations contradicting the "one-China" policy, pragmatic approaches to trade and investment relations with Taiwan suggest a broad approach of accommodation. Such contending perspectives on Taiwan's position in China's Outer Periphery will continue to dictate conditions for economic change and development.

Normative and organizational perspectives

In the Outer Periphery, factors of selective adaptation and institutional capacity are evident, revealing normative and organizational dimensions of PRC law and policy on governance, the economy, and culture.

Selective Adaptation

The dynamics of selective adaptation are evident in China's law, policy, and practices on political authority in the Outer Periphery. In each of these elements of governance, factors of perception, complementarity, and legitimacy play a role.

Political authority

In matters of political authority, factors of perception influence the central government's reactions to political initiatives on such matters as elections in Hong Kong and the so-called independence movement in Taiwan. Thus, the democracy movement in Hong Kong is depicted as "unpatriotic" and aimed at overthrowing Party leaders (Kahn 2004), while political campaigns in

Taiwan centered on identity issues are deemed a threat to China's territorial integrity (Jia 2005). As well, idealistic perceptions about solidarity between overseas Chinese and Taiwan "compatriots" (*tongbao*) on the one hand and China's national integration program on the other helped to inform norms about both methods and standards for the one China policy. Perceptions borne of historical circumstances—particularly the colonial experience in both Hong Kong and Taiwan—have done much to fuel perceptions about the hostile intentions of international forces and their collusion with local communities seeking more meaningful autonomy. These perceptions were evident in China's negotiating positions on the Sino-British declaration for Hong Kong (Roberti 1996), and in legislative initiatives resulting in the basic law of Hong Kong SAR and the anti-secession law regarding Taiwan.

Dynamics of complementarity have also been evident, particularly in China's reliance on interpretations of international law norms as a basis for supporting its claims to sovereignty over Taiwan. Both the State Council's 2000 Taiwan White Paper and the 2005 Anti-Secession Law rely heavily on international law justifications for China's assertion of the right to use force to protect sovereignty and territorial integrity. International law standards on constitutional interpretation and sovereignty are also complementary with China's assertions of the right to intrude on constitutional arrangements for Hong Kong and to retain the final authority in interpreting the Basic Law through the NPC Standing Committee.

The factors of legitimacy are also evident as China remains keenly sensitive to international criticism of its handling of the resumption of sovereignty over Hong Kong and its policies toward Taiwan. Repeated efforts at the United Nations and in bilateral and multilateral fora to depict China's policies as lawful and to reject as interventionist criticisms from the United States and other observers reveal the extent to which legitimacy remains a key determinant in China's selective adaptation of international norms of governance. Legitimacy remains a critical factor in China's claims to political sovereignty – based in no small part on commitments to accept the autonomy of Hong Kong and ultimately Taiwan. Frequent statements about preserving local economic autonomy and development are presented as key elements of China's governance proposals and are intended to assuage local concerns about PRC intrusion. Models of shared interest in economic growth are fundamental underpinnings of China's claims to legitimacy in governance of the Outer Periphery.

Social regulation and religion

As with China's positions on governance and the economy, perception and complementarity with international law norms are key elements in China's normative position. The fact that uniform standards of human rights and religious freedoms are largely absent from the international legal discourse allows China to be selective in its use of international norms as a basis for explaining its behavior. Yet the disparity between China's restrictive approach to religious practice and the broader international recognition of freedoms of religious belief and behavior standards as a barrier to full complementarity of PRC and international standards. As well, repeated references to scientific discourse draw closely on international academic and intellectual discourses of secularism that are used to challenge the privileges attributed to organized religion in the Outer Periphery.

Legitimacy also plays a role, particularly in China's criticism of US support for religious freedoms in the outer periphery. Depicting the United States as abusing support for religious freedom as a basis for political intervention reflects China's effort to compete with the US for legitimacy in social regulation. As it has done in the Inner Periphery, China's efforts to rebut US criticisms and to raise independent critiques of its own about US human rights and religious policy reflect the extent to which legitimacy remains important as a source of Chinese selective adaptation behavior.

Economic relations

Perceptions about essential affinities between Chinese communities in Taiwan and Hong Kong and counterparts in the Mainland have much to do with the PRC's policies encouraging investment and trade exchanges among overseas Chinese. The fact that these are managed through the United Front Work Department of the CPC Central Committee suggests that such confidence is not unlimited. Nonetheless perceptions about ethnic affinity play a large role in China's policies on trade and investment in the Outer Periphery. As well, perceptions about the inherent strengths and potential for economic autonomy of Taiwan and Hong Kong have had a significant impact on China's policies toward integration. Thus, expanding Chinese investment in Hong Kong and tolerance of ever closer cross-strait economic ties reflect an effort to constrain potential for economic and ultimately political autonomy of Hong Kong and Taiwan. Perceptions about potential links between economic and political integration continue to inform PRC efforts to establish an economic cooperation framework across the Taiwan Strait.

Complementarity also plays a role in China's efforts to conform its economic regulatory standards and processes to economic conditions in Taiwan and Hong Kong. The fundamental similarity of the civilian legal systems in Taiwan and mainland China offer a major example of complementarity. Indeed, China's own legal reform activities particularly in areas of property and business law are heavily influenced by the Taiwan experience. With Hong Kong, by contrast, the common law system of Hong Kong has many features that are contrary to practices in the PRC. Nonetheless, significant efforts have been made by China to build complementarity between the two systems—notably intensive and wide ranging support for economic and business exchanges, joint training programs, and efforts at legislative coordination.

Legitimacy also plays a role, particularly in the ways that China has relied on accession to the WTO as a talisman for its legitimacy as the sovereign trade authority for the greater China region, to which are attached Hong Kong and Taiwan as customs territories. Mindful of potential challenges, China has been loath to be drawn into the WTO dispute settlement process by Taiwan (Hsieh 2005), and been careful to avoid concessions on statutory jurisdiction and interpretation on matters of commercial law that overlap the Mainland–Hong Kong border (Zhang and Smart 2006).

As with circumstances of political relations, China's policies of governance on economic relations in the Outer Periphery reveal the effects of selective adaptation. While the elements of selective adaptation in the Inner and Outer Periphery vary considerably, the general pattern has many similarities. In each region, China's governance programs for economic development reveal the ways in which international standards on local development and on globalized trade and investment relations are mediated by value preferences of interpretive communities.

Institutional Capacity

Institutional capacity factors are evident in China's practices of political authority in the Outer Periphery.

Political authority

Issues of institutional purpose around issues of reunification, state sovereignty and territorial integrity are evident in policies and practice with regard to Hong Kong and Taiwan (one country–two systems). China's positions on the legislative council, elections for the chief executive, and political and legal institutional reform in Hong Kong reflect tensions over the extent to which imperatives of sovereignty are to be tempered by legal commitments to local autonomy under the Basic Law and the Sino-British Joint Declaration. Repeated visits by constitutional and legal scholars to Hong Kong to articulate China's legal interpretations of constitutional arrangements and policy preferences are often met with highly sophisticated legal arguments from the Hong Kong Bar that often suggest the mainland and Hong Kong perspectives are couched in different institutional languages. Delegations from the PRC repeatedly indicate China's right and authority to intervene at the point where local assertions of autonomy exceed Beijing's tolerance, whereas Hong Kong law specialists continue to focus on legal analysis of agreed constitutional texts as limitations on the behavior of the state. These differences of institutional purpose unavoidably have an impact on the effectiveness of China's practices in Hong Kong.

Similarly, with regard to issues of cross-strait relations, factors of institutional purpose are evident in official interpretations of the PRC Anti-Secession

Law and reactions to political developments in Taiwan asserting varying claims to autonomy. In contrast to the well-trained, well-prepared, and well-staffed cohorts of legal specialists on issues ranging from trade relations to constitutional interpretation that are used to bolster Taiwan's negotiating positions (Chen 2003), China's resources seem directed toward generally single-purpose issues of sovereignty and territorial integrity. As a result, similarly with Hong Kong, the complexity of issues suggested by Taiwan negotiators tends to be boiled down to single issue debates by counterparts from the PRC. These conflicts of institutional purpose have an impact on the capacity of China to achieve its institutional goals.

Naturally, institutional location plays an important role. The embeddedness of a southern China/Guangdong social culture in Hong Kong poses innumerable obstacles to Beijing's attempt to manage the region. Few officials within the State Council Hong Kong/Macau affairs office speak Cantonese well, or have lengthy experience in the region. This tends to privilege perspectives centered on North China and central government sensibilities regards Hong Kong that stand significantly at variance from the localized perceptions (that include globalized sensitivities) of Hong Kong counterparts. With regard to Taiwan, although the important role of Jia Qinglin as coordinator for Taiwan policy draws upon Jia's lengthy experience in Fujian Province, the uneven extent of local knowledge on Taiwan among China's central government units—including the CASS Taiwan Research Institute (*Taiyansuo*), and the NPC and State Council offices on Taiwan leads frequently to miscalculations about electoral politics and social behavior.

Institutional orientation is of particular importance. China's governance culture may be described in terms of patrimonial sovereignty (Potter 2004). Drawing on traditional norms of Confucianism combined with ideals of revolutionary transformation drawn from Marxism–Leninism and Maoism, regulatory culture in China tends to emphasize governance by a political authority that remains largely immune to challenge (Lieberthal 1995; SCIO 2001). During the first 30 years of the PRC, law and regulation served primarily as instruments for enforcing policies of the Party/state. Norms and processes for accountability were dismissed as bourgeois artifacts deemed inappropriate to China's revolutionary conditions. By the turn of the twenty-first century, even after 20 years of legal reform, the supremacy for the Party/state remains a salient feature in the regulatory process (Potter 2001). Whether the policy aim is military re-strengthening, economic growth or social welfare, accountability is determined nearly exclusively by Party and governmental leaders rather than through popular participation. The patrimonialism of Confucianized Marxism–Leninism Mao Zedong Thought combines with the sovereignty of Party/state supremacy to establish a powerful modality of governance in the PRC. Patrimonial sovereignty is thus a typology of governance by which regulators are accountable primarily to their bureaucratic and political superiors, and as a result have few obligations to heed the subjects of rule in the process or substance of regulation.

By contrast, the legal systems of Hong Kong and Taiwan are grounded in principles of liberalism (Ma 1996; Hsu 1994). Liberalism proceeds from tenets about human equality and natural law, the liberal tradition of political ideology asserts that government should be an agency of popular will (Kymlicka 1991). Such agency requires accountability, from political leaders through democratic elections and from administrative agencies acting within the limits of lawfully delegated authority. Responsible Agency is thus a typology by which regulators and their political superiors are accountable to the subjects of regulation, and as a result are expected to exercise regulatory authority broadly in accordance with norms of transparency and the rule of law (Potter 2004). The influence of liberal norms on the legal and political cultures of Hong Kong and Taiwan remains powerful, ever more so as these areas of the Outer Periphery engage ever more closely with the realities or prospects of governance from Beijing. The complexities of integrating the normative and operational dimensions of the Taiwan and Mainland legal systems (Zheng 2007; Fu 2005; Wang and Chen 2000) reflect differences of institutional orientation and pose a significant obstacle to China's willingness to accommodate the relatively liberal rule of law system that operates in Taiwan. Similarly questions arise over closer integration of the Hong Kong and PRC legal systems (Tang 2004).

The legal instrumentalism that characterizes the operation of the Chinese legal system generally informs China's interpretations of constitutional principles on local autonomy in the Outer Periphery. China's policy preferences remain the final determinant in discussions about local autonomy in Hong Kong. The law of the PRC on stationing troops in Hong Kong ("Zhu jun fa") also adopts a generally accommodating perspective on local concerns, expressed as a matter of text but with significant uncertainty as to implementation. Similarly with Taiwan, the State Council White Paper (2000) and the Anti-Secession Law and its attendant policy prescriptions express an institutional orientation of formalism that underscores China's discretion to limit assertions of local autonomy in name of national sovereignty. Such orientation works effectively to articulate and justify China's policy preferences, but remains of limited effect in furthering practical or conceptual engagement with counterpart legal and political communities in the outer periphery and beyond.

Tensions between responsible agency and patrimonial sovereignty suggest that conflicts over governance models in the Outer Periphery will remain strong. While gradual convergence is possible, China's insistence on application of its Constitutional norms of the unitary state suggests resistance to liberal influences that would permit significant local autonomy. While China's law and policy approach to relations with the Outer Periphery will continue to be influenced by the international context, the underlying tension between liberal and socialist approaches to law and governance suggest that mutual accommodation will be a complex and difficult process.

Institutional cohesion remains a key element in China's policy practice. Factors of bureaucratic politics influence the staffing, mission, and political influence of the leading small groups charged with policy management on Hong Kong and Taiwan (Lam 2004). Personnel changes in State Council and NPC departments governing Hong Kong and Taiwan, as well as differences in policy interpretation between and within these units affect their capacity. Interpretations of the Hong Kong Basic Law emerging from the State Council Hong Kong and Macau Affairs Office can be seen to differ in modest ways from those expressed in Hong Kong by delegations from Beijing. For example the assertions by the State Council Hong Kong and Macao Affairs Office that Hong Kong's autonomy would be protected under the Hong Kong Basic Law supported Office directives supporting a general hands off policy in the first years after the handover. In contrast, statements by visiting delegations as well as by national leaders criticizing conduct of the Hong Kong government and suggesting that intervention from Beijing was a real possibility suggest a lack of cohesion in policy interpretation and application (Pan 2004; Kahn 2004). Personnel changes—particularly the role of Zeng Qinghong on Hong Kong affairs—raise a host of political questions involving loyalties to Jiang Zemin and Hu Jintao that invite policy conflict. With regard to Taiwan, Hu Jintao's leadership over the Taiwan affairs leading small group invites potential conflict with supporters of Jia Qinglin, a long-standing Jiang Zemin appointee. As well, personnel changes in the CASS *Taiyansuo* also have resulted in emergence of harder line positions than had been the case in the past, inviting questions about institutional cohesion. Thus on both issues of political governance and social regulation, institutional cohesion remains a factor. As a result, China's effectiveness in building support for its policies remains a matter of political loyalty rather than substantive constitutional discourse.

Social regulation and religion

Factors of institutional capacity are also evident in China's social regulatory practices regarding expectations about freedom of religion. Factors of institutional purpose arise around the goals of regulation of religion, which in turn are tied closely to issues of political authority and also raise tension about the meaning of local autonomy. This invites questions about the boundaries between social autonomy and political regulation which come into sharp relief on issues of religious education, and the freedom of political activity by religious organizations. China's positions on the role of the *Falun Gong* in Hong Kong, and also China's efforts to limit communication with international organizations supporting local autonomy in Tibet and Xinjiang draw unavoidably on discourses of suppression of religious extremism and terrorism, which draw upon China's policy preferences on control of religion in the Inner Periphery. The extent to which China's institutional purposes on control of religion reflect differences of perspective between a central government and local communities in the Outer Periphery manifest issues of institutional location, which in turn affect other elements of institutional capacity. Lack of local knowledge, wariness about the motives of local communities, and preoccupation with central policy imperatives invite particular tensions over questions about institutional location.

As with other elements of China's governance in the Outer Periphery, institutional orientation—particularly the formalism of constitutional legal arrangements—continues in evidence. As with its policies on religion in the Inner Periphery, China insists on compliance with PRC law which in turn invites the application of formalistic discourses on what such compliance requires. The fact that China's approach to legislative supremacy is coupled with the realities of Party dominance over legislative processes in content and the general absence of democratic restraints, means in effect that the state legislates its own policy preferences and then imposes these on social relations such as freedom of religion, all in the name of compliance with law. The extent to which such orientation stands at variance with the rule of law discourses and practices well entrenched in Hong Kong and Taiwan simply underscores the potential for conflict and lack of communication. In part, this explains the position of both the Taiwan government and the Hong Kong Bar that relations with China will depend on the emergence of a genuine rule of law system.

Institutional Cohesion questions also arise, as China's government departments charged with regulation of religion (particularly the State Council Religious Affairs Bureau and the Party's United Front Work Department) confront the vagaries of bureaucratic politics and personnel changes. These departments also face the challenges of maintaining disciplined enforcement among their constituent members for policy ideals separating religion from socio-economic and political relations under circumstances where, on both the Mainland and in the Outer Periphery, religious organizations and believers are deeply embedded in daily life.

Economic relations

Institutional capacity is also evident in China's policies for economic relations in the Outer Periphery. Factors of institutional purpose are evident in economic regulatory relations with Hong Kong and Taiwan on questions as to whether the purpose of economic links is further economic development and growth alone or rather to support broader aims of political integration and control. Thus, legislative and administrative cooperation between the government of the Hong Kong SAR and the central government on issues of economic regulation often run into questions about the purpose of central government demands which can be perceived as driven by issues of political control rather than economic facilitation. Similarly, PRC institutions charged with managing cross-straits economic ties often face questions about the underlying policy agenda of political integration, or economic growth. Naturally institutional location also plays a role as the government agencies of China charged with governance of economic relations in the

Outer Periphery remain headquartered in Beijing with little on-site presence in Hong Kong, let alone Taiwan. These factors of institutional location have an impact on the relative effect of policy proposals coming from the region itself and policy direction coming from Beijing. Factors of institutional orientation are also evident, as preferences for more laissez-faire economic policies in Hong Kong and Taiwan confront lingering preferences for ongoing state control from PRC policy officials and regulators. Institutional cohesion is also a key factor, as evidenced by the examples of PRC-nominated officials and business leaders in China invested companies operating in Hong Kong who face corruption charges and complaints. Links with Taiwan are too attenuated to address with certainty, although indicators from the Taiwan community in Shanghai are that the institutional cohesion of China's regulatory institutions charged with overseeing Taiwan investments in the mainland is affected by factors of corruption.

Summary

Thus, despite obvious differences of history, location, and local conditions, PRC law, policy, and practices for governance in Hong Kong and proposed for Taiwan suggest fundamental similarities with central government approaches to governance in the Inner Periphery areas of Tibet, Xinjiang, and Inner Mongolia. The dominance of a constitutional arrangement dependent on interpretation by the central government, the primacy of national sovereignty and security imperatives, and the efforts to legalize relations between the Mainland and the regions of the Outer Periphery echo approaches adopted for the Inner Periphery. The resiliency of Party and government perspectives on regulation of religion in the Inner Periphery is also evident in central government positions on the role of religion in Hong Kong and Taiwan. The relationship between local development and the pursuit of national development goals suggests patterns of similarity in economic affairs that link central governance of the Inner and Outer Peripheries. As with the Inner Periphery, normative and organizational elements of selective adaptation and institutional capacity help explain the content and operation of PRC law, policy, and practice in the Outer Periphery.

In light of China's increased participation in an ever-widening range of bilateral and multilateral political, socio-cultural and economic relationships with direct relevance to Hong Kong and Taiwan, understanding China's approach to governance of the Outer Periphery will be increasingly important. Since central government jurisdiction over Hong Kong is of relatively recent vintage and remains a matter of proposal with regard to Taiwan, understanding and the potential for prediction can be furthered through comparisons with China's record of governance in the Inner Periphery. The implications for the Outer Periphery are complex, but real and not to be ignored.

6 Conclusion

China's approaches to governance in the periphery are manifested in areas of political authority, socio-cultural relations, and economic regulation. People's Republic of China (PRC) law, policy and practice of governance reveal patterns of similarity and difference across the regions of the Inner Periphery, borne largely of interaction with local conditions. PRC governance in the Inner Periphery has important implications for changing relations with the Outer Periphery. These relationships in turn invite discussion of opportunities for international engagement and local reform.

Governance in the Inner Periphery

In the Inner Periphery, as exemplified by the minority nationality autonomous regions of Tibet, Xinjiang, and Inner Mongolia, local conditions include historical factors of relations with Han China, institutional arrangements for the exercise of political authority, issues of accommodation and assimilation of local minority communities into a broader Han cultural world, complex interactions between religious identity and minority culture and identity and questions about economic development and local living standards. Much of China's legal and policy architecture for the exercise of political authority in the Inner Periphery is driven by policy imperatives of national integrity and sovereignty and resistance to separatism. Whereas these issues remain highly contested in Tibet and Xinjiang, they appear less so in Inner Mongolia such that IMAR is often depicted as a model for China's nationalities autonomy policy. Policies and practices of the Party/state on minority nationalities and minority cadre recruitment and management are key elements of governance in the Inner Periphery. Central government perspectives on the regulation of religion, a key element in ethnic culture and identity in Tibet and Xinjiang, and to a lesser extent in Inner Mongolia, are essential elements of governance. Regulation of the economy is given high priority by the central government, reflecting conclusions that raising living standards will help resolve tensions over the assertion of Beijing's political authority in the Inner Periphery. On these and other issues, China's law, policies, and practices of governance in the

172 Conclusion

Inner Periphery reflect influences of both selective adaptation and institutional capacity.

Selective Adaptation

Selective adaptation dynamics of perception, complementarity, and legitimacy are evident in the political, socio-cultural, and economic dimensions of PRC rule. While these tend to overlap, a summary of the operation of elements of selective adaptation in the various dimensions of Chinese governance in the Inner Periphery is nonetheless helpful to build understanding of the characteristics and contours of PRC rule.

Perception

China's policies and practices on political authority, nationalities and religion, and economic development in the Inner Periphery subordinate local goals and conditions to national policy imperatives. In the realm of political authority, selective adaptation dynamics of perception are evident in policy imperatives that give primacy to national unity over local diversity, particularly in Tibet and Xinjiang. In these two regions as well, separatism is linked with local ethnic nationalism, while central government perceptions about local ethnic diversity are limited or dismissive. Perceptions on political authority also tend to associate separatism with the influence of the Dalai Lama in Tibet and the "East Turkistan Movement" in Xinjiang. Perception dynamics are evident in central government conclusions about the role of "international hostile forces" in encouraging the Westernization and division of China. Separatism is also perceived as linked with religious extremism and radical international Islam. Official perceptions on political authority pertaining to Inner Mongolia, by contrast, emphasize the assimilation of Mongol culture and society with Han culture and society, and present IMAR as a model of autonomy. Perceptions around political authority in the Inner Periphery also reveal Party and government perspectives on the scope and operation of autonomy for local political subdivisions. Limits to meaningful local autonomy are underscored by the orthodox discourses on the unitary state and by the restricted meaning of the term "*zizhi quan*."

Government regulation of minority nationality affairs also reveals factors of perception in official responses to international standards. International standards are viewed as particular to Western values, and not relevant to China's needs for stability and a foundation for development. In all three autonomous regions, minority nationalities are perceived as potentially or inherently hostile to the Han. Mutual hostility of Han and minority nationalities in the Inner Periphery are attributed to historical errors (including Han chauvinism and the Cultural Revolution) rather than failures of contemporary policy and practice. Han-minority relations are perceived as affecting other elements of PRC rule in the Inner Periphery, but are also perceived as subject to resolution through education, political work, and policy. Nationality policy reveals perceptions about the "quality" (*suzhi*) of local minorities, primarily challenges of political reliability and education and technical training. Perceptions about religion in the Inner Periphery tend to link religion with separatism. Religious believers and organizations are perceived as a threat to Party and government administration. This is especially the case in Tibet and Xinjiang, although this perception is evident in Inner Mongolia as well. Nonetheless religion is perceived as a temporary phase of social development that can be controlled and harnessed to the will of the Party/state.

In the economy, as well, factors of perception are evident in official responses to international discourses of development and links between development and suppression of separatism. Perceptions on the economy tend to view economic development as a means to resolve nationalism and separatism issues in Xinjiang and Tibet, and to pacify and assimilate local nationalities in Inner Mongolia. Perceptions concerning economic development also prioritize capital-intensive approaches to development though dynamics of marketization, infrastructure, and urbanization. While there is uncertainty as to the resource base on which to build development in Tibet, perceptions about natural resource wealth (oil and gas, minerals in Xinjiang; and minerals, rare earths, and agricultural husbandry in Inner Mongolia) are seen as a basis for development. Central government perceptions on the economy in all three regions tend to subordinate local economic conditions to national development needs.

Complementarity

The dynamics of complementarity are evident as well. In the dimension of political rule, China's unitary state doctrines are seen as supported by international and constitutional discourses while international policies and programs on security and anti-terrorism are seen as supporting the exercise of political dominance in the Inner Periphery. Complementarity is also evident in the ways that nationality and religion policies in the Inner Periphery are portrayed officially as consistent with certain international human rights discourses on minority rights. This tends to support a rather instrumentalist application of PRC policies on nationalities and religion, encouraging doctrines on the right to development that disregard international standards which conflict with PRC policy priorities. Complementarity in regulatory practice is also evident in the selection of international discourses purportedly limiting freedom of religious behavior on grounds of public security and anti-terrorism. Factors of complementarity are also evident in the application of international discourses on development and economic policies for the Inner Periphery. Global neo-liberal discourses on development are drawn upon to support the priorities of China's Western Development Program in areas of marketization, infrastructure development and natural resource development. Global growth priorities also complement

174 Conclusion

China's policies encouraging accumulation and consumption as measures of development.

Legitimacy

Factors of legitimacy are evident in the central government's ongoing efforts to justify its exercise of political authority over the Inner Periphery in terms of historical claims and international law discourses, as well as its active resistance to international criticism on issues concerning Tibet and Xinjiang. Legitimacy dynamics are evident in China's efforts to base its claims to sovereignty over the regions of the Inner Periphery on particularistic historical interpretations. Legitimacy is also closely linked to "legalization of governance" and the reliance on the Nationality Region Autonomy Law (NRAL) and local legislation in the governance of institutions. Tensions between legitimacy sought from superiors in the hierarchy of the Party/state and legitimacy from local communities complicates the processes of negotiation that inform local implementation of central directives. In the area of nationality policy and religion, legitimacy is sought through assertions about compliance with international standards on governance, human rights, nationalities, and religion, which in turn are used to bolster China's resistance to international criticism. Legitimacy dynamics are evident in China's responses to international criticism of its policies and practices on religion. Legitimacy dynamics also affect economic policy as the "right to development" discourse is used to support Western Development policies and the use of economic development indicators based on elevated incomes and living standards. Legitimacy dimensions emerge through policy programs aimed at elevating numerical measures of local living standards and through efforts to proclaim internationally China's success in achieving the right to development.

Institutional Capacity

China's governance of the Inner Periphery can also be understood in terms of organizational perspectives of institutional capacity. Dynamics of institutional purpose, Location, Orientation, and Cohesion are evident in policy directives and their expression through law and regulation.

Institutional Purpose

Factors of institutional purpose are evident in the political sphere where primacy is given to national unity over local diversity, while separatism and local ethnic nationalism are suppressed. As well, the broad consensus within governance institutions on the need to resist international support for local ethnic nationalism (particularly US support for the Dalai Lama and Tibet, and support for Uighur nationalism and the "East Turkistan Movement" in Xinjiang). Institutional purposes is also furthered by consensus over goals of unity and stability that take precedence over other goals and influence policy design and implementation in economic and social policy.

On nationalities and religion, institutional purpose issues are evident in the broad consensus on supposed links between local religion and separatism, as well as suppression of "unlawful" religious behavior that is hostile to Party and government administration. The consensus around the need to control behavior (worship and education) of religious believers and organizations in order to minimize threat to party and government administration is a further indicator of the strength of institutional purpose. Institutional purposes of control over the influence of religion are revealed through the emphasis on economic growth, ideology, science, and education that inform policy and law.

In the economic realm, institutional purpose is evident in the use of policies of economic development to resolve nationalism and separatism issues, and the reliance on the Western Development Program to support goals of infrastructure development and urbanization. Broad consensus around reliance on marketization, price reform and natural resource development as a basis for economic development reflects positively on the dynamic of institutional purpose, as does the broad consensus on issues of subordinating local economic development programs to national development needs and the gradually diminishing attention to providing preferences for local nationality communities in development.

Institutional Location

Institutional capacity is generally challenged by the influences of institutional location. In the political realm, tensions between national and local conditions and goals play an important role. Factors of institutional location are particularly evident in the tensions between central and local perspectives on governance in the Inner Periphery—particularly as these affect analysis of local conditions and the design of regulatory and policy responses. As well, factors of the Inner Periphery's distance from Beijing (particularly for Tibet and Xinjiang) affect the capacity of central government actors to understand local conditions. In areas of nationalities and religion policy, tensions between national priorities and local goals, as well as language barriers impede understanding of local society by the central government. Cultural differences between local nationalities and Han officials impede social integration, while the potential for local religion to serve as a potential agent for building mutual understanding between Han and local nationalities is not available to communist party cadres, another feature of institutional location that may tend to undermine institutional capacity. Similarly, in the economy, tensions between national priorities and local goals reflect the influence of institutional location and have the potential to undermine institutional capacity.

Institutional Orientation

Factors of institutional orientation are evident in tensions between national priorities and local goals and in the tensions between the formalization of legal regulation and the informal realities of local socio-economic conditions. These dynamics affect both the exercise of political authority and the management of the economy, as measures protecting political orthodoxy and regulating economic behavior rely on formal measures that are not particularly relevant to local political and socio-economic relations. In nationality and religion policy as well, tensions between Han-dominated Party and government policy processes on nationalities conflict with the aspirations of local communities. As well, institutional orientation is also evident in tensions over questions about assimilation and accommodation, and ongoing concerns over questions about "quality" of local nationality cadres. The Party's denial of the legitimate role of religion and the dismissal of deeply embedded religious sensibilities in local communities also reflects issues of institutional orientation and may undermine institutional capacity.

Institutional Cohesion

Factors of institutional cohesion are also evident—particularly in relations between Han and minority cadres. Institutional cohesion is a key dimension of programs on minority cadre training and bilingualism. Ongoing dilemmas of language training for Han cadres, "quality" (*suzhi*) assessments of local nationality cadres, and the scope, intent, and operation of minority cadre training programs reflect issues of institutional cohesion and have an impact on institutional capacity. Evidence of continuing difficulties in securing "reliable" performance by local minority cadres—particular in respect of enforcement of restrictions against religious practice speak to fundamental issues of institutional cohesion. This also affects the ongoing process of negotiated enforcement of central edicts as the loyalties of local administrators is conflicted. This tends to entrench tensions between leading cadres in the nationality autonomy regions of the Inner Periphery and their local minority subordinates.

Implications for the Outer Periphery

The influence of selective adaptation and institutional capacity on China's governance of the Inner Periphery has important implications for China's management of the Outer Periphery. Under the constitutional model in place in Hong Kong and proposed for Taiwan, the "one country–two systems" approach and policy operations to implement it suggest a pattern of consistency with the basic norms and ideals underlying constitutional arrangements for governance in the Inner Periphery. In Hong Kong, despite the "high degree" of autonomy (*gaodu zizhi*) promised in the Basic Law, the scope and operation of autonomy remains subject to the limitations on the term *zizhi quan*. As is the case in the Inner Periphery, such notions of autonomy are limited to matters of implementation rather than conceptualization of law, policy, and governance. While empowered to take into account local conditions and to adjust implementation in light of them, government agencies in China's political sub-divisions operating under grants of "autonomy" have limited authority to conceptualize policies and programs without approval from the central government. The central government's commitment to this approach is evident in Hong Kong on matters of political authority such as elections, the authority of the courts, and public security; rights to freedom of religious action and education; and matters of the economy such as monopoly policy and integration with Mainland opportunities and interests. The potential for resolving cross-straits issues on Taiwan will depend significantly on the manner in which China's management of governance in Hong Kong gives meaning to ideals of autonomy—in a very real sense the wariness of the political community on Taiwan is the result of its appreciation of importance of this issue and the disquieting fashion in which the PRC government has handled it.

Selective Adaptation in the Outer Periphery

Factors of selective adaptation are evident in China's perspectives and actions on governance in Hong Kong and Taiwan, revealed in dynamics of perception, complementarity, and legitimacy. Selective adaptation dynamics of perception are evident in areas of political authority, where central government expectations about inherent and potential alliances with local compatriot (*tongbao*) communities in Hong Kong and Taiwan are coupled with apprehension about foreign collusion with hostile and unpatriotic elements. Factors of perception are evident in the political realm as colonialism is perceived as a cause of the dismembering of China, while international hostile forces comprised largely of the United States are seen as displacing Britain as a watchdog for Hong Kong autonomy. Perception also is evident in the tension between suspect loyalties of local Chinese communities, and the assumed commonality of interest between compatriot Chinese and mainland China. Perception also plays a role in social and religious matters, as religion is perceived as hostile to Party and government administration, albeit a dynamic that is seen as temporary and controllable. In the economic realm, perception plays a role in the linkages between economic development and local support for reunification. Perceptions about political loyalty are influential in the awarding of economic preferences and opportunities, while local economic development is perceived as linked with regional mainland development.

Complementarity between international law standards on national sovereignty and territorial integrity are evident in central government positions on political authority in Hong Kong and Taiwan. International security discourses also complement central government intervention in Hong Kong and the potential use of force to reunify Taiwan and the mainland. Complementarity also plays a role in social and religious matters as international human rights discourses on religion are relied upon selectively as a basis for PRC policy, whereas international secularist trends are seen as marginalizing the role of religion. Globalization discourses on economic development support pretensions to liberal market policies in Hong Kong and Taiwan and their impact on reunification.

Legitimacy factors are also evident, not only in China's effort to ground its policies in legal institutionalism and international law standards, but also to emphasize the colonial legacy that resulted in the separation of both Hong Kong and Taiwan from the Chinese mainland. Legitimacy dynamics are also evident in building support for central government policies and practices on Hong Kong and Taiwan through an emphasis on legalization. In Hong Kong, legitimacy for PRC policies is sought by reference to the Hong Kong Basic Law and the PRC Constitution, while Taiwan policy is legitimated through reference to the Anti-Secession Law and various State Council White Papers. Legitimacy of central government law policy and practice in areas of society and religion is claimed through the assertions of compliance with international standards and through the resistance and rebuttal of international criticism. Legitimacy for central government law policy and practice on Hong Kong and Taiwan is also claimed through a commitment to protecting economic growth, income and living standards.

Institutional Capacity in the Outer Periphery

Institutional capacity factors of institutional purpose, Location, Orientation, and Cohesion are also evident in the Outer Periphery. In Hong Kong SAR and Taiwan, issues of institutional purpose affect questions about whether resumption of sovereignty alone is sufficient to satisfy goals of national reunification or require more intrusive limits on local autonomy. Factors of institutional purpose are evident in the broad consensus around the imperative of national reunification, but are potentially undermined by tensions over the extent of mainland policy intrusion in local affairs. With regard to society and religion, institutional purpose dynamics are evident in the consensus around managing local religious behavior deemed hostile to Party and government administration, including suppression of alleged support for separatism and unlawful religious activity in the mainland, suppression of religious education, and assumptions around parallels between local conditions and goals and those that exist on the mainland. Institutional purpose is a positive contributor to capacity in areas of economic policy, as economic development is pursued through neo-liberal growth models associated with the WTO. Tensions arise however over political implications of economic growth models, and in tensions between the interests of mainland and local actors.

Factors of institutional location are also evident and tend to undermine institutional capacity. Institutional location factors are frequently evident when central government policy makers appear at odds with local experts or curiously out of touch with local issues. Tensions between local conditions and goals and those assumed or imposed by mainland authorities are evident in the political, socio-cultural, and economic realms.

Factors of institutional orientation are apparent in tensions between legalization and local conditions—particularly in the tension between the formalism that informs China's legalization of "one country–two systems" and the flexible nuances that more often characterize operation of the more mature legal system of Hong Kong and Taiwan. Tensions between national priorities and local goals are also indicators of the role of institutional orientation in religion and economic policy and their potential effect on institutional capacity. Institutional cohesion is also evident in bureaucratic politics and personnel changes in central government departments responsible for policy making on Hong Kong and Taiwan.

Opportunities for engagement and reform

The paradigms of selective adaptation and institutional capacity offer possibilities for building understanding about China's policies and practices of governance in the Peripheries. The normative challenges of selective adaptation present opportunities for more effective international engagement, while the dynamics of institutional capacity raise possibilities for policy reform.

Selective Adaptation

Appreciation of the ways that selective adaptation affects China's engagement with international standards on governance can help construct the contours for international engagement on policies pertaining to the Periphery. The elements of perception, complementarity and legitimacy can support positive engagement with China by international organizations and foreign governments on issues of governance in the Inner and Outer Peripheries. Appreciation of the importance of perception can contribute to efforts at education, participation, and confidence building in China's relations with the international legal system, as a way to diminish assumptions about exclusion and hostility that distort China's acceptance of international law standards. Expanded support for multilateral processes for communication and dialogue to diminish threat perception can also be helpful, along with dissemination of standards on participatory governance, federalism, and models of local autonomy. Perception dynamics can also be affected through the dissemination of information and best practice models on religious freedom and church–state relations, which can acknowledge Chinese government perceptions about links between religion and ethnic separatism while also providing information on religious matters that contribute to social cohesion and well-being. Appreciation of perception dynamics may also contribute to engagement on economic issues, through dissemination of compliance models for GATT/WTO regimes and regional economic integration.

On the issue of complementarity, acceptance of the variability and imprecision of international standards on human rights and local governance can temper critical assertions about China's compliance with international law, even as a continued reliance on international law as a source of standards can restrain temptations toward relativism in assessments of local governance practices. In the political realm, providing information on authoritative policy/law discourses and dissemination of best practices on local autonomy might strengthen complementarity between Chinese and international standards. Such efforts might extend as well to issues of religious freedoms and economic autonomy.

International engagement can also be furthered by reference to the dynamic of legitimacy. Attention to the PRC government's search for international and domestic legitimacy offers opportunities for engagement and influence. In the political realm, identifying the legitimacy dynamics of Chinese policy behavior, and incorporating legitimacy inducements in multilateral and bilateral engagement would be helpful. The same approach can be taken in religious and economic issues. As well, appreciation of the dynamics of legitimacy can inform efforts to recognize the importance of members of local administrative units and civil society institutions and empower their capacity to intensify the myriad informal processes of negotiated compliance that characterize local enforcement of central laws and policies. Responding to the legitimacy dimensions of China's governance in the Inner and Outer Peripheries will not admit to easy solutions and cannot be achieved through rote copying, or rejection, of governance models from abroad. But attention to best practices that capture elements of pragmatic, normative, and cognitive legitimacy with adjustments to meet China's specific conditions will certainly help. China's policies and practices on governance in the Periphery are neither immutable nor sacred, but simply the result of political decisions made to address the complex problems of political authority, socio-cultural relations and economic development. Appreciating the legitimacy dimensions of these processes will undoubtedly aid effective and productive engagement.

Institutional Capacity

Understanding the ways in which institutional capacity affects China's governance behavior in the Inner and Outer Peripheries can strengthen the possibilities for internal reform. Appreciation of the sources and content of institutional purpose can contribute significantly to strengthening the application of Chinese law and policy. Dynamics of institutional purpose can be taken into account in dissemination of standards on governance transparency, rule of law, and national unification in the political realm. Institutional purpose dynamics in society and religion policy can be affected through consideration of effective approaches to religious freedoms and church–state

Conclusion 181

relations, while institutional purpose factors in economic policy can also be affected through dissemination of compliance models for GATT/WTO disciplines and models of regional economic integration.

Elements of institutional location are critical elements in weighting the importance of varying policy positions on governance emerging from Beijing and the Periphery. Factors of institutional location can affect engagement in political matters through support for research and analysis on institutional mapping and personnel assignments and through dissemination of best practices on central–local relations in law and policy-making. Similarly in matters of religion and economic relations, attention to location-based best practices and authoritative law and policy discourses on religious freedoms and church–state relations and on economic autonomy and regional integration can be helpful.

Factors of institutional orientation can also be taken into account through dissemination of best practices and authoritative policy/law discourses on the operation of formal institutions and on substantive justice, rule of law and policy operations. Appreciation of the importance of institutional orientation in China's relations with its peripheral areas can help resolve tensions between formalistic law and policy texts and complex operational realities at local levels.

Dimensions of institutional cohesion can alert policy-makers to the internal political and bureaucratic factors that lead to inconsistencies in law and policy. Factors of institutional cohesion—particularly challenges of deployment of minority cadres and the issues of negotiated compliance—can usefully be taken into account in research, analysis, and program support on cadre recruitment and training as well as in accounting for the role of organizational politics in law and policy-making. Support for exchange programs and confidence building measures in organizational development can be helpful steps forward. In each of these areas, specific terms of policy and program engagement can be informed by factors of institutional capacity.

***

International engagement with China and ongoing policy reform within China will remain key realities of international law and politics for the twenty-first century. Understanding of PRC law, policy, and practice of governance in China's Inner and Outer Peripheries will be an integral part of this effort. Normative and organizational dynamics of selective adaptation and institutional capacity can be helpful to build effective international engagement and local reform. A hoped-for conclusion will be that equipped with tools for clearer analysis, stakeholders that engage with China over the coming decades will be able to interpret PRC behavior more clearly and will thereby be better able to build a global community of interest and understanding. One might hope as well that China's law and policy on governance in the Peripheries might become something more than simply an instrument of control. Returning to the *doucai* metaphor suggested in the Introduction, we might recall that the word "*dou*" can also mean "join," replacing implications of controlling conflict with those of facilitating interaction (Cort and Stuart 1993: 16). Thus, instead of serving as a mechanism to confine the "contending colors" of diverse socio-economic and political relationships that characterize China's peripheries, China's systems of law and regulation could potentially become vehicles for joining together the varying normative and organizational elements of human experience in the Inner and Outer Peripheries into a stronger whole. Such a transition from control to community would go far to redress the challenges that beset China's governance in the Periphery and elsewhere.

Notes

1 Overview

1 An earlier version of this chapter appeared as Pitman B. Potter, "China's Peripheries: Challenges of Central Governance and Local Autonomy," in Diana Lary, ed., *China at the Borders* (Vancouver: UBC Press, 2007).

2 Political authority in the Inner Periphery

1 An earlier version of this chapter appeared as Pitman B. Potter, "Governance of the Periphery: Balancing Local Autonomy and National Unity," *Columbia Journal of Asian Law* (2006).
2 Portions of this section are drawn from Pitman B. Potter, "Courts in Xinjiang: Institutional Capacity in China's Periphery," in Nicholson and Harding, ed., *New Courts in Asia* (London: Routledge, 2009).

3 Socio-cultural relations in the Inner Periphery

1 Kong was a Party functionary from Shandong who was appointed deputy Party secretary in Ganpa county in Xigaze Tibet in 1979 and later became deputy Mayor of Lhasa. He has been celebrated as a worker-martyr in style of Lei Feng after his untimely death in an auto accident in 1994 while en route to Xinjiang, and has been the subject of government campaigns to exhort people to study the "old Tibet spirit" of Kong and other Communist heroes in the region. Union News Net (www.unn.com.cn/GB/channel326/329/753/782/200010/19/2883.html) [Jan. 4, 2010].
2 This section draws on Pitman B. Potter, "Belief in Control: Regulation of Religion in China," in *The China Quarterly* no. 174 (July 2003).

Bibliography
Chinese

Bai, Yongli, 2001, "Huhehaote shi minzu jiaoyu de fazhan gaikuan" (Survey of development of nationalities education in Hohehot city), in Liu Jinghai and Shi Wenzheng, ed., *Lun wanshan minzu quyu zizhi* (On improving autonomy in nationality regions) (Huhehaote: Inner Mongolia People's Press): 167–75.
——2005, "Chazouhou qi zai tuigeng, tuimu huancao zhong de wenti" (Problems existing in the converting arable land to forestry and converting grazingland to grassland in Chazouhou Banner), in Shi Wenzheng, ed., *Caoyuan huanjin de falu baohu* (Legal Protection of the Grasslands environment) (Huhehaote: Inner Mongolia People's Press): 161–67.
Bu, He 1993, "Jiaqiang minzu fazhi jianshe, cuzin ge minzu gongtongfanrong" (Strengthen establishment of minority legal system, promote the wellbeing of all nationalities) (Dec. 17, 1993), in Guojia Minzu Shiwu Weiyuanhui (State Nationalities Affairs Commission) and Zhonggong Zhongyang Wenxian Yanjiu Shi (CPC Central Archives Research Office), *Minzu gongzuo wenjian xuanbian 1990–2002* (Collection of documents on nationalities work – 1990–2002) (Beijing Central Archives Press, 2003) (hereafter, "SNAC and CCARO 2003"): 98–111.
——2003 *Minzu lilun yu minzu zhengce* (Nationalities theory and nationalities policy) (Huhehaote: Inner Mongolia University Press).
CCARO-GRU and RAB-PRD, 2003, Zhonggong Zhongyang Wenxian Yanjiushi Zonghe Yanjiuzu (General research unit of CPC Central Archives Research Office) and Guowuyuan Zongjiao Shiwu Ju Zhengce Fagui Si (Policy and law division of State Council Religious Affairs Bureau), ed., *Xin shiqi zongjiao gongzuo wenxian xuanbian* (Compilation of documents on religion work in the new period) (Beijing: Religion and Culture Press).
CCC-OTW and SC-TAO, 2005, Zhonggong Zhongyang Taiwan Gongzuo Bangongshi (CPC Central Committee Office on Taiwan Work) and Guowuyuan Taiwan Shiwu Bangongshi (State Council Taiwan Affairs Office), ed., *"Fa fenlie guojia fa" ji zhongyao wenxian xuanbian* (Anti-Secession Law and compilation of important documents) (Beijing: Jiuzhou Press,).
CCTV, 2003, *Zhongguo Xibu* (The West of China) (Beijing: Youth Publishing).
CDRO and TARCC, 2005, Zhonggong Zhongyang Wenxian Yanjiushi (Central Documents Research Office) and Zhonggong Xizang Zizhiqu Weiyuanhui (TAR CPC Committee), ed., *Xizang gongzuo wenxian xuanbian* (Collection of documents on Tibet work) (Beijing: Central Documents Press).
Chen, Fucheng, 2004, *Dalu zhengce yu liangge guanxi* (Mainland policy and cross-strait relations) (Taipei: Liming).

Chen, Rongzhuan, 2003, *Liang'an falu chongtu de xianqing yu shiwu* (Cross-strait legal conflicts: present conditions and types) (Taipei: Xuelin).
"Chengshi minzu gongzuo tiaoli" (Regulations on nationalities urban work) in SNAC and CCARO 2003: 85–90.
Dai, Xiaoming, 2002, *Minzu fazhi wenti tansuo* (Inquiry on nationalities issues) (Beijing: Nationalities Press).
"Dalai jituan pohuai Xizang shehui wending zhuding yao shibai" (The Dalai group's destruction of social stability in Tibet doomed to fail) Renmin ribao (People's Daily) Mar. 17, 2008 (http://news.sina.com.cn/c/2008-03-17/022115161350.shtml) [Jan. 4, 2010].
Deng, Xiaoping, 1983, "Jianchi sixiang jiben yuanze" (Uphold the four basic principles), in *Deng Xiaoping wenxuan–yijiuqiu–yijiu ba'er* (Collected works of Deng Xiaoping: 1975–82) (Beijing: People's Press): 144–70.
Ding, Jianwei, 2004, *Diyuan zhengzhi zhong de xibei bianjiang anquan* (Security of the northwest periphery in geopolitics) (Beijing: Nationalities Press).
Du, Huanfang, 2004, "Zhongguo quji falu wenti yanjiu de zuixin jinzhan: Ping Zhongguo de quji falu wenti yanjiu" (Latest developments in the study of the issue of regional law in China: Reviewing "Study of Questions of Regional Law in China)," Faxue pinglun (Law Review) no. 5: 159–160.
Du, Shiwei, "Xiandaihua de tuijin yu shaoshu minzu wenhua shiye de fazhan" (Promoting modernization and the development of minority nationality cultural affairs), in Guo Shiyuan and Wan Xien 2006: 194–211.
Dui Taiwan diqu maoyi guanli banfa" (Administrative measures for trade with the region of Taiwan) (Dec. 29, 2000), in Zhang Wanming: 205–6.
Dui Taiwan diqu xiao'e maoyi de guanli banfa" (Administrative measures on small-scale trade with the region of Taiwan) Sep. 25, 1993 (http://law.baidu.com/pages/chinalawinfo/0/63/8e0295c31875a2f969d51cfcbf245bf4_0.html) [Jan. 5, 2010].
Fang, Li, 2004, "Xin shiqi tongyi zhanxian de zhongyao fazhan" (Important developments in the united front in the new era), in *Xianfa he xianfa xiuzheng an: Pudao duben* (Authoritative reader on the constitution and constitutional revision) (Beijing: China Law Press):170–83.
Fu, Houmin, 2000, "Jianchi [yi zhong] yuanze tuijin liang'an jingmao guanxi" (Insist on 'one China' principle and promote economic and trade relations across the Taiwan Strait) (Unification Forum no. 4).
Fu, Houmin 1999, "Ru shi tuidong liang'an san tong" (WTO entry prods cross-strait three-links) (HK *Wenhui Bao* Dec. 4).
Fu, Kuncheng, 2003, *Yifa zhiguo: kuayue haiyan de xinnian* (Ruling the country by law: belief in surmounting the two coasts) (Taipei: State Press).
"Gansu sheng zongjiao shiwu guanli zanxing guiding" (Provisional regulations of Gansu Province on management of religious affairs) (Nov. 16, 1991), in Guowuyuan Zongjiao Shiwu Ju Zhengce Fagui Si (Policy and Research Division of State Council Religious Affairs Office), ed., *Quanguo zongjiao xingzheng fagui guizhang huibian* (Compilation of national laws, regulations and charters for administration of religion) (Beijing: Religion and Culture Press, 2002) (hereafter, "RAB-PRD 2002"): 123–29
Gao, Gangjun, 2006, "Zhongguo de heping fazhan yu guoji fa de jiazhi tixi" (China's peaceful development and the value system of international law," *Faxue pinglun* (Law Review) no. 3: 104–10.
Gao, Zhang, 2002, *Dalu jing gai yu liang'an jingmao guanxi* (Economic reform on the mainland and cross-strait economic and trade relations) (Taipei: Wunan).

Gao, Zhaoping, Liu Zhong, and Chen Shaoxue, 2000, *Zhongguo Xibu da kaifa zhanlue yanjiu* (Study of China's western development strategy) (Xining: Qinghai People's Press).

"Gonggu he fazhan shehui zhuyi de minzu guanxi" (Consolidate and development socialist nationality relations), in SNAC and CCARO 2003: 53–56.

Guan, Shouxin, Liang Junyan, and Zhang Wenya, 2001, *Kashi fengwu zhi* (Scenery of Kashgar) (Kunming: Yunan People's Press).

"Guangxi zhuang zizhiqu zongjiao shiwu xingzheng guanli zanxing guiding" (Provisional regulations of Gaungxi Zhuang Autonomous Region on administration and management of religious affairs) (Mar. 22, 1994), in RAB-PRD 2002: 145–52.

"Guanyu chuban Taiwan tongbao zuopin banquan wenti de zanxing guiding" (Provisional regulations on copyrights for publishing works of Taiwan compatriots) (Feb. 8, 1988) http://law.baidu.com/pages/chinalawinfo/1/8/ d64ed3068403d35438730f7cb5e51eeb_0.html [Jan. 5, 2010].

"Guanyu dui haiyan liang'an zhuanli jiaoliu huodong guanli de yijian" (Opinion on strengthening management of coastal and cross-strait patent exchange activities) (nd) www.edu.cn/20010101/21391.shtml [Jan. 5, 2010].

"Guanyu fangkai dui Tai maoyi jinchukou jingyingquan de tongzhi" (Notice on expanding managerial authority in import-export trade with Taiwan) (July 11, 1999) (www.cctv.com/news/special/C14328/20050711/102836.shtml) [Jan. 5, 2010].

"Guanyu guli Taiwan tongbao touzi de guiding" (June 25, 1988), in Zhang Wanming: 192–94.

"Guanyu jiaqiang haiyan liang'an guanggao jiaoliu guanli de tongzhi" (Notice on strengthening management of coastal and cross-strait advertising exchange) (July 20, 1994) http://law.baidu.com/pages/chinalawinfo/2/55/ ee06f2fbbe02f1ccd852005686196217_0.html [Jan. 5, 2010].

"Guanyu jiaqiang Taiwan haiyan liang'an jianjie jizhuangxiang banlun yunshu guanli de tongzhi" (Notice on strengthening administration of regular container transport on the Taiwan coast and across the strait) (Jun. 8, 2004) (http://law.baidu.com/pages/ chinalawinfo/5/33/d48421ee0922f59234351bbf7c9402ec_0.html) [Jan. 5, 2010].

"Guanyu shenru guanche luoshi zhongyang fupin kaifa gongzuo huiyijingshen de tongzhi" (Circular on thoroughly implementing the spirit of the central work conference on poverty) (Jun. 22, 2001), in Tianjin Shi Minzu Shiwu Weiyuanhui (Tianjin Municipal Minorities Affairs Commission *Xin shiqi chengshi minzu gongzuo zhengce fagui xuanbian* (Collection of policies and laws on urban minorities work in the new era) (Beijing: Nationalities Press, 2004) (hereafter, "Tianjin 2004"): 156–60.

"Guanyu shouli Taibao zhuanli shenqing de yijian" (Opinion on accepting patent applications from Taiwan compatriots) (Dec. 18, 1987) Wang and Chen: 189.

"Guanyu Taiwan haiyan liang'anjian jian huowu yunshu dailiye guanli banfa" (Administrative measures for Taiwan coastal and cross-straits trade agency) (Aug. 21, 1996) (http://law.baidu.com/pages/chinalawinfo/1/47/ a389746359458199f15e39ab1ca49f22_0.html) [Jan. 5, 2010].

"Guanyu woguo shehui zhuyi shiqi zongjiao wenti de jiben guandian he jiben zhengce" (Basic Viewpoints and Policies on Religious Issues During Our Country's Socialist Period" (March 31, 1982) (Document 19), in Zhonggong Zhongyang Wenxian Yanjiushi Zonghe Yanjiuzu (General Research Unit of CPC Central Archives Research Office) and Guowuyuan Zongjiao Shiwu Ju Zhengce Fagui Si (Policy and Research Division of State Council Religious Affairs Office), ed., *Xin shiqi zongjiao gongzuo wenxian xuanbian* (Selected documents on religion work in

the new period) (Beijing: Religion and Culture Press, 2003) (hereafter "CCARO-GRU and RAB-PRD 2003"): 54–73.
Guojia Huanjing Baohu Ju (State Environmental Protection Bureau), "Guanyu xibu da kaifa zhong jiaqiang jianshe xiangmu huanjing baohu guanli de ruogan yijian" (Various opinions on strengthening environmental protection administration in construction projects under the Western Development Program) (Jan. 8, 2001) (www.xjwd.gov.cn/sjmb.php?id=47) [Nov. 7, 2007].
"Guojia Jihua Weiyuan Hui guanyu xibei diqu jingji guihhua wenti de baogao" (State Planning Commission report on issues of economic programming in the northwest), in SNAC and CCARO 2003: 58–65.
"Guojia Jiwei chutai zhengce cujin xibu kaifa" (The State Planning Commission issues policies to promote western development) (Xinhuanet) (Sept. 1, 2000) (www.xjbz.gov.cn/wmfw/zcxx/2000/09/090102.html) [Nov. 7, 2007].
"Guojia Minwei, Jiaoyubu guanyu jiakuai shaoshu minzu he minzu diqu zhiye jiaoyu gaige he fazhan de yijian" (Opinion of the State Nationalities Affairs Commission and the Ministry of Education on accelerating reform and development of professional education for minorities and minority areas) (Jul. 28, 2000), in SNAC and CCARO 2003: 271–80.
Guojia Minwei Zhengfa Si Diaoyanzu (Investigation and research organ of State Nationalities Commission Politics and Law Department), "Guanyu Xinjiang minzu gongzuo de diaoyan baogao" (Investigation and research report on nationalities work in Xinjiang), in Tiemuer and Mao Gangning, ed., *Xinjiang yanjiu wenlun xuan – di yi ji* (Collection of essays on the study of Xinjiang – vol. 1) (Beijing: Nationalities Press, 2003) (hereafter, "Tiemuer and Mao 2003"): 225–34
Guojia Minzu Shiwu Weiyuanhui (State Nationalities Affairs Commission), 2002, *Zhongguo gongchandang guanyu minzu wenti de jiben guandian he zhengce* (Basic approaches and policies of the Chinese Communist Party on nationalities issues) (Beijing: Nationalities Press, 2002) (hereafter, "SNAC 2002").
Guojia Minzu Shiwu Weiyuanhui (State Nationalities Affairs Commission) and Zhonggong Zhongyang Wenxian Yanjiu Shi (CPC Central Archives Research Office), 2003. *Minzu gongzuo wenjian xuanbian 1990–2002* (Collection of documents on nationalities work – 1990–2002) (Beijing Central Archives Press, 2003) ("SNAC and CCARO 2003").
"Guojia Minzu Shiwu Weiyuanhui zhineng peizhi neishe jigou he renyuan bianzhi guiding" (Regulations of the State Nationalities Commission on staff functions and assignments, internal institutions and staff complements) (Jun. 20, 1998) in SNAC and CCARO 2003: 187–92.
Guojia Zongjiao Shiwu Ju Zhengce Fagui Si (Policy and Research Division of State Council Religious Affairs Office), ed., *Quanguo zongjiao xingzheng fagui guizhang huibian* (Compilation of national laws, regulations and charters for administration of religion) (Beijing: Religion and Culture Press, 2002) ("RAB-PRD 2002").
"Guowuyuan fupin fazhan lingdao xiaozu guanyu zuzhi jingji jiao fada diqu yu jingji qian fada diqu fazhan fupin xiezuo de tongzhi" (Notice of the State Council Leading Small Group on poverty alleviation and development concerning organizing poverty alleviation cooperation between relatively economically developed and undeveloped areas) (Feb. 13, 1996), in SNAC and CCARO 2003: 157–60.
"Guowuyuan guanyu guli waishang touze de guiding" (State Council regulations on encouraging foreign investment) (Nov. 11, 1986), in Zhonghua renmin gongheguo

fagui huibian (Compilation of laws and regulations of the PRC) (Beijing: Law Publishing, 1987): 1–6.
"Guowuyuan guanyu minzu xueyuan gongzuo de jibe zongjie he jinhou fangzhen renwu de baogao" (Report on basic summary of work at the nationalities academy and policy tasks for the future) (Nov. 1979) (www.seac.gov.cn/gjmw/mzjykj/2004-06-29/1194334511366639.htm) [Jan. 5, 2010].
"Guowuyuan guanyu shenhua gaige jiakuai fazhan minzu jiaoyu de jueding" (State council decision on deepening reform and accelerating development of nationalities education) (July 7, 2002), in SNAC and CCARO 2003: 384–93.
"Guowuyuan guanyu shishi xibu da kaifa ruogan zhengce cuoshi de tongzhi" (Circular on various policy measures concerning western development), in SNAC and CCARO 2003: 281–90.
Guowuyuan guanyu Zhonghua renmin gongheguo jingnei waiguo ren zongjiao huodong guanli guiding" (State Council Regulations on the Management of Religious Activities of Foreigners in the PRC) (Jan. 31, 1994), in Xu Yucheng, *Zongjiao zhengce falu*: 306–7. [English text appears in Human Rights Watch Asia, *China: State Control of Religion* (1997): 104–5.]
"Guowuyuan guanyu zongjiao huodong changsuo guanli tiaoli" (State Council Regulations Regarding the Management of Places of Religious Activities) (Jan. 31, 1994), in Xu Yucheng, *Zongjiao zhengce falu* : 308–10.
Guowuyuan Taiwai Bangongshi Xinwenju, ed, 2002, *Chen Shuibian "Yibian yiguo lun" pipan* (Critique of Chen Shuibian's "One state on each side theory") (Beijing: Jiuzhou Press).
Guowuyuan Xibu Diqu Kaifa Lingdao Xiaozu Bangongshi (Office of the State Council Western Development Leading Small Group), "'Shi Wu' xibu kaifa zongti guihua" (General plan for western development under the Tenth Five Year Plan) (Jul. 10, 2002).
Guowuyuan Xibu Kaifa Ban (State Council Western Development Office), 2003, "Shishi xibu kaifa de jinzhan he renwu" (Progress and tasks for implementation of western development) (Mar. 8, 2003) (www.chinawest.gov.cn/web/NewsInfo.asp?NewsId=182) [Nov. 7, 2002].
Guowuyuan Xibu Kaifa Ban (State Council Western Development Office), 2000, "Guanyu xibu da kaifa ruogan zhengce cuoshi de shishi yijian) (Opinion on the Implementation of Certain Policy Measures on the Great Development of the Western Regions" (Aug. 28, 2001) (http://news.xinhuanet.com/politics/2006-04/13/content_4418585.htm) [Nov. 7, 2007].
Hao, Shiyuan and Wang Xien, ed., 2006, *Zhongguo minzu fazhan baogao 2001–2006* (Report on nationalities development in China 2001–6) (Beijing: Social Sciences Academic Press).
Hao, Shiyuan, ed., 2002, *Zhongguo shaoshu minzu fenbu tuji* (Atlas of distribution of national minorities in China) (Beijing: China Maps Press).
Hao, Tiechuan, 2006, "'Wuquan fa (caoan)' weixian wenti zhi wojian" (My perspectives on the issue of the 'Property Rights Law (draft)' contravening the constitution), *Faxue* (Legal studies) 2006 no. 8 (Aug. 10,): 41–42.
Hao, Weimin, 1997, *Neimenggu geming shi* (The history of the revolution in Inner Mongolia) (Hehuhaote: Inner Mongolia University Press).
Hao, Weimin, ed.,1991, *Neimenggu Zizhi Qu lishi: 1947–1987* (The history of Inner Mongolia Autonomous Region: 1947–87) (Huhehaote: Inner Mongolia University Press).

He, Husheng, 2004, *Zhongguo gongchandang de zongjiao zhengce yanjiu* (Study of CPC policy on religion) (Beijing: Religion and Culture Publishers).
He, Longqun, 2005, *Zhongguo Gongchandang minzu zhengce shilun* (History and theory of CPC nationality policy) (Beijing: People's Press).
He, Qinghua, 2002, "Fa de yizhi yu fa de bentuhua," (Legal transplanting and localization of law"), *Zhongguo faxue* (Chinese Legal Studies) no. 3: 3–15.
He, Qinglian, 1998, *Xiandaihua de xianjing: Dangdai Zhongguo de jingji shehui wenti* (The trap of modernization: Economic and social issues in contemporary China) (Beijing: Today's China Press).
He, Zhipeng, 2006, "Ren de huigui: Geren guojifa shang diwei zhi shensi" (The return of man: Reflections on the status of the individual in international law), *Faxue pinglun* (Law Review) no. 3: 56–63.
Hu, Jintao, 2005a, "Xiwang di shiyi jie Banchan Gerdini chengwei aiguo aijiao de dianfan" (I hope the 11th Panchen Gerdini will be a model of patriotism and love of learning) (Feb. 3, 2005), Zhongong Zhongyang Wenxian Yanjiushi (Central Documents Research Office) and Zhonggong Xizang Zizhiqu Weiyuanhui (TAR CPC Committee), ed., *Xizang gongzuo wenxian xuanbian* (Collection of documents on Tibet work) (Beijing: Central Documents Press) (hereafter, "CDRO and TARCC 2005"): 622–624.
Hu, Jintao 2005b, "Zai zhongyang minzu gongzuo huiyi jia Guowuyuan di si ci quanguo minzu tuanjie jinbu biaozhang dahui shang de jianghua" (Speech at meeting of central nationalities work conference and 4th State Council meeting commending progress in unity of nationalities) (May 27), in CDRO and TARCC 2005: 629–646.
Hu, Jintao, 2004, "Shuli he luoshi kexue fazhan guan, jinyibu shishi hao xibu da kaifa zhanlue" (Establish and carry out an ethic of scientific development, steadily implement well the Western Development Program) (Mar. 5), in CDRO and TARCC 2005: 617–621.
Hu, Jintao, 2002a "Gaodu zhongshi, qieshi zuohao shaoshu minzu ganbu de peiyang xuanba gongzuo" (Raise the emphasis and completely excel in minority cadre training and selection work), in SNACand CCARO 2003: 66–81.
Hu, Jintao, 2002b "Zhuazhu youli shiji, tuidong Xizang kuayue shi fazhan" (Grasp the opportune moment, prod leapfrog development for Tibet) (Mar. 5, 2002), in CDRO and TARCC 2005: 612–616.
Hu, Jintao, 2001a, "Zai qingzhu Xizang heping jiefang wushi zhounian dahui shang de jianghua" (Speech at the meeting for the 50th anniversary of the peaceful liberation of Tibet) (Jul. 19), in SNACand CCARO 2003: 590–595.
Hu, Jintao, 2001b, "Xizang guangda ganbu yao zai cujin fazhan he weihu wending zhong fahui mofan daitou zuoyong" (Tibet cadres must restore the role of models and taking the lead in the course of promoting development and preserving stability) (Jul.19), in CDRO and TARCC 2005: 596–599.
Hu, Jintao, 2000, "Jinyibu tigao dui peiyang shaoshu minzu ganbu zhongyaoxing he jinpoxing de renshi" (Steadily raise awareness of the importance and urgency of training minority cadres) (Oct. 26), in CDRO and TARCC 2005: 537–541.
Hu, Jintao, 1998, "Fazhan xuyao wending, wending baozhang fazhan" (Development requires stability, stability ensures development) (Mar. 6, 1998), in SNACand CCARO 2003: 512–514.
Hu, Jintao, 1993, "Gaodu zhongshi, qieshi zuohao shaoshu minzu ganbu de peiyang xuanba gongzuo" (Raise attention and earnestly do a good job in the work of training and selection of minority cadres), in CDRO and TARCC 2005: 66–81.

"Hu Jintao tiqu xin xingshi xia fazhan liang'an guanxi sidian yijian" (Hu Jintao issues four point opinion on development of cross-strait relations under the new situation) (Mar. 4, 2005), *Renmin ribao* (People's Daily) Mar. 3, 2005, in Zhonggong Zhongyang Taiwan Gongzuo Bangongshi (CPC Central Committee Office on Taiwan Work) and Guowuyuan Taiwan shiwu bangongshi (State Council Taiwan Affairs Office), ed., ≪*Fa fenlie guojia fa*≫ *ji zhongyao wenxian xuanbian* (Anti-Secession Law and compilation of important documents) (Beijing: Jiuzhou Press, 2005) (hereafter, "CCC-OTW and SC-TAO 2005"): 5–9.

"Huhehaote shi renmin zhengfu guanyu guli jinru kaifaqu xingban qiye de youhui banfa" (Preferential methods of Huhehaote municipal government for setting up enterprises entering the development zone) (author's copy).

Huang, Jilian, 2002, *Dazao Taiwan* (Constructing Taiwan) (Hong Kong: Joint Publishing).

"Hubei sheng zongjiao shiwu guanli zanxing guiding" (Provisional regulations of Hubei Province on management of religious affairs) (Dec. 3, 1992), in RAB-PRD 2002: 136–44.

IM Laws, 2000, *Neimenggu zizhiqu difangxing fagui guizhang xuanze* (Volume of selected local laws and regulations of Inner Mongolia Autonomous Region) (Huhehaote: Inner Mongolia People's Press).

Ji, Ping and Gao Bingzhong, 1994, "Xinjiang wei han minzu jiaoyizhe yinsu de lianghua fenxi" (Analysis of quantitative factors in intermingling of Uighur and Han nationalities in Xinjiang), in Pan Naigu, Ma Rong *Zhongguo bianyuan diqu kaifa yanjiu* (Study of development in China's frontiers) (Hong Kong: Oxford University Press): 183–260.

Jia, Qinglin, 2005, "Jianjue ezhi 'Taidu' fenlie huodong weihu Taihai diqu heping wending jixu zhengqu liang'an guanxi chaozhe heping tongyi de fangxiang fazhan" (Resolutely limit secessionist activities of Taiwan independence, protect peace and stability in the Taiwan Sea region, strive for cross-strait relations to develop toward peaceful unification) *Renmin ribao* (People's Daily) Jan. 29, in CCC-OTW and SC-TAO 2005: 17–28.

Jiang, Zemin, 2001a, "Cujin Xizang shixian kuayueshi fazhan he changzhi jiuan" (Promote Realization of leapfrog development and longterm political stability) (Jun. 25), in CDRO and TARCC 2005: 547–560.

Jiang, Zemin, 2001b, "Qieshi zuohao zongjiao gongzuo we gaige fazhan wending daju fuwu" (Conscientiously do a good job in religion work to serve the main situation of reform, development and stability) (Dec. 10), in CDRO and TARCC 2005: 603–611.

Jiang, Zemin, 1999, "Zai zhongyang minzu gongzuo huiyi ji guowuyuan di sanci quanguo minzu tuanjie jinbu biaozhang dahui shang de jianghua (Speech to the central nationalities work conference and the third State Council meeting on recognizing progress in the unity of nationalities) (Sep. 29), in SNAC and CCARO 2003: 209–18.

Jiangl Zeminl 1998a, "Xizang renmin de qiantu he mingyun shizhong shi tong zuguoo de qiantu he mingyun jinmi lianxi zai yiqi de" (The future and destiny of Tibet are from beginning to end intimately linked with the future and destiny of the motherland) (Mar. 7), in CDRO and TARCC 2005: 515–517.

Jiang, Zemin, 1998b, "Guanyu Zhongguo zhengfu dui Dalai wenti de lichang he zhengce" (The standpoint and policy of the Chinese government on the Dalai Lama question) (Nov. 16), in CDRO and TARCC 2005: 518–520.

Jiang, Zemin, 1994a, "Weirao fazhan he wending liangjian dashi, kaichuang Xizang gongzuo xin jumian" (Centre on the two major issues of development and stability, seize the new breakthrough in Tibet work) (Jul. 20, 1994), in CDRO and TARCC 2005: 457–464.

Jiang, Zemin, 1994b, "Zai guwuyuan di erci quanguo minzu tuanjie jinbu biaozhang dahui shang de jianghua" (Speech to the State Counci's second national conference on stead expression of unity of nationalities) (Sep. 29, 1994), in SNAC and CCARO 2003: 126–28.

Jiang, Zemin 1993a, "Gaodu zhongshi minzu gongzuo he zongjiao gongzuo" (Emphasize to a high degree nationalities work and religion work) (Nov.7, 1993), in Guojia Minzu Shiwu Weiyuan Hui (State Nationalities Affairs Commission), ed., *Zhongguo gongchandang guanyu minzu wenti de jiben guandian he zhengce* (Basic approaches and policies of the Chinese Communist Party on nationalities issues) (Beijing: Nationalities Press, 2002): 295–302.

Jiang, Zemin, 1993b. "Yao shanyu ba Zhongyang de fangzhen zhengce tong Xizang de Shiji henhaode jieheqilai" (We must perfect the excellent linkage of program and policy with the actual conditions in Tibet) (Mar. 16), in CDRO and TARCC 2005: 455–456.

Jiang, Zemin, 1992a, "Jinyibu jiaqiang ge minzu de da tuanjie, jianjue weihu zuguo de tongyi" (Steadily strengthen the unity of all nationalities, resolutely safeguard the unity of the motherland) (Jan. 14) in CDRO and TARCC 2005: 442–44.

Jiang, Zemin, 1992b, "Jiaqiang ge minzu da tuanjie, wei jianshe you Zhongguo tese de sheihuizhuyi xieshou qianjin," (Strengthen unity of all nationalities, move forward hand in hand to establish socialism with Chinese characteristics) (Jan. 14), in SNACand CCARO 2003: 24–41.

Jiang, Zemin, 1991, "Baochi Dang de zongjiao zhengce de wendingxing he lianxux- ing" (Preserving the stability and continuity of Party policy on religion) (Jan. 30, 1991), in CCARO-GRU and RAB-PRD 2003: 208–12

Jiang, Zemin, 1990, "Yiding yao zuohao zongjiao gongzuo" (We definitely need to do well in religion work) (Dec. 7, 1990), in CCARO-GRU and RAB-PRD 2003: 198–204.

Jiang, Guoqing, 2001, "Luetan zhuquan yu liang'an guanxi" (Sketch on sovereignty and cross-strait relations), *Faxue pinglun* (Law Review) no. 3: 39–43, 79.

Jin, Binggao and Gong Xuezeng, 2004, *Minzu lilun minzu zhengce xuexi gangyao* (Study outline on nationalities theory and nationalities policy) (Beijing: National- ities Press).

Lai, Bangfan, ed., 2002. *Xibu kaifa zhengfu guanli yanjiu* (Study of government administration in China's western development) (Beijing: National Administration Institute).

Lan, Zou, 2000, *Zongguo xibu gulu* (Alone in China's West) (Hong Kong: Mirror Books).

Li, Baojun, 1999, *Dangdai Zhongguo waijiao gailun* (Treatise on contemporary Chinese foreign policy) (Beijing: People's University Press).

Li, Dexi, Qian Zhen, and Lin Zhe, 2005, *Quanqiu beijing xia de Zhongguo minzhu jianshe* (Development of democracy in China under the global background) (Chongqing: Chongqing Press), based on a policy conference at the authoritative Central Party School.

Li, Dezhu, 2000, "Xibu dakaifa yu woguo minzu wenti" (Western development and our nationalities issues) *Qiushi* (Seeking truth) no. 288, June 1.

Li, Hong, 2004, *Zhongguo minzu fazhan lungang* (Outline views on development of China's nationalities) (Hohehaote: Inner Mongolia University Press).

Li, Jingui, 2001, "Nei Menggu xumuye de zhenqing yu fazhan" (Promotion and development of animal husbandry in Inner Mongolia), in Zhonggong Ningxia Hui Zizhiqu Weiyuanhui Dang Shi Yanjiu Shi (Party History Research Office of CPC Ningxia Hui Autonomous Region Committee), ed., *Zhongguo gongchandang yu shaoshu minzu diqu de gaige kaifang* (The Communist Party of China and reform and opening up in the minority areas) (Beijing: CPC Party History Press) (hereafter, "Ningxia 2001"): 379–87.

Li, Lanqing, 2003, "Jiakuai minzu jiaoyu shiye fazhan, cujin ge minzu tuanjie jinbu yu gongtong fanrong" (Accelerate development of nationality education activities, promote progress in the unity and common prosperity of nationalities), in SNACand CCARO: 394–406.

Li, Minggan, Chen Yahui, and Lu Zhifang, eds., 2001, *WTO yu liang'an jinghe* (WTO and cross-straits anxiety) (Taipei: Tianxia Press).

Li, Minggan, 2001, "Liang'an keji zhengfeng" (Cross-strait competition in science and technology), in Li Minggan, Chen Yahui, Lu Zhifang, eds., *WTO yu liang'an jinghe* (WTO and cross-straits anxiety) (Taipei: Tianxia Press,): 15–32.

Li, Peng, 1994, "Zhuazhu jiyu, tuanjie fendou, jiakuai Xizang jianshe" (Seize the opportunity, struggle for unity, accelerate Tibet construction) (July 22), in CDRO and TARCC 2005: 465–77.

Li, Peng, 1992, "Zi zhongyang minzu gongzuo huiyi tuanmuhui shang de jianghua" (Speech at the closing session of the central nationalities work conference) (Jan. 18), in SNACand CCARO 2003: 42–52.

Li, Peng, 1990, "Jinyibu zhongshi, guanxin he zuohao zongjiao gongzuo" (Progressively focus, attend to and do a good job in religion work) (Dec. 5), in CCARO-GRU and RAB-PRD 2003: 189–97.

Li, Ruihuan, 2001, "Jizhong jingli fazhan jingji, gaishan shenghuo" (Concentrate forces to develop the economy and improve living standards) (Jun. 27), in CDRO and TARCC 2005: 571–9.

Li, Ruihuan, 1995, "Zai Banchan zhuanshi lintong xunfang lingdao xiaozu di sanci huiyi shang de jianghua" (Speech to third meeting of leading small group on search for the reincarnated Panchen Lama) (Nov. 10), in CDRO and TARCC 2005: 501–507.

Li, Ruihuan, 1994, "Xin xingshi xia de minzu zongjiao wenti" (Nationalities and religion issues under new conditions), in Zhongyang dangxiao minzu zongjiao lilun shi (Central Party School nationalities and religion theory office) ed., *Xin shiqi minzu zongjiao gongzuo xuanchuan shouce* (Propaganda manual for nationalities and religion work in the new period) (Beijing: Religion and Culture Press, 2002): 300–6.

Li, Shantong, ed., 2003, *Xibu da kaifa yu diqu xietiao fazhan* (Western Development and regional coordinated development) (Beijing: Commercial Press).

Li, Shaobo, 2002, "Xinjiang youxu min dingju zhengce de yanbian" (Development of Xinjiang's policies on fixed residency for nomadic herders), *Xinjiang xhifan daxue xuebao* (Journal of Xinjiang Normal University) vol. 23 no. 4: 83–89.

Li, Shuang and Liu Baoqiong, "Lun dang de di sandai lingdao ren weihu Xinjiang wending de sixiang," in Tiemuer and Mao: 1–9.

Li, Wanqiang, 2006, "Lun quanqiuhua qushi xia guojifa de xin fazhan" (New developments in international law under the trend of globalization), *Faxue pinglun* (Law Review) no. 6: 55–62.

Li, Zhanrong, 2003, *Minzu jingji fa yanjiu* (Research on nationalities economic law) (Beijing: Nationalities Press,): 181–94.

Lian, Xiangmin, 2006, "'Xizang wenti' de youlai he zhuangkuang" (Origins and present situation of the 'Tibet Question'), in Hao Shiyuan and Wang Xien: 273–90.
Liang'an san tong (Cross-strait three links) (Taipei: Legislative Yuen 2003) (2 vols).
Lin, Ziyang, ed., 2004, *Yi guo mei liang zhi, geng meiyou xin Xianggang* (One country without two systems and even more so without a new Hong Kong) (Hong Kong: Shi Publishing).
Ling, Jun, "Xitong yanjiu he zhengque xuanquan Xinjiang de lishi wei Xinjiang de wending he fazhen fuwu" (Systematic research and precise propaganda on Xinjiang's history serve stability and development in Xinjiang), in Tiemuer and Mao 2003: 43–51.
Liu, Hantai and Du Xifu, ed., *Zhongguo daji 'Dong Tu' bagao* (Report on China's attack against the East Turkestan Movement).
Liu, Jian and Hao Jianyun, 2001, "Lun woguo laodong jiaopei zhidu yu guoji renquan gongyue de chongtu ji qi tiaozheng" (On conflicts between our labor education and training system and international human rights treaties and their adjustment), *Faxue pinglun* (Law Review) no. 5: 29–32.
Liu, Jianlan, Wang Zongli, 1998. *Zhongguo xibei minzu diqu xiang zhen zhengquan jianshe yanjiu* (Study of building political power at the village and township level in minority areas of northwest China) (Lanzhou: Gansu People's Press).
Liu, Jie, 2004, *Renquan yu guojia zhuquan* (Human rights and national sovereignty) (Shanghai: Shanghai People's Press).
Liu, Jinghai and Shi Wenzheng, 2003, *Xibu dakaifa zhong de minzu zizhi difang jingji zizhiquan yanjiu* (Study of economic autonomy of nationality autonomy areas in the Western Development Program) (Huhehaote: Inner Mongolia People's Press).
Liu, Jinghai and Shi Wenzheng, ed., 2001, *Lun wanshan minzu quyu zizhi* (On perfecting autonomy in nationality regions) (Huhehaote: Inner Mongolia People's Press)
Liu, Shuguang, 2003, *Quanqiuhua yu fan quanqiuhua* (Globalization and anti-globalization) (Changsha: Hunan People's Press).
Liu, Xinhui and Wang Yanbin, 2001, "Secretary of Xinjiang Uygur Autonomous Regional CPC Committee Wang Lequan: Press on at the Opportune Moment Brought About Through the Large-scale Development of the West," *Liaowang* (Outlook) No. 26 (Jun. 25) FBIS-CHI-2001-0710 (July 25, 2001).
Liu, Zhigang, ed. 2003, *Yida zhisheng de shixian tujing yanjiu* (Realize the ruling of provinced through law via research) (Baoding: Hebei University Press).
Liu, Jun, 2003, "Xinjiang guanche luoshi dang de minzu zhengce de qingkuang ji duice" (Situation and countermeasures concerning full implementation of Party nationalities policies in Xinjiang), in Tiemuer and Mao 2003: 255–78.
Lu Gongdong and Siwei zhengce yanjiu suo (Civic Exchange Research Institute), ed., 2003, *Chuangjian minzhu* (Building democracy) (Hong Kong: Civic Exchange).
Lu Gongdong and Siwei zhengce yanjiu suo (Civic Exchange Research Institute), ed., 2002, *Rang minyi shengyin xiangqilai* (Let the voice of the people ring out) (Hong Kong: Civic Exchange).
Lu, Zhifang and Li Minggan, 2001, "Jingzheng duishou: Liangxiang jituan, Hai'er jituan" (The adversaries: Legend Group, Hai'er Group), in Li Minggan, Chen Yahui, Lu Zhifang, eds., *WTO yu liang'an jinghe* (WTO and cross-straits anxiety) (Taipei: Tianxia Press): 133–60.
Lu, Jian, Wang Weisheng, and Jiang Guoli, 2003, "Xibu dakaifa yu Xinjiang jingji fazhan (The Western development program and Xinjiang's economic development), in Tiemuer and Mao 2003, 311–48.

Luo, Guangwu, 2001, *Xin Zhongguo zongjiao gongzuo da shi yaojian* (Outline of major events in religious work in the new China) (Beijing: Chinese culture (*huawen*) press): 298–304.

Ma, Dazheng 2005, "Bianjiang yu minzu wenti: Lishi yu xianshi cengmian de sikao (The frontier and nationalities issues: Considerations of history and the present statge), in Zhang Zhirong, *Zhongguo bianjiang yu minzu wenti: Dangdai Zhongguo de taozhan ji qi lishi youlai* (China's frontiers and nationalities issues: China current strategy and its historical origins) (Beijing: Peking University Press):1–8.

Ma, Dazheng, 2003, *Guojia liyi gaoyu yiqie* (The national interest is paramount) (Urumqi: Xinjiang People's Press).

Ma, Rong, 1994, "Xizang jumin shouru xiaofei zhong de cheng xiang chabie" (Urban-rural disparities in income and consumption amoung residents of Tibet), in Pan Naigu, Ma Rong *Zhongguo bianyuan diqu kaifa yanjiu* (Study of development in China's frontiers) (Hong Kong: Oxford University Press): 323–86.

Ma, Rong and Pan Naigu, 1994, "Nei Menggu bannong banxu qu de shehui jingji fazhan" (Social and economic development in semi-agricultural semi-pastoral regions of Inner Mongolia), in Pan Naigu, Ma Rong *Zhongguo bianyuan diqu kaifa yanjiu* (Study of development in China's frontiers) (Hong Kong: Oxford University Press): 63–124.

Ma, Yue, 2003, "Minzhu fazhan yu shangjie liyi" (Democratic development and the interests of the business community), in Lu Gonghui and Civic Exchange (eds.), *Chuangjian minzhu* (Establishing democracy) (Hong Kong: Hong Kong University Press): 74–81.

Ma, Zifu, ed., 2003, *Xibu kaifa yu duominzu wenhua* (Western China development and multi-ethnic cultures) (Beijing: Huaxia Press).

Miao, Jiafu, 2005, *Quanqiuhua yu minzu wenhua duoyangxing* (Globalization and multiculturalism of nationality culture) (Beijing: People's Press).

Miao, Pusheng, 2003, "Xinjiang zai Zhongguo tongyi de duominzu guojia xingcheng, fazhan, he gonggu guocheng zhong de lishi diwei" (Xinjiang's historic role in the process of the formation, development, and consolidation of unified China as a multi-ethnic state), in Tiemuer and Mao 2003: 52–64.

"Minzu gongzuo zhong guojia mimi yi qi mimi juti fanwei de guiding" (Regulations on the specific scope of state secrecy and other secrecy in nationalities work), in Tianjin 2004: 96–97.

"Minzu xiang xingzheng gongzuo tiaoli" (Regulations on administration work in nationality villages), in SNACand CCARO 2003, 82–85.

Na, La, 2004, *Xinjiang youmu minzu shehui fenxi* (Analysis of Xinjiang's nomadic herder nationality societies) (Beijing: Nationalities Press).

"Neimenggu zizhiqu (hereafter, "NMAR") caoyuan guanli tiaoli" (Inner Mongolia Measures for Grasslands Management) (1984, rev. 1991, rev. 2004), in Shi Wenzheng, ed., *Caoyuan huanjin de falu baohu* (Legal Protection of the Grasslands environment) (Huhehaote: Inner Mongolia People's Press, 2005): 320–33.

NMAR difangxing fagui guizhang xuanze (Volume of selected local laws and regulations of Inner Mongolia Autonomous Region) (Huhehaote: Inner Mongolia People's Press, 2000) (hereafter, "IM Laws 2000").

"NMAR geji renmin daibiao dahui changwu weiyyuanhui jiandu gongzuo tiaoli" (Regulation on inspection work for different levels of IMAR People's Congress Standing Committees) (1995), in IM Laws 2000: 23–33).

"NMAR geji renmin daibiao dahui changwu weiyyuanhui zhifa jiancha tiaoli" (Inspection regulations for different levels of IMAR People's Congress Standing Committees on enforcement of law) (1994) in IM Laws 2000): 18–22.

"NMAR guanyu guli waishang touze de youhui zhengce" (Preferential policies on encouraging foreign investment) Nov. 11, 20005 (http://manzhouli.gov.cn/2005-11/2005112114758.htm) [Jan. 4, 2010].

"NMAR guanyu jinyibu kuangda hengxiang lianhe de youhui zhengce" (On progressively expanding lateral coordination of preferential policies) (Aug. 17, 1995) (http://law.baidu.com/pages/chinalawinfo/1678/31/2850fa2e5b4d721b1003e35364c6f833_0.html) [Jan. 4, 2010]

"NMAR guli Taiwan tongbao touze de guiding" (Regulations of Inner Mongolia Autonomous Region on encouraging investment by Taiwan compatriots), (Dec. 6, 1999) http://law.baidu.com/pages/chinalawinfo/1679/30/650e54c62802b6c59c1f9aca2dc4c3bc_0.html) [Jan. 4, 2010].

"NMAR 'jiu wu' dui wai kaifang zhanlue guihua" (Strategic program for Inner Mongolia opening up to the outside world under the 9th Five Year Plan) (Jan. 15, 1996), in Ningxia 2001: 201–2.

"NMAR 'jiu wu' mingpai jinxing zhanlue guihua" (Strategic program for implementing famous brands in Inner Mongolia under the 9th Five Year Plan) (Jan. 16, 1996), in Ningxia 2001: 210–12.

"NMAR 'jiu wu' rencai kaifang zhanlue guihua" (Strategic program for human resource development in Inner Mongolia under the 9th Five Year Plan) (Jan. 15, 1996), in Ningxia 2001: 202–7.

"NMAR 'jiu wu' ziyuan zhuanhuan zhanlue guihua" (Strategic program for transformation of natural resources in Inner Mongolia under the Fifth Five Year Plan) (Jan. 15, 1996), in Ningxia 2001: 199–201.

"NMAR Renmin Daibiao Dahui Changwu Weiyyuanhui pizhun difangxing fagui he zizhi tiaoli, danxing tiaoli de guiding" (Regulations of the IMAR People's Congress Standing Committee on approval of local laws and regulations, autonomous measures, and individual measures), in IM Laws 2000: 40–42.

NMAR Renmin Daibiao Dahui Changwu Weiyyuanhui zhiding difangxing fagui de guiding" (Regulations of the IMAR People's Congress Standing Committee on enactment of local laws and regulations), in IM Laws 2000: 34–39.

"NMAR Renmin Zhengfu he Neimenggu Zizhiqu gonghui lianxi huiyi zhidu ruogan guiding" (Several regulations of IMAR Government and IMAR General Trade Union on integrated chairperson system) (Jan. 14, 2004) (www.lawbook.com.cn/lawhtm/2004/83944.htm) [Jan. 4, 2010].

"NMAR Renmin Zhengfu yiding difangxing fagui caoan he zhiding guizhang guiding" (Regulations of the IMAR People's Government on drafting local laws and regulations and enacting regulations and rules), in IM Laws 2000: 178–84.

"NMAR shishi xibu dakaifa ruogan zhengce shishi de guiding" (Implementing regulations of Inner Mongolia Autonous Region for carrying out certain policies of Great Western Development) (Feb. 21, 2003) (http://law.baidu.com/pages/chinalawinfo/1682/58/2bcd59ed37c333376e3d58f82fcd19e9_0.html) [Jan. 4, 2010].

"NMAR shixing 'Zhonghua Remin Gongheguo Shuifa' Banfa" (Methods of Inner Mongolia Autonomous Region for Implementing the 'Water Law of the PRC') (Aug. 1, 2004) (www.law-lib.com/law/law_view1.asp?id=86632) [Jan. 4, 2010].

"NMAR zhengfu changwu huiyi tongguo sanxiang difangxing fagui caoan" (IMAR government standing meeting enacts three draft local regulations) (*Xinhua Inner*

Mongolia Desk) (Aug. 2004) (www.gl.cei.gov.cn/westKF/Policy/locoal/2004/08/0902. htm) [jan. 4, 2010]
"NMAR zongjiao huodong changsuo guanli shishi banfa" (IMAR implementing measures on management of sites for religious activities) (Jan. 23, 1996), in RAB-PRD 2002: 279–82.
Ni, Guoliang, 1998, *Zhongguo xibei diqu xiandaihua zhong de jingji yu wenhua guanxi* (Relations between economy and culture in the course of modernization in China's northwest) (Lanzhou: Gansu People's Press).
Ningxia, 2001, Zhonggong Ningxia Hui Zizhiqu Weiyuanhui Dang Shi Yanjiu Shi (Party History Research Office of CPC Ningxia Hui Autonomous Region Committee), ed., *Zhongguo gongchandang yu shaoshu minzu diqu de gaige kaifang* (The Communist Party of China and reform and opening up in the minority areas) (Beijing: CPC Party History Press).
"Ningxia hui zizhiqu zongjiao shiwu guanli zanxing guiding" (Provisional regulations of Ningxia Hui Autonomous Region on management of religious affairs) (Jun. 7, 1994), in RAB-PRD 2002: 153–60.
Pan, Naigu, Ma Rong, 1994, *Zhongguo bianyuan diqu kaifa yanjiu* (Study of development in China's frontiers) (Hong Kong: Oxford University Press).
Peng, Zhen, 1991, *Peng Zhen wenxuan* (Collected Works of Peng Zhen) (Beijing: Peoples' Press).
Peng, Zhen, 1989a, "Guanyu Zhonghua renmin gongheguo xianfa xiugai cao'an de shuoming" (Explanation of the draft revisions to the Constitution of the PRC), in Peng Zhen, *Lun xin shiqi de shehui minzhu yu fazhi jianshe* (On building socialist democracy and legal system during the new period) (Beijing: Central Archives Press): 100–115.
Peng, Zhen, 1989b, *Lun xin shiqi de shehui minzhu yu fazhi jianshe* (On building socialist democracy and legal system during the new period) (Beijing: Central Archives Press).
Peng, Zhen 1982a, "Guanyu Zhonghua renmin gongheguo xianfa xiugai cao'an de shuoming" (Explanation of the draft revisions to the Constitution of the PRC), in *Renmin ribao* (People's Daily) Dec. 6.
Peng, Zhen, 1982b, "Wo guo gongmin you zongjiao xinyang de ziyou." (Our citizens enjoy the freedom of religious belief), in CCARO-GRU and RAB-PRD 2003: 74–76.
Peng,Zhen, 1991, "Guanyu difang ren da changweihui de gongzuo" (On the work of local people's congress standing committees) (Apr. 18 1980), in *Peng Zhen wenxuan* (Collected Works of Peng Zhen) (Beijing: Peoples' Press): 383–91.
Pu, Hao *et al.*, 2000, *Xinjiang* (Xinjiang) (Beijing: Nationalities Press).
Qing, Jue *et al.*, 2003, "Xinjiang jingji shehui fazhen due minzu guanxi de yingxiang" (Effects of economic and social development on nationalities relations in Xinjiang), in Tiemuer and Mao 2003: 196–224.
Qu, Haiyuan, 1997, *Taiwan zongjiao bianqian de shehui zhengzhi fenxi* (Socio-political analysis of changes in Taiwan religions) (Taipei: Guiguan Publishers).
"Quanguo minwei 'shi wu' qijian jingji gongzuo guihua" (Economic work plan for nationalities commissions across the country during the Tenth Five Year Plan), in Tianjin 2004: 163–70.
"Quanguo zongjiao gongzuo huiyi zai jing juxing" (National work conference on religion convenes in Beijing) *Renmin wang* (People's Net) (electronic service) (Dec. 12, 2001) (www.people.com.cn/GB/paper39/4949/531577.html) [Jan. 5, 2010].

RAB-PRD, 2002, Guojia Zongjiao Shiwu Ju Zhengce Fagui Si (Policy and Research Division of State Council Religious Affairs Office), ed., *Quanguo zongjiao xingzheng fagui guizhang huibian* (Compilation of national laws, regulations and charters for administration of religion) (Beijing: Religion and Culture Press).
Rao, Geping and Huang Yao, 2002, "Lun quanqiuhua jincheng yu guoji zuzhi de hudong guanxi" (On mutual impacts of globalization processes and international organizations), *Faxue pinglun* (Law Review) no. 2: 3–13.
Re, Like and Tie Muer, 2003, "Gaoju minzu datuanjie he zuguo tongyi de qizhi, shenru chijiu di kaizhan fafenlie douzheng" (Raise the banner of unity among nationalities and unity of the motherland, deepen and prolong the development of the struggle against separatism), in Tiemuer and Mao 2003: 10–28.
RMET. Zhonggong Xizang Zizhiqu Weiyuanhui Dangshi Yanjiushi (Party history office of CPC TAR Committee) (ed.), *Zhongguo gongchandang xizang lishi da shiji – 1949–2004* (Record of major events in the history of the CPC in Tibet – 1949–2004) (Party History Press, 2005) (2 vols).
Renda jiao-ke-wen-wei weiyuanhui he jiaoyubu (NPC Committee on Education, Science, Culture and Health and Ministry of Education), ed., Zhonghua renmin gonghe guo guojia tongyong yuyan wenzi fa xuexi duben (Study reader on the Simultaneous Language Law of the PRC) (Beijing: Language Press, 2001).
Sheng, Lang, Tao Ying, 2002, *Zhongguo xibu da kaifa zhong de renkou yu kezhixu fazhan* (Population and sustainable development in China's western development) (Beijing: People's Press).
Shi, Shengtan 2001a, *Xibu kaifa zhengce* (Policies on China's western development) (Lanzhou: Gansu People's Press).
Shi, Shengtan 2001b, *Xibu shengtai huanjing* (The Ecology and Environment of the West) (Lanzhou: Gansu People's Press).
Shi,Wenzheng, ed., 2005, *Caoyuan huanjin de falu baohu* (Legal Protection of the Grasslands environment) (Hohhot: Inner Mongolia People's Press, 2005).
Shi, Zhengyi, ed., 2002, *Minzu jingjixue yu xibu da kaifa luntan* (Forum on nationalities economics and the western development) (Beijing: Nationalities Press).
Si Da shihua jidi chengwei Xinjiang zhaoshang zhongdian" (The four great petroleum basins constitute important points for Xinjiang's attracting business), *Xinjiang jingji bao* (Xinjiang economic news) Nov. 11, 2004 (http://xjbz.gov.cn/html/news/jjxx/2004-11/11/11_32_0018094.html) [Nov. 7, 2007].
SNAC. 2002, Guojia Minzu Shiwu Weiyuanhui (State Nationalities Affairs Commission), 2002, *Zhongguo gongchandang guanyu minzu wenti de jiben guandian he zhengce* (Basic approaches and policies of the Chinese Communist Party on nationalities issues) (Beijing: Nationalities Press).
SNAC and CCARO, 2003, Guojia Minzu Shiwu Weiyuanhui (State Nationalities Affairs Commission) and Zhonggong Zhongyang Wenxian Yanjiu Shi (CPC Central Archives Research Office), 2003. *Minzu gongzuo wenjian xuanbian 1990–2002* (Collection of documents on nationalities work – 1990–2002) (Beijing: Central Archives Press).
Song, Caifa, ed., 2003, *Minzu quyu zizhifa tonglun* (General Survey on the Law on Autonomy in Minority Areas) (Beijing: Nationalities Press).
Su, Taiheng, ed., 2001, *Zoujin Xibu: Xibu da Kaifa yu Xinan minzu wenti* (Go West: The Western Development Program and nationalities issues in the Southwest) (Guiyang: Guizhou Nationalities Press).
Sun, Shichen, 2001, "Lun guoji renquan fa xia guojia de yiwu" (On state responsibility under international human rights law), in *Faxue pinglun* (Law Review) no. 2: 91–96.

Sun, Yi, 2006, "Xin shiji chu de shaoshu minzu ganbu duiwu jianshe" (Establishing minority cadre corps at the turn of the new century), in Hao Shiyuan and Wang Xien, ed., *Zhongguo minzu fazhan baogao 2001–2006* (Report on nationalities development in China 2001–6) (Beijing: Social Sciences Academic Press): 132–47.

Sun, Yi, Jiao Yacheng, Ma Zhengyi, Sun Jiwei, 2003, "Xinjing peiyang shaoshu minzu ganbu ji shaoshu minzu daibiaorenshi wenti" (Issues in training minority cadres and minority representatives in Xinjiang), in Tiemuer and Mao 2003: 285–310.

Sun, Yu, Guo Chenjie, Liu Hongbi, 2001. *Zhongguo xibu diqu fazhi huanjing yanjiu* (Study of the legal system environment in China's western regions) (Chongqing: Chongqing Press).

Sun, Zhonglin, 2001, "Lun shaoshu minzu ganbu de peiyang yu shiyong" (On training and use of minority nationality cadres), Liu Jinghai and Shi Wenzheng, ed., *Lun wanshan minzu quyu zizhi* (On improving autonomy in nationality regions) (Huhehaote: Inner Mongolia People's Press): 68–81.

"Taiwan haiyan liang'anjian hangyun guanli banfa" (Administrative measures for air transport on the Taiwan coast and across the straits), Zhang Wanming: 206–7.

Tang, Jiahua, 2004, *Falu, zhengzhi yu wo* (Law, politics and me) (Hong Kong: et press).

Tang, Jiahua, 2003, *Renquan,minzu yu fazhi* (Human rights, democracy and rule of law) (Hong Kong: et press).

Tang, Tianri, 2003, "Zhongguo he xifang zai renquan wenti shang de yuanze fenqi" (Divergence of principles between China and the West on human rights questions), in China Human Rights Development Foundation ed., *Xifang renquan guan yu renquan waijiao* (Western human rights concepts and human rights diplomacy) (Beijing: New World Press): 60–65.

Tian, Weijiang, 2001, *Zhengque chanming Xinjiang lishi* (Correctly explaining Xinjiang's history) (Urumqi: Xinjiang People's Press).

Tian, Weijiang, Chen Chao, Ma Pinyan, 2001, *Zhengque chanming Xinjiang lishi, Xinjiang minzu shi, Xinjiang yixilanjiao shi* (Correctly explaining Xinjiang history, Xinjiang ethnic history, and Xinjiang Islamic history) (Urumqi: Xinjiang People's Press).

Tianjin, 2004: Tianjin Shi Minzu Shiwu Weiyuanhui (Tianjin Municipal Minorities Affairs Commission *Xin shiqi chengshi minzu gongzuo zhengce fagui xuanbian* (Collection of policies and laws on urban minorities work in the new era) (Beijing: Nationalities Press).

Tibet Propaganda Department, 2003, "Shixian kuayue shi fazhan" (Implement leapfrog style development), in CCTV, *Zhongguo Xibu* (The West of China) (Beijing: Youth Publishers): 337–38.

Tiemuer, Dawamaiti, 2005, *Lun minzu gongzuo yu minzu wenhua* (On nationalities work and nationalities culture) (Beijing: Central Party School Press).

Tiemuer, Dawamaiti, 2001a, "Quanmian guanche shizing minzu quyu zizhifa" (Fully implement in an all round way the Nationality Region Autonomy Law) in Tiemuer Dawamaiti, ed., *Lun minzu gongzuo yu minzu wenhua* (On nationalities work and nationalities culture (Beijing: Central Party School Press, 2005): 518–27.

Tiemuer, Dawamaiti, 2001b, "Jiejue Zhongguo minzu wenti de chenggong zhilu" (The road to success in resolving China's nationaties issues) in Tiemuer Dawamaiti, ed., *Lun minzu gongzuo yu minzu wenhua* (On nationalities work and nationalities culture (Beijing: Central Party School Press, 2005): 528–45.

Tiemuer, Dawamaiti, 1997, "Wei jianshe tuanjie, furao, wenming de shehui zhuyi Xinjiang er fendou" (Struggle for construction of a united, prosperous and cultured socialist Xinjiang), in Tiemuer Dawamaiti, ed., *Lun minzu gongzuo yu minzu wenhua* (On nationalities work and nationalities culture (Beijing: Central Party School Press, 2005): 472–89.

Tiemuer, Dawamaiti, 1996, "Quanmian guanche he huoshi zongyang qihao wenjian jingsheng, quebao Xinjiang de zhangqi wending" (Fully implement in an allround way the spirit of Central Document No. 7, ensure long-term stability in Xinjiang), in Tiemuer Dawamaiti 2005: 448–71.

Tiemuer, Dawamaiti, 1990, "Renzhen zhixing Dang de minzu zhengce" jinyibu zengqiang minzu tuanjie, wei wending he fazhan Xinjiang er shili fendou (Consciensciously implement Party policy on nationalities and progressively strengthen unity of nationalities, and energetically struggle for stability and development in Xinjiang, in Tiemuer Dawamaiti 2005: 269–91.

Tiemuer, and Mao Gangning, ed., *Xinjiang yanjiu wenlun xuan – di yi ji* (Collection of essays on the study of Xinjiang – vol. 1) (Beijing: Nationalities Press, 2003) ("Tiemuer and Mao").

Tung, Chen-yuan, 2003, "Quanqiuhua xia de liang an jingji guanxi" (cross-strait economic relations in the era of globalization) (Taipei: Sheng-Chih Book,).

Tung, Zhenyuan, 2003, *Quanqiuhua xia de liang'an jingji guanxi* (Cross-straits economic relations under globalization) (Taipei: Shengzhi Wenhua Press).

Wang, Guangxian, 2002, "Diyue guo zai shishi guoji renquan tiaoyue fangmian de jingyan yu wenti" (Experience and problems of signatory states implementing human rights treaties), *Faxue pinglun* (Law Review) no. 2: 116–25.

Wang, Zuoan, 2002, *Zhongguo de zongjiao wenti he zongjiao zhengce* (China's religious issues and policies on religion) (Beijing: Religion and Culture Press,).

Wang, Jianmin, Wang Gang, 2003, "Xianggang, Taiwan, yu Zuguo dalu jingji guanxi de fazhan ji ziben ronghe" (Development of economic relations and capital merger among Hong Kong, Taiwan, and the Motherland) in Yu Keli, ed., *Taiwan yanjiu lunwenji* (Collection of essays on Taiwan studies) vol. 12 (Beijing: China Population Press): 181–94.

Wang, Lixiong, 2009, *Wo de xiyu ni de dong tu* (My western region, your East Turkestan) (Taipei: Dakuai pub. 2007).

Wang, Luolin et al., 2003, *Zhongguo xibu dakaifa zhengce* (China's western development policy) (Beijing: Economic Management Publishing).

Wang, Ningxiong, 2002, *Xibu dakaifa yu Hexi Zouxiang jingji fazhan yanjiu* (Study of western development and economic development in the Gansu Corridor) (Lanzhou: Lanzhou University Press,).

Wang, Shuanqian, 2003, *Huihuang Xinjiang* (Splendid Xinjiang) (Urumqi: Xinjiang People's Press).

Wang, Taiquan and Chen Yueduan, ed., 2000, *Liang'an guanxi falu* (Cross-straits law) (Taipei: Greater China Press).

Wang, Tianjin, 2002, *Xibu huanjing ziyuan chanye* (Environmental and resource industries of the Western Region) (Dalian: Northeast Finance and Economics University Press).

Wang, Yinzhou, 2003, *Quanqiu zhengzhi he Zhongguo waijiao* (Global politics and China's foreign policy) (Beijing: World Knowledge Press).

Wang, Zhaoguo, 2005, "Guanyu ' Fan fenlie guojia fa (Caoan)' de shuoming" (Explanation of the draft Anti Secession Law), in CCC-OTW and SC-TAO 2005: 33–39.

Wang, Zhaoguo, 2003, "Zai guazhi duanlian shaoshu minzu ganbu peixun ban shang de jiaghua" (Speech to leadership tempering minority cadre training class), in Chengshi minzu gongzuo tiaoli") in SNACand CCARO 2003: 85–90.

Wang, Zhaoguo, 2000, "On PRC United Front Work," Beijing *Xinhua* Domestic Service Jan. 8, 2000, in *FBIS Daily Report – China* (FBIS-CHI-2000-0110) Jan. 11.

Wang, Zhaoguo, 1996, "Zai guazhi duanlian shaoshu minzu ganbu peixunban shang de jianghua" (Speech to minority cadre training class on tapping knowledge and exercising the body) (Nov. 14), in SNAC and CCARO 2003: 161–70.

Wang, Zhenmin, 2002, *Zhongyang yu tebie xingzhengqu guanxi* (Relations between the Centre and special administrative regions) (Beijing: Qinghua University Press).

Wang, Zitou, 1985, *Badashanren shu hua ji* (Collection of calligraphy and paintings of Badashanren) (Beijing: People's Arts Publishing).

Wang, Zongli, Liu Jianlan, Jia Yingsheng, 1995. *Zhongguo xibei nong xu min zhengzhoo xingwei yanjiu* (Study of political behaviour among peasants and herdsmen in China's northwest) (Lanzhou: Gansu People's Press).

Wang, Zongli, Tan Zhenhao, Liu Jianlan, 1998, *Zhongguo xibei minzu diqu zhengzhi wending yanjiu* (Study of political stability in China's northwest minority areas) (Lanzhou: Gansu People's Press).

Wei, Yifan, 2009, "Too late to talk about Xinjiang?" *Nanfang Zhoumo* (Southern Weekend) Aug. 2, 2009, reprinted in *China Digital Times* http://chinadigitaltimes.net/2009/08/wei-yifan-tim-too-late-to-talk-about-xinjiang/ [Nov. 28, 2009].

"Wenhuabu, Guojia minwei guanyu jinyi bu jiaqiang shaoshu minzu wenhua gongzong de yijian" (Opinion of the Ministry of Culture and the State Nationalities Commission on progressively strengthening minority nationality cultural work) (Dec. 13, 2000), in SNACand CCARO 2003: 253–62.

"Woguo shoubu jieshui guangai difang fagui chutai" (Our fist local regulations for water conservation in irrigation are tabled) *Zhongguo shuli bao* (China water power news) Feb. 27, 2003 (http://shuizheng.chinawater.com.cn/zhxw/20030227/200302270074.asp) [Jan. 5, 2010].

Wu, Bangguo, 2005, Quanmian guanche zhongyang dui Tai gongzuo dazheng fangzhen renzhen zuohao fanfenlie guojia lifa gongzuo" (Fully implement CPC political policy on Taiwan work and do a good in anti-secession legislation) *Renmin ribao* (People's Daily) Dec. 30, 2004, in CCC-OTW and SC-TAO 2005: 10–12).

Wu, Bangguo, 1995, "Jianshe tuanjie, fuyu, wenming de xin Xizang" (Establish a unified, prosperous, and cultured new Tibet) (Aug. 31, 1995), in CDRO and TARCC 2005: 492–497.

Wu, Jianli, 2001, "Xizang zizhiqu gaige kaifang 20 nian shulue" (Narrative on twenty years of reform and opening up in Tibet Autonomous Region), in Ningxia 2001: 343–75.

Wu, Shimin, 1998, *Zhongguo minzu zhengce duben* (Reader on China's nationalities policy) (Beijing: Central Nationalities University Press).

"Wujia hui shang Xinjiang shengchan jianshe bingtuan chutai zhaoshang yinze youhui zhengce" (The Wujia meeting tables preferential regulations for attracting business and investment in the production and construction corps) *Xinhua wang* (New China News Agency Net) (Sep. 3, 2001) (www.cein.gov.cn/news/show.asp?rec_no=2346) [Nov. 7, 2007].

"Wulumuqi shi zhaokai le ganbu dahui kongqi fan fenlie douzheng tongqiang tiebi" (Urumqi city convenes candres conference, constructs a bastion of iron in the

Bibliography: Chinese 201

struggle to resist separatism) *Xinjiang ribao* (Xinjiang daily) Sep. 13, 2008 (http://news.xinhuanet.com/legal/2008-9/13/content_9968788.htm) [Jan. 5, 2010].).

Xiandai Xueshu Yanjiu Jijinhui (Council on Formosa Studies), ed., 2002, *Taiwan yu Zhongguo jingji guanxi* (Economic relations between Taiwan and China) Xiandai xueshu yanjiu (Contemporary academic research), no. 12.

Xianfa he xianfa xiuzheng an: Pudao duben (Authoritative reader on the constitution and constitutional revision) (Beijing: China Law Press, 2004).

"Xianggang tebie xingzheng qu jumin de quanli he ziyou" (Rights and freedoms of residents of Hong Kong Special Administrative Region) (Dec. 19, 1984), in CCARO-GRU and RAB-PRD 2003: 121.

Xianggang Wenwei Bao teyue pinglun yuan (Hong Kong Wenwei Pao special commentator), ed., *Quanguo renda changweihui [ze fa] wenda* (Questions and answers on the NPC Standing Committee's legal interpretation) (Hong Kong: Wenwei press, 2005).

Xiao, Weiyun, 1993a, *Yiguo liangzhi yu Aomen tebie xingzhengqu jiben fa* (One country two systems and the Macao Basic Law (Beijing: Peking University Press).

Xiao, Weiyun, 1993b, *Yiguo liangzhi yu Xianggang jiben falu zhidu* (One country two systems and the Hong Kong basic legal system (Beijing: Peking University Press).

Xiao, Yongping, 2003, "Falu de jiao yu xue zhi geming" (Revolution in teaching and studying law), *Faxue pinglun* (Law Review) no. 3: 153–60.

Xibu Xinwen (Western News), 2003, "Manzhouli jiancheng quanguo zuida de lulu kouyan" (Manzhouli constitutes the largest overland port in the country), in CCTV *Zhongguo Xibu* (The West of China) (Beijing: Youth Publishing): 517.

Xie, Junqun, Ma Kelin, 2002, *Xibu renwen huanjing youhua yanjiu* (Study of improving the human environment in the West) (Lanzhou: Gansu Peoples Press).

Xie, Weiwu, 2003a, ed., *Zhongguo tongyi de tonglu* (Common road to unification of China) (Hong Kong: HK Literary News,).

Xie, Weiwu 2003b, "[Xiao santong] chengguo you xian jiu bu liao Tai zheng jing kun ju" (The results of 'mini three links' limits the resolution of Taiwan's political and economic difficulties) (HK Ta Kong Bao Dec. 13, 2000), in Xie Weiwu, ed., *Zhongguo tongyi de tonglu* (Common road to unification of China) (Hong Kong: HK Literary News).

Xie, Zhengguan, 1999, *Zhongguo de bianjiang kaifa yu biancheng guihua* (Development of the periphery and planning for border cities in China) (Taipei: Tangshan Press).

Xin, Chunying, 2004, "Zunzhong he baozhang renquan, shixian shehui quanmian jinbu" (Respect and protect human rights, carry out all round social progress), in *Xianfa he xianfa xiuzheng an: Pudao duben* (Authoritative reader on the constitution and constitutional revision) (Beijing: China Law Press): 218–30.

Xingzheng Yuan Dalu Weiyuanhui (Mainland committee of the Administrative Yuan), ed., 2003, *Zhengfu dalu zhengce zhongyao wenjian* (Important documents on the government's mainland policy) (Taipei: Xinzheng Yuan Dalu Weiyuanhui).

"Xinjiang jiang chutai Xibu Da Kaifa shuishou youhui zhengce" (Xinjiang will table regulations on tax preferences under the Western Development Program), Zhongjingwang Xinjiang zhongxin (Xinjiang centre for China economy net) May 21, 2002 (www.gddoftec.gov.cn/wjmxx/Detail.asp?ID=951) [Nov. 7, 2007].

Xinjiang keji kecheng bangongshi (Xinjiang Science and Technology Program Office, "'Xinjiang nongye zhanlue diwei yanhua ji nongye chanyehua jingying yanjiu' chengguo jianshao" (Brief introduction to the results of ' Research on strategic

202 Bibliography: Chinese

positioning of agriculture and management of agricultural commercialization in Xinjiang'," Tianshannet (Feb. 13, 2004).

Xinjiang tuichu sishi tiao guiding gaishan touze ruan huanjing" (Xinjiang tables 40 regulations to improve the soft climate for investment) *Xinjiang jingji bao* (Xinjiang economic news) (Jan. 31, 2003) (www.gl.cei.gov.cn/westKF/2003/01/2101.htm) [Nov. 7, 2007].

"Xinjiang Weiwuer Zizhiqu (hereafter, "XUAR") cheng zhen zhigong shengyu baoxian banfa" (Methods for maternity insurance for staff and workers ini cities and towns of Xinjiang Uighur Autonomous Region), Art. 1 (XUAR Information Centre Mar. 12, 2004).

"XUAR guanyu Xibu Da Kaifa shuishuo youhui zhengce youguan wenti de shishi yijian" (Implementing opinion of XUAR on issues related to income tax preference policies under the Western Development Program), Apr. 18, 2002 (http://bt.xinhuanet.com/2006–9/15/content_8046552.htm) [Nov. 7, 2007].

"XUAR guli waishang touze banfa (shixing) (Provisional methods of Xinjiang Uighur Autonomous Region for encouraging foreign investment) (China Western Development 2002–3) (Western Development net, Aug. 10, 2004) (http://sdb.llas.ac.cn/xb/zhengce_10.htm) [Jan. 5, 2010].

"XUAR jiti hetong tiaoli" (Regulations on collective contracts for Xinjiang Uighur Autonomous Region) Mar. 1, 2004 (XUAR Information Centre) (www.law-lib.com/law/law_view.asp?id=113873) [Jan. 5, 2010].

"XUAR minzu yuwen shiyong guanli zanxing guiding" (Provisional XUAR Regulations on administration of use of nationality languages) (Dec. 1988) (www.cnki.com.cn/Article/CJFDTotal-YYFY198902001.htm) [Jan. 5, 2010].

"XUAR shishi 'Zhonghua Renmin Gongheguo tudi guanli fa' banfa" (Methods of Xinjiang Autonomous Region for implementing the 'Land Administration Law of the PRC'" (Feb. 13, 2004) (www.xjht.gov.cn/flfg/xjdffg109.htm) [Nov. 7, 2007].

"XUAR shixing 'Gongshang baoxian tiaoli' Banfa" (Methods of Xinjiang Uighur Autonomous Region for Implementing the 'Regulations on Workers Injury Insurance') (XUAR Information Centre, Mar. 12, 2004) (www.chinaacc.com/new/63/69/113/2004/1/ad587338501111140026380.htm) [Jan. 5, 2010].

"XUAR shixing 'Zhonghua Remin Gongheguo Jieyue Nengyuan Fa' banfa" (Methods of Xinjiang Uighur Autonomous Region for Implementing the 'Law of the PRC on Energy Conservation') (XUAR Information Centre, Oct. 20, 2003) http://law.baidu.com/pages/chinalawinfo/1682/68/887985b52d2206cc014577df26ec8525_0.html) [Jan. 5, 2010].

"XUAR shixing 'Zhonghua Remin Gongheguo Xiaofeizhe Quanyi Baohu Fa' banfa" (Methods of Xinjiang Uighur Autonomous Region for Implementing the 'Law of the PRC on Protecting Consumer Rights and Interests') (XUAR Information Centre, Oct. 20, 2003) (http://law.baidu.com/pages/chinalawinfo/1678/44/1807326c1ef247812599971849958759b_0.html) [Jan. 5, 2010].

"XUAR shixing 'Zhonghua Remin Gongheguo Yesheng Zhiwu Baohu Tiaoli' banfa" (Methods of Xinjiang Uighur Autonomous Region for Implementing the 'Regulations of the PRC on Natural Plant and Animal Conservation') (XUAR Information Centre, Oct. 17, 2003) (http://law.148365.com/146769.html) [Jan. 5, 2010].

"XUAR shixing 'Zhonghua Remin Gongheguo Shuifa' Banfa" (Methods of Xinjiang Uighur Autonomous Region for Implementing the 'Water Law of the PRC') Mar. 1, 2004 (XUAR Information Centre) (http://law.baidu.com/pages/chinalawinfo/1678/67/f8ea501a9ad8f0da29147f2f20b3b6a7_0.html) [Jan. 5, 2010].

XUAR Minzu Shiwu Weiyuan Hui (XUAR Minorities Affairs Commission) 2003, "Xinjiang weiwuwe zizhiqu minzu guanxi jiben qingkuang" (Basic situation of relations among nationalities in Xinjiang Uighur Autonomous Region), in Tiemuer and Mao 2003: 183–93.
"XUAR yuwen wenzi gongzuo tiaoli" (XUAR regulations on spoken and written language work) (Sept. 25, 1993) (http://law.baidu.com/pages/chinalawinfo/1678/67/ 8f1a21dc98aa06c61e3ff304cc743a6e_0.html) [Jan. 5, 2010].
"XUAR yuwen wenzi gongzuo tiaoli" (XUAR regulations on spoken and written language work) (rev. 2002) (http://law.baidu.com/pages/chinalawinfo/1681/83/ a0742129d2eea261328a791eba89db38_0.html) [Jan. 5, 2010].
"XUAR yuwen shiyong guanli zanxing guiding" (XUAR provisional regulations on application and management of language) (1988).
XUAR zongjiao huodong guanli zanxing guiding" (Aug. 23, 1990) (Provisional XUAR regulations on administration of religious activities), in RAB-PRD 2002: 228–31.
XUAR zongjiao shiwu guanli tiaoli" (XUAR regulations on administration of religious affairs) (July 16, 1994), in RAB-PRD 2002: 24–28.
XUAR zongjiao zhiye renyuan guanli zanxing guiding" (Provisional XUAR regulations on administration of religious staff) (Sept. 16, 1990) (Provisional XUAR regulations on administration of religious activities), in RAB-PRD 2002: 232–35.
Xinjiang xuanchuan bu (Xinjiang Propaganda Department), 2003a, "Chang hao keji ying mianxian" (Song of science and technology promoting cotton thread), in CCTC, *Zhongguo Xibu* (The West of China) (Beijing: Youth Publishers): 764–65.
Xinjiang xuanchuan bu (Xinjiang Propaganda Department), 2003b, "Fazhan youqi kan Xinjiang" (Viewing Xinjiang from the perspective of developing oil and gas), in CCTC, *Zhongguo Xibu* (The West of China) (Beijing: Youth Publishers): 762–64.
"Xinjiang zhiding youhui cuoshi xiyin waishang touze" (Xinjiang enacts preferential measures to attract foreign investment) (New China News Agency) (Oct. 6, 2007) www.chinapcn.com/htms/zhuanyieqikan/docc/eee/viewarticle.asp?id=72) [Nov. 7, 2007].
Xinjiang zhonggong xuanchuan bu (Xinjiang CPC Propaganda Department) 2004. *"Si ge rentong" duben* (Reader on 'four identities') (Urumqi: Xinjiang People's Press, 2004).
"Xizang de xiandaihua fazhan" (Development of modernization in Tibet) (2001), in SNAC and CCARO 2003: 447–74).
"Xizang jiakuai difang lifa bufa" (Tibet quickens its steps in enacting local legislation) *Xinhua* net (Jan. 20, 2003) (http://news.sina.com.cn/c/2003-01-18/091034917s.shtml) [Jan. 5, 2010].
Xizang Zizhiqu Dangshi Ziliao Zhengqi Weiyuanhui (Tibet Autonomous Region Party History Materials Collection Committee) and Xizang Junqu Dangshi Ziliao Zhengqi Lingdao Xiaozu (Tibet Military Region Party History Materials Collection Leading Small Group), ed., *Heping jiefang Xizang* (Peaceful Liberation of Tibet) (Lhasa: Tibet People's Press, 1995).
Xizang Zizhiqu Dangshi Ziliao Zhengqi Weiyuanhui (Tibet Autonomous Region Party History Materials Collection Committee) and Xizang Junqu Dangshi Ziliao Zhengqi Lingdao Xiaozu (Tibet Military Region Party History Materials Collection Leading Small Group), ed., *Pingxi Xizang panluan* (Pacification of Armed Rebellion in Tibet) (Lhasa: Tibet People's Press, 1995).
"Xizang Zizhiqu Dangwei, Zizhiqu Renmin Zhengfu guanyu jiakuai nongxuye he nongxuqu jingji de jueding" (Decision of the TAR CPC committee and TAR

peoples government on accelerating the economy of agricultural and herding enterprises and regions) (Feb. 2, 1994), in Ningxia 2001: 184–85.

"Xizang Zizhiqu guomin jingji he shehui fazhan di shige wu nian jihua gangyao" (Outline of the Tenth Five Year Plan for Economic and Social Development in Tibet) (May 21, 2001) (www.tibetinfor.com/xzrb/200106/01060903/010609030.htm) [Jan. 5, 2010].

"Xizang Zizhiqu Renmin Zhengfu guanyu dali fazhan xiang zhen qiye de jueding" (Decision of the TAR people's government on actively developing village and township enterprises) (Aug. 5, 1992), in Ningxia 2001: 173–74.

"Xizang Zizhiqu Renmin Zhengfu guanyu jiakuai fazhan di san chanye de shishi yijian" (Opinion of the TAR people's government on the situation of accelerating development of tertiary production), in Ningxia 2001: 174–76.

"Xizang Zizhiqu Renmin Zhengfu guanyu jiakuai geti, siying jingji fazhan de ruogan guiding" (Regulation of the TAR people's government on various issues of accelerating development of the individual and private economy) (Nov. 7, 1993), in Ningxia 2001: 179–84.

"Xizang Zizhiqu Renmin Zhengfu guanyu jinyibu kuoda kaifang jiaqiang jingji jishu lianhe de ruogan guiding" (Various regulations of the TAR people's government on steadily expanding opening up and strengthening integration of technology and economy) (June 25, 1995), in Ningxia 2001: 190–95.

"Xizang Zizhiqu Zongjiao Shiwu guanli zanxing banfa" ("Provisional Measures on Management of Religious Affairs") (Dec. 20, 1991), in RAB-PRD 2002: 130–35).

Xu, Bingxun and Wang Songtao, 1999, *Inner Mongolia* (Huhehaote: Inner Mongolia University Press).

Xu, Mingxu, 1999, *Yinmou yu qiancheng: Xizang sangluan de lai long qu mai* (Intrigue and devotion: The Origins and effects of the Tibet riots) (Missasauga ONT: Mirror Books).

Xu, Xianming and Qu Xiangfei, 2001, "Renquan zhuti jie shuo" (Speaking on the boundaries of the subject of human rights), *Zhongguo faxue* (Chinese Legal Science) no. 2: 53–62.

Xu, Yucheng, 1997, *Zongjiao zhengce falu zhishi dawen* (Responses to questions about knowledge of law and policy on religion) (Beijing: Chinese Academy of Social Sciences Press).

"Xuexiao shi guanche shishi 'Guojia tongyong yuyan wenzi fa' de jiben zhendi" (Schools are the basic front for fully implementing the Law on Simultaneous Language Usage by the State), in NPC Committee on Education, Science, Culture and Health and Ministry of Education: 34–36.

Yan, Tianling, 2004, *Hanzu yimin yu jindai Neimenggu shehui bianqian yanjiu* (Study of Han migrants and changes in contemporary Inner Mongolia society) (Beijing: Nationalities Press).

Yan, Yuanyang, Zhang Guanhua, 2004, "Jiaru WTO dui liang'an jingji guanxi de yingxiang" (Effects of WTO accession on cross-straits economic relations" in Yu Keli, ed., *Taiwan yanjiu lunwenji* (Collection of essays on Taiwan studies) vol. 13 (Beijing: China Population Press): 94–103.

Yang, Kaizhong, 2001, *Zhongguo xibu da kaifa zhanlue* (China's Western Development Program) (Guangzhou: Guangdong Education Press): 1–15.

Yang, Shenglong, 2004, *Minzu wenti minzu wenhua lunji* (Collection of essays on nationalities issues and nationalities culture) (Beijing: Nationalities Press).

Yao, Huan, 2005, *Dang de zhizheng nengli jianshe jiaocheng* (Teaching course on the Party's governance capacity) (Beijing: People's Press).
Ye, Xiaowen, 2001, "Dui zongjiao lilun he zhengce yaodian de fenxi he guilei" (Analysing and classifying the main points of religious theory and policy), in Luo Guangwu: 1–8.
"Yili Zhou guoshui houshi shuishou youhui zhengce" (Yili Zhou tax bureau adopts preferential income tax policies) *Yili ribao* (Yili daily) (May 9, 2003) (www2.yb.jl.cn/ybxx/ybxbkf/kfdt/xbdt56.hmt) [Nov. 7, 2007].
Yin, Sheng, 2006, "Zhongguo heping fazhan zhong funu renquan de guoji falu baohu," (International legal protection of the human rights of women during China's peaceful development), *Faxue pinglun* (Law Review) no. 2: 116–21.
Yu, Yuanzhou, 2002, "Scholar's Proposal: National Unification Promotion Law of the People's Republic of China" (Nov. 1). Thanks to Professor Richard Baum (UCLA) and ChinaPol for this draft.
Yuan, Gujie, 2002, "Tiaoyue zai Zhongguo neidi yu Kang, Ao, Tai shiyong zhi bijiao" (Comparison of the application of treaties in China's interior and in Hong Kong, Macao, and Taiwan), *Faxue pinglun* (Law Review) no. 5: 129–37 at pp. 134–35.
Yuan, Jifu, 2001, "Minzu diqu shaoshu minzu ganbu jiaoyu yanjiu – yi Neimenggu jiceng shaoshu minzu lingdao ganbu peixun wei li" (Research on education of minority nationality cadres in nationality areas – the example of training basic level minority leading cadres in Inner Mongolia), in Liu Jinghai and Shi Wenzheng, ed. 2001, *Lun wanshan minzu quyu zizhi* (On perfecting autonomy in nationality regions) (Huhehaote: Inner Mongolia People's Press): 82–92
Yuan, Sifang, 2001, "Nei Menggu zizhiqu gaige kaifang 20 nian shulue" (Narrative on 20 years of reform and opening up in Inner Mongolia), in Ningxia 2001: 233–63.
"Zai 16 da xinwen zhongxin juxing de jizhe zhaodaihui, Guowuyuan Xibu Da Kaifa Bangongshi ji Chongqing, Xizang, Shaanxi, Xinjiang, deng sheng qu shi fuzeren jieshao xibu kaifa qingkuang" (State Coucil Western Development Program Office introduces the situation of western development to responsible persons from Chongqing, Tibet, Shaanxi, Xinjiang and other provinces and regions at the news conference called by the new centre for the 16th Party Congress) (Nov. 12, 2002) (http://news.xinhuanet.com/zhengfu/2002-11/12/content_628026.htm) [Nov. 7, 2007].
Zai zuguo dalu xingban dui Taiwan jingji jishu zhanlanhui zanxing guanli banfa" (Provisional administrative measures on setting up Mainland exhibitions on Taiwan's economy and technology) (Jan. 14, 1999) (http://law.baidu.com/pages/chinalawinfo/2/19/6234337f86d05c85da10508e460a5d85_0.html) [Jan. 5, 2010].
Zeng, Lingliang, 2001, "21 shijie falu fuwu maoyi de fazhan qushi yu Zhongguo faxue rencai peiyang de yong you gaige" (Development trends in 21 century trade in legal services and needed reforms in training of China's legal talents), *Faxue pinglun* (Law Review) no. 1: 3–8.
Zeng, Peiyan, ed., 2003, *Guojia xibu kaifa baogao* (Report on national western development) (Beijing: Water Publishing).
Zeng, Xianyi, 2002, *Minzu diqu xiandai jingcheng de minzhu fazhi jianshe* (Establishment of democracy and legal system in the course of modernization of minority areas) (Beijing: Nationalities Press).
Zhang, Degui, 2001, "Nei Menggu ganbu renshi zhidu de gaige" (Reform of Inner Mongolia's systems for cadres and personnel), in Ningxia 2001: 396–403.

206   Bibliography: Chinese

Zhang Jiliang, 2004, *Zhong gong renquan lilun yu Zhongguo requan lifa* (Party policy on human rights and China's human rights legislation) (Beijing: Chinese Academy of Social Sciences Press).

Zhang, Laosheng, ed., 2004, *Difang guojian quanli jiguan juedingquan yanjiu* (Study on the decisionmaking powers of organs of local and central authority) (Beijing: China Democracy and Legal System Press).

"Zhang Qingli zuoke Xinhua wang: Gongchandang cai you laobaixing zhenzheng de Huopusa" (Zhang Qinglin visits Xinhua net: The Communist Party is the living Bodhisatva of the common people) *Xinhua* (New China News Agency) Mar. 2, 2008 http://news.xinhuanet.com/misc/2007–03/02/content_5792651.htm [Dec. 31, 2009].

Zhang, Shaodong, 2001, "Ye lun guoji tiaoyue zai woguo de shiyong," (Again examining the application of international treaties in China), *Faxue pinglun* (Law Review) no. 6: 73–79.

Zhang, Shulin and Bao Guirong, 2004, *Neimenggu minzu minjian wenhua baohu de lifa yanjiu* (Sudy of legislation on the protection of popular nationality culture in Inner Mongolia) (Huhehaote: Inner Mongolia Finance and Economic Institute Department of Law).

Zhang, Wanming, 2003, *She Tai falu wenti zonglun* (Summary of Taiwan-related legal issues) (Beijing: Law Publishers).

Zhang, Wenshan, 2005, *Zizhiquan lilu yu zizhi tiaoli yanjiu* (Study of theories and conditions of self-rule) (Beijing: Law Publishing).

Zhang, Wenxiang, 2005, "Shilun dui shaoshu minzu de suquan baohu" (Provisional views on protecting litigation rights of minorities), in Zhang Wenshan: 176–84.

Zhang, Wuyue, ed., 2003, *Liang'an guanxi yanjiu* (Perspectives of the Relationship Across the Strait) (Taipei: New Wun Ching Development Publishing).

Zhang, Xukai, 2001, "Xinjiang Weiwuer Zizhiqu gaige kaifang 20 nian shulue" (Narrative on twenty years of reform and opening up in Xinjiang Uighur Autonomous Region), in Ningxia 2001: 264–81.

Zhang, Yisheng, 2005, "Jinuoqi de quanyi baozhang wenti – shenglun minzu zizhi difang nei sangju shaoshu minzu quanli de baohu" (Issues of protecting rights and interests in Jinuo Banner – Concurrent views on safeguarding minority rights dispersed communities in nationality autonomy areas), in Zhang Wenshan 2005: 185–204.

Zhang, Zhirong, 2005, *Zhongguo bianjiang yu minzu wenti: Dangdai Zhongguo de taozhan ji qi lishi youlai* (China's frontiers and nationalities issues: China current strategy and its historical origins) (Beijing: Peking University Press).

Zhang, Zifeng, 2003, "Jiaqiang jingmao hezuo, zujin gongton fanrong" (Strengthen cooperation in economics and trade, promote common prosperity), in Yu Keli, ed., *Taiwan yanjiu lunwenji* (Collection of essays on Taiwan studies) vol. 12 (Beijing: China Population Press): 167–80 at pp. 177–78.

Zhao, Wenyuan, 2004, "Yi fa xingxhi zhongda shixiang juedingquan de shixian yu sikao" (Implement and consider handling the authority to make decisions on major matters according to law), in Zhang Laosheng, ed., *Difang guojian quanli jiguan juedingquan yanjiu* (Study on the decisionmaking powers of organs of local and central authority) (Beijing: China Democracy and Legal System Press): 13–19.

Zheng, Zhengzhong, 2002, *Liang'an sifa zhidu zhi bijiao yu pingxi*(Comparison and analysis of the cross-straits judicial systems) (Taipei: Wunan Press).

"Zhenfeng xiangdui jianjue huiji, quebao Xizang zizhiqu shehui wending" (Give tit for tat and resolutely fight back, guarantee social stability in Tibet Autonomous

Region) *Xizang ribao* (Tibet daily) March 17, 2008 (www.chinadaily.com.cn/hqzg/ 2008-03/21/content_6556677.htm) [Jan. 5, 2010].

"Zhonggong Neimenggu Zizhiqu Weiyuanhui guanyu guanche <Zonggong zhongyang guanyu nongye he nongcun gongzuo ruogan zhongda wenti de jueding> de yijian" (Opinion of the Inner Mongolia CPC Committee on fully implementing the <Decision of the CPC Central Committee on Various Urgent Problems of Agriculture and Rural Work>) (Oct. 23, 1998) in Ningxia 2001: 228–29.

Zhonggong Ningxia Hui Zizhiqu Weiyuanhui Dang Shi Yanjiu Shi (Party History Research Office of CPC Ningxia Hui Autonomous Region Committee), ed., *Zhongguo gongchandang yu shaoshu minzu diqu de gaige kaifang* (The Communist Party of China and reform and opening up in the minority areas) (Beijing: CPC Party History Press, 2001) (hereafter, "Ningxia 2001")

'Zhonggong Xinjiang Weiwuer Zizhiqu ("XUAR") Weiyuanhui guanyu guanche <Zonggong zhongyang guanyu nongye he nongcun gongzuo ruogan zhongda wenti de jueding> de yijian" (Opinion of the XUAR CPC Committee on fully implementing the <Decision of the CPC Central Committee on Various Urgent Problems of Agriculture and Rural Work>) (Dec, 4, 1998), in Ningxia 2001: 229–30.

"Zhonggong XUAR Weiyuanhui, Zizhiqu Renmin Zhengfu <Guanyu jiakuai fazhan muxu ruogan wenti de jueding> " (Decision of XUAR CPC Committee and People's Government on several issues of speeding up development in herding areas) (July 7, 1996), in Ningxia 2001: 212–13.

"Zhonggong XUAR Weiyuanhui, Zizhiqu Renmin zhengfu <Guanyu jiakuai fazhan nongxuqu shehui zhuyi shichang jingji de jueding> " (Decision of the XUAR CPC Committee and the XUAR People's Government on speeding up the development of the socialist market economy in agricultural and herding areas) (Feb. 3, 1993), in Ningxia 2001: 178–79.

"Zhonggong XUAR Weiyuanhui, Zizhiqu Renmin Zhengfu <Guanyu jinyibu kuoda duiwai kaifang de jueding> " (Decision of the XUAR CPC Committee and the XUAR People's Government on steadily expanding opening up to the outside world) (Nov. 6, 1991) in Ningxia 2001: 161–67.

"Zhonggong XUAR Weiyuanhui, Zizhiqu Renmin Zhengfu <Guanyu shenhua gaige, qianghua guanli, jinyibu gaohao zizhiqu guoyou qiye de jueding> " (Decision of the XUAR CPC Committee and the XUAR People's Government on deepening reform strengthening management, and steadily improving state-owned enterprises) (Sept. 21, 1995), in Ningxia 2001, pp. 196–99.

Zhonggong Xizang Zizhiqu Weiyuanhui Dangshi Yanjiushi (Party history office of CPC TAR Committee) (ed.), *Zhongguo gongchandang xizang lishi da shiji – 1949–2004* (Record of major events in the history of the CPC in Tibet – 1949–2004) (Party History Press, 2005). (2 vols) ("RMET").

"Zhonggong Xizang Zizhiqu Weiyuanhui Zizhiqu Renmin Zhengfu guanyu shenhua gaige kuoda kaifang de jueding" (Decision of the TAR CPC committee and the TAR people's government on deepening reform and expanding opening up) (July 14, 1992), in Ningxia 2001: 170–73.

"Zhonggong Zhongyang Guowuyuan zhaokai di sici Xizang gongzuo zuotanhui" (The CPC Central Committee and State Council Convene 4th national Tibet work conference), *Renminwang* (People's Net) Jun. 30, 2001 (www.cctv.com/news/china/ 20010630/65.html) [Jan. 5, 2010].

"Zhonggong Zhongyang Guowuyuan guanyu jiakuai Xizang fazhan, weihu shehui wending de yijian" (Opinion of CPC CC and State Council on accelerating Tibet development and preserving social stability) (Oct. 29, 1994), in CDRO and TARCC 2005: 478–91.

"Zhonggong Zhongyang Guowuyuan guanyu jinyibu zuohao zongjiao gongzuo ruogan wenti de tongzhi" (Notice on several issues in progressively doing a good job in religion work) (Document No. 6), in CCARO-GRU and RAB-PRD 2003: 213–21.

"Zhonggong Zhongyang Guowuyuan guanyu zuohao xin shiji chu Xizang fazhan wending gongzuo de yijian" (CPC CC and State Council opinion on doing good work in Tibet development and stability at the beginning of the new century) (July 13, 2001), in CDRO and TARCC 2005: 581–589.

"Zhonggong Zhongyang Quanguo Renda Changweihui Guowuyuan Zhonggong Junwei qingzhu Xizang heping jiefang sishi zhounian hedian" (Congratulatory telegram of the CPC Central Committeee, NPC Standing Committee, State Council and Central Military Commission on the 40th Anniversary of the peaceful liberation of Tibet) (May 22, 1991), in CDRO and TARCC 2005: 438–41.

"Zhonggong Zhongyang Quanguo Renda Changweihui Guowuyuan Quanguo Zhengxie Zhongyang Junwei qingzhu Xizang jianshe sanshi zhounian hedian") zizhiqu chengli sanshi zhounian hedian" (Congratulatory telegram from CPC CC, NPC SC, State Council, CPPCC, Central Military Commission on 30th anniversary of establishment of TAR) (Sep. 1, 1995), CDRO and TARCC 2005: 498–500.

"Zhonggong Zhongyang Quanguo Renda Changweihui Guowuyuan Quanguo Zhengxie Zhongyang Junwei qingzhu Xizang heping jiefang wushi zhounian hedian" (Congratulatory telegram from CPC CC, NPC SC, State Council, CPPCC, CMC on the 50th anniversary of the peaceful liberation of Tibet) (Jul. 19, 2001), CDRO and TARCC 2005: 600–602.

Zhonggong Zhongyang Taiwan Gongzuo Bangongshi (CPC Central Committee Office on Taiwan Work) and Guowuyuan Taiwan Shiwu Bangongshi (State Council Taiwan Affairs Office), ed., <Fa fenlie guojia fa> ji zhongyao wenxian xuanbian (Anti-Secession Law and compilation of important documents) (Beijing: Jiuzhou Press, 2005) ("CCC-OTW and SC-TAO 2005").

"Zhonggong Zhongyang Tongzhanbu, Guowuyuan Zongjiao Shiwuju 'Zang quan fojiao gongzuo zuotanhui jiyao'" (Abstract of work conference on Tibetan Buddhism' of the CPC CC United Front Work Committee, State Council Religious Affairs Bureau) (Dec. 5, 1992), in CDRO and TARCC 2005: 445–54.

Zhonggong Zhongyang Wenxian Yanjiushi Zonghe Yanjiuzu (General research unit of CPC Central Archives Research Office) and Guowuyuan Zongjiao Shiwu Ju Zhengce Fagui Si (Policy and law division of State Council Religious Affairs Bureau), ed., Xin shiqi zongjiao gongzuo wenxian xuanbian (Compilation of documents on religion work in the new period) (Beijing: Religion and Culture Press, 2003) ("CCARO-GRU and RAB-PRD 2003").

Zhonggong Zhongyang Wenxian Yanjiushi (CPC Central Archives Research Office) and Zhonggong Xizang Zizhiqu Weiyuanhui (TAR CPC Committee), ed., Xizang gongzuo wenxian xuanbian (Collection of documents on Tibet work) (Beijing: Central Documents Press, 2005) ("CDRO and TARCC 2005").

Zhonggong Zhongyang Zuzhi Bu (CPC Central Organization Department), "Guanyu shaoshu minzu diqu ganbu gongzuo de jidian yijian" (Various opinions on cadre work in minority regions) (Oct. 1978) (author's copy).

"Zhonggong Zhongyang Zuzhi Bu guanyu toushan jiejue gongchandang yuan xinyang zongjiao wenti de tongzhi" (Notice of the CPC Central Organization Department

on the problem of Party members believing in religion) (Jan. 28, 1991), in CCARO-GRU and RAB-PRD 2003: 205–7.
"Zhonggong Zhongyang Zuzhi Bu, Zhonggong Zhongyang Tongzhanbu, Guojia Minwei guanyu jinyibu zuohao paiyang, xuanba shaoshuminzu ganbe gongzuo de yijian' (Opinion of the CPC Central Organization Department, CPC Central United Front Work Department and State Council Nationalities Affairs Commission on continuing to do a good job in the work of training and selecting minority nationality cadres) (Dec. 30, 1993), in Zhongyang Dangxiao Minzu Zongjiao Lilun Shi (Central Party School nationalities and religion theory office) ed., *Xin shiqi minzu zongjiao gongzuo xuanchuan shouce* (Propaganda manual for nationalities and religion work in the new period) (Beijing: Religion and Culture Press, 2002): 136–41.
"Zhongguo Gongchandang di shi yi jie zhongyang weiyuanhui di san ci quanti huiyi gongbao" (Communique of the Third Plenum of the Eleventh CCP Central Committee), *Hongqi* (Red Flag), 1979, no. 1: 14–21.
"Zhongguo gongmin wanglai Taiwan diqu guanli banfa" (Administrative Methods for Chinese Citizens Travelling To and From Taiwan), in Zhang Wanming: 210–15.
Zhongguo Shehui Kexue Yuan Falu Yanjiu Suo (Chinese Academy of Social Sciences Law Institute (ed.), *Guoji renquan wenjian yu Guoji renquan jigou* (International Human Rights Documents and International Human Rights Institutions) (Beijing: Chinese Academy of Social Sciences Press, 1993).
Zhongguo Renquan Fazhan Jijinhui (China Human Rights Development Foundation) ed., *Xifang renquan guan yu renquan waijiao* (Western human rights concepts and human rights diplomacy) (Beijing: New World Press, 2003).
"Zhonghua Renmin Gongheguo ("ZRG") caoyuan fa" (PRC Grasslands Law) in Shi Wenzheng, ed., *Caoyuan huanjin de falu baohu* (Legal Protection of the Grasslands environment) (Hohhot: Inner Mongolia People's Press, 2005): 302–19.
"ZRG Fazhan Gaige Wei ZRG Guowuyuan di 13 mingling" (Order No. 13 from the PRC Development and Reform Commission and the PRC State Council) (July 23, 2004).
"ZRG Taiwan tongbao touzi baohu fa" (Law of the PRC on protection of investments from Taiwan compatriots) (Mar. 5, 1994), in Zhang Wanming: 186–87.
"ZRG Taiwan tongbao touzi baohu fa shishi xize" (Implementing regulations for the Law of the PRC on protection of investments from Taiwan compatriots) (Dec. 5, 1999), in Zhang Wanming: 188–91.
"ZRG zongjiao shiwu tiaoli" (Regulations of the PRC on Religious affairs) (Nov. 30, 2004) (www.gov.cn/gongbao/content/2005/content_63293.htm) [Jan. 5, 2010].
"Zhong Na di yi jie Zhongguo minzu quyu zizhi zhidu yantaohui' zongshu" (Summary of the first China-Norway conference on the autonomy system in China's nationality regions), in Zhang Wenshan, *Zizhiquan lilu yu zizhi tiaoli yanjiu* (Study of theories and conditions of self-rule) (Beijing: Law Publishing, 2005): 205–10.
Zhongyang Dangxiao Minzu Zongjiao Lilun Shi (Central Party School nationalities and religion theory office) ed., *Xin shiqi minzu zongjiao gongzuo xuanchuan shouce* (Propaganda manual for nationalities and religion work in the new period) (Beijing: Religion and Culture Press, 2002).
Zhou, Chonghai and Xie Haibao, 2001, "Lun guoji fa shang de renquan baohu) (On human rights enforcement in international law), in *Zhongguo faxue* (Chinese Legal Science) no. 1: 164–68.
Zhou, Gangzhi, 2006. "Gongwu gainian ji qi zai woguo de shiyong" (The concept of public property and its application in our country) *Xiandai faxue* (Modern legal studies) vol. 28 no. 4: 62–67.

210 Bibliography: Chinese

Zhou, Hongge, 2005, "Caoyuan quanshu zhidu de baohuxing wanshan yu chuangxin" (Perfection and creation of the safeguarding of the grasslands ownership system), in Shi Wenzheng, ed., *Caoyuan huanjin de falu baohu* (Legal Protection of the Grasslands environment) (Huhehaote: Inner Mongolia People's Press,): 145–54.

Zhou, Yue, 2002, *Difang renda jiandu jizhi yanjiu* (Study of the structure of supervision by local people's congresses) (Beijing: People's Press): 152–56.

"Zhu jun fa" [Zhonghua renmin gongheguo Xianggang tebie xingzhengqu zhu jun fa] (Law of the PRC on the military garrison in Hong Kong Special Administrative Region) (Dec. 30, 1996), in Wang Zhenmin, "Zhongyang yu tebie xingzhengqu guanxi" (Relations between the Centre and special administrative regions) (Beijing: Qinghua University Press, 2002): 453–58.

Zhu, Peimin, Chen Xiong, Yang Hong, 2004, *Zhongguo gongchangdang yu Xinjiang minzuwenti* (The Chinese Communist Party and nationality issues in Xinjiang) (Urumqi: Xinjiang People's Press).

Zhu, Rongji, 2001, "Guanyu jiakuai Xizang jingji fazhan" (On accelerating Tibet economic development) (Jun. 25), in Central Documents Office and TAR CPC Committee pp. 561–70.

Zhu, Rongji, 2000, "Tongyi sixiang, mingque renwu, bushi shiji shishi xibu diqu dakaifa zhanlue" (Unify thought, clarify tasks, do not lose time or opportunity to carry out the great development strategy for the western regions), in SNACand CCARO 2003: 237–51.

Zhu, Rongji, 1999, "Jiakuai shaozhu minzu he minzu diqu fazhan, ba minzu tuanjie jinbu shiye tuixiang xinshiji" (Accelerate development of minorities and nationality regions, push the activities of promoting unity of nationalities into the new century) (Oct. 3, 1999), in SNACand CCARO 2003: 219–31.

Zhu, Weijiu and Wang Chongli, 2003, *Haiyan liang'an guanxi zhengce falu yanjiu* (Legal study of cross-straits policy) (Coastal Academic Press).

"Zongjiao shehui tuanti dengji guanli shishi banfa" (Provisional measures for registration of religious societies and groups) (May 6, 1991), in RAB-PRD 2002: 8–9.

Zou, Jiahua, "Zai qingzhu Neimenggu Zizhiqu chengli wushi zhounian ganbu dahui shang de jianghua" (Speech to cadres meeting celebrating the 50th anniversary of the founding of IMAU) (July 19, 1997), in SNACand CCARO 2003: 173–86.

Bibliography
English

A Collection of Selected Translation of the IMAR Local Legal Regulations (Hohehaote: Inner Mongolia People's Press, 2000).
"A Report on the Development of Christian Sects in China," Human Rights Watch/Asia, *Freedom of Religion in China* (Washington: Human Rights Watch/Asia, 1992): 76.
"A Voice for the Uyghurs," *China Rights Forum* 2006 no. 4: 58–59.
Abulkhatin, Marat, "Ten Executed in Xinjiang-Uygur District," *ITAR-TASS World Service*, March 3, 1999 (FBIS-CHI-1999-0303).
"Action Agenda on 'China's 11th Five-Year Plan and the Development of Hong Kong'," Annex 1: "Guiding Principles and Selected Key Strategies of the National 11th Five Year Plan," Office of the Chief Executive, Hong Kong Special Administrative Region (www.info.gov.hk/info/econ_summit/eng/pdf/annex1.pdf) [Dec. 22, 2009].
"Address at the Press Conference by the State Council Information Office," Nov. 10, 2008 (file copy).
Adger, W. Neil, "Social and Ecological Resilience: Are they Related?" *Progress in Human Geography* vol. 24 no. 3 (2000): 347–64.
Agence France Presse (AFP), "Cites Xinjiang Legal Daily on Anti-Crime Campaign," Hong Kong Agence France Presse (Nov. 14, 2001) FBIS-CHI-2001-1114 (Nov. 15, 2001).
AFP: "10 Moslem Separatists in Xinjiang Executed," Hong Kong Agence France Presse Mar. 1, 1999, FBIS-CHI-1999-0301 (Mar. 2, 1999).
AFP: "Circular Urges Scrutiny of Muslim Religious, Folk Ceremonies in China's Xinjiang," Hong Kong Agence France Presse (Jan. 8, 2002), FBIS-CHI-2002-0108 (Jan. 9. 2002).
AFP: "PRC Executes Two Moslem Separatists after Rally," Hong Kong Agence France Presse (Feb. 5, 1999), in *FBIS Daily Report – China* (WNC Doc #: 0F6VIIO00FBP2Q (Feb. 8, 1999).
AFP: "PRC FM Statement Rebukes US Congress Over Resolution on Uighur Dissident," Hong Kong Agence France Presse July 26, 2000, FBIS-CHI-2000-0726 (July 27, 2000).
AFP: "PRC Sentences 18 Moslems for Separatist Activities," Hong Kong Agence France Presse (Aug. 17, 1999), *FBIS Daily Report – China* (FBIS-CHI-1999-0817 (Aug. 18, 1997).
Ai, Yu, "Kosovo Crisis and Stability in China's Tibet and Xinjiang," *Da Gong Bao* (HK) June 2, 1999, FBIS-CHI-1999-0624 (Jun. 25, 1999).

Bibliography: English

Allen, David, "A Vital Place Called Xinjiang," *Asia Times* Feb. 27, 2007 (www.info.gov.hk/info/econ_summit/eng/pdf/annex1.pdf) [Dec. 22, 2009].

Amnesty International (AI) 2005a, "China: Human Rights – A Long Way to Go before the Olympics," (Aug. 5, 2005).

Amnesty International, 2005b, *China Report 2005* (www.amnestyusa.org/annualreport.php?id=ar& yr=2005& c=CHN) [Dec. 28, 2009].

Amnesty International, 2002, "Urgent Action Update: Death Penalty/Fear of Imminent Execution," Jan. 4, 2002.

Amnesty International, 1992a, *Secret Violence: Human Rights Violations in Xinjiang (1992)*.

Amnesty International, 1992b, *People's Republic of China: Repression in Tibet, 1987–1992* (1992).

Amnesty International UK, "EU-China Summit: EU Must Continue Pressing for Real Progress on Human Rights in China" (Sep. 2, 2005).

"Apparent Text of 'Plan for Distribution of Quotas of Deputies of Minority nationalities to 10th NPC'," *Xinhua* Domestic Service (Apr. 28, 2002) FBIS-CHI-2002-0428 (Jun. 24, 2002).

"Apparent Text of PRC State Council Article on 'East Turkestan' Terrorists," *Xinhua* (New China News Agency) Hong Kong Service (Jan. 21, 2002), FBIS-CHI-2002-0121 (Jan. 22, 2002).

Arias, Jose Tomas Gomez, 1998, "A Relationship Marketing Approach to *Guanxi*," *European Journal of Marketing* vol. 32: 145–56.

"Article on Kosovo Crisis vs. Tibet Xinjiang «Hong Kong," *Ta Kong Pao* (Jun. 2, 1999) FBIS-CHI-1999-0624 (Jun. 25, 1999).

"At National Meeting on Political, Legal Work, Luo Gan Calls for Comprehensively Enhancing Politics, Legal Work, Ensuring Smooth Process of Reform, Opening Up, Modernization," *Xinhua* (New China News Agency) Domestic Service (Dec. 1, 2000) FBIs-CHI-2000-1201 (Jan. 18, 2002).

Backhouse, Constance, *Color-Coded: A Legal History of Racism in Canada, 1900–1950* (Toronto: University of Toronto Press, 1999).

Baehr, P.R., Fried van Hoof, Liu Nanlai, and Tao Zhenghua (eds.), *Human Rights: Chinese and Dutch Perspectives* (The Hague: Kluwer, 1996).

Balbus, Isaac D., 1977, "Commodity Form and Legal Form: An Essay on the 'Relative Autonomy' of the Law," *Law & Society Review* vol. 11: 571–88.

Bao, Lisheng, "Three Evil Forces Threatening Xinjiang' Stability – Interview with Pan Zhiping, Director of the Central Asia Research Institute of Xinjiang Academy of Social Sciences," Hong Kong *Ta Kung Pao* (Aug. 10, 2001) FBIS-CHI-2001-0810 (Aug. 16, 2001).

Barboza, David, "China Says It has Evidence Dalai Lama Incited Riots," *New York Times* March 31, 2008.

Barnett, Doak, *China's Far West: Four Decades of Change* (Boulder, CO: Westview Press, 1993).

Barnett, Robert, 2008a, "The Tibet Protests of Spring 2008," *China Perspectives* no. 3, 2009: 6–23.

Barnett, Robert, 2008b, "Did Britain Just Sell Tibet?" *New York Times* Nov. 24, 2008 www.nytimes.com/2008/11/25/opinion/25barnett.html [Dec. 22, 2009].

Barnett, Robert, 2008c, "Thunder from Tibet," *New York Review of Books* vol. 55 no. 9, 2008.

Bartlett, Richard H., *Indian Reserves and Aboriginal Lands in Canada: A Homeland* (Saskatoon: University of Saskatchewan Native Law Centre, 1990).
"Basic Law of the Hong Kong Special Administrative Region of the People's Republic of China," (1990) (Hong Kong: Constitutional Affairs Bureau, 2006).
Becquelin, Nicholas, 2004, "Staged Development in Xinjiang," *The China Quarterly* no. 178: 358–77.
Becquelin, Nicolas, 2000, "Xinjiang in the Nineties," *The China Journal* no. 44 (July 2000): 65–90.
"Beijing Commentary: Dalai Lama is Spewing Lies," *China Daily* May 1, 2008.
"Beijing formally OK's HK Leader," *Hong Kong Standard* June 21, 2005, www.thestandard.com.hk/stdn/std/Front_Page/GF22Aa01.html [Dec. 22, 2009].
"Beijing–Dalai Lama Talks Postponed because of Quake," *South China Morning Post* June 5, 2006.
"Beijing–Taipei Sign Flight, Cargo Agreements," *China Daily* Nov. 4, 2008, http://chinadaily.cn/china/2008-11/04/content_7172951.htm [Dec. 22 2009].
Bellows, Thomas J., *Taiwan and Mainland China: Democratization, Political Participation and Economic Development in the 1990s* (Jamaica, NY: Center of Asian Studies St. Johns University, 2000).
Berman, Sheri, 2003 "We Didn't Start the Fire: Capitalism and Its Critics, Then and Now," *Foreign Affairs* vol. 82 no. 4: 176–81.
Betancourt, Ernesto F., 1997, "A New Approach to Developing Institutional Structure," *Studies in Comparative International Development* vol. 32: 3–29.
Blomquist, William and Elinor Ostrom, 1999, "Institutional Capacity and the Resolution of the Commons Dilemma," in Michael D. ed., *Polycentric Governance and Development: Readings from the Workshop in Political Theory and Policy Analysis* (Ann Arbor: University of Michigan Press).
Bohr, Niels H. D., 1963, *Essays, 1958–1962, on Atomic Physics and Human Knowledge* (New York, NY: Interscience Publishers).
Borchigud, Wurlig, 1995, "The Impact of Urban Ethnic Education on Modern Mongolian Ethnicity, 1949–66," in Stevan Harrell, ed., *Cultural Encounters on China's Ethnic Frontiers* (Seattle: University of Washington Press): 278–300.
Bovington, Gardner, 2004a, "Heteronomy and Its Discontents: 'Minzu Regional Autonomy' in Xinjiang," in Rossabit, Morris 2004. *Governing China's Multiethnic Frontiers* (Seattle: University of Washington Press): 117–54.
Bovington, Gardner, 2004b, "Contested Histories," in Starr, S. Frederick ed., *Xinjiang: China's Muslim Borderland* (Armonk, NY: M.E. Sharpe): 353–74.
Bradsher, Keith and Edward Wong, "Taiwan Leader Urges Rapid Expansion of Economic Ties with China," *International Herald Tribune* June 18, 2008.
Bradsher, Keith, "China Tensions Could Sway Vote in Taiwan," *New York Times* March 21, 2008 (www/nytimes.com/2008/03/21/world/asia/19cnd-taiwan.html?hp) [March 21, 2008].
Braithwaite, John and Peter Drahos, 2000, *Global Business Regulation* (New York, NY: Cambridge University Press).
Branigan, Tania, "China Plans String of Dams in South Tibet," *The Guardian* Oct. 13, 2008.
Brogaard, Sara and Zhao Xueyong, 2002, "Rural Reforms and Changes in Land Management and Attitudes: A Case Study from Inner Mongolia, China," *Ambio* (Royal Swedish Academy of Sciences) vol. 31 no. 2: 219–25.

Bromley, Nicholas K., 2002, *Law, Space, and the Geographies of Power* (New York, NY: Guilford).
Brookes, Adam and Susan V. Lawrence, 1999, "Gods and Demons," *Far Eastern Economic Review* May 13: 38–40.
Brown, Deborah A., 2006, "Hong Kong's Catholic Church and the Challenge of Democratization in the Special Administrative Region," in Cheng, Tun-jen and Deborah A. Brown, eds., *Religious Organizations and Democratization: Case Studies from Contemporary Asia* (Armonk NY: M.E. Sharpe): 180–220.
Brown, Michael E., 1997, "The Impact of Government Policies on Ethnic Relations," in Brown and Ganguly, S., eds., *Government Policies and Ethnic Relations in Asia and the Pacific* (Cambridge: MIT Press): 511–75.
Buckley, Chris, 2004, "China's Central Bank Nears Bailout of Private Company," *New York Times* Aug. 24.
Buergenthal, Thomas, Shelton Dinah, and Stewart David, 2002, *International Human Rights*, 3rd edn. (St. Paul, MN: West Group,).
Bulag, Uradyn E., 2006, "The Yearning for 'Friendship': Revisiting 'the Political' in Minority Revolutionary History in China," *Journal of Asian Studies* vol. 65 no. 1: 3–32.
Bulag, Uradyn E., 2004, "Inner Mongolia: The Dialectics of Colonization and Ethnicity Building," in Morris Rossabit, ed., *Governing China's Multiethnic Frontiers* (Seattle: University of Washington Press): 84–116.
Bulag, Uradyn E., 2003, "Mongolian Ethnicity and Linguistic Anxiety in China," *American Anthropologist*, vol. 105 no. 4: 753–63.
Bulag, Uradyn E., 2002a, *The Mongols at China's Edge: History and the Politics of National Unity* (Lanham, MD: Rowman and Littlefield).
Bulag, Uradyn E., 2002b, "From Yeke-juu League to Ordos Municipality: Settler Colonialism and Alter/native Urbanization in Inner Mongolia," in *Provincial China* vol. 7 no. 2: 196–234.
Bush, Susan, 1971, *The Chinese Literati on Painting: Su Shi (1037–1101) to Tung Ch'i-ch'ang (1555–1636)* (Cambridge MA: Harvard University Press).
Callahan, William A., 2004, *Contingent States: Greater China and Transnational Relations* (Minneapolis, MN: University of Minnesota Press).
Carlson, Allen, 2005, *Unifying China, Integrating with the World: Securing Chinese Sovereignty in the Reform Era* (Stanford, CA: Stanford University Press, 2005): 124–45.
Cass, Deborah Z., Brett G. Williams, George Barker, eds., 2003, *China and the World Trading System: Entering the New Millenium* Cambridge: Cambridge University Press).
CASS (Chinese Academy of Social Sciences) Law Institute (ed.), *Guoji renquan wenjian yu Guoji renquan jigou* (International Human Rights Documents and International Human Rights Institutions) (Beijing: Chinese Academy of Social Sciences Press, 1993).
Cau, Kwai-cheong, 2004, "Xinjiang," in Y. M. Yeung and Shen Jianfa, eds., *Developing China's West: A Critical Path to Balanced National Development* (Hong Kong: The Chinese University Press): 251–75.
CCICED Secretariat, *China Council for International Cooperation on Environment and Development: Success Story* (2005). www.harbour.sfu.ca/dlam/index.html [Dec. 22, 2009] and www.secretariat@cciced.org [Dec. 22, 2009].
Chan Kam-nga and Others v. Director of Immigation [1999] 1 HKLRD 304.

Chan, Carrie, "Beijing Seeks Change for 07–08 Elections: Lam," *Hong Kong Standard* Feb. 11, 2005.

Chan, Hon S., "Christianity in Post-Mao Mainland China," *Issues & Studies* vol. 29 no. 3: 106–32.

Chan, Johannes, Fu Hualing, and Yash Ghai, 2000, *Hong Kong's Constitutional Debate: Conflict over Interpretation* (Hong Kong: Hong Kong University Press).

Chan, Kim-Kwong and Alan Hunter, 1995, "New Light on Religious Policy in the PRC," *Issues & Studies* vol. 31 no. 2: 21–36

Chan, Vivien Pik-Kwan, 2001a, "War on Terrorism: Local Foes in Mainland's Sights," *South China Morning Post* September 19.

Chan, Vivien Pik-Kwan, 2001b, "China Steps up 'Political Ee-education Campaign' for Xinjiang Mosque Leaders," in *South China Morning Post*, in *BBC World Monitoring* (Doc. # bbcapp0020011114dxbe0012x) (Nov. 14, 2001).

Chang, Anita, 2008, "China: Separatists behind Jet Crash Plot," Associated Press Mar. 20, 2008.

Chang, Felix K., 1997, "China's Central Asian Power and Problems," *Orbis* vol. 47 no. 3: 401–26.

Charney, Jonathan and J.R.V. Prescott, 2000, "Resolving cross-strait Relations Between China and Taiwan," *American Journal of International Law* vol. 94: 453–477.

Cheek, Timothy, 2007, *Living with Reform: China Since 1989* (New York, NY: Zed Books).

Chen, Daojun, "Officials Forced the People to Rebel: A Salute to the Heroic Resistance of the Tibetan People," *Hong Kong Chinese Affairs* Apr. 2008 http://2newcenturynet.blogspot.com/2008/04/blog-post_7713.html. [Dec. 22, 2009].

Chen, Maodi and Qian Yong Hong, 2000, "Huang Ju Says Shanghai Should Take an Active Part in the Large-scale Development of the Western Region and is Duty-Bound to Serve the Whole Country," *Xinhua* Jul. 8, 2000, in *FBIS Daily Report – China* (FBIS-CHI-2000-0708) July 11.

Chen, Albert HY, 2004, *An Introduction to the Legal System of the People's Republic of China* (3d edn.) (Hong Kong: Butterworth's).

Chen, Albert HY, 1997, "The Provisional Legislative Council of the SAR," *Hong Kong Law Journal* vol. 27: 1.

Cheng, T.J., 2005, "China-Taiwan Economic Linkage: Between Insulation and Superconductivity," in Nancy Bernkopf Tucker, ed., *Dangerous Strait: The US–Taiwan – China Crisis* (New York, NY: Columbia University Press): 93–132.

Cheng, Tun-jen and Deborah A. Brown, eds., 2006, *Religious Organizations and Democratization: Case Studies from Contemporary Asia* (Armonk, NY: M.E. Sharpe).

Chi Maohua, Yin Hongdong, and Zhang Sutang, 1998, "Zhu Rongji Inspects Inner Mongolia and Shanxi," *Xinhua* Aug. 2, 1998, in *FBIS Daily Report – China* (FBIS-CHI-98-226) Aug. 17.

"China Claims 'Big Victory' over Separatists in Xinjiang," Agence France Presse (Oct. 25, 2001).

"China Condemns Dalai Lama Ahead of Planned Talks," *Reuters* May 3, 2008.

"China Conducts Training Courses for Xinjiang Mosque Leaders," *Xinhua* (New China News Agency) domestic service (Jan. 11, 2002), in BBC Worldwide Monitoring (Document #bbcapp00200200112dy1c003pd) (Jan. 12, 2002).

216 Bibliography: English

"China in Dalai Lama Talks Offer," *BBC News* Oct. 29, 2008 www.bbc.co.uk/go/pr/fr/-/2/hi/asia-pacific/7696771.stm [Oct. 29, 2008].

"China Lays out Ground Rules for Tibet Talks," *Agence France Presse* May 5, 2008 (http://afp.google.com/article/ALeqM5hA3PnmCHgh_ysL4_bbnfJ7m8I98A?index=0) [Dec. 28, 2009].

"China Passes Law to 'Smash' Falungong, Other Cults," Agence France Presse HK Oct. 30, 1999, in *FBIS Daily Report – China* (FBIS-CHI-1999-1030), Nov. 20, 1999.

"China Rejects Prominent Xinjiang Businesswoman's Jail Appeal," Hong Kong Agence France Presse (Dec. 11, 2000) FBIS-CHI-2000-1211 (Dec. 13, 2000).

"China Said to Arrest 21 in Koranic Schools in Xinjiang," Hong Kong Agence France Presse (Feb. 18, 1997) FBIS-CHI-97-0033 (Feb. 20, 1997).

"China Says Serious Differences in Talks with Private Envoys of the Dalai Lama," *Xinhua* (New China News Agency) Beijing Nov. 10, 2008.

"China Sentences Son of Nobel Nominee," *The Times of India* Apr. 17, 2007 (http://timesofindia.indiatimes.com/Top_Headlines/China_sentences_son_of_Nobel_nominee/articleshow/1918800.cms) [Dec. 22, 2009].

"China: Inner Mongolia Viewed," *Xinhua* Dec. 25, 1996, in *FBIS Daily Report – China* (FBIS-CHI-96-249) Dec. 27, 1996.

"China: Jiang Zemin Inspects Xinjiang 5–9 July," *Xinhua* New China News Agency (July 10, 1998) FBIS-CHI-98-194 (July 14, 1998).

"China: Official Says Religion Going Through 'Golden Period'," *Xinhua* (New China News Agency) (Oct. 13, 1997), FBIS-CHI-97-286 (nd).

"China: On CPC Report, Nationality Autonomy System," *Renmin Ribao* (People's Daily) (Jan. 22, 1998) FBIS-CHI-98-050 (Feb. 25, 1998).

"China: Raidi, Wang Lequan Comment on Situation in Tibet, Xinjiang," *Xinhua* (New China News Agency) (Sep. 17, 1997), FBIS-CHI-97-261 (nd).

"China: Report on Ethnic Minority Economic Success," *Xinhua* Dec. 24, 1997, in *FBIS Daily Report – China* (FBIS-CHI-98-001) Jan. 6, 1998.

"China: Xinjiang To Bolster Anti-Separatism Reeducation in Schools," *Xinjiang Ribao* (Xinjiang Daily) Feb. 9, 2002, FBIS-CHI-2002-0227 (Mar. 25, 2002).

"China: Zou Jiahua Speaks in Hohhot," *Xinhua* July 22, 1997, in *FBIS Daily Report – China* (FBIS-CHI-97–205) July 29, 1997.

"China's Luo Gan Outlines Tasks of Political Legal Work in 2002," Beijing *Xinhua* Domestic Service Dec. 4, 2001, in *FBIS Daily Report – China* (FBIS-CHI-2001-1204) Dec. 7, 2001.

"China's Premier Invites Taiwan for 'Big-Issue' Talks: Report," Agence France Presse March 31, 2008.

China's Tibet: Facts and Figures 2003 (Beijing: New Star Press, 2003).

"*China's Tibet: World's Largest Remaining Colony,*" (Unrepresented Nations and Peoples Organization, 1997).

"China-Dalai Lama Dialogue: Prospects for Progress," Roundtable before the Congressional-Executive Commission on China (Mar. 13, 2006) (Washington, DC: US Government Printing Office, 2006).

"China-Tibetan Monk," Associated Press Wire Service (Sep. 27, 1991).

"Chinese Central Government Officials Meet with Dalai Lama's Private Representative," *Xinhua* (New China News Agency) Jul. 3, 2008.

Chinese Human Rights Defenders, 2008, "Tibetans Sentenced Without Fair Trial, Lawyers Offering Aid Face Punishment," (May 1).

"Chinese Leader May Talk With Dalai Lama," *Associated Press* March 19, 2008.

"Chinese Official Outlines Keys of Western Region Development," *Xinhua* English Service (July 28, 2000), FBIS-CHI-2000–0728 (Jul. 31, 2000).

"Chinese Police Killed, Wounded in New Xinjiang Clash," *Radio Free Asia* Aug. 28, 2008.

Ching, Cheong, 2004. "China Warns HK: Don't Stray Too Far," *Straits Times* Feb. 7, 2004 (http:straitstimes.asia1.com.sg/topstories/story/0,4386,235755.00.html) [Feb. 19, 2004].

Chiu, Hongdah, 1993, "Koo-Wang Talks and the Prospect of Building Constructive and Stable Relations Across the Taiwan Straits," *Issues and Studies* vol. 29 no. 8: 1–36.

Choukroune, Leila, 2005, "Justifiability of Economic, Social, and Cultural Rights," *Columbia Journal of Asian Law* vol. 19 no. 1: 30–49.

Christoffersen, Gaye, 1994, "Xinjiang and the Great Islamic Circle: The Impact of Transnational Forces on Chinese Regional Economic Planning," *The China Quarterly*.

Chu, Bo, 2002, "Correctly Handle 'Three Relationships' and Further Open Up Wider to the Outside World," *Renmin ribao* June 1, 2002 in *FBIS-Daily Report – China* (FBIS-CHI-2002–0601) June 5.

Chu, Yun-han, 1999–2000, "The Challenge of the 1997 Hong Kong Handover for Taiwan," *Pacific Affairs* vol 72 no. 4 (Taiwan Strait: Special Issue): 553–69.

Chung, Chien-peng, 2002, "China's 'War on Terror': September 11 and Uighur Separatism," *Foreign Affairs* vol. 81 no. 4: 8–12.

Chung, Chien-peng, 2004, "The Shanghai Co-Operation Organization: China's Changing Influence in Central Asia," *The China Quarterly*: 989–1009.

Clark, Cal and K.C. Roy, 1997, *Comparing Development Patterns in Asia* (Boulder, CO: Lynne Rienner).

Clarke, Donald C., 2009, "China and the World Trade Organization," in Michael Mosher, ed., *Doing Business in China* (Huntington NY: Juris Publishing, looseleaf).

Coates, Austin, 1968, *Myself a Magistrate: Memoirs of a Special Magistrate* (Hong Kong: Oxford University Press).

Cody, Edward, 2008a, "China Shuts Out 2 Lawyers Over Tibetans' Cases: Activists Had Offered to Defend Those Arrested After Crackdown," *Washington Post* June 4: A14.

Cody, Edward, 2008b, "Across China, Security Instead of Celebration: Policy Crack Down on 'Hostile Forces', Apply New Safety Measures," *Washington Post* July 19: A1).

Cody, Edward, 2005, "China Says US Has Double Standard on Rights," *Washington Post* March 3.

Cohen, Jerome A. and Hungdah Chiu, eds., 1974, *People's China and International Law: A Documentary* Survey (Princeton: Princeton University Press).

Collis, Maurice, 1946, *Foreign Mud: The Opium Imbroglio at Canton in the 1930s and the Anglo-Chinese War* (New York, NY: W.W.Norton).

"Commentary: Miscalculation of public opinion," *China Daily HK Edition* July 10, 2003.

"Computer Information Network and Internet Security, Protection and Management Regulations," (December 30, 1997).

Congressional Research Service, 2008, "Tibet: Problems, Prospects, and US Policy," Apr. 10.

Congressional Executive Commission on China (CECC), 2009a "Special Topic Paper: Tibet 2008–9," (Washington: CECC).
CECC, 2009b, *Annual Report 2009* (Oct. 10, 2009) www.cecc.gov/pages/annualRpt/annualRpt09/CECCannRpt2009.pdf [Nov. 19, 2009].
CECC, 2007, *Annual Report 2007* "Freedom of Religion," Religion (Washington, DC: Government Printing Office).
CECC, 2006, *Annual Report 2006* Section V(d) "Freedom of Religion." Religion (Washington, DC: Government Printing Office).
CECC, 2005, *Annual Report 2005* Section III(d) Freedom of Religion (Washington, DC: Government Printing Office).
CECC, 2004, *Annual Report 2004* (Washington, DC: Government Printing Office).
CECC, 2003, *Annual Report 2003* (Washington, DC: Government Printing Office).
"Constitution of the China Christian Council," (Jan. 1, 1997), in Pik-wan Wong, Wing-ning Pang and James Tong, eds., "The Three-Self Churches and 'Freedom' of Religion in China, 1980–97," pp. 39–42.
"Constitution of the National Committee of the Three Self Patriotic Movement of the Protestant Churches of China," (Jan. 2, 1997), in Pik-wan Wong, Wing-ning Pang and James Tong, eds., "The Three-Self Churches and 'Freedom' of Religion in China, 1980–97," *Chinese Law and Government* vol. 33 no. 6 (Nov./Dec. 2000): 37–39.
"Constitution of the People's Republic of China," (1982) (Beijing: Publishing House of Law, 2004).
"Controversial Tibetan Railway Moving Ahead Full Steam," Agence France Presse (HK) Dec. 20, 2002, in *FBIS Daily Report – China* (FBIS-CHI-2002-1220) Dec. 23, 2002.
Cooke, Susette, 2003, "Great Western Development in the Tibet Autonomous Region: Merging Tibetan Culture into the Chinese Economic Fast-lane," (CQ manuscript).
Corne, Peter, 1997, "Legal System Reforms Promise Substantive – But Limited – Improvement," *China Law and Practice* June.
Corson, Trevor, 2004, "Strait Jacket," *The Atlantic* December 1, (http://web.me.com/trevor_corson/articles/published/Entries/2004/12/1_Strait-jacket.html) [April 12, 2010].
Cort, Louise Allison and Jan Stuart, 1993, *Joined Colors: Decoration and Meaning in Chinese Porcelain* (Washington, DC, Smithsonian Institution).
"Council of Heads of SCO Member States Meets in Shanghai," SCO Website (www.sectsco.org) (2006) [Dec. 22, 2009].
"CPC Constitution" (rev. 2007), (www.china.org.cn/english/congress/229722.htm#1) [Dec. 22, 2009].
"CPC Political Bureau Alternate Member Wu Yi Inspects Inner Mongolia's Manzhouli," *Xinhua* Sep. 27, 2002, in *FBIS Daily Report – China* (FBIS-CHI-2002-0927) Oct. 7, 2002.
CPC United Front Work Department and State Council Religious Affairs Bureau 1988, "Circular on Stepping Up Control Over the Catholic Church to Meet the New Situation," (February 24, 1988), in Human Rights Watch/Asia, *Freedom of Religion in China* (Washington, London and Brussels: Human Rights Watch/Asia, 1992): 46–51.
Crossing the Line: China's Railway to Lhasa, Tibet (Washington: International Campaign for Tibet, nd).
D.T., 2007, "Uyghur Culture Faced With Endless Campaigns," *China Rights Dialogue* no. 4: 97–107.

"Dalai Lama May Appoint a Regent to Succeed Him," *Times Online* Nov. 23, 2008 (www.timesonline.co.uk/tol/comment/faith/article/5217495.ece) [Nov. 23, 2008]
"Dalai Lama Says He Has Given Up on China Talks," *Associated Press* Oct. 25, 2008 www.washingtonpost.com/wp-dyn/content/article/2008/1025/AR2008102500912. html [Oct. 28, 2008]
"Dalai Lama Threatens to Resign over Tibet Violence," *The Guardian* Mar. 18, 2008.
"Dalai Lama Urged to Truly not Support 'Tibet Independence'," Beijing *Xinhua* (New China News Service) Nov. 6, 2008.
Davis, Michael, 2008, "Establishing a Workable Autonomy in Tibet," *Human Rights Quarterly* no. 30: 227–58.
Davis, Michael (Dai Dawei), 2003, "Jiben fa, renquan he minzhu: Lilun yu shijian," (The Basic Law, Human Rights, and Democracy: Theory and Practice) in Lu Gonghui and Civil Exchange, eds., *Chuangjian minzhu* (Establishing democracy) (Hong Kong: Hong Kong University Press): 9–19 at p. 15.
Davis, Michael, 1999, "The Case for Chinese Federalism," *Journal of Democracy* vol. 10 no. 2.
"Decision of the Standing Committee of the National People's Congress on Issues Relating to the Methods for Selecting the Chief Executive of the Hong Kong Special Administrative Region in the Year 2007 and for Forming the Legislative Council of the Hong Kong Special Administrative Region in the Year 2008," (Apr. 26, 2004).
DeLisle, Jaques, 2008, "King of Blue? Implications of Taiwan's 2008 Elections," Foreign Policy Research Institute Jan. 24 (www.fpri.org/research/asia) [Dec. 22, 2009].
Desveaux, J.A., 1995, *Designing Bureaucracies: Institutional Capacity and Large-Scale Problem Solving* (Cambridge: Cambridge University Press).
"Development of West China to Bring Changes to Minorities," *Xinhua* English Service (Mar. 8, 2000), FBIS-CHI-2000-0308 (Mar. 9, 2000).
Dezalay, Yves and Bryant Garth, 2001, "The Import and Export of Law and Legal Institutions: International Strategies in National Palace Wars," in David Nelken and Jahannes Fees, eds., *Adapting Legal Cultures* (Oxford: Hart Publishing): 241–53.
Diamant, Neil, Stanley Lubman and Kevin O'Brien, eds., 2005, *Engaging the Law in China: State, Society, and Possibilities for Justice* (Stanford).
Dickie, Mure, 2006, "China Delays Property Law Amid Rights Dispute," *Financial Times* March 9.
Dicks, Anthony, 1989, "The Chinese Legal System: Reforms in the Balance," *The China Quarterly* vol. 199: 540.
Ding, Guangen, 2000, "Makes Inspections, Studies in Xinjiang," *Renmin Ribao* (People's Daily) Aug. 17, 2000, FBIS-CHI-2000-0817 (Aug. 18).
Dirlik, Arif and Maurice Meisner, eds., 1989, *Marxism and the Chinese Experience* (Armonk, NY: M.E. Sharpe).
"Disappearances Continue across Tibet: Tibetan Woman Sentenced for Talking on Telephone," *International Campaign for Tibet*, Nov. 17, 2008.
"Document 11: Laws Exist for the Banning of Falun Gong," in Ming Xia and Shiping Hua, Guest Editors, "The Battle Between the Chinese Government and the Falun Gong," *Chinese Law and Government* vol. 32 no. 5 (1999): 43–45.
"Document 6: CPC Central Committee/State Council, Circular on Some Problems Concerning Further Improving Work on Religion," (Feb. 5, 1991), Appendix 1 in Mickey Spiegel, "Freedom of Religion in China," (Washington, London and Brussels: Human Rights Watch/Asia, 1992): 27–32.
"Doubts over Sinopec Oil Find in Tarim," *The Standard* Jan. 4, 2005.

Dougherty, S. and R. McGuckin, 2002, "Federalism and the Impetus for Reform in China," *China Law and Practice* vol. 15 no. 4.

Dougherty, S., R. McGuckin, and J. Radzin, 2002, "How Federalism-Not Just Privatization-Is Driving China's Economy," *Zhongguo jingji pinglun* (China Economic Forum) vol. 1 no. 2.

"Draft Anti-Secession Law Explained," *Xinhua* (New China News Agency) March 8, 2005, www.chinadaily,com,cn/english/doc/2005–03/08/content_422875.htm. [Dec. 22, 2009].

Drew, Jill, 2008a, "China Sentences 30 for Involvement in Tibet Riots," *Washington Post* Apr. 29.

Drew, Jill, 2008b, "China Unlike to Loosen Its Grip in West: Experts Anticipate Unyielding Response to Latest Fatal Attacks in Xinjiang Province," *Washington Post Foreign Service* Aug. 30: A4.

Dreyer, June Teufel, 2000, "Ethnicity and Economic Development in Xinjiang," in *Inner Asia* vol. 2 no. 2: 137–54.

Dreyer, June Teufel, 1976, *China's Forty Millions: Minority Nationalities and National Integration in the People's Republic of China* (Cambridge MA: Harvard University Press).

Drover, Glen and K.K. Leung, 2001, "Nationalism and Trade Liberalization in Quebec and Taiwan," *Pacific Affairs* vol 74 no. 2: 205–24.

Dumbaugh, Kerry, 2008a, "Taiwan: Recent Developments and US Policy Choices," *Congressional Research Service Report to Congress* May 23.

Dumbaugh, Kerry, 2008b, "Taiwan-US Relations: Recent Developments and Their Policy Implications," *Congressional Research Service Report to Congress* Oct. 27.

Dutton, Michael, 1989, *Streetlife China* (Cambridge: Cambridge University Press).

Dwyer, Arienne, 2005, *The Xinjiang Conflict: Uyghur Identity, Language Policy, and Political Discourse* (Washington: East West Center).

"Editorial Views PRC Comments against Falungong Activities in Hong Kong," *Hong Kong iMail* Jan. 31, 2001, in *FBIS Daily Report – China* (FBIS-CHI-2001-0131) Jan. 31, 2001.

Edmonds, Richard Louis and Steven M. Goldstein, eds., 2001, *Taiwan in the Twentieth Century: A Retrospective View* (Cambridge: Cambridge University Press).

"Education for Ethnic Minorities: Diversity Neglected in Stress on Manufactured Unity," *China Rights Forum* Summer 2001: 12–15.

"Education Regulations for Ethnic Minorities Practices in Hohhot City," (Apr. 7, 2000), in *A Collection of Selected Translation of the IMAR Local Legal Regulations* (Hohehaote: Inner Mongolia People's Press, 2000): I: 298–305; II: 173–77.

Elegant, Simon, 1996, "The Great Divide," *Far Eastern Economic Review* June 6: 53.

Elvin, Mark, 1973, *The Pattern of the Chinese Past: A Social and Economic Interpretation* (Stanford, CA: Stanford University Press).

Eskildsen, Robert, 2005, "Taiwan: A Periphery in Search of a Narrative," *Journal of Asian Studies* vol. 64 no. 2: 281–94.

Etzioni, Amitai, 2000, "Social Norms: Internalization, Persuasion, and History," *Law & Society Review* vol. 34 no. 1: 157–78.

"Excerpts from Questions and Answers on the Patriotic Education Program in Monasteries," (May 25, 1997), in Human Rights Watch/Asia, *China: State Control of Religion* (1997): 100–103.

"Experts Say PRC's Leadership 'Increasingly Alarmed' by Falun Gong's Strength," Agence France Presse HK Jan. 22, 2001, in *FBIS Daily Report – China* (FBIS-CHI-2001-0122) Jan. 23, 2001.
Fairbank, John King, 1953, *Trade and Diplomacy on the China Coast: The Opening of the Treaty Ports 1842–1854* (Stanford, CA: Stanford University Press).
Feinerman, James V., 1992, "Taiwan and the GATT," in 1 *Columbia Bus. L. Rev.* 39.
Feinerman, James V., 1995, "Chinese Participation in the International Legal Order: Rogue Elephant or Team Player?" in *The China Quarterly* no. 141: 186–210.
Feuchtwang, Stephan, 2000, "Religion as resistance," in Elizabeth J. Perry and Mark Selden, eds., *Chinese Society: Change Conflict and Resistance* (London: Routledge): 161–77.
Fewsmith, Joseph and Stanley Rosen, 2001, "The Domestic Context of Chinese Foreign Policy: Does 'Public Opinion' Matter?" in David M. Lampton, ed., *The Making of Chinese Foreign and Security Policy* (Stanford, CA: Stanford University Press): 151–87.
"Final Declaration of the Regional Meeting for Asia of the World Conference on Human Rights," (Bangkok Declaration) (April 2, 1993), *Human Rights Law Journal* vol. 14 (1993): 370.
Fischer, Andrew, 2002, "Poverty by Design: The Economics of Discrimination in Tibet," Canada Tibet Committee.
Fish, Stanley, 1980, *Is There a Text in This Class: The Authority of Interpretive Communities* (Cambridge MA: Harvard University Press).
Florcruz, Jamie et al., 1999, "Inside China's Search for Its Soul," *Time* vol. 15 no. 14: 68–72.
Ford, Peter, 2009, "China Cracks Down on Human Rights Lawyers," *Christian Science Monitor* Feb. 25.
Ford, Peter, 2008, "Uighurs Struggle in a World Reshaped by Chinese Influx," *Christian Science Monitor* Apr. 28.
"Foreign Trade Law of the PRC," (2004) at www.chinadaily.com.cn/bizchina/2006-04/17/content_569437.htm. [Dec. 22, 2009].
"Foreign Trade Law of the PRC," (1994), in *China Economic News*, May 23, 1994: 8, May 30, 1994: 7.
Forney, Matt, 1996, "God's Country," *Far Eastern Economic Review* June 6: 46–48.
"Four Point Guidelines on Cross-strait Relations Set Forth by President Hu (full text)," (Mar. 4, 2005) Xinhuanet
"Fourteen Points from Christians in the People's Republic of China to Christians Abroad," in Donald E. MacInnis, *Religion in China Today: Policy and Practice* (Maryknoll, NY: Orbis, 1989): 61–70.
"Freedom of Religious Belief in China," in *White Papers of the Chinese Government, 1996–1999* (Beijing: Foreign Languages Press, 2000): 227–57.
Friedman, Edward, Paul G. Pickowicz, Mark Selden, 1991, *Chinese Village, Socialist State* (New Haven and London: Yale University Press).
French, Howard, 2008a, "Protest in Muslim Province in China," *New York Times* Apr. 2.
French, Howard, 2008b, "China Confirms Protests by Uighur Muslims," *New York Times* Apr. 3.
Friedman, Thomas L., 1999, *The Lexus and the Olive Tree* (New York, NY: Farrar, Straus, Giroux).

"From Telephones to Fibre Optics, Tibet Gets Wired," *Xinhua* Oct. 23, 2002, in *FBIS Daily Report – China* (FBIS-CHI-2002-1023) Oct. 24, 2002.

Fu Hualing, 2005, "Counter-Revolutionaries, Subversives, and Terrorists: China's Evolving National Security Law," in Fu Hualing, Carole J. Peterson and Simon N.M. Young, eds., *National Security and Fundamental Freedoms: Hong Kong's Article 23 Under Scrutiny* (Hong Kong: Hong Kong University Press): 63–92.

Fu Hualing, Carole J. Peterson and Simon N.M. Young, eds., 2005, *National Security and Fundamental Freedoms: Hong Kong's Article 23 Under Scrutiny* (Hong Kong: Hong Kong University Press).

"Full Text of Anti-Secession Law," Third Session of the 10th National People's Congress and National Political Consultative Congress (www.china.org.cn/english/2005lh/122724.htm) [Dec. 22, 2009].

"Full text of Hu Jintao's report at 17th Party Congress," *Xinhua* (New China News Agency) Oct. 24, 2007 (www.chinadaily.com.cn/china/2007-10/24/content_6204564.htm) [Dec. 31, 2009].

Fung, Archon, 2004, *Empowering Democracy* (Chicago: University of Chicago Press).

Garnett, Sherman W., ed., 2000, *Rapprochement or Rivalry: Russia-China Relations in a Changing Asia* (Washington, DC: Carnegie Endowment for International Peace): 371–402.

"Genghis Khan's Tribe Fears for His Honor," *The Age* Nov. 13, 2004.

Ghai, Yash, 2000, *Autonomy and Ethnicity: Negotiating Competing Claims in Multi-Ethnic States* (Cambridge: Cambridge University Press).

Ghai, Yash, 1999, *Hong Kong's New Constitutional Order: The Resumption of Chinese Sovereignty and the Basic Law* (Hong Kong: Hong Kong University Press).

Gladney, Dru, 2004a, *Dislocating China: Muslims Minorities and Other Subaltern Subjects* (Chicago: University of Chicago Press).

Gladney, Dru, 2004b, "Chinese Program of Development and Control, 1978–2002," in S. Frederick Starr, ed., *Xinjiang: China's Muslim Borderland* (Armonk, NY: M.E. Sharpe): 101–19.

Gladney, Dru, 2003, *China's Minorities: The Case of Xinjiang and the Uyghur People* (UN Commission on Human Rights, 2003) E/CN.4/Sub.2/AC.5/2003/WP.16 May 5, 2003.

Gladney, Dru, 1991, *Muslim Chinese: Ethnic Nationalism in the People's Republic* (Cambridge, MA: Harvard Council on East Asian Studies).

"Gloom Descends on Tibet's Exiled Leader," *Financial Times* May 25, 2008.

Gold, Thomas B., 1986, *State and Society in the Taiwan Miracle* (Armonk, NY: M.E. Sharpe).

Gold, Thomas B., Doug Guthrie, and David Wank, eds., 2002, "Social Connections in China," (Cambridge: Cambridge University Press).

Goldstein, Melvyn, 1997, *The Snow Lion and the Dragon: China, Tibet and the Dalai Lama* (Berkeley, CA: University of California Press).

Goldstein, Melvyn, 1995, "Tibet, China and the United States: Reflections on the Tibet Question," *Atlantic Council Occasional Paper* April: 38–48.

Goldstein, Melvyn and Matthew T. Kapstein, eds., 1998, *Buddhism in Contemporary Tibet* (Berkeley: University of California Press).

Goldstein, Melvyn, William Siebenschuh, and Tashi Tsering, 1999, *The Struggle for Modern Tibet: The Autobiography of Tashi Tsering* (Armonk, NY: M.E. Sharpe).

Goodman, David S.G., 2004, "The Campaign to 'Open Up the West': National, Provincial-level and Local Perspectives," in *The China Quarterly* no. 178 (Jun.): 317–34.

Goodman, David S.G., 1997, *China's Provinces in Reform: Class, Community and Political Culture* (London: Routledge).
Goodman, David S.G. and Gerald Segal, 1994, *China Deconstructs: Politics, Trade, and Regionalism* (London: Routledge).
Goodman, Peter, 2006, "Natives Feel Left Out of China's New West," *Washington Post* Jun. 5.
Gossett, David, 2007, "The Xinjiang Factor in the New Silk Road," *Asia Times* May 22 (www.atimes.com/atimes/Central_Asia/IE22Ag01.html) [Dec. 28, 2009].
Greenfeld, Liah, 2001, *The Spirit of Capitalism: Nationalism and Economic Growth* (Cambridge, MA: Harvard University Press).
Grunfeld, A. Thomas, 1996, *The Making of Moden Tibet* (rev. ed.) (Armonk, NY: M.E. Sharpe).
Gyari, Lodi, 2008a, "Turning Point for Tibet," *International Herald Tribune* Apr. 3.
Gyari, Lodi, 2008b, "Tibet at a Crossroads: The Current Status of Discussions between His Holiness the Dalai Lama and the Government of the People's Republic of China," Oct. 8.
"Hada in Prison: A Visitation Report from His Son, Uiles," *China Rights Forum* 2007 no. 4: 31–32.
Haggard, Stephan, 1990, *Pathways from the Periphery* (Ithaca, NY: Cornell University Press).
Han, Nianlong, ed.,1990, *Diplomacy of Contemporary China* (Hong Kong: New Horizon Press).
Hannum, Emily and Yu Xie, 1998, "Ethnic Stratification in Northwest China: Occupational Differences between Han Chinese and National Minorities in Xinjiang 1982–90," *Demography* vol. 35 no. 2: 323–33.
Harrell, Stevan, ed., 1995, *Cultural Encounters on China's Ethnic Frontiers* (Seattle: University of Washington Press).
Harris, Paul, 2008a, "Is Tibet Entitled to Self-Determination?" Apr. 25 (folio).
Harris, Paul, 2008b, "Tibet Has Stronger Self-rule Case than Kosovo," May 8 (folio).
Harvard Project on Cold War Studies, "The Cold War and Its Legacy in Tibet: Great Power Politics and Regional Security," (conference papers, 2001).
Hattaway, Paul, 200, *Operation China: Introducing All the Peoples of China* (Carlisle UK: Piquant).
He, Yanji, 1991, "Adapting Islam to Socialism in Xinjiang," in Luo Zhufeng, ed., *Religion under Socialism in China* (MacInnis and Zheng tr.) (Armonk, NY: M.E. Sharpe): 224–31.
Healey, P., 1998, "Building Institutional Capacity through Collaborative Approaches to Urban Planning," in *Environment and Planning* vol. 30: 1531–46.
Heer, P., 2000, "A House Divided," *Foreign Affairs* vol. 79: 18–24.
Held, David, Anthony McGrew, David Goldblatt, and Jonathan Perraton, 1999, *Global Transformations: Politics, Economics and Culture* (Stanford, CA: Stanford University Press).
Helfer, Laurence and Anne-Marie Slaughter, 1997, "Toward a Theory of Effective Supranational Litigation," *Yale Law Journal* vol. 107: 273.
Henderson, Robert, Andre Laliberte, Scott Simon, Fu-Chang Wang, Joseph Wong, 2004, "Domestic and International Considerations of Taiwan's 2004 Presidential Election: An Interdisciplinary Roundtable" ["From Ruling Party to Opposition Party: The KMT and Democratic Consolidation"], *Pacific Affairs: An International Review of Asia and the Pacific* vol. 77, no. 4: 683–713.

224 Bibliography: English

Hewitt, Duncan, 1999, "Clash as Hong Kong Court Bars Immigrants," BBC News Dec. 3.

Hille, Kathrin, 2008b, "China and Taiwan Move Big Step Closer," *Financial Times* June 12, www.ft.com/cms/s/0/809628b4-38a4-11dd-8aed-0000779fd2ac.html [June 13, 2008].

Hille, Kathrin, 2008a, "China and Taiwan Close to Bank Deal," *Financial Times* Feb. 21.

Hille, Kathrin, 2007, "Taiwan Court Clears Ma of Corruption," *Financial Times* Aug. 14 (www.ft.com/cms/s/1cf3f986-4a0b-11dc-9ffe-0000779fd2ac,dwp_uuid=7f5f6b12-2f66-11da-8b51-00000e2511c8,print=yes.html) [November 28, 2009].

Hirsch, Max, 2009, "cross-strait Crackdown: Taiwan's Law Enforcement Cooperation Agreement with China," *Jane's Intelligence Review* no. 10 (20 Aug).

Hirsch, Max 2008, "Focus: Tibet Issue Forces Taiwan Presidential Frontrunner to Shift Rhetoric," Kyodo News Service Taipei Mar. 19.

"Historic China-Taiwan Talks Held," BBC Apr. 12, 2008 http://newws.bbc.co.uk/2/low/asia-pacific/7343945.stm. [Dec. 22, 2009].

"HK Election Needs Approval from Central Government," *China Daily* Feb. 9, 2004 (www.chinadaily.com.cn/english/doc/2004-02/09/content_304396.htm) [Dec. 28, 2009].

Ho, Stephanie, 2008, "China, Taiwan to Hold Regular Talks," *Voice of America* May 29, (www.voanews.com/english/archive/2008-05/2008-05-29-voa5.cfm?CFID=65550947& CFTOKEN=45594508) [June 3, 2008].

Hogg, Chris, 2005, "China to Settle New HK Chief Row," BBC Apr. 6, http://news.bbc.co.uk/1/hi/world/asia-pacific/4415257.stm [Dec. 28, 2009].

Holbig, Heike, 2004,"The Emergence of the Campaign to Open Up the West: Ideological Formation, Central Decision-making and the Role of the Provinces," *The China Quarterly* no. 178: 333–57.

"Hong Kong Lawmaker to Legally Challenge China," *Taipei Times* Mar. 25, 2005."

Hong Kong's Bill of Rights: Problems and Prospects (Hong Kong: University of Hong Kong Law Faculty, 1990).

Howell, Jude and Jenny Pearce, 2002, *Civil Society and Development: A Critical Exploration* (Boulder, CO: Lynne Rienner, 2002).

Hsieh, Pasha L., 2005, "Facing China: Taiwan's Status as a Separate Customs Territory in the World Trade Organization," *J. World Trade* vol. 39 no. 6: 1195–1221.

Hsing, Youtien, 1996, "Blood, thicker than water: interpersonal relations and Taiwanese investment in southern China," *Environment and Planning* vol. 28: 2241–2261.

Hsu, Berry, 2004, "Judicial Independence under the Basic Law," *Hong Kong Law Journal* vol. 34 pt. 2: 279–302.

Hsu, Berry, 1992, *The Common Law System in Chinese Context: Hong Kong in Transition* (Armonk, NY: M.E. Sharpe, 1992).

"Hu Jintao Addresses CPC Politburo Study Session, Calls for Common Prosperity," *Xinhua* Domestic Service Oct. 22, 2004, in *FBIS Daily Report – China* FBIS-CHI 2004–1022 (Oct. 22, 2004).

"Hu Jintao Inspects Inner Mongolia, Stresses Importance of Re-Employment," *Xinhua* Jan. 5, 2003, in *FBIS Daily Report – China* (FBIS-CHI-2003-0105) Jan. 6, 2003.

"Hu Jintao Stresses Work Style, Urges to Crack Down on Separatist in Xinjiang," Beijing *Xinhua* Domestic Service Jun 16, 2001, in *FBIS Daily Report – China* FBIS-CHI 2001–0616 (Jun. 19, 2001).

"Hu Meets Taiwan Delegation, Hails cross-straits Talks," *Xinhua* (New China News Agency) Jun. 13, 2008 (http://news.xinhuanet.com/english/2008–06/13/content_8362629.htm) [Dec. 22, 2009].

"Hu Stresses Full Implementation of Free Religious Policy," *Xinhua* (New China News Agency) Dec. 19, 2007 (www.wsichina.org/morningchina/archive/20071221.html) [Dec. 22, 2009].

Huang, Yafeng, 2001, "Political Institutions and Fiscal Reforms in China," *Problems of Post-Communism* vol. 48 no. 1.

Hughes, Christopher, 2007, "Hu Report-national Unification Section," (via Chinapol: CHINAPOL@weber2.sscnet.ucla.edu (Oct. 25, 2007).

Hui, Chin and George Graen, 1997, "*Guanxi* and Professional Leadership in Contemporary Sino-American Joint Ventures in Mainland China," *Leadership Quarterly* vol. 8: 451–65.

"Hui Liangyu Inspects Inner Mongolia," *Xinhua* Sep. 3, 2004, in *FBIS Daily Report – China* (FBIS-CHI-2004-0903) Sep. 8, 2004.

"Human Rights Accusations Refuted," *China Daily*, March 29. 1995: 4; State Council Information Office, "The Human Rights Record of the United States in 2002," (Beijing: 2003).

Human Rights in China, 1998, "Report on the Implementation of CEDAW in the People's Republic of China."

Human Rights Watch (HRW), 2009, *"We are Afraid to Even Look for Them": Enforced Disappearances in the Wake of Xinjiang's Protests* (Oct.).

Human Rights Watch, 2008, "'Walking on Thin Ice:' Control, Intimidation, and Harassment of Lawyers in China," (Apr.).

Human Rights Watch, 2006a, "China: A Year after New Regulations, Religious Rights Still Restricted," (Mar. 1)

Human Rights Watch, 2006b, "China: Events of 2006," in *World Report 2007* (http://hrw.org/englishwr2k7/docs/2007/01/11/china14867.htm) [Dec. 22, 2009].

Human Rights Watch, 2006c, "China: Curbs on Lawyers Could Intensify Social Unrest – New Regulations Cast Doubt on Legal Reforms," (Dec. 12, 2006).

Human Rights Watch, 2005, "Devastating Blows: Religious Repression in Xinjiang."

Human Rights Watch, 2002, "Dangerous Meditation: China's Campaign against Falungong."

Human Rights Watch, 2000, *HRW World Report 2000: China* (February).

Human Rights Watch, 1999, "China Uses 'Rule of Law' to Justify Falun Gong Crackdown," (Nov. 9).

Human Rights Watch, 1996, *Cutting Off the Serpent's Head: Tightening Control in Tibet, 1994–1995*.

Human Rights Watch/Asia, 1997, "China: State Control of Religion," (Washington, DC: Human Rights Watch/Asia).

Humphrey, Caroline and David Sneath, 1999, *The End of Nomadism? Society, State and the Environment in Inner Asia* (Durham, Duke University Press): 54–58, 103–9.

Information Office of PRC State Council, "East Turkistan Terrorist Forces Cannot Get Away With Impunity," Beijing *Xinhua* English Service Jan. 21, 2002, in *FBIS Daily Report – China* (FBIS-CHI-2002-01-21) Jan. 21, 2002.

"Inherited Persecution: China Imprisons the Son of a Human Rights Activist," *The Washington Post* Apr. 26, 2007: A28.

"Inner Mongolia's Uyunqimg on Economic, Social Development," *Xinhua* Mar. 14, 2001, in *FBIS Daily Report – China* (FBIS-CHI-2002-0314) Mar. 16, 2001.

226 Bibliography: English

International Campaign for Tibet (ICT), 2008a, "Aggressive Anti-Dalai Lama Campaign in Kham; Imminent Food Shortages Feared as Result of Security Sweep," *ICT Report Apr. 17, 2008* (http://savetibet/org/news/newsitem.php?id=1292) [Dec.22, 2009].

International Campaign for Tibet, 2008b, "'A Choked Silence:' Images from Tibet of Crackdown," ICT Report Oct. 31, http://savetibet.org/media-center/behind-news/a-choked-silence-images-tibet-crackdown [Nov. 3, 2008].

International Commission of Jurists, *Tibet: Human Rights and the Rule of Law* (Geneva: International Commission of Jurists, 1997).

International Committee of Lawyers for Tibet (ICLT), "Legal Materials on Tibet," (2nd ed.) (1997).

"International Covenant on Civil and Political Rights," ("ICCPR"), G.A. res. 2200A (XXI), 21 U.N. GAOR Supp. (no. 16) at 52, U.N. Doc. A/6316 (1966), 999 U.N.T.S. 171, *entered into force* Mar. 23, 1976, (www.1.umn.edu/humanrts/instree/b3ccpr.htm) [Dec. 22, 2009].

"International Covenant on Economic, Social and Cultural Rights," ("ICESCR"), United Nations, *Treaty Series*, vol. 993: 3.

International Rehabilitation Council for Torture Victims (ed.), 1999, *Torture in Tibet 1949–1999* (Copenhagen: IRCT).

"Jailed Inner Mongolian Dissident Claims Torture," (South China Morning Post/Reuters Apr. 22, 2008).

Jameson, Fredric and Masao Miyoshi eds., 1998, *The Cultures of Globalization* (Durham, NC: Duke University Press).

Jayasuriya, Kanishka, ed., 1999, *Law Capitalism and Power in Asia* (London: Routledge).

Jenner, W.J.F., 1992, *The Tyranny of History: The Roots of China's Crisis* (London: Penguin Press): 193–201.

Jensen, Rian and Erich Marquardt, 2009, "The Sino-Russian Romance," *Asia Times On-Line* Mar. 21, 2006, www.atimes.com/atimes/Central_Asia/HC21Ag02.html. [Dec. 22, 2009].

"Jiang Meets NPRC Ethnic, Religious Leaders," *Xinhua* (New China News Agency) Domestic Service (Mar. 4, 1999), FBIS-CHI-1999-0307 (Mar. 8, 1999).

Jiang, Xiyuan, 2005, "An Analysis on Changing International System and Its Acceptance of China," *International Review* vol. 39: 19–36.

"Jiang Zemin, Zhu Rongji Address Religious Work Conference, Other Leaders Take Part," Beijing *Xinhua* Domestic Service Dec. 12, 2001 in *FBIS Daily Report – China* (FBIS-CHI-2001-1212) Dec. 19, 2001.

Job, Brian, Andre Laliberte and Michael Wallace, 1999–2000, "Assessing the Risks of Conflict in the PRC-ROC Enduring Rivalry," *Pacific Affairs* vol. 72 no. 4 (Taiwan Strait-Special Issue): 513–35.

Johnson, Chambers, 1982, *MITI and the Japanese Miracle* (Stanford, CA: Stanford University Press).

Johnston, Alistair I., 1993, "Independence through Unification: On the Correct Handling of Contradictions across the Taiwan Strait," *Fairbank Centre for East Asian Research, Contemporary Issues* no. 2.

Jones, Susan Mann and Philip A. Kuhn, 1978, "Dynastic Decline and the Roots of Rebellion," in John K. Fairbank, ed., *The Cambridge History of China: Volume 10 – Late Ch'ing 1800–1911 Part I* (Cambridge: Cambridge University Press): 107–62.

Kahn, Joseph, 2004, "Criticism by China Raises Questions about Hong Kong Freedom," *New York Times* Feb. 26.
Kaplan, Edward H. and Donald W. Wisenhunt, eds., 1994, *Opuscula Altaica: Essays Presented in Honor of Henry Schwartz* (Bellingham, WA: Western Washington University Centre for East Asian Studies).
Karmel, Solomon M., 1995–96, "Ethnic Tension and the Struggle for Order: China's Policies in Tibet," *Pacific Affairs* vol. 68 no. 4: 485–508.
Keith, Ron and Zhiqiu Lin, 2001, *Law and Justice in China's New Marketplace* (New York, NY: Palgrave).
Kelly, David and Anthony Reid, ed., 1998, *Asian Freedoms: The Idea of Freedom in East and Southeast Asia* (Cambridge: Cambridge University Press).
Kennedy, David, 1994, "Receiving the International," *Connecticut Journal of International Law*, vol. 10, no. 1:1.
Kennedy, Duncan, 1976, "Form and Substance in Private Law Adjudication," *Harvard Law Review* vol. 89: 1685–1778.
Kipnis, Andrew, 2006, "*Suzhi*: A Keyword Approach," *The China Quarterly* no. 186 (Jun.): 295–323.
Kong, Qingjiang, 2002, *China and the World Trade Organization* (Singapore: World Scientific).
Kristof, Nicolas D., 2008, "An Olive Branch from the Dalai Lama," *New York Times* Aug. 7.
Kuczynski, Pedro-Pablo, 2002, "Reforming the State," in Kuczynski and Williamson, *After the Washington Consensus: Restarting Growth and Reform in Latin America* (Washington, DC: Institute for International Economics): 33–47.
Kuo, Tai-chun and Ramon Myers, 2004, "Peace Proposal One: The China Commonwealth Model," in Steve Tsang, ed., *Peace and Security Across the Taiwan Strait* (London: Palgrave Macmillan): 189–94.
Kwong, Julia, 1997, *The Political Economy of Corruption in China* (Armonk NY and London: M.E.Sharpe).
Kymlicka, Will, 1991, *Liberalism, Community and Culture* (Oxford: Clarendon Press).
Lague, David, 2008, "China Premier Blames Dalai Lama for 'Appalling' Violence in Tibet," *New York Times* Mar. 18.
Lai, Hongdah Harry, 2002, "China's Western Development Program: Its Rationale, Implementation, and Prospects," *Modern China* vol. 28 no. 4: 432–66.
Laliberte, Andre, 2006, "'Buddhism in the Human Realm' and Taiwanese Democracy," in Cheng, Tun-jen and Deborah A. Brown, eds., *Religious Organizations and Democratization: Case Studies from Contemporary Asia* (Armonk, NY: M.E. Sharpe): 55–82.
Lam, Janus, 2005, "Beijing Misstep over New Hong Kong Head," *Asia Times On-Line* (Apr. 2).
Lam, Willy, 2008a, "Hope for a Better Tibet Policy," *Far Eastern Economic Review* Apr.: 13–16.
Lam, Willy, 2008b, "Beijing Intensifies 'People's War' Against 'Splittism' as Nationalism Rears its Head," *China Brief* vol. 8 no. 9 (www.jamestown.org/china_brief/article.php?articleid=2374129) [Apr. 29, 2008].
Lam, Willy, 2004, "Hu, Jiang and Hong Kong," *Wall Street Journal* Sep. 22.
Lam, Willy, 2001, "Terrorism Fight Used to Target China Secessionists," CNN e-mail newsletter (Oct. 23).

Lampton, David M., ed., 2001, *The Making of Chinese Foreign and Security Policy* (Stanford, CA: Stanford University Press).
Landes, David, 1998, *The Wealth and Poverty of Nations: Why Some are So Rich and Some So Poor* (New York, NY: W.W. Norton).
Lanteigne, Mark, 2005, *China and International Institutions: Alternate Paths to Global Power* (New York, NY: Routledge).
Laogai Research Foundation, "The World Bank and the Chinese Military," (Apr. 4, 1996).
Lary, Diana, ed., 2007, *China at the Borders* (Vancouver: UBC Press).
Lau, Siu-kai, ed., 2002, *The First Tung Chee-hwa Administration: The First Five Years of the Hong Kong Special Administrative Region* (Hong Kong: Chinese University Press).
Lau, Siu-kai and Kuan Hsin-Chi, 1989, *The Ethos of the Hong Kong Chinese* (Hong Kong: Chinese University Press).
"Leaders on PRC's Western Development," *Xinhua* Mar. 7, 2000, in *FBIS Daily Report – China* (FBIS-CHI-2000-0307) Mar. 28, 2000.
Lechner, Frank J. and J. Boli eds., 2000, *The Globalization Reader* (Malden, MA: Blackwell).
Lee, Che-fu, 1998, "China's Perception of the Taiwan Issue," *New England Law Review* vol. 32: 695–706.
"Legal System Publicity Viewed in Xinjiang," *Renmin Gongan Bao* (Public Security Report) (Feb. 23, 1990) FBIS-CHI-90-076 (Apr. 19, 1990): 51–52.
Leung, Beatrice and Shun-hing Chan, 2003, *Changing Church and State Relations in Hong Kong, 1950–2000* (Hong Kong: Hong Kong University Press).
Leung, Priscilla MF and Zhu Guobin, eds., 2002, *The Basic Law of HKSAR: From Theory to Practice* (Singapore: Butterworths).
Lewis, Philip, ed., 1994, *Law and Technology in the Pacific Community* (Boulder, CO: Westview).
Li, Jialu, 2001, "Vice Premier Wen Jiabao Visits Inner Mongolia, Comments on Forestry under New Situation," *Xinhua* Apr. 17 2001, in *FBIS Daily Report – China* (FBIS-CHI-2001-0417) Apr. 23.
"Li Peng Says PRC Not to Permit Opposition Parties," AFP Dec. 1, 1998, in FBIS-CHI-98-335, Dec. 1, 1998.
"Li Peng Stresses the Need to Strengthen National Unity, Seize New Opportunity, and Boost Economic Development When Joining Xinjiang Delegation in Its Discussion of Government Work Report," *Xinhua* Domestic Service (Mar. 8, 2000) FBIS-CHI-2000-0208 (Mar. 13, 2000).
"Li Ruihuan Meets Religious Leaders," *Xinhua* Domestic Service (Jan. 31, 2000), FBIS-CHI-2000-0201 (Feb. 1, 2000).
Li, Shixiong and Xiqiu (Bob) Fu, 2002, "Religion and National Security in China: Secret Documents from China's Security Sector," (New York, NY: Committee on Investigation of Persecution of Religious Freedom in China).
Liao, Hollis, 1995, "The Case of the Two Panchen Lamas – A Religious or Political Issue?" *Issues & Studies* vol. 31 no. 12: 115–17.
Lieberthal, Kenneth, 1995, *Governing China* (New York, NY: W.W. Norton).
Lim, Louisa, 2003, "China's Uighurs Lose Out to Development," *BBC News World Edition* (Dec. 19) (http://news.bbc.co.uk/2/hi/asia-pacific/3330803.stm) [Dec. 22, 2009].
Lim, Weiyi and Janet Ong, 2009, "Taiwan Ex-President Chen Sentenced to Life for Graft," *Bloomberg News* (Sep. 11) www.bloomberg.com/apps/news?pid=20601080& sid=amY.tLT6_t.I# [November 28, 2009].

Lindblom, Charles E., 1977, *Politics and Markets* (New York, NY: Basic Books).
Link, Perry, 2009, "China's Charter 08," *New York Review of Books* vol. 56 no. 1.
Lipman, Jonathan N., 2004, "White Hats, Oil Cakes, and Common Blood: The Hui in the Contemporary Chinese State," in Morris Rossabi (ed.), *Governing China's Multiethnic Frontiers* (Seattle, WA: University of Washington Press).
Liu, Liangming, 1996, "Grain Output in Inner Mongolia Increases by Big Margin," *Renmin ribao* Dec. 8, in *FBIS Daily Report – China* (FBIS-CHI-96-249) Jan. 23, 1997.
Liu, Mingzu, 1996, "Taking Truly Effective Measures to Speed up Development in Minority Nationality Regions," *Renmin ribao* Aug. 10, 1996, in *FBIS Daily Report – China* (FBIS-CHI-96-164) Aug. 24.
Liu, Melinda and Katharine Hesse, 2001, "A Blessing for China," *Newsweek* (Jun. 11): 27–31.
Lo, Chang-fa, 2006, T*he Legal Culture and System of Taiwan* (Alphen aan den Rijn: Kluwer).
Lubman, Sarah, 2001, "A Chinese Battle on US Soil: Persecuted Group's Campaign Catches Politicians in the Middle," *San Jose Mercury News* Dec. 23: 1A
Lubman, Stanley, 1999, *Bird in a Cage: Legal Reform in China after Mao* (Stanford, CA: Stanford University Press).
Lung, Hua, 1999, "The Challenge of China Joining the WTO: China Will Pay a High Price for Joining the WTO," *Hsin Pao* (HK), May 27 1999 in *FBIS Daily Report: China* (FBIS-CHI-1999-0528), 1 Jun.
Luo, Shuze, 1997, "Some Hot Issues in Our Work on Religion," (Jun., 1996) in Human Rights Watch/Asia, *China: State Control of Religion* (Washington: Human Rights Watch/Asia, 1997): 65–70.
Luobu, Ciren, 2001, "To Run the Country Well, We need Stability; for the Country to Prosper, We Need to Enrich the People – Deputies from Tibet, Xinjiang Talk About Stability, Development in Frontier Minority Regions," *Xinhua* Domestic Service (Mar. 14, 2001) FBIS-CHI-2001-0314 (Mar. 16).
Ma, Herbert H.P., 1996, *Law and Contemporary Society: Essays in Honor of the Seventieth Birthday of Professor Herbert Han-pao Ma* (Taipei).
MacInnis, Donald E., 1989, *Religion in China Today: Policy and Practice* (Maryknoll, NY: Orbis).
MacInnis, Donald E., 1996, "From Suppression to Repression: Religion in China Today," *Current History* vol. 95: 284–89;
"MacKay to Raise Celil's Case in Beijing," *CBC News* Apr. 29, 2007.
MacKerras, Colin, 2004, "What is China? Who is Chinese? Han-minority Relations, Legitimacy, and the State," in Peter Hays Gries and Stanley Rosen, ed., *State and Society in 21st Century China* (London: Routledge): 216–34.
MacKerras, Colin, 2003, *China's Ethnic Minorities and Globalisation* (London: Routledge).
MacKerras, Colin, 1999, "The Minorities: Achievements and Problems in the Economy, National Integration and Foreign Relations," in Joseph Y. S. Cheng, ed., *China Review 1998* (Hong Kong: Chinese University of Hong Kong Press): 281–311.
MacKerras, Colin, 1994, "Religion, Politics, and the Economy in Inner Mongolia and Ningxia," in Edward H. Kaplan and Donald W. Wisenhunt, eds., *Opuscula Altaica: Essays Presented in Honor of Henry Schwartz* (Bellingham, WA: Western Washington University Centre for East Asian Studies): 437–64.

Madsen, Richard, 2000, "Editor's Introduction," in Richard Madsen and James Tong, eds., "Local Religious Policy in China, 1980–97," *Chinese Law and Government* vol. 33 no. 3: 5–11.

Madsen, Richard, 1998, *China's Catholics: Tragedy and Hope in an Emerging Civil Society* (Berkeley: University of California Press): 108

Madsen, Richard and James Tong, eds., 2000, "Local Religious Policy in China, 1980–97," *Chinese Law and Government* vol. 33 no. 3.

Magnier, Mark, 2008, "China Tightening Control in Tibet Region, Exiles Say," *Los Angeles Times* Nov. 20 (www.latimes.com/news/nationworld/world/la-fg-tibet21-2008nov21,0,5660367.story) [Dec. 22, 2009].

Magnier, Mark, 2006, "Muslims Feel the Long Arm of Beijing," *Los Angeles Times* Oct. 23.

Mainland Affairs Council, 2008a, "Mainland Policy and cross-strait Relations in the Current Phase," Oct. (folio).

Mainland Affairs Council, 2008b, "Explanations Concerning the Forthcoming Second Chiang-Chen Talks," Oct. (folio).

Makris, G. P., 2007, *Islam in the Middle East: A Living Tradition* (Malden, MA: Blackwell).

Malloy, R. P., 1995, "A New Law and Economics," R. P. Malloy and C. R. Braun (eds.) *Law and Economics: New and Critical Perspectives* (New York, NY: Peter Lang): 1.

Marquand, Robert, 2003a, "Go West: China Looks to Transform Its Frontier," *Christian Science Monitor* (Sep. 26).

Marquand, Robert, 2003b, "Pressure to Conform in West China: China's 'Go West' Effort Poses a Challenge to the Identity of Eight Million Ethnic Muslim Uighurs," *Christian Science Monitor* (Sep. 29).

Martin, Lisa L. and Beth A. Simmons, 1998, "Theories and Empirical Studies of International Institutions," *International Organization* vol. 52: 729–57.

McCabe, Eileen, 2009, "Obama Postpones Meeting with Dalai Lama," *Montreal Gazette* (Sep. 15) www.montrealgazette.com/news/Obama+postpones+meeting+with+Dalai+Lama/1996254/story.html. [Nov. 19, 2009].

McCarthy, Susan K., 2002, "The State, Minorities, and Dilemmas of Development in Contemporary China," *Fletcher Forum on World Affairs* vol. 26 no. 2.

McCorquodale, Robert and Nicolas Orosz, eds., 1993, *Tibet: The Position in International Law* (London: Report of the Conference of International Lawyers on Issues relating to Self-Determination and Independence for Tibet).

McGinnis, Michael D., ed., 1999, *Polycentric Governance and Development: Readings from the Workshop in Political Theory and Policy Analysis* (Ann Arbor, MI: University of Michigan Press).

"Memorandum on Genuine Autonomy for the Tibetan People" (translated from the original Tibetan) Oct. 29, 2008 (file copy).

Mendes, Errol P. and A-M Traeholt, eds., 1997, *Human Rights: Chinese and Canadian Perspectives* (Ottawa: Human Rights Research and Education Centre).

"Mentor Urges Taiwan's Ma to Ensure Trial Fairness," *Associated Press* (Taipei) Jan. 17, 2009.

Meng, Yang, 2002, "Patriotism is an Important Part of Religious Beliefs," *Renmin ribao* (People's Daily) (Mar. 10), FBIS-CHI-2002-0311 (Mar. 20, 2002).

Merwin, Wallace C. and Francis P. Jones, 1963, *Documents of the Three-Self Movement* (New York, NY: National Council of the Churches of Christ in the USA).

"Method for Annual Inspection of Places of Religious Activity," July 29, 1996, in Human Rights Watch/Asia, *China: State Control of Religion* (1997): 112–14.
"Miliband Clears up Britain's Tibet Policy," (www.china.org./international/news/2008-11/02/content_16700275.htm) [Dec. 28, 2009].
Military to crush attempt to split Taiwan" *Renmin wang* (People's Daily Net) (Dec. 27 2004) http://english.people.com.cn/200412/27/eng20041227_168785.html
Miller, H. Lyman, 1996, *Science and Dissent in Post-Mao China* (Seattle and London: University of Washington Press).
Miller, H. Lyman and Liu Xiaohong, 2001, "The Foreign Policy Outlook of China's 'Third Generation' Elite," in David M. Lampton, ed., *The Making of Chinese Foreign and Security Policy* (Stanford, CA: Stanford University Press): 123–50.
Millward, James A., 2007, *Eurasian Crossroads: A History of Xinjiang* (Hurst).
Millward, James A., 2004, "Violent Separatism in Xinjiang: A Critical Assessment," (Washington, DC: East-West Center).
Millward, James A., 1994, "A Uyghur Muslim in Qianlong's Court: The Meanings of the Fragrant Concubine," *Journal of Asian Studies*, vol. 53 no. 2: 427–58.
Millward, James A. and Nabijan Tursun, 2004, "Political History and Strategies of Control, 1884–1978," in S. Frederick Starr, *Xinjiang: China's Muslim Borderland* (Armonk, NY: M.E. Sharpe): 63–98.
Millward, James A. and Peter Perdue, 2004, "Political and Cultural History of the Xinjiang Region through the Late 19th Century," in S. Frederick Starr, ed., *Xinjiang: China's Muslim Borderland* (Armonk, NY: M.E. Sharpe): 27–62.
Ming Xia and Shiping Hua, Guest Editors, 1999, "The Battle Between the Chinese Government and the Falun Gong," *Chinese Law and Government* vol. 32 no. 5.
Minnow, Martha, 1993, "Partial Justice," in Austin Sarat and Thomas R. Kearns, *The Fate of Law* (Ann Arbor: University of Michigan Press): 15 – 78, at p. 70.
Mirsky, Jonathan, 2000, "A Lamas' Who's Who," *New York Review of Books* Apr. 27: 15.
Moneyhon, Matthew D., 2002–3, "China's Great Western Development Project in Xinjiang: Economic Palliative or Political Trojan Horse?" *Denver Journal of International Law and Policy* vol. 31 no. 3: 491–519.
Moneyhon, Matthew D., 2002, "Controlling Xinjiang: Autonomy on China's 'New Frontier,'" *Asia Pacific Law & Policy Journal* vol. 3 no. 1: 120–52
"Mongols Resist Government's Plan of Privatizing Chinggis Khaan Mausoluem, Police Impose Curfew on College Campuses in Inner Mongolia," New York Southern Mongolia Human Rights Information Centre (Oct. 31, 2004).
Monti, Mario, ed., 1989, *Fiscal Policy, Economic Adjustment, and Financial Markets* (Washington, DC: International Monetary Fund).
"More on China Issues Anti-Cult Law," Beijing *Xinhua* English Service Oct. 30, 1999, in *FBIS Daily Report – China* (FBIS-CHI-1999-1030), Nov. 20, 1999.
"More Suspects Prosecuted while Urumqi Syringe Attacks Described as 'Violent, Terrorist' Crimes," *Xinhua* Sep. 9, 2009 http:/xinhuanet.com/English/2009–09/09/content_12018378.htm [Sep. 11, 2009].
"Moves to Save Mongolian Language," South China Morning Post/Reuters Mar. 8, 2008.
Munro, Ross, 2006, "China's Relations with Its Neighbors: Some Observations Regarding Its Strategy and Tactics," *International Journal* Spring: 320–28.
Mushkat, Roda, 2006, "Hong Kong's Exercise of External Autonomy: A Multi-Faceted Approach," *International and Comparative Law Quarterly* vol. 55: 945–62."

Bibliography: English

"Muslim Terrorists Executed in Xinjiang," Hong Kong Agence France Presse (Oct. 7, 1999), (FBIS-CHI-1999-1007) (Oct. 7, 1999).

Naquin, 1976, *Millenarian Rebellion in China: The Eight Trigram Uprising of 1813* (New Haven, CT, Yale University Press).

"National Forum Held To Make Arrangements for Cultivation and Selection of Ethnic Minority Cadres," *Xinhua* Domestic Service (Jun. 27, 2000) FBIS-CHI-2000-0627 (Jun. 30, 2000).

"National Public Work Conference Held in Beijing," *Xinhua* (New China News Agency) Domestic Service (Apr. 3, 2001) FBIS-CHI-2001-0403 (Apr. 5, 2001).

"New Historic Chapter of China National Solidarity," People's Daily Online Mar. 11, 2005. (http://english.peopledaily.com.cn/200410/18/eng20041018_160550.html) [November 28, 2009].

Nelken, David and Jahannes Fees, eds., 2001, *Adapting Legal Cultures* (Oxford: Hart Publishing).

Ng, Ka Ling v *Director of Immigration* [1999] (1HKLRD 315).

Ng, Wing-fai and Zhou Yixing, 2004, "Tibet," in Y.M. Yeung and Shen Jianfa, eds., *Developing China's West: A Critical Path to Balanced National Development* (Hong Kong: Chinese University Press): 549–79.

Noble, Gregory W. and John Ravenhill, eds., 2000, *The Asian Financial Crisis and the Architecture of Global Finance* (Cambridge: Cambridge University Press).

Norbu, Dawa, 2001, *China's Tibet Policy* (Richmond: Curzon).

"Notice on the Prevention of Some Places Using Religious Activities to Hinder School Education," (Nov. 26, 1991), in Human Rights Watch/Asia, *Freedom of Religion in China* (1992): 68–70.

"NPC Mulls Law to Promote Legislation in Minority Regions," Beijing *Xinhua* English Service (Mar. 14, 2000) FBIS-CHI-2000-0314 (Mar. 15, 2000).

"NPC Standing Committee Issues Anti-Cult Law," Beijing *Xinhua* English Service Oct. 30, 1999, in *FBIS Daily Report – China* (FBIS-CHI-1999-1030), Nov. 20, 1999.

O'Brien, Kevin J., 1990, *Reform without Liberalization: The National People's Congress and the Politics of Institutional Change* (New York, NY: Cambridge University Press).

Ocampo, Jose Antonio and Juan Martin, 2003, *Globalization and Development* (Santiago: UN Economic Commission for Latin America and the Caribbean).

OECD (Organization for Economic Cooperation and Development), ed., 1998, *21st Century Technologies: Promises and Perils of a Dynamic Future* (Paris: OECD,).

Ogutsu, Mehmet, 2002, "Foreign Direct Investment and Importance of the 'Go West' Strategy in China's Energy Sector," (Paris: OECD).

Olcot, Martha Brill, 2000, "Russian-Chinese Relations and Central Asia," in Sherman W. Garnett, ed., *Rapprochement or Rivalry: Russia-China Relations in a Changing Asia* (Washington, DC: Carnegie Endowment for International Peace): 371–402.

"Olympic Crackdown: China's Secret Plot to Tame Tibet," *The Sunday Times* July 13, 2008, (www.timesonline.co.uk/tol/news/world/asia/article4322538.ece) [Dec. 22, 2009].

"Once Hostile Taiwan, China Set to Sign More Deals," Reuters Oct. 31, 2008.

"'One Country' Key to 'Two Systems'," *China Daily HK Edition* Feb. 23, 2004 (www.china.org.cn/english/China/88132.htm) [Dec. 28, 2009].

Onishi, Yasuo, ed., 2001, *China's Western Development Program: Issues and Prospects* (Chiba: Institute of Developing Economies).

"Opinion on the Implementation of Certain Policy Measures on the Great Development of the Western Regions," Aug. 28, 2001, in *CCH Laws for Foreign Business – Special Zones and Cities* (loosleaf).
"Opposition's Ma Wins Taiwan Poll," BBC March 22, 2008 (http://news.bbc.co.uk/2/hi/asia-pacific/7309113.stm) [Dec. 22, 2009].
Ostrom, Eleanor, Basudeb Guha-Khasnobis and Ravi Kanbur, eds., 2006, *Linking the Formal and the Informal Economy* (Oxford, UK: Oxford University Press).
Ostry, Sylvia, Alan S. Alexandroff, and Raphael Gomez, eds., 2002, *China and the Long March to Global Trade: The Accession of China to the World Trade Organization* (New York, NY: Routledge).
Overholt, William H., 2004, "Hong Kong at the Crossroads," Testimony to Subcommittee on Asia and the Pacific, House of Representatives Committee on International Relations (Jun. 23).
Ownby, David, 2008, *Falungong and the Future of China* (New York, NY: Oxford University Press,).
Ownby, David, 1996, *Brotherhoods and Secret Societies in Early and Mid-Qing China: The Formation of a Tradition* (Stanford, CA: Stanford University Press).
Pan, Philip, 2004, "Jiang Puts Hard Line to Test in China," *Washington Post* May 31: A01.
Pao, Wenwei, 2001, "Stressing International Cooperation and Opposing Double Standards, China Has Clear-Cut Stand on Combating Terrorism," Hong Kong *Ta Kung Pao* Sep. 21, 2001, FBIS-CHI-2001-0921 (Sep. 26).
Parry, Richard Lloyd, 2009, "China's Uighur Rebels Switch to Suicide Bombs," *Times on line* (www.timesonline.co.uk/tol/news/world/asia/article 4499762.ece) [Aug. 19, 2009].
"Party Congress Delegates Laud Efforts to Develop China's Western Region," *Xinhua* Nov. 12, 2002, FBIS-CHI-2002-11-12 (Nov. 14, 2002).
"Party Warns Chinese Communists against Professing a Religion," Asia News IT March 7, 2006, www.asianews.it/view.php?l=en& art=5573 [Nov. 26, 2009].
Perdue, Peter C., 2005, *China Marches West: The Qing Conquest of Central Eurasia* (Cambridge, MA: Harvard University Press).
Perkins, Dwight, 1991, "The Lasting Effect of China's Economic Reforms, 1979–89," in Kenneth Lieberthal et al., *Perspectives on Modern China* (Armonk, NY: M.E. Sharpe): 341–63.
Perry, Elizabeth J., 2001, "Challenging the Mandate of Heaven: Popular Protest in Modern China," *Critical Asian Studies*, vol. 33 no. 2: 163–80.
Perry, Elizabeth J., 1980, *Rebels and Revolutionaries in North China, 1845–1945* (Stanford, CA: Stanford University Press, 1980).
Perry, Elizabeth J. and Mark Selden, 2000, *Chinese Society: Change, Conflict and Resistance* (London: Routledge).
"Police Station Raided in West China's Xinjiang, Terrorist Plot Suspected" *Xinhua* (New China News Agency) Aug. 4, 2008.
Policy and Law Office of State Development and Planning Commission, ed., *Xibu da kaifa zhanlue yanjiu* (Study of the Western Development Program) (Beijing: China Prices Press, 2002).
Pomfret, John, 2008, "Dalai Lama Envoy Upbeat on China Talks," *International Herald Tribune* May 6.
Pomfret, John, 2002a, "China Holds 40 Foreign Falun Gong Protesters: Use of Westerners Marks New Tactic," *Washington Post* Feb. 15: A26.

Pomfret, John, 2002b, "China Church Chief Said to Protest in Prison," *International Herald Tribune* Dec. 7–8: 2.
Potter, Pitman B., 2004, "Legal Reform in China – Institutions, Culture, and Selective Adaptation," *Law & Social Inquiry* vol. 28 no. 4: 465–95.
Potter, Pitman B., 2003a, "Belief in Control: Regulation of Religion in China," in *The China Quarterly* no. 174 (Jul.).
Potter, Pitman B., 2003b, "Globalization and Economic Regulation in China: Selective Adaptation of Globalized Norms and Practices," *Washington University Global Studies Law Review*, vol. 2 no. 1: 119–50.
Potter, Pitman B., 2002, "*Guanxi* and the PRC Legal System: From Contradiction to Complementarity," in Thomas Gold, Doug Guthrie, and David Wank, eds., Social Connections in China (Cambridge: Cambridge University Press).
Potter, Pitman B., 2001, *The Chinese Legal System: Globalization and Local Legal Culture* (London: Routledge).
Powell, Gareth, 2007, "Not Everyone Supports Law on Privatization," *China Economic Review* Feb. 25 (www.chinaeconomicreview.com/property/2007/02/25/not-everyone-supports-law-on-privatization/html [Feb. 24, 2007].
"PRC Refutes Charges on Religious Affairs," Beijing *Xinhua* English Service Dec. 8, 1999, in *FBIS Daily Report – China* (FBIS-CHI-1999-1208) Dec. 9, 1999.
"PRC Spokesman on Asylum in India for Karmapa Lama," Agence France Presse HK, Jan. 11, 2000, FBIS-CHI-2000-0111 (Jan. 12, 2000).
"PRC State Council Notice on Implementing Policy on Opening Western Regions," *Xinhua* Domestic Service (Dec. 27, 2000), FBIS-CHI-2000-1227 (Jan. 4, 2001).
"PRC State Council Opinions on West Region Development Policies," *Xinhua* Domestic Service (Dec. 20, 2001) FBIS-CHI-2002-0805 (nd).
"PRC to Intensify 'Strike Hard' in Xinjiang," *Xinjiang Ribao* (Xinjiang Daily) (May 29, 2001) FBIS-CHI-2001-0618 (Jul. 16, 2001).
"PRC to Maintain Freedom of Religion until It Disappears," *Xinjiang ribao* (Xinjiang Daily) (Nov. 14, 2002), FBIS-CHI-2002-1129 (Dec. 11, 2002).
"PRC: Inner Mongolian Chairwoman Views Economic Restructuring," *Xinhua* Mar. 13, 2002, in *FBIS Daily Report – China* (FBIS-CHI-2002-0313) Mar. 20, 2002.
"PRC: Li Peng Joins Xinjiang NPC Delegation's Deliberations," *Xinhua* Domestic Service (Mar. 12, 2002) FBIS-CHI-2002-0314 (Mar. 18, 2002).
"PRC: Wang Lequan, Abulahat Abdurixit Speak at XUAR Religious Work Conference," *Xinjiang ribao* (Xinjiang Daily) (Oct. 13, 2002), FBIS-CHI-2002-1029 (Nov. 5, 2002).
"PRC: Xinjiang's Hotan Prefecture Develops New Ways to Train 'Patriotic' Islamic Clery," *Xinjiang ribao* (Xinjiang Daily) (Oct. 17, 2001), FBIS-CHI-2001-1123 (Nov. 27, 2001).
"PRC's Ding Guangen Urges Propaganda Departments to Service West Development," *Xinhua* (New China News Agency) Aug. 20, 2000, FBIS-CHI-2000-0820 (Aug. 30, 2000).
"PRC's Urumqi City Reports Successes in 'Strike Hard' Campaign against Crime," *Xinjiang Ribao* (Xinjiang Daily) May 29, 2001, FBIS-CHI-2001-0618 (Sep. 12, 2001).
"PRC's Wang Zhaoguo Discusses Religious Belief, Politics," *Xinhua* (New China News Agency) English Service (Sep. 2, 2001), FBIS-CHI-2001-0902 (Sep. 4, 2001).
"PRC's Xinjiang Arrests 1,000-plus 'Terrorists' since Sep. 11," Hong Kong *Ming Pao* (Dec. 11, 2001) FBIS-CHI-NES-2001-1211 (Dec. 12, 2001).

"President Chen's Cross-century Remarks," (Dec. 31, 2000), in Mainland Affairs Council, ed., *Seeking Constructive cross-strait Relations: Taipei Current Mainland Policy Documents* (Taipei: Mainland Affairs Council, 2001): 1–1 – 1–3.

"President Ma's Inaugural Address," Office of the President Republic of China, May 20, 2008 (file copy).

"Protocol of Accession of the People's Republic of China to the Marrakesh Agreement Establishing the World Trade Organization," WLI/100 2 (Nov. 10, 2001).

"Provisional Regulations for the Registration and Management of Places of Religious Activity in Fujian Province," in Human Rights Watch/Asia, *Continuing Religious Repression in China* (Washington, DC: Human Rights Watch/Asia, 1993): 50–54

"Provisional Regulations on the Administration of Religious Activities in the Xinjiang Uighur Autonomous Region," (1990), in Human Rights Watch/Asia, *Freedom of Religion in China* (Washington, DC: Human Rights Watch/Asia, 1992): 64–65.

"Provisions for Encouraging Domestic and Foreign Investments in Tibet," (July 14, 1992), *China Economic News* no. 34 (1992): 6–8.

"Provisions of the State Council of the People's Republic of China for the Encouragement of Foreign Investment," (1986), *The China Business Review*, Jan.-Feb. (1987): 14–15.

Pun, Pamela, 2002, "China Announces Tax Incentives to Lure Investment to Western Region," *Hong Kong I-Mail* (internet) May 25, 2002, in *FBIS Daily Report – China* (FBIS-CHI-2002-525) May 28.

"Putonghua Taken as Key Factor to Booming Western China's Economy," *Xinhua* English Service (Sep. 18, 2002) FBIS-CHI-2002-0918 (Sep. 19, 2002).

Putterman, Louis, 2001, *Dollars and Change: Economics in Context* (New Haven, CT: Yale University Press).

"Qian Qichen Inspects Three Western Provinces, Speaks on Tourism, Environment," *Xinhua* (July 30, 2000) FBIS-CHI-2000-730 (Aug. 1, 2000).

"Qiao Shi Stresses Efforts against Separatism in Xinjiang," *Xinhua* (New China News Agency) (Apr. 13, 1997) FBIS-CHI-97-103 (nd).

"Qiao Shi Stresses Xinjiang 'Indivisible' Part of Nation," *Zhongguo Xinwen She* (China News Agency) (Nov. 8, 1996) FBIS-CHI-96-218 (Nov. 8, 1996).

Rajan, D.S., 2008, "Tibet Unrest: Counter-measures by Chinese in Lhasa," *South Asia Analysis Group* (Mar. 20) www.southasiaanalysis.org/papers27/paper2635.html. [Dec. 22, 2009].

Ramcharan, Bertrand, 2005, "The United Nations High Commissioner for Human Rights and International Humanitarian Law," occasional paper no. 3 of the Harvard University Program on Humanitarian Policy and Conflict Resolution (Spring).

Reardon-Anderson, James, 2005, *Reluctant Pioneers: China's Expansion Northward 1644–1937* (Stanford, CA: Stanford University Press).

"Record of the Meeting of the Standing Committee of the Political Bureau of the Chinese Communist Party Concerning the Maintenance of Stability in Xinjiang (Document 7)," reproduced in Human Rights Watch, "China: State Control of Religion: Update #1" (1998) www.asylumlaw.org/docs/china/hrw_china_religion98. pdf [Dec. 28, 2009].

"Registration Procedures for Venues for Religious Activities," (May 1, 1994) in Human Rights Watch/Asia, *China: State Control of Religion* (1997): 109–11.

"Regulations from the Shanghai Religious Affairs Bureau," (Nov. 30, 1995), in Human Rights Watch/Asia, *China: State Control of Religion* (1997): 90–99;

"Regulations Governing Labour Cooperation with Hong Kong Region," *China Economic News* (Jan. 6, 1997): 8–10.

"Regulations on Mainland Tourists' Travel to Taiwan Published," *Xinhua* (New China News Agency) June 22, 2008, (http://news.xinhuanet.com/english/2008-06/22/content_8416514.htm) [Dec. 22, 2009].

"Reincarnation of Living Buddha Requires Gov't Approval," *Xinhua* (New China News Agency) Aug. 4, 2007 (www.chinadaily.com.cn/china/2007-8/04/content_5448242.htm) [Dec. 22, 2009].

Religious Affairs Bureau of the State Council ("RAB") 1988, "Comments on Enhancing the World of Religious Academies," (January 15, 1988), in Chan Kim-Kwong and Alan Hunter, "New Light on Religious Policy in the PRC," *Issues & Studies* vol. 31 no. 2 (1995): 21–36 at pp. 29–30.

RAB, 1990, "Comments on the Protestant Church Sending of Students Overseas," (May 21, 1990), in Chan Kim-Kwong and Alan Hunter, "New Light on Religious Policy in the PRC," *Issues & Studies* vol. 31 no. 2 (1995): 31–32.

RAB and Ministry of Public Security, "Notification on Stopping and Dealing With Those Who Use Christianity to Conduct Illegal Activities," (Oct. 18, 1988), in Chan Kim-Kwong and Alan Hunter, "New Light on Religious Policy in the PRC," *Issues & Studies* vol. 31 no. 2 (Feb. 1995): 30–31.

RAB and Taiwan Affairs Office, "Secret, National Edict on Religion," (*guo zhongfa*) no. 128, 1989 (Nov. 13, 1989), in Chan Kim-Kwong and Alan Hunter, "New Light on Religious Policy in the PRC," *Issues & Studies* vol. 31 no. 2 (Feb. 1995): 21–36 at pp. 30–31.

Religious Affairs Office, "Comments on Handling Religious Publications that Enter Our Borders," (Jun. 16, 1990), in Chan Kim-Kwong and Alan Hunter, "New Light on Religious Policy in the PRC," *Issues & Studies* vol. 31 no. 2 (Feb. 1995): 30 and 32, respectively.

"Report of the Working Party on Accession of China," WT/MIN (01)/31 (Nov. 10, 2001).

"Report Says CPC Plans to Allow Religious Figures to Join Party," Hong Kong Sing Tao Jih Pao (internet version), in *FBIS Daily Report – China* (FBIS-CHI-2001-1224) Dec. 26, 2001.

"Reviewing a Quarter Century of Political Crime," *Human Rights Forum* (2003) no. 2: 54–57.

Rhodes, Richard, 1986, *The Making of the Atomic Bomb* (New York, NY: Simon and Schuster): 13 *et seq*.

Rigger, Shelley, 1999–2000, "Social Science and National Identity: A Critique," *Pacific Affairs* vol 72 no. 4 (Taiwan Strait-Special Issue): 537–52.

Roberti, Mark, 1996, *The Fall of Hong Kong: China's Triumph & Britain's Betrayal* (New York, NY: John Wiley & Sons).

Rocamora, Joel, 2002, "A Clash of Ideologies; International Capitalism and the State in the Wake of the Asian Crisis," in Joseph S. Tulchin, ed., *Democratic Governance and Social Inequality* (Boulder, CO: Lynn Rienner): 75–88.

Rose, Nikolas, 2000, "Governing Liberty," in Richard V. Ericson and Nico Stehr, eds., *Governing Modern Societies* (Toronto: University of Toronto Press): 141–75.

Rosett, A., 1991, "Legal Structures for Special Treatment of Minorities in the People's Republic of China," *Notre Dame Law Review* vol. 66, no. 5: 1503–28.

Rossabi, Morris, 2004, *Governing China's Multiethnic Frontiers* (Seattle: University of Washington Press).

"'Roundup': Falungong Urged to Abide by Hong Kong Law," *Hong Kong China News Service*, Hong Kong *Zhongguo Tongxun She* (China Advisory Service) (Dec. 11, 1999), FBIS-CHI-1999-1211 (Dec. 11, 2001).

Rubenstein, Murray A., "The Presbyterian Church in the Formation of Taiwan's Democratic Society, 1945–2004," in Cheng, Tun-jen and Deborah A. Brown, eds., *Religious Organizations and Democratization: Case Studies from Contemporary Asia* (Armonk NY and London: M.E. Sharpe, 2006): 109–35.

Rudelson, Justin and William Jankowiak, "Acculturation and Resistance: Xinjiang Identities in Flux," in S. Frederick Starr, *Xinjiang: China's Muslim Borderland* (Armonk NY and London: M.E. Sharpe, 2004): 299–319.

Russian Ministry of Foreign Affairs, "Text of Putin – Hu Jintao Joint Declaration," (FBIS May 28, 2003).

Saiget, Robert, 2000a, "China Hoping Development of West Will Dampen Xinjiang Separatist," Hong Kong Agence France Presse (Aug. 21) FBIS-CI-2000-0821 (Aug. 22, 2000).

Saiget, Robert, 2000b, "Muslim Separatists Still Bubbling under Repression in Western China," Hong Kong Agence France Presse (Aug. 27) FBIS-CHI-2000-0827 (Aug. 28, 2000).

Sautman, Barry, 2001, "Tibet: Myths and Realities," *Current History* Sep.: 278–83.

Sautman, Barry, 2000, "Is Xinjiang an Internal Colony?" *Inner Asia* vol. 2 no. 2: 239–71.

Sautman, Barry, 1999, "Ethnic Law and Minority Rights in China: Progress and Constraints," *Law & Policy* vol. 21, no. 3.

Sautman, Barry, 1998, "Preferential Policies for Ethnic Minorities in China: The Case of Xinjiang," *Nationalism and Ethnic Politics* vol. 4 nos 1–2: 88–118.

Sautman, Barry and June Teufel Dreyer, eds., 2006, *Contemporary Tibet: Politics, Development, and Society in a Disputed Region* (Armonk, NY: M.E. Sharpe).

Savitch, H.V., 1998, "Global Challenge and Institutional Capacity: Or How We Can Refit Local Administration for the Next Century," *Administration and Society* vol. 30: 248–73.

Scharpf, Felix, 2000, "Interdependence and Democratic Legitimation," in Susan J. Pharr and Robert D. Putnam, eds., "Disaffected Democracies: What's Troubling the Trilateral Countries," Princeton, NJ: Princeton University Press).

Schichor, Yitzhak, 2004, "The Great Wall of Steel: Military and Strategy in Xinjiang," in S. Frederick Starr, ed., *Xinjiang: China's Muslim Borderland* (Armonk, NY: M.E. Sharpe): 120–60.

Scott, Rosemary E., 1993, *The Porcelain of Jingdezhen* (London: Percival David Foundation).

Segal, George and David S.G. Goodman, eds., 2000, *Towards Recovery in Pacific Asia* (London: Routledge,

Seliktar, Okifira, 1986, "Identifying a Society's Belief System," in Margaret Herman, ed., *Political Psychology* (San Francisco, CA: Jossey-Bass).

Seymour, James D., 2000, "Xinjiang's Production and Construction Corps and the Sinification of East Turkestan," *Inner Asia* vol. 2 no. 2: 171–93.

Seytoff, Alim, 2006, "Pride, Prejudice, Protest and Progress," *China Rights Forum* no. 4: 60–61.

Shakya, Tsering, 2008, "Tibet Questions," *New Left Review* no. 51: 5–27

Shakya, Tsering, 1999, *The Dragon in the Land of Snows: A History of Modern Tibet Since 1947* (London: Pimlico).

238 Bibliography: English

Shi, Jiangtao, 2005, "Beijing Reviews Key Human Rights Treaty," *South China Morning Post* (Sep. 6,).
Shirk, Susan, 1993, *The Political Logic of Economic Reform in China* (Berkeley, CA: University of California Press).
Si Liang, 2001a, "Notes on a Journey to Xinjiang, Part One – Xinjiang Develops Steadily, Focuses on Promoting Economy," Hong Kong *Zhongguo Tongxun She* (China Advisory Service) (Oct. 3, 2001) FBIS-CHI-2001-1003 (Oct. 4,).
Si Liang, 2001b, "China Is Taking Effective Steps to Crack Down on and Contain 'East Turkestan'," Hong Kong *Zhongguo Tongxun She* (China Advisory Service) (Dec. 20, 2001) FBIS-NES-2001-1220 (Dec. 26,).
Silbey, Susan S., 1997, "'Let Them Eat Cake': Globalization, Postmodern Colonialism, and the Possibilities of Justice," *Law & Society Review* vol. 31, no. 2: 207–35.
Simon, Denis Fred and Michael Y.M. Kau, eds., 1992, *Taiwan: Beyond the Economic Miracle* (Armonk, NY: M.E. Sharpe).
Sines, Abigail, 2002, "Civilizing the Middle Kingdom's Wild West," *Central Asian Survey* vol. 21 no. 1: 5–18.
Singh, Praksh, 2008, "Dalai Lama, China Keep Channel Open," *Los Angeles Times* Apr. 18.
"Sinopec Oil Find Could Lift China Reserves by Third," Reuters (HK) Jan. 2, 2005,
"Sino-Russian Border Port Does Record High of Foreign Trade," *Xinhua* Jan. 8, 2005, in *FBIS Daily Report – China* (FBIS-CHI-2005-0108) Jan. 10, 2005.
"Sino-Russian Border Treaty," (Xinhuanet, Oct. 14, 2004).
Sisci, Francesco, 2009, "Who is Hitting at Hu?" *Asia Times* Jul. 24.
Sloane, Robert D., 2002, "The Changing Face of Recognition in International Law: A Case Study of Tibet," *Emory Law Review* vol. 16: 107–86.
Sautman, Craig S., 2001, "China, in Harsh Crackdown, Executes Muslim Separatists," *New York Times* Dec. 16.
Smith, Craig S., 2001, "China, in Harsh Crackdown, Executes Muslim Separatists," *New York Times* Dec. 16,
Smith, Warren, 2008, *China's Tibet? Autonomy or Assimiliation* (Lanham, MD: Rowman & Littlefield).
Sneath, David, 2000, *Changing Inner Mongolia: Pastoral Mongolian Society and the Chinese State* (Oxford: Oxford University Press,).
Soete, Luc, 1998, "Global Possibilities: Technology and Planet-Wide Challenges," in Organization for Economic Cooperation and Development, ed., *21st Century Technologies: Promises and Perils of a Dynamic Future* (Paris: OECD): 147–69.
Solinger, Dorothy, 2002, "The Cost of China's Entry into WTO," *Asian Wall Street Journal* Jan. 4.
Song, X., 2000, "Thinking Federal: The Relevance of Federalism to China," *Regional and Federal Studies* vol. 10.
Sorensen, Theodore C. and David L. Phillips, 2004, *Legal Standards and Autonomy Options for Minorities in China: The Tibetan Case*.
"Special Message of His Holiness the Dalai Lama for Tibetans In and Outside of Tibet," 14 Nov. 2008 (www.tibet.net/index.php?id=530& articletype=flash& rmenuid=morenews) [Nov. 14, 2008].
"Speech by Li Zhibin, Deputy Director of the Office of the Leading Group for Western Regional Development of the State Council and Vice Minister of National Development and Reform Commission, Oct. 14, 2004," *Xinhua* (English version), in *FBIS Daily Report – China* (FBIS-CHI-2004–1014), Oct. 18, 2004.

Sperling, Elliot, 2008. "He Has Got it Wrong," *Times of India* Nov. 27 (http://timesofindia.indiatimes.com/Editorial/TOP_ARTICLE_He_Has_Got_It_Wrong/articleshow/3760696.cms) [Nov. 27, 2008].
Spencer, Richard, 2007, "China Demands Veto on Tibet's 'Living Buddhas'," *The Telegraph* (Aug. 5), www.telegraph.co.uk/news/main.jhtml?xml=/news/2007/08/04/wtibet104.xml) [Dec. 22, 2009].
Spiegel, Mickey, 1998, "Control 'According to Law': Restrictions in Religion," *China Rights Forum* Spring 1998: 22–27.
Spiegel, Mickey, 1992 "Freedom of Religion in China," (Washington, DC: Human Rights Watch/Asia).
Starr, S. Frederick, 2004a, *Xinjiang: China's Muslim Borderland* (Armonk, NY: M.E. Sharpe).
Starr, S. Frederick, 2004b, "Introduction," in Starr, ed. *Xinjiang: China's Muslim Borderland* (Armonk, NY: M.E. Sharpe): 3–24.
SCIO 2009a, "White Paper: Development and Progress in Xinjiang," (http://news.xinhuanet.com/english/2009-09/21/content_12090477.htm) [Sep. 22, 2009].
SCIO, 2009b, "White Paper on Ethnic Policy," (Sep. 27), (www.chinadaily.com.cn/china/2009-09/27/content_8743072.htm) [Oct. 22, 2009].
SCIO, 2008a, "White Paper: China's Efforts and Achievements in Promoting the Rule of Law," (Feb. 28) http://news.xinhuanet.com/english/2008-02/28/content_7687418_1.htm [Nov. 19, 2009].
SCIO, 2008b, "Protection and Development of Tibetan Culture," (Beijing, Sep.) (http://news.xinhuanet.com/english/2008-9/25/content_10108734.htm) [Dec. 22, 2009].
SCIO, 2005a, "White Paper on Political Democracy," (www.chinadaily.com.cn/english/doc/2005-10/19/content_486206.htm) [Nov. 19, 2009].
SCIO 2005b, "Regional Autonomy for Ethnic Nationalities in China" (Beijing, February 2005) (http://english.gov.cn/official/2005-07/28/content_18127.htm) [Apr. 10, 2010].
SCIO, 2004a, "National Minorities Policy and Its Practice in China," (May 20, 2004).
SCIO, 2004b, "Regional Ethnic Autonomy in Tibet," (Beijing: New Star Publishers).
SCIO, 2004c, "China's National Defense in 2004," (www.fas.org/nuke/guide/china/doctrine/natdef2004.html) [Dec. 22, 2009].
SCIO, 2003a, "History and Development of Xinjiang," (Beijing: Xinhua News Agency).
SCIO, 2003b, "Ecological Improvement and Environmental Protection in Tibet," *Xinhuanet* (Mar. 11).
SCIO, 2002a, "Tibet's March toward Modernization," (Beijing: New Star Press, 2002).
SCIO, 2002b, "The Human Rights Record of the United States in 2001," (Beijing)
SCIO, 2002c, "'East Turkistan' Terrorist Forces Cannot Get Away With Impunity," (Beijing, Jan.).
SCIO, 2001, "White Paper: Progress in China's Human Rights Cause," (Beijing).
SCIO, 2000, "White Paper: Fifty Years of Progress in China's Human Rights," (Beijing).
SCIO, 1999, "White Paper on National Minorities Policy and Its Practice in China," (Beijing).
SCIO, 1998, "New Progress in Human Rights in the Tibet Autonomous Region," (Beijing).
SCIO, 1996, "Freedom of Religious Belief in China," (www.china.org.cn/e-white/Freedom/index.htm).

SCIO and State Council Taiwan Affairs Office, "The One-China Principle and the Taiwan Issue," (Feb. 21, 2000).

"Shanghai Outlines Steps to Develop Global Financial Center Status," *Shanghai Daily* (May 20, 2009) www.nyconsulate.prchina.org/eng/xw/t563437.htm [Apr. 14, 2010].

"Statement by Ms. Che Ying, Advisor of the Chinese Delegation at the 61st Session of the Commission on Human Rights (Item 5: Right to Self-Determination)," (Mar. 1995).

Stein, Janice, *The Cult of Efficiency* (Toronto: House of Anansi Press, 2001).

Steiner, Henry J. and Philip Alston, 2000, *International Human Rights Law in Context: Law, Politics, Morals* (Oxford: Oxford University Press).

Stewart, Cameron, 2008, "Tibet's Looming Eruption," *The Australian* Nov. 13, (www.theaustralian.news.com.au/story/0,24642115-25837.00.html) [Nov. 13, 2008].

Stiglitz, Joseph E., 2002, *Globalization and Its Discontents* (New York, NY: W.W. Norton): 10.

"Strategic Direction for Central Asia," Hong Kong *Ta Kung Pao* Aug. 4, 1999, FBIS-CHI-1999-0829 (Aug. 30, 1999

Su, Yigong, 1999, "The Application of Chinese Law and Custom in Hong Kong," *Hong Kong Law Journal* vol. 29 pt. 2: 267–93.

Suchman, Mark, 1995, "Managing Legitimacy: Strategic and Institutional Approaches," in *Academy of Management Review* vol. 20 no. 3: 577–85.

Sunahara, Ann Gomer, 1981, *The Politics of Racism* (Toronto: James Lorimer & Co).

Tai Benny, 1999, "Why Second-Generation Mainland Children Have No Right of Abode in Hong Kong," *Hong Kong Law Journal* vol. 29 pt. 2: 208–15.

"Taiwan, China sign MOUs," *Straits Times* Nov. 16, 2009 (www.straitstimes.com/BreakingNews/Asia/Story/STIStory_455164.html) [Nov. 28, 2009].

"Taiwan Leader Ma Vows No War with China in His Term," Reuters Oct. 21, 2008 www.washingtonpost.com/wp-dyn/content/article/2008/10/21/AR2008102100274.html [Oct. 22, 2008].

"Taiwan Leader Ma Ying-jeou Meets ARATS Chief," *Xinhua* (New China News Service) Nov. 6, 2008 http://chinadaily.cn/china/2008-11/06/content_7180625.htm. [Dec. 22, 2009].

"Taiwan's Ruling Party Chief Arrives in China," *Voice of America* May 26, 2008. www.channelnewsasia.com/stories/afp_asiapacific/view/350107/1/.html. [Dec. 22, 2009].

Tan, Qingshan, 2004, "Controversial Taiwan Election," *EAI Bulletin* May: 1–8 at p. 1.

Rajahee, Farhand, (2000) *Globalization on Trial: The Human Condition and the Information Civilization* (Ottawa: International Development Research Council).

Tanner, Murray Scot, 1998, *The Politics of Law-Making in Post-Mao China: Institutions, Processes, and Democratic Prospects* (Oxford: Oxford University Press).

"Tashkent Declaration of Heads of Member States of Shanghai Cooperation Organization," (Jun. 17, 2004) (www.sectsco.org) [Dec. 22, 2009].

"Teams Sent to China's Xinjiang Southern Areas to 'Rectify Order'," Xinjiang People's Broadcasting Station (Mar. 31, 1999), in *BBC Worldwide Monitoring* (Doc. # bbcapp0020010901dv4100ltw) (Apr. 2, 1999).

Tennant, Paul, 1990, *Aboriginal Peoples and Politics: The Indian Land Question in British Columbia, 1849–1989* (Vancouver: UBC Press).

"Three Murdered in China's Restive Northwest: State Media," Agence France Presse Beijing Aug. 12, 2008 (Oly-2008-China-Xinjiang-attacks // AFP 120917 GMT AUG 08.

Thwaites, Rik, Terry De Lacy, Li Yonghong, and Liu Xianhua, 1998, "Property Rights, Social Change, and Grassland Degradation in Xilingol Biosphere Research, Inner Mongolia China," *Society and Natural Resources* vol. 11: 319–38.

"Tibet – Tracking Dissent on the High Plateau: Communications Technology on the Gormo-Lhasa Railway," Rights and Democracy, ed., *Human Rights Impact Assessments for Foreign Investment Projects* (Montreal: International Centre for Human Rights and Democratic Development, 2007: 59–80.

"Tibet Envoy: Beijing Talks 'Difficult'," *Associated Press* Jul. 4, 2008.

Tibet Information Network (TIN), 2003a, "Despite Economic Boom, Rural Standards of Living in the Tibet Autonomous Region still Below 1992 Levels," TIN News Update, Feb. 6 (www.tibet.ca/en/newsroom/wtn/archive/old?y=2003& m=2& p=6_3) [Jan. 4, 2010].

Tibet Information Network, 2003b, "Deciphering Economic Growth in the Tibet Autonomous Region," TIN Special Report, Apr. 9 (www.tew.org/development/eco.growth.tar.html) [Jan. 4, 2010].

Tibet Information Network, 2003c, "The Rich Get Richer and the Poor? Rural Poverty and Inequality in Tibet – Indications from Recent Official Surveys," TIN News Update, May 31.

Tibet Information Network, 2001, "Serthar Teacher now in Chengdu: New Information on Expulsions of Nuns at Buddhist Institute," (Nov. 8) www.reversespins.com/serthar.html [Jan. 4, 2010].

Tilly, Chris, 1999, "Power – Top Down and Bottom Up," *Journal of Political Philosophy* vol. 7: 330–52.

"Time to Reconsider the Meaning of 'Autonomy'," *China Development Brief* vol. X no. 7: 2006: 1–2.

Tomlinson, John, 999, *Globalization and Culture* (Oxford: Polity).

"Top Advisor Reiterates Resolute Opposition to 'Taiwan Independence," *Xinhuanet* March 9, 2007. (www.gwytb.gov.cn:8088/detail.asp?table=headlines& title=Headlines&m_id=678) [Dec. 22, 2009].

"Top Envoy Trapped as Protests Flare," *South China Morning Post* Nov. 6, 2008.

"Top Trade Official Arrives in Bejing," *China Post* Nov. 5, 2009 www.chinapost.com.tw/taiwan/china-taiwan-relations/2009/11/05/231489/Top-trade.htm [Jan. 4, 2010].

Tracking the Steel Dragon: How China's Economic Policies and the Railway are Transforming Tibet (Washington, DC: International Campaign for Tibet, nd).

"True Colors of 'East Turkestan" Terrorist Forces Exposed," *China Daily* Jan. 21, 2002 SCIO 2002 (http://english.peopledaily.com.cn/200201/21/eng20020121_89079.shtml) [Nov. 25, 2009].

Tsai, Ing-wen, 2001, "Current cross-strait Relationship," (Speech to Taiwanese Chamber of Commerce, San Francisco Bay Area), Jan. 21, 2001, in Mainland Affairs Council, ed., *Seeking Constructive cross-strait Relations: Taipei Current Mainland Policy Documents* (Taipei: Mainland Affairs Council): 6.1–6.7.

Tsang, Donald, 2005, "2005 Policy Address," (Oct. 12), 2005–6 Policy Address: www.policyaddress.gov.hk. [Dec. 22,2009].

Tsang, Steve, 2004a, ed., *Peace and Security across the Taiwan Strait* (London: Palgrave Macmillan).

Tsang, Steve, 2004b, "Peace Proposal Two: The China Union Model," in Steve Tsang, ed., *Peace and Security across the Taiwan Strait* (London: Palgrave Macmillan): 195–208.

Tsang, Steve and Hung-Mao Tien, 1999, *Democratization in Taiwan: Implications for China* (New York, NY: St. Martin's Press).

Bibliography: English

Tsering, Buchung K., 2008a, "The Time Has Come for the Tibetan Struggle to Show Its Maturity," *International Campaign for Tibet*, Nov. 20.

Tsering, Buchung K., 2008b, "A Way Forward for Tibet: Perspectives from Inside China," *International Campaign for Tibet*, Nov. 20.

Tucker, Nancy Bernkopf, ed., 2005, *Dangerous Strait: The US–Taiwan – China Crisis* (New York, NY: Columbia University Press).

Tulchin, Joseph S., ed., 2002, *Democratic Governance and Social Inequality* (Boulder and London: Lynn Rienner).

Tung, Chee-hwa, 2004, "Policy Address by the Chief Executive," (Jan. 7) www.info.gov.hk/gia/general/200401/07/0107001.htm. [Dec. 22, 2009].

"Twelve Suggestions for Dealing with the Tibetan Situation by Some Chinese Intellectuals," (Mar. 22, 2008) *New York Review of Books* vol. 55 no. 8 May 15, 2008 (www.nybooks.com/articles/21379) [Dec. 28, 2009].

Tyler, Christian, 2004, *Wild West China: The Taming of Xinjiang* (New Brunswick, NJ: Rutgers University Press).

"US Charges on Religious Freedom Refuted," *Xinhua* (New China News Agency) English Service (Oct. 15, 1998), FBIS-CHI-1999-1014 (Nov. 27, 2000).

US Department of State, Bureau of Democracy, Human Rights and Labor (USS-DHRL), 2005, "Country Reports on Human Rights Practices: China (includes Tibet, Hong Kong and Macao) 2004," (Feb. 28, 2005).

US Department of State, Bureau of Democracy, Human Rights and Labor, 2000, Annual Report on International Religious Freedom: Taiwan (Sep. 5).

"Uighur Leader Says China Fabricated Terrorism Plots," (Agence France Press March 10, 2008).

UN Commission on Human Rights, "Civil and Political Rights, Including the Question of Torture and Detention: Report of the Special Rapporteur on Torture and Other Cruel, Inhumane, or Degrading Treatment or Punishment – Mission to China," (Mar. 10, 2006).

UN Committee against Torture, 2008a, "List of Issues to be Considered during the Examination of the Fourth Periodic Report of CHINA (CAR/C/CHN4)," (4 Aug.).

UN Committee against Torture, 2008b, "Consideration of Reports Submitted By States Parties under Article 19 of the Convention," CAT/C/CHN/CO/4 (21 Nov.).

UN Development Programme, *Human Development Report* (2001).

"UN Human Rights Chief Stresses Collective Responsibility to Protect Civilians," *UN News Centre* July 22, 2009 www.un.org/apps/news/story.asp?NewsID=31554&Cr=protection+of+civilians& Cr1=[Nov. 27, 2009].

"UN World Conference on Human Rights: Vienna Declaration and Programme of Action," U.N. Doc. A/CONF.157/24 (1993), *International Legal Materials* vol. 32: 1661.

Unger, Roberto, 1975, *Knowledge and Politics* (New York, NY: Free Press).

"Urumqi Mayor on Existence of Xinjiang Independence," Hong Kong *Zhongguo Tongxun She* (China Advisory Service) (Aug. 30) FBIS-CHI-1999-0902 (Sep. 3, 1999).

"US Report on Religious Freedom Seen as 'Power Politics'," Beijing *Xinhua* English Service Dec. 11, FBIS-CHI-1999-1210 (Dec. 13, 1999).

"Uyghur Language Banned from University," Agence France Presse (May 28, 2002).

Vajda, Mihaly, 1988, "East-Central European Perspectives," in John Keane, *Civil Society and the State* (London: Verso Press): 333–60 at p. 346.

Van Ness, Peter, ed., 1999, *Debating Human Rights: Critical Essays from the United States and Asia* (London: Routledge).
Van Wie Davis, Elizabeth, 2008, "China Confronts Its Uyghur Threat," *Asia Times* Apr. 18.
"Vice Premier Huang Ju Stresses Macroecoomic Control Policies in Inner Mongolia," *Xinhua* June 13, 2004, in *FBIS Daily Report – China* (FBIS-CHI-2004-0614) Jun. 15, 2004.
"Vigilance against Infiltration by Religious Forces from Abroad," (March 15, 1991), in Human Rights Watch/Asia, *Freedom of Religion in China* (Washington, DC: Human Rights Watch/Asia, 1992): 52–54.
"Vocal Government Critic Dismissed from China's Top Think Tank," Human Rights in China Dec. 21, 2009 (www.hrichina.org/public/contents/press?revision_id=172630&item_id=172628) [Jan. 4, 2010].
Waldron, Arthur, 1998, "Religious Revivals in Communist China," *Orbis* vol. 42 no. 2: 323–32.
Wang, Hongwei, 2002, "11th Plenary Meeting of Ninth Regional Government Calls for Ensuring Sound Economic and Social Development By Laying Stress on Key Points and Grasping Key Links – Ablet Abdureshit Delivers Important Speech," *Xinjiang Ribao* (Xinjiang Daily) (Apr. 16), FBIS-CHI-2002-0515 (May 17, 2002).
Wang, Jing'ai and Yang Mingchuan, 2004, "Inner Mongolia," in Y.M. Yeung and Shen Jianfa, eds., *Developing China's West: A Critical Path to Balanced National Development* (Hong Kong: Chinese University Press): 373–407.
"Wang Lequan" *New York Times* July 13, 2009 (http://topics.nytimes.com/topics/reference/timestopics/people/w/wang_lequan/index.html?inline=nyt-per) [Nov. 19, 2009].
Wang, Lixiong, 2008, "A True 'Middle-Way' Solution to Tibetan Unrest," *China Security* vol 4 no. 2: 27–37.
Wang, Lixiong, 1998, *Sky Burial: The Fate of Tibet* (Hong Kong: Mirror Books)
Wang, Tay-sheng, 2002, "The Legal Development of Taiwan in the 20th Century: Toward a Liberal and Democratic Country," *Pacific Rim Law & Policy Journal* vol. 11 no. 3: 531–59.
"Wang Zhaoguo on PRC United Front Work," Beijing *Xinhua* Domestic Service Jan. 8, 2000, in *FBIS Daily Report – China* (FBIS-CHI-2000-0110) Jan. 11, 2000.
Wang, David, 1999, *The Yining Incident: Under the Soviet Shadow* (Hong Kong: The Chinese University Press).
Wang, David, 1998, "Han Migration and Social Changes in Xinjiang," *Issues & Studies* vol. 34 no. 7: 33–61.
"War of Words after Call for Independence," *The Times* Mar. 7, 2007, (www.gwytb.gov.cn:8088/detail.asp?table=headlines& title=Headlines&m_id=678) [Dec. 22, 2009].
Watts, Jonathan, 2009, "Chinese Human Rights Activist Liu Xiaobo Sentenced to 11 Years in Jail," *The Guardian* Dec. 25 (www.guardian.co.uk/world/2009/dec/25/china-jails-liu-xiaobo) [Dec. 26, 2009].
Weber, Max, 1978, *Economy and Society* (Roth and Wittich, eds.) (Berkeley, CA: University of California Press).
"Wei Jianxing, Luo Gan Address Conference on Public Security, Judicial Work," Beijing *Xinhua* Domestic Service Dec. 2, 2000, in *FBIS Daily Report – China* (FBIS-CHI-2000-1202) Dec. 13, 2000.

Weiler, Calla, 2004, "The Economy of Xinjiang," in S. Frederick Starr, *Xinjiang: China's Muslim Borderland* (Armonk, NY: M.E. Sharpe): 163–89.

Weller, Robert, 1999, *Alternate Civilities: Democracy and Culture in China and Taiwan* (Boulder, CO: Westview Press).

Wesley-Smith, Peter, ed., 1990, *Hong Kong's Basic Law: Problems and Prospects* (Hong Kong: Hong Kong University Faculty of Law).

Weston, Timothy B., 2008, "Growing Up Han: Reflections on a Xinjiang Childhood," *The China Beat* Apr. 28 (www.thechinabeat.org/?p=94) [Dec. 28, 2009].

"What We Learned from the Trial of the Case of the Zhu Hongsheng Counter-revolutionary Clique," in Human Rights Watch/Asia, *Continuing Religious Repression in China* (Washington, DC: Human Rights Watch/Asia, 1993): 41–47.

White, Lynn III. *Unstately Power* (Armonk NY and London: M.E. Sharpe, 1998).

White, Randy, 1995, *Global Spin: Probing the Globalization Debate.* (Toronto: Dundurn Press).

Whitfield, Susan, 1999, *Life along the Silk Road* (London: John Murray Publishers).

Williams, Dee Mack, 2002, *Beyond Great Walls: Environment, Identity, and Development of the Chinese Grasslands of Inner Mongolia* (Stanford, CA: Stanford University Press): Chapter 2.

Williams, Dee Mack, 1996, "The Barbed Walls of China: A Contemporary Grassland Drama," *Journal of Asian Studies*, vol. 55 no. 3: 665–91.

Wilson, Richard W., 1992, *Compliance Ideologies: Rethinking Political Culture* (Cambridge: Cambridge University Press).

Wing, L. P. and J. Sims, 1992, "Human Rights in Tibet: An Emerging Foreign Policy Issue," *Harvard Human Rights Journal*, vol. 5: 193–203.

Wong, Betty L., 2001, "A Paper Tiger? An Examination of the International Religious Freedom Act's Impact on Christianity in China," *Hastings International and Comparative Law Review* vol. 24: 539.

Wong, Edward, 2009a, "Intellectuals Call for Release of Uighur Economist," *New York Times* Jul. 15,

Wong, Edward, 2009b, "China Court Sentences 6 to Death in Rioting," *New York Times* Oct. 12 (www.nytimes.com/2009/10/13/world/asia/13china.html?_r=1) [Nov. 19, 2009].

Wong, Edward, 2008a, "Doubt Arises in Account of an Attack in China," *New York Times* Sep. 29.

Wong, Edward, 2008b, "China Has Sentenced 55 Over Tibet Riot in March," *New York Times* Nov. 6.

Wong, Edward, 2008c, "Taiwan and China Draw Closer with New Agreements," *International Herald Tribune* Nov. 4, 2008 (www.iht.com/bin/printerfriendly.php?id=17506116) [Nov. 5, 2008].

Wong, Edward, 2008d, "Taiwan President and Chinese Envoy Meet in Effort to Strengthen Ties," *International Herald Tribune* Nov. 6, (www.iht.com/bin/printfriendly.php?id=17582204) [Nov. 7, 2008].

"Working Regulations of the People's Congress of Sumu, Township, Township of Minority Nationality, and Town of Inner Mongolia Autonomous Region," (Jun. 2, 1995), in *A Collection of Selected Translation of the IMAR Local Legal Regulations* (Hohehaote: Inner Mongolia People's Press, 2000): I: 132–40 // pp. II: 79–84,

"Working Regulations of the People's Governments Sumu, Township, Township of Minority Nationality, and Town of Inner Mongolia Autonomous Region," (April 20, 1991), in *A Collection of Selected Translation of the IMAR Local Legal*

Bibliography: English 245

Regulations (Hohehaote: Inner Mongolia People's Press, 2000): I:141–46 // pp. II: 85–88.

World Bank, 2009, *World Development Indicators* (http://siteresources.worldbank.org/DATASTATISTICS/Resources/front.pdf) [Nov. 19, 2009].

Wu-Hu meeting in China in June a possibility: KMT," Agence France Presse Apr. 28, 2008, https://www.taipeitimes.com/News/taiwan/archives/2008/04/28/2003410468. [Apr. 28 2008].

Wunsch, James S., 1999, "Institutional Analysis and Decentralization: Developing an Analytical Model for Effective Third World Administrative Reform," in Michael D. McGinnis ed., *Polycentric Governance and Development: Readings from the Workshop in Political Theory and Policy Analysis* (Ann Arbor, MI: University of Michigan Press).

Xin, Dingding, 2008, "Qinghai-Tibet Railway to Get Six New Lines," *China Daily* Aug. 17.

Xin, Catherine R., Jane L. Pearce, 1996, "*Guanxi*: Connections as Substitutes for Formal Institutional Support," *Academy of Management Journal* vol. 39: 1641–58.

"Xinhua: Bio of Wang Lequan – Politburo Member of CPC Central Committee," Beijing *Xinhua* English Service (Nov. 15, 2002), FBIS-CHI-2002-1115 (Nov. 15, 2002).

"Xinjiang Boss Warns of 'Life and Death' Battle with Terror," *South China Morning Post* // *Reuters* Beijing, Aug. 14, 2008.

"Xinjiang Chairman Calls for Early Enactment of Anti-Terror Law," Hong Kong *Wen Wei Po* (Mar. 9, 2002) FBIS-CHI-2002-0309 (Mar. 11, 2002).

Xinjiang CPC Propaganda Department, 2004, *"Si ge rentong" duben* (Reader on 'four identities') (Urumqi: Xinjiang People's Press).

"Xinjiang Crackdown for Ramada," Agence France Presse (Sep. 6, 2008).

"Xinjiang Daily Says 11 Separatists Executed," Hong Kong Agence France Presse (Jan. 27, 1998) *FBIS Daily Report – China* (FBIS-CHI-98–027) (Feb. 27, 1998).

"Xinjiang Dispatches Agents to Fight Independence," Hong Kong *Sing Tao Jih Pao* (Jun. 21, 2000) FBIS-CHI-2000-0621 (Jun. 27, 2000).

"Xinjiang Educates 8,000 Muslim Imams in CPC's Religious Policy," *Xinhua* (New China News Agency) Domestic Service (Jan. 11, 2002), FBIS-CHI-2002-0111 (Jan. 14, 2002).

"Xinjiang Leader Promises Crackdown on Separatism, Religious Extremism," *Zhongguo Xinwen She* (China News Agency) (Oct. 24, 2001) FBIS-CHI-2001-1024 (Oct. 25, 2001).

"Xinjiang Leaders Denounce Separatism, Stress Economic Development, Hong Kong," *Ta Kung Pao* (Jul. 19, 2001) FBIS-CHI-2001-0719 (Jul. 20, 2001).

"Xinjiang Leaders, NPC Delegates Discuss Splittist, Religious, Terrorist Forces," Hong Kong *Zhongguo Tongxun She* (China Advisory Service) (Mar. 13, 2002), FBIS-CHI-2002-0313 (Mar. 25, 2002).

"Xinjiang Party Committee holds Meetings on Anti-Separatism in Ideological Sphere," *Xinjiang Ribao* (Xinjiang Daily) (Apr. 5, 2002) FBIS-CHI-2002-0508 (May 22, 2002).

"Xinjiang Party Official Addresses Training Class for Patriotic Muslims, Calls for Opposing Separatism," *Xinjiang ribao* (Xinjiang Daily) (Oct. 10, 2001, FBIS-CHI-2001-1123 (Nov. 27, 2001).

"Xinjiang Party Secretary Addresses Meeting on Public Order," *Xinjiang Ribao* (Xinjiang Daily) (Apr. 16, 2001) FBIS-CHI-2001-0521 (May 29, 2001).

"Xinjiang Party Secretary's Speech on Employment Role for Xinjiang Production and Construction Corps," *Xinjiang Ribao* July 23 2002 pp. 1,4/ Xinjiang Radio July 23, 2002 (FBIS-CHI-2002-0807) Aug. 15, 2002.

"Xinjiang People's Congress Hears Report on Procuratorate Reform," *Xinjiang Ribao* (Xinjiang Daily) (May 31, 2002) FBIS-CHI-2002-0710 (July 16. 2002).

"Xinjiang Prefecture Mounts Crackdown on Separatists, Terrorists, Extremists," *Zhongguo Xinwen She* (China News Agency) (Jan. 3, 2002) FBIS-CHI-2002-0103 (Jan. 4, 2002).

"Xinjiang Region Sees Targeted Atheist 'Education' Campaign," *Xinjiang ribao* (Xinjiang daily) (Apr. 9, 1997), in *BBC Monitoring Summary of World Broadcasts* (Doc. # bbcfe0020010929dt6100d5h).

"Xinjiang Regional Law Court Presidents' Meeting Ends," *Xinjiang Ribao* (Xinjiang Daily) (Feb. 16, 1994) FBIS-CHI-94-056 (Mar. 23, 1994): 64–65.

"Xinjiang Regulations on Party Discipline in Anti-Separatism Efforts," *Xinjiang Ribao* (Xinjiang Daily) (May 8, 2001) FBIS-CHI-2001-0529 (Sep. 17, 2001).

Xinjiang Ribao Editorial on Importance of Region's Religious Work," Xinjiang Ribao (Xinjiang Daily) (Oct. 13, 2002), FBIS-CHI-2002-1029 (Nov. 4, 2002)

"Xinjiang Secretary Sees Continuing Separatist Fight," Hong Kong Agence France Press (Mar. 31, 1997) FBIS-CHI-97-090.

"Xinjiang United Front Heads Attend Forum on National Religious Work," *Xinjiang ribao* (Xinjiang Daily) (Jul. 21, 2002), FBIS-CHI-2002-0809 (Aug. 13, 2002).

Xinjiang Urumqi Intermediate Court Executes 3 Separatists, 3 Other Criminals," *Zhongguo Xinwen She* (China News Agency) (Jul. 7, 2000) FBIS-CHI-2000-0707 (Jul. 10, 2000).

"Xinjiang's Official Urges Religious Personages to Enhance Political Quality," *Xinjiang ribao* (Xinjiang Daily) (Dec. 5, 2001), FBIS-CHI-2001-1227 (Jan. 10, 2002).

"Xizang Ribao Commentator Views Implementation 'Outline' on Ethics Building, Tibet's Religious Policy," *Xizang ribao* (Tibet Daily) Dec. 13, 2001, in *FBIS* Doc. ID: CPP20011217000175, Dec. 17, 2001.

Xu, Jilin, 2004, "What Future for Public Intellectuals?" *China Perspectives* no. 42 (http://chinaperspectives.revues.org/document799.html) [Nov. 20, 2009].

Yan, Jiaqi, 1996, "China's National Minorities and Federalism," *Dissent* Summer: 139–44.

Yan, Jiaqi, 1998, "Federalism and the Future of Tibet," in Cao Changching and Seymour, James D., eds., *Tibet through Dissident Chinese Eyes* (Armonk, NY: M.E. Sharpe): 107–20.

Yardley, Jim, 2008a, "Simmering Resentments Led to Tibetan Backlash," *New York Times* Mar. 18.

Yardley, Jim, 2008b, "In Shift, China Offers to Meet with Dalai Lama Envoys," *New York Times* Apr. 26.

Yardley, Jim, 2008c, "Tibet Talks Resume, but with Few Hopes for Breakthrough," *International Herald Tribune* Jul. 1.

Ye, Xiaowen, 1997, "China's Current Religious Question: Once Again an Inquiry into the Five Characteristics of Religion," (March 22, 1996) in Human Rights Watch/Asia, *China: State Control of Religion* (Washington, DC: Human Rights Watch/Asia): 116–44 at pp. 117–18.

Yermukanov, Marat, 2007a, "Amid Mounting Criticism in Kazakhstan, Beijing and Astana Seal New Deals," *Eurasia Daily Monitor* vol. 4 issue 6

Yermukanov, Marat, 2007b, "New Government in Kazakhstan Heralds No Radical Changes," *Eurasia Daily Monitor* Jan. 11, 2007.
Yeung, Y.M., 2004, "Introduction" in Y.M.Yeung and Shen Jianfa, eds., *Developing China's West: A Critical Path to Balanced National Development* (Hong Kong: The Chinese University Press): 1–25.
Yeung Y.M. and Shen Jianfa, eds., 2004, *Developing China's West: A Critical Path to Balanced National Development* (Hong Kong: The Chinese University Press).
Yom, Sean L., 2001, "Uighur Muslims in Xinjiang," *Foreign Policy in Focus* no. 14 (www.hartford-hwp.com/archives/55/455.html) [Dec. 28, 2009].
York, Geoffrey, 2008, "Why Tibet is Boiling Over," *Globe and Mail* Mar. 21.
You, Ji, 2004, "China's Post 9/11 Terrorism Strategy," *China Brief* vol. IV no. 8: 7–9.
Yu, Fei, 1999, "Analysts Note Science, Education Gap in Minority Regions," *Xinhua (HK)* May 19, 1999, in *FBIS Daily Report–China* (FBIS-CHI-1999-0519) May 21.
Yu, Yuanzhou, 2002, "Scholar's Proposal: National Unification Promotion Law of the People's Republic of China," (Nov. 1).
Zhang, Boshu, 2008, "The Way to Resolve the Tibet Issue," Apr. 22–28 (Chinese text: "Xizang wenti de genben chulu").
Zhang, Qingyang, 2008, "Attorney Zhu Jiuhu Speaks in defense of Dalai Lama in Chengdu Courtroom," 11 Nov. http://news.boxun.com/news/gb/china/2008/11/200811071107.shtml. [Dec. 22, 2009].
Zhang, Xianchu, and Philip Smart, 2006, "Development of Regional Conflict of Laws: On the Arrangement of Mutual Recognition and Enforcement of Judgments in Civil and Commercial Matters between Mainland China and Hong Kong SAR," *Hong Kong Law Journal* vol. 36 no. 3: 585–612.
Zhang, Xudong, 2008, *Post-socialism and Cultural Politics: China in the Last Decade of the 20th Century* (Durham, NC: Duke University Press).
Zhao, Cheng and Han Zhenjun, 2002, "A Brilliant Chapter on the Great Cause of Rejuvenating the Nation – Written on the Third Anniversary of Implementatioon of Western Development (1)," *Xinhua* Domestic Service (Mar. 31), FBIS-CHI-2002-0331 (Apr. 2, 2002).
Zhao, Linglin, "Central Asia: The Focus of Future International Contention," Hong Kong *Da Kung Pao* Oct. 25, 2001, FBIS-CHI-2001-1025 (Nov. 16, 2001).
Zhao Suisheng, 1999–2000, "Military Coercion and Peaceful Offence: Beijing's Strategy of National Reunification with Taiwan," *Pacific Affairs* vol 72 no. 4 (Taiwan Strait-Special Issue): 495–512.
Zheng, Yongnian, 2007, *Defacto Federalism in China: Reforms and Dynamics of Central-Local Relations* (Hackensack, NJ: World Scientific).
Zhou Minglang, "The Politics of Bilingual Education in the People's Republic of China since 1949," *Bilingual Research Journal* Winter 2001.
Zweig, David, 2000, "The 'Externalities of Development': Can New Political Institutions Manage Rural Conflict?" in Perry and Seldon, *Chinese Society: Change, Conflict and Resistance* (London: Routledge, 2000).

Index

'110 Command Center' 37
'17 Point Agreement' (Tibet) 4
'1992 consensus' 147

Abdiriyim, Ablikim 49
'Action Agenda' 155, 157
'Administrative Measures for Trade with the Region of Taiwan' (2000) 158
'Administrative Methods for Chinese Citizens Travelling To and From Taiwan' ('*Zhongguo gongmin*') 154
alienation 44, 57, 61, 71, 83, 87
Anglo-Tibet treaty (1904) 4
Anti-Japanese War 6
Anti-Secession Law (for Taiwan) (2005) 3, 148–9, 163. 165–6, 167, 178
'anti-separatism' 29, 44, 88
'anti-terrorism' 7, 44, 51, 60, 110, 173
Asian financial crisis (1997) 155
'Asian Values' discourse 15
Association for Relations Across the Taiwan Strait (ARATS) 150
Autonomous Region Religion Work Conference (2001) 97, 104
Autonomous Region Status 4
'autonomy' (*zizhi quan*) 30, 58, 85, 172, 177
Autonomy Region People's Congresses 26

Badashanren 109
Bangkok Declaration on Human Rights ('Final Declaration') (1993) 15, 56
Beg, Yakub 6
Britain: recognition of China's sovereignty over Tibet 41; rule in Hong Kong 10, 153, 156, 177
Buddhism 93, 97, 99, 151, 153

CASS Taiwan Research Institute (Taiyansuo) 166, 168
Catholicism 93, 152
Celil, Huseyin ('MacKay') 110
Central Ideological and Political Work Conference 128
Central Nationalities Work Conference 45; (1992) 42, 82, 83, 88; (1999) 117; (2001) 73–5, 103
Central Public Order Work Conference (April 2–3, 2001) 44
Chan Kam Nga and Others v. Director of Immigration 145
Charter 08 document 40
Chen Kuiyuan 34
Chen Shui-bian 12, 13 150, 151, 158
Chen Yunlin 161
'Chiang-Chen' talks (November 2008) 161
China Christian Council 152; Constitution 152
China Islamic Association 103
'China-Dalai Lama Dialogue' 5
Chinese Academy of Social Sciences 91
Chinese Buddhist Association 151
Chinese Catholic Patriotic Association 152
Chinese Conference of Catholic Bishops 152
Chinese People's Political Consultative Congress (CPPC) 97
Cho-Yan priest-patron relationship 4
Christianity 63, 93, 151
collectivization 4, 15, 54–5, 57, 94, 134
Communist Party of China (CPC) 24; Central Committee Document No. 6 95–6, 98, 101; Central Committee Document No. 7 86–7, 102; Central Committee Document No. 19 98;

Index   249

Constitution 33, 67, 68–70; on ethnic issues 70; leadership 29; National Congress, Fifteenth 27; National Congress, Sixteenth 49; National Congress, Seventeenth 94; policies on society and culture 67; Politburo Political-Legal Committee 43, 141; Politburo Standing Committee 43; Tibet Committee on governance activities in Tibet ('RMET'), 34; United Front regime 17; United Front Work Department 5, 19, 35, 36, 37, 71, 103
'community of developing economies' 61
Complementarity 18–19, 20, 179, 180; between Taiwan and the Mainland 161; in Inner Periphery 57, 58–9, 65, 109, 110, 137, 172, 173–4; in Outer Periphery 162, 163, 164–5, 177–8
Confucianism 166
Constitution *see* Communist Party of China (CPC): Constitution; PRC Constitution
Cooperative Enterprises 123, 128, 158
cotton, Xinjiang 128, 129
Court of Final Appeal 146
Criminal Law of the PRC 43, 102, 159
cross-straits Economic Cooperation Framework Agreement (ECFA) 160
'cultural genocide' 40
Cultural Revolution 4, 8, 67, 78, 172
'culture halls' (*wenhua gong*) 72

Dalai Lama 19, 35, 36, 39, 65, 73, 83, 123, 151, 172; authority of 98; Chinese vilification 37–8, 40, 41; flight to to India (1959) 4; 'government in exile' 5; 'Middle Way' 5, 40, 41–2; Nobel Peace Prize 5; speech at the Third Tibet Work Conference in July 1994 99; 'splittism' of 126
Daoism 93
'Decision of the XUAR CPC Committee and People's Government on Expanding the Opening Up Policy' (1991) 128
Deng Xiaoping 5, 10, 123, 134
Ding Guangen 129
'double responsibility system' (Inner Mongolia) 133
Du Qinglin 38, 39, 65

East Turkestan Islamic Movement 51; in Xinjiang 52, 172, 174
'East Turkistan Movement' in Xinjiang 172, 174
'Eastern' Mongols 8
Eastern Turkistan Republic (ETR) 6–7
Economic Cooperation Framework Agreement (ECFA) 160
economic development 16; in Inner Periphery 122–36: Inner Mongolia 132–6; Tibet 122–7; Xinjiang 127–32; in Outer Periphery 164–5, 169–70: globalization and development 154–62; Hong Kong Special Administrative Region 154–6; Taiwan 156–62
education: ideological 48–9, 88, 102–3; of minority nationalities 70, 76, 81, 88–92; religious 48, 95, 98–9, 103–5, 107, 168, 178
'ethnic autonomy' (*minzu zizhi*) 28
ethnic nationalism 19, 33, 37, 43, 73, 83, 100, 140, 174

Fa Gong Wei 141
Falun Gong movement 95, 153, 168
Fazhi ju 141
'federalism' (lianbang zhuyi) 18, 19, 21, 28; discourses of 14–15
'fenlie zhuyi' ('splittism,' 'separatism,' and 'secessionism.') 7–8, 43, 83
Five Year Plan: Fifth 35; Eighth (1991–95) 128; Ninth (1996–2000) 71, 87, 125, 126, 128, 133, 134; Tenth (2000–5) 118, 125, 126, 129, 135; Eleventh 157
'foreign invested enterprise' (FIE) system 128
Four Basic Principles 29, 70, 94, 101
'Fourteen Points' 152
'Fragrant Concubine' 6
'frontier' (*bianjiang*) 2

General Agreement on Tariffs and Trade (GATT) 156, 160, 161, 180, 181
Genghis Khan 92
globalization 16, 18, 20, 63, 71, 109, 136, 154–62; Hong Kong Special Administrative Region 154–7; Taiwan 157–62
'Go West' program 120
'governance capacity' (*zhizheng nengli*) 32–3

250 *Index*

'Great Game' of British and Russian imperialism 6
Great Wall of China 8
Guanxi 22

Han chauvinism (*Da Hanzu zhuyi*) 2, 15, 67, 76, 83, 88, 172
hegemony 21, 141
Hong Kong and Macao Affairs Office 17
Hong Kong Basic Law 9, 142–6, 153, 155–6, 165, 168, 176, 178
Hong Kong Lawyer 41
Hong Kong Special Administrative Region (SAR) 9–11, 141; globalization and development 154–7; political authority 142–7; religion and 153–4
Hu Jintao 34, 43, 49, 57, 59, 84, 113, 125, 132, 135, 149–51, 168; 'Inspection Tour' of Xinjiang (June 8–16, 2001) 48
Hu Qili 123
Hu Yaobang 122; six-point reform proposal (1980) 5
Hui Nationality 4
human rights 15, 18, 20, 24, 57, 108–11, 126, 154; international 61, 63, 107, 108, 111; for minorities 40–1, 78, 108, 173; religious 41, 94, 105, 178

ICCPR Article 18 109
Idhkah Mosque 7
'Implementing Measures' (1999) 157–8
Inner Mongolia: economic development 132–6; political authority in 53–5, PRC nationalities policies 89–92; religion in 106–7
Inner Mongolia Autonomous Region (IMAR) 8–9, 53, 171
Inner Mongolia Grasslands Law (1984, rev. 2002) 54, 55
Institutional Capacity 20–2, 23, 56, 112–15, 136, 180–1; factors of 181; in Inner Periphery 61–5, 66, 107, 137–40, 171, 174–6; in Outer Periphery 162, 165–70, 178–9
Institutional Cohesion 22, 113; dimensions of 181; factors of 181; in Inner Periphery 65, 140, 176; in Outer Periphery 167–8, 169, 170
Institutional Location 112; in Inner Periphery 62–4, 138, 175; in Outer Periphery 166, 178, 179

Institutional Orientation 21–2, 61; factors of 181; in Inner Periphery 64–5, 139, 176; in Outer Periphery 166, 169, 170
Institutional Purpose 21, 112, 114, 178, 180, 181; in Inner Periphery 61–2, 137–8, 174–5; in Outer Periphery 165, 166, 169
International Campaign for Tibet 5
International Convention on the Elimination of All Forms of Racial Discrimination (ICERD) 108
International Covenant on Civil and Political Rights (ICCPR) 108, 109, 153
International Covenant on Economic, Social and Cultural Rights (ICESC) 108
international human rights standards 24
International Monetary Fund 136
'international socialist movement' 61
Islam 46–7, 63, 93, 172; restrictions on travel to Mecca for Hajj 47, 50

Jia Qinglin 149, 166, 168
Jiang Zemin 5, 10, 34, 42, 43, 44, 79, 83, 84, 85, 95, 97, 99, 104, 124, 134, 168
Joint Ventures 123, 128, 158

Kadeer, Mrs Rebiya 49–50, 60, 65, 132
Kelsang Gyaltsen 38, 41
KMT (Kuomintang) 12, 13
Kong Fansen 84
Kowloon-Canton Railway (KCR) 11

language 7, 9, 12, 40, 51, 55, 70, 78; bilingual policy 31–2, 91; local minority 16, 27, 32, 64, 65, 69–70, 76, 79, 88–9
Lanzhou Military District CPC Committee 86
'Law on Protecting Investments by Taiwan Investors' (1994) 157–8
Leading Small Group on Hong Kong Affairs (Xianggang shiwu lingdao xiaozu) 11
Lee Teng-hui 150
'legalization of governance' 174
Legitimacy 19, 20, 21, 25, 28–9, 65, 76, 109, 110–12, 115; in Inner Periphery 57, 59–61, 137, 138, 172, 174; in Outer Periphery 162, 163, 165, 178, 179, 180
Li Peng 34, 79, 124

Index 251

Li Ruihuan 42
Li Zhi 51
Liang Kai 109
Lien Chan 13
Liu Mingzu 134
Liu Xiaobo 40
Liu Yaohua 51
local Autonomous Region governments 26
'local autonomy' (*difang zizhi*) 28
Lodi Gyari 5, 38, 41
Luo Gan 34, 35, 97, 104

Ma Ying-jeou 12, 13, 150, 151, 161, 162
Macao Basic Law 9
Mandarin for Han-dominated governance 89
Maoism 166
Marxism-Leninism Mao Zedong Thought 29, 70, 94, 166
Memoranda of Understanding 160
'Middle Way' 5, 40, 41–2
Ministry of Culture 70
Ministry of Public Security 37
'Mini-Three-Links' 150
Minority Autonomy Law 114
minority cadre policy: in Inner Periphery 78–82, 84, 113; in Inner Mongolia 90–2; training classes 80–1, 90–2
minority nationalities, governance in Inner Periphery 3–9, 67–92
Minority Nationalities Work Conference (1992) 33, 45
'minority nationality autonomy regions' 4
Minority Nationality Law 138
Minority Nationality White Paper (2004) 108
multiculturalism, discourses of 15, 16
Muslims *see* Islam

National Conditions (*guoqing*) Research Institute in the Chinese Academy of Sciences 117
National Defense White Paper (2005) 149
National Development and Reform Commission (NDRC) 17
National Forum on Cultivating and Selecting Ethnic Minority Cadres (June 26–27, 2000) 81
National Law Use Law 131

National Minority Nationalities Work Conference (1992) 79
National People's Congress (NPC) 28, 142; Ninth 84, 99, 125, 126; 'NPC Mulls Law' 28, 29; Party Committees in the 141; Standing Committee (NPCSC) 25, 26, 29, 145, 146, 154, 163
National Regional Autonomy Law (NRAL) 24
National Tibet Work Conference: First (March 1980) 122; Second (February 1984) 122; Third (July 1994) 124
National Work Conference: (2001) 106; (2005) 76; on Nationality Policy (1992) 61, 71; on Religion (1990) 96; on Religious Affairs (December 2001) 97, 104, 106
'nationalist separatism' 37
Nationalities Affairs Commission 29, 79
Nationalities Work Conference (1992) 71–2, 73, 79
Nationality Region Autonomy Law (NRAL) (1984, 2001) 24, 27–31, 33, 35, 36, 39, 42, 63, 64, 67, 68, 70, 98, 116, 138, 140–2, 144, 145, 174
NATO 57
Ng Ka Ling v. Director of Immigration 145
'nonaligned movement,' 61
'normalcy' 40
'NPC Mulls Law' 28, 29

Olympic Games, Beijing (2008) 37, 38, 39, 50
'one China' principle 12, 147, 158
'one country–two systems' 3, 10, 36, 39, 142, 143, 147–9, 165, 176, 179
Ordos Mongols 8

'Pan-Blue' team 13
Panchen Lama 35
'patrimonial sovereignty' 137, 166, 167
Peng Zhen 93
People First Party (PFP) 13
People's Armed Police (PAP) 37, 44, 57, 86
People's Liberation Army (PLA) 5, 7, 37, 44, 57, 130; resistance to social control mandates 86–7
perception 18, 20, 109, 179; in Inner Periphery 57–8, 172–3; in Outer Periphery 162, 164, 177

political authority in Outer Periphery 142–51,162–3, 165–8
'post-Socialism' 15–16
poverty 34, 72, 77, 83, 121, 122, 124, 127, 129, 139
PRC Constitution (1982) 14, 15, 24–7, 30, 42, 93, 141, 143, 144, 178; Article 1 148; Article 4 68; Article 4.1 68; Article 4.2 68; Article 4.3 69; Article 4.4 69; Article 4.5 69; Article 4.6 69–70; Article 31 142; Article 33 93; Article 36 153; Article 36 93; Article 62(13) 142; Articles 117–19 26–7; Article 100 145; Article 113 24–5; Article 114 25; Article 115 25–6; Article 116 26; Article 120 27, 146; Article 121 27; Article 122 27; Article 126 145
proletariat, dictatorship of, principle 29
Protestantism 93, 152
Public Security organs 44

Qiao Shi 43–4, 56
Qinghai-Tibet Railway 126, 127
'quality' of minority cadres 81

RAB 102, 103
Re Di, Governor 36
Red Guards 5
'Regulations on Encouraging Investment by Taiwan Compatriots' (1988) 157
religion, PRC policy on 46–7, 92–107; Constitution and law 93–5; in Inner Mongolia 106–7; in Inner Periphery 98–107; in Outer Periphery 163–4, 168–9; party policy 95–7; in Tibet 98–100; in Xinjiang 100–6
Religious Affairs Bureau 17, 95; Document No. 5 of 2007 100
Ren Jianxin 34
Responsible Agency 167
riots: in Lhasa (1987, 1989, 2008) 5, 6, 98; in Tibet (1989, 2008) 6, 36–7, 40–1, 65, 83; in Urumqi (July 2009) 50–1; in Xinjiang (2009) 62, 65; in Yining and Urumqi (February 1997) 43

'Security Administration Punishment Regulations,' 102
Selective Adaptation 17–20, 23, 115, 179–80, 181; in Inner Periphery 56–61, 65, 66, 107, 108–12, 136–7, 140, 171, 172; in Outer Periphery 162–5, 166, 170, 177–8
self-determination (*zijuequan*) 58, 59
separatism ('*fenlie zhuyi*') 7–8, 43, 83, 172
September 11, 2001 60
Shanghai Cooperation Organization (SCO) 44, 57–8, 59, 87, 131
Sheng Shicai 7
Sichuan earthquake 38
Siew, Vincent 150
Silk Road 6
Sino-British Declaration 153, 165
social unrest *see* riots
socialist road principle 29
Soong, James 13
sovereignty (*zhuquan*) 2, 4, 10, 12–13, 20, 30, 57–61, 110, 111; patrimonial 137, 166, 167; over Hong Kong 141, 163, 165; over Taiwan 147–9, 163; over Tibet 33, 36, 41, 42, 61, 77; over Xinjiang 49, 61, 77
'splittism' ('*fenlie zhuyi*') 7–8, 43, 83, 172
'Special Administrative Region' 14
State Council Hong Kong and Macau Affairs Office 11, 168
State Council Religious Affairs Committee 35
State Council Religious Affairs Office (RAB) 95
State Council White Papers: Ethnic Policy (2009) 76–8, 82, 108; 'Freedom of Religious Belief in China' (1997) 97; National Minority Policies (SCIO 1999) 27–8; Nationalities Policy 111; Protection of Tibetan Culture (2008) 39–40; Regional Autonomy 31–3; 'The One-China Principle and the Taiwan Issue' (2000) 147, 163; Tibet 35, 111; Xinjiang 51, 89, 111
State Nationalities Affairs Commission, Politics and Law Department 88
State Planning Commission 72
State Secrets Bureau 29
Strike Hard campaign 45
Sun Yat-sen 1
Supreme People's Court 30

Taiwan 11–13; Anti-Secession Law for (2005) 3, 148–9, 163, 165–6, 167, 178; Constitution, Article 13 154; Fubon Bank 161; globalization and development 157–62; investment 52;

Mainland Affairs Council 150;
  political authority in 147–51;
  religion and 154
tax 70 117, 119, 121, 123, 129,
  130, 133, 155
Thondup, Gyalo 5
'three adherences' 38
Three-Self Patriotic Movement 152
Tian Jiyun 123
Tiananmen crisis (1989) 86
Tibet: Chinese military occupation
  (1959) 4; economic development in
  122–7; fiftieth anniversary of the
  'peaceful liberation' 33, 57, 84;
  governance in 33–42; PRC policy on
  82–5; religion in 98–100
Tibet Autonomous Region 4–6
Tibet Autonomous Region (TAR)
  Party 34, 36
Tibet Daily 100
Tibet Work Conference: Third (July
  1994) 34–5, 83–4; Fourth (2001)
  84, 126
Trade Union organization 52
Tsang, Donald 155
Tung Chee-hwa 146, 155
'Twelve Suggestions' 40
'two German states' model 147

Ulanhu 8
unitary state principle 29–30
united front work 5, 19, 35, 36,
  37, 71, 103
United Nations Committee Against
  Torture 110
United Nations Human Rights
  Commission (Human Rights
  Council) 56
United Nations World Conference
  on Human Rights 15
Universal Declaration of Human Rights
  Article 18 109
USA: and Soviet hegemony 59; State
  Department Annual Report on
  Religious Freedom (1999) 111;
  support for the Dalai Lama and Tibet
  Uighur nationalism 174

Wang Lequan 43, 45, 50, 51, 59, 104,
  129, 131
Wang Lixiong 40
Wang Yaoguo 34
Wang Zhaoguo 149
'war on terror' 110

Wen Jiabao 38, 150
Western Development Program 16, 17,
  30, 53, 58, 71, 73, 78, 116,117–22,
  128, 129, 130, 136, 138, 139, 140,
  173, 175
Western Development Strategy
  (*Xibu da kaifa*) 6, 26, 52, 82, 139
'Western' Mongols 8
Wholly Foreign- Owned Enterprises
  123, 128, 158
World Bank 136
World Health Organization (WHO) 144
World Trade Organization (WTO) 144,
  156, 159, 160, 161, 165, 178; China's
  entry to 134; Dispute Resolution
  Understanding 161; regimes 180, 181
Wu 84
Wu Bangguo 149
Wu Po-hsiung 150
'Wuhan Draft' 148

Xiamen Commercial Bank 161
Xinjiang 42–53; China's nationalities
  policies 85–9; economic development
  in 127–32; religion in 100–6
Xinjiang Autonomous Region
  High Court 45
Xinjiang CPC Committee 86; 'Interim
  Provisions on Disciplinary
  Punishments for Party Members and
  Organs that Violate Discipline in
  Fighting Separatism and
  Safeguarding Unity' 46, 48;
  Propaganda Department 1997
  campaign on atheism education 103
Xinjiang Party Committee and People's
  Government 43
Xinjiang Production and Construction
  Corps (XPCC; *Bingtuan*) 45, 86,
  117, 130–1
'Xinjiang Regulations on Party
  Discipline' 60, 65
Xinjiang Uighur Autonomous
  Region 6–8, 43, 87

Yili Kazakh Autonomous Prefecture 7
Yuan Shikai, General 1

Zeng Qinghong 168
Zhang Boshu, Dr 41
Zhang Qingli 36, 37, 52, 59
Zhu Rongji 42, 44–5, 104, 118, 135
Zhu Yuanzhang 1
Zuo Zongtang, General 6

A library at your fingertips!

eBooks are electronic versions of printed books. You can store them on your PC/laptop or browse them online.

They have advantages for anyone needing rapid access to a wide variety of published, copyright information.

eBooks can help your research by enabling you to bookmark chapters, annotate text and use instant searches to find specific words or phrases. Several eBook files would fit on even a small laptop or PDA.

NEW: Save money by eSubscribing: cheap, online access to any eBook for as long as you need it.

Annual subscription packages

We now offer special low-cost bulk subscriptions to packages of eBooks in certain subject areas. These are available to libraries or to individuals.

For more information please contact webmaster.ebooks@tandf.co.uk

We're continually developing the eBook concept, so keep up to date by visiting the website.

www.eBookstore.tandf.co.uk